# Business Environment

Pippa Riley

Viva Books
New Delhi | Mumbai | Chennai | Kolkata | Bengaluru | Hyderabad | Kochi | Guwahati

**First Indian Edition 2011**

VIVA BOOKS PRIVATE LIMITED

- 4737/23 Ansari Road, Daryaganj, New Delhi 110 002
  E-mail: vivadelhi@vivagroupindia.net, Tel. 42242200
- 76, Service Industries, Shirvane, Sector 1, Nerul, Navi Mumbai 400 706
  E-mail: vivamumbai@vivagroupindia.net, Tel. 27721273, 27721274
- Jamals Fazal Chambers, 26 Greams Road, Chennai 600 006
  E-mail: vivachennai@vivagroupindia.net, Tel. 28290304, 28294241
- B-103, Jindal Towers, 21/1A/3 Darga Road, Kolkata 700 017
  E-mail: vivakolkata@vivagroupindia.net, Tel. 22836381, 22816713
- 7, Sovereign Park Apartments, 56-58, K. R. Road, Basavanagudi, Bengaluru 560 004
  E-mail: vivabangalore@vivagroupindia.net, Tel. 26607409, 26607410
- 101-102 Mughal Marc Aptt., 3-4-637 to 641, Narayanguda, Hyderabad 500 029
  E-mail: vivahyderabad@vivagroupindia.net, Tel. 27564481, 27564482
- First Floor, Beevi Towers, SRM Road, Kaloor, Kochi 682 018, Kerala
  E-mail: vivakochi@vivagroupindia.net, Tel: 0484-2403055, 2403056
- 232, GNB Road, Beside UCO Bank, Silpukhuri, Guwahati 781 003
  E-mail: vivaguwahati@vivagroupindia.net, Tel: 0361-2666386

*Published by arrangement with*

BPP Learning Media Ltd.
BPP House, Aldine Place
London W12 8AA



ISBN : 978 81 309 1754-2

Published by Vinod Vasishtha for Viva Books Private Limited, 4737/23, Ansari Road, Daryaganj, New Delhi - 110 002.

Printed and bound by Raj Press, R-3, Inderpuri, New Delhi - 110 012.

# Contents

# Introduction

**Viva-BPP Learning Media's Business Essentials** range is the ideal learning solution for students studying for business-related qualifications and degrees. The range provides concise and comprehensive coverage of the key areas that are essential to the business student.

Qualifications in business are traditionally very demanding. Students therefore need learning resources which go straight to the core of the topics involved, and which build upon students' pre-existing knowledge and experience. The BPP Learning Media Business Essentials range has been designed to meet exactly that need.

Features include:

- In-depth coverage of essential topics within business-related subjects
- Plenty of activities, quizzes and topics for discussion to help retain the interest of students and ensure progress
- Up-to-date practical illustrations and case studies that really bring the material to life
- A glossary of terms and full index

**Each chapter** contains:

- An introduction and a list of specific study objectives
- Summary diagrams and signposts to guide you through the chapter
- A chapter roundup, quick quiz with answers and answers to activities

# Study Guide

This Course Book includes features designed specifically to make learning effective and efficient.

- Each chapter begins with a summary diagram which maps out the areas covered by the chapter. There are detailed summary diagrams at the start of each main section of the chapter. You can use the diagrams during revision as a basis for your notes.
- After the main summary diagram there is an introduction, which sets the chapter in context. This is followed by learning objectives, which show you what you will learn as you work through the chapter.
- Throughout the Course Book, there are special aids to learning. These are indicated by symbols in the margin:

**Signposts** guide you through the book, showing how each section connects with the next.

**Definitions** give the meanings of key terms. The *glossary* at the end of the book summarises these.

**Activities** help you to test how much you have learned. An indication of the time you should take on each is given. Answers are given at the end of each chapter.

**Topics for discussion** are for use in seminars. They give you a chance to share your views with your fellow students. They allow you to highlight holes in your knowledge and to see how others understand concepts. If you have time, try 'teaching' someone the concepts you have learned in a session. This helps you to remember key points and answering their questions will consolidate your knowledge.

**Examples** relate what you have learned to the outside world. Try to think up your own examples as you work through the Course Book.

**Chapter roundups** present the key information from the chapter in a concise format. Useful for revision.

- At the end of each chapter, there is a **chapter roundup** and a **quick quiz** with answers. Use these to revise and consolidate your knowledge. The chapter roundup summarises the chapter. The quick quiz tests what you have learned (the answers often refer you back to the chapter so you can look over subjects again).
- At the end of the book, there is an index.

Part A

# Business Environment

# Chapter 1:
# ORGANISATIONS AND THEIR OBJECTIVES

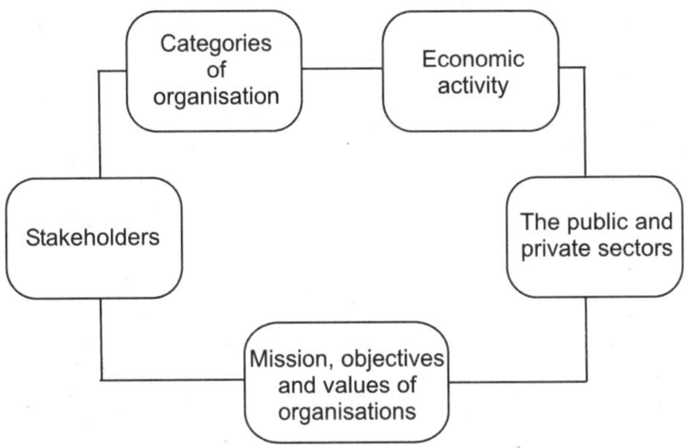


## Introduction

In our lives we come into contact with a great assortment of organisations with many forms, types and usually with very different objectives. The business organisations we encounter range from huge multinational organisations, employing thousands all over the world and with a turnover larger than some nations' gross national product, to modest business organisations employing just a few people and operating in a small locality.

What is the purpose of all these organisations, why were they set up, how is it that they can and usually do continue? In this chapter we shall consider the advantages and disadvantages in the UK context of the principal legal forms of organisation, sole trader, partnership and limited liability companies. We also identify differences between the public and private sectors, explain the functions of primary, secondary and tertiary industries and explore the changing balance of power between them.

An organisation's mission – why it exists in society at all – is the guiding idea behind the organisation's activities. Goals and objectives are devised to fulfil the mission. They also interpret the organisation's mission to a number of different client groups or stakeholders, who all have an interest in what the organisation does. The mission must reflect the legitimate expectations of these stakeholders.

## Your objectives

In this chapter you will learn about:

(a) The size and types of organisations

(b) The nature of the public and private sectors

(c) The nature of the primary, secondary and tertiary sectors

(d) Business mission and objectives

(e) Stakeholder expectations

## 1 CATEGORIES OF ORGANISATION

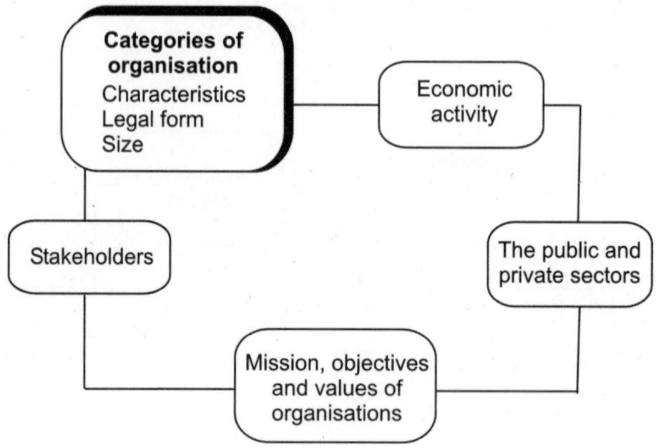


### 1.1 Characteristics

**Definition** 

> An **organisation** is an arrangement of people, pursuing common goals, achieving results and standards of performance.

There are many different types of organisations that are set up to serve a number of different purposes and to meet a variety of needs. They come in all forms, shapes and sizes. All businesses try to achieve their objectives, are accountable to stakeholders, need to be managed, have to meet legal requirements and have a formal structure.

Any business involves people and resources to do one of two things. These are:

(a) To make (produce) items or goods to be sold eg shirt factory, shoe factory, furniture maker, jeans factory, computer manufacturer, boat builder and dairy farmer;

(b) To provide services to be sold eg banks, building societies, dentists, police, hospitals and insurance companies.

Here are some possible differences between organisations.

| Factor | Example |
|---|---|
| Ownership (public vs. private) | Private sector: owned by private owners/shareholders<br>Public sector: owned by the government |
| Control | By the owners themselves, by people working on their behalf, or indirectly by government-sponsored regulators |
| Activity (what they do) | Manufacturing, healthcare |

| Factor | Example |
|---|---|
| Profit or non-profit orientation | Business exists to make a profit. The army, on the other hand, is not profit-oriented |
| Legal status | Limited company, partnership, sole trader or public limited company |
| Size | Size can be measured in many ways eg, the number of staff, number of branches, sales revenue each year, number of customers and market share |
| Sources of finance | Borrowing, government funding, share issues |
| Technology – the equipment and associated techniques used for carrying out certain tasks. | Some organisations eg mobile telephone manufacturers, have a high technology usage compared to others eg a window cleaning company. |

All organisations are affected by the environment (both nationally and internationally) and by the government of the day. They react and interact to each other and to professional bodies such as those of accountants and solicitors.

Thus the nature and type of organisation will be constantly changing and developing in reaction to environmental changes; a business that starts as a sole trader may develop into a partnership, then a limited company, then become part of a group of companies, then be taken into state ownership and then, following a change of government, be privatised and returned to the status of a company.

## 1.2 Legal form

Depending on how it is legally constituted an organisation may have a legal existence separate from that of its owners and/or its members. This is not the case for sole traders or partnerships where unlimited liability means that the individual or partner is personally liable to the full extent of his or her private assets for the debts of the business. Neither can provide a type of investment that allows for a share of the ownership to be readily marketable. This shortcoming is removed by the formation of a limited company.

*Sole traders*

Sole traders are single individuals carrying on a business on their own. Such businesses are usually small, although large ones with some managerial delegation do exist. The sole trader earns the profit or covers the losses of his or her venture. Legally, the business affairs of sole traders are not distinguished in any way from their personal affairs. If they incur a debt in their business dealings and the earnings of that business are not adequate to pay the debt then the creditor can require payment out of the trader's non-business property (eg their house). The advantages of being a sole trader are as follows.

(a) **No formal procedures** needed to begin trading

(b) **Independence and self-reliance** – the owner has no need to consult with others about his/her decisions and, except for tax purposes, is not required to issue trading results

(c) **Commitment and motivation** are encouraged by the solely accountable nature of the business

(d) Often such businesses are **close to their customers** and can respond quickly to market changes

The *disadvantages* of sole tradership are as follows.

(a) **Total personal liability** to the full extent of the private assets for the business debts. A sole trader can lose his/her home and all possessions as a result of business failure.

(b) **Financial problems** include difficulties in raising finance and expansion is only possible by ploughing back profits. Borrowed capital for expansion is often limited by lack of collateral.

(c) The individual usually has **one skill** eg an inventor or a good salesperson but the sole trader needs to be adequate in all areas (eg advertising, purchasing and maintaining accounts).

(d) **Lack of cover** in the case of illness and lack of succession in the case of death is a major problem.

*Partnership*

Legally, a partnership is two or more persons associated for the purpose of a business or profession. It is one stage beyond the sole trader and often arises from the need to introduce more capital or to combine skills eg a garage proprietor may introduce a marketing partner. Each partner contributes an agreed amount of capital and there is an agreed method of sharing profits, salaries and interest. Like a sole trader, the partners exert considerable influence over the business and are fully liable to outside parties in the event of financial failure. Sole traders who develop into a partnership often find difficulty in adapting to the need to consult others before any major decisions can be taken.

The **Limited Liability Partnerships Act** 2000 introduced the concept of the limited liability partnership into English and Scots law. It created a Limited Liability Partnership (LLP) as a body with a legal personality separate from its members (unlike a normal partnership). Unlike normal partnerships, the liability of members of LLP on winding up is limited to the amount of capital they contributed to the LLP.

*Companies or corporations*

Companies or corporations are distinct artificial 'persons' created in order to separate legal responsibility for the affairs of a business from the personal affairs of the individuals who own or operate it. Since a company exists only to establish legal responsibilities, it can only be created, operated and dissolved in accordance with the legal rules governing it (eg the Companies Acts in the UK).

Consequently, the business debts and liabilities are those of the company and not those of its members (shareholders). In other words, if the assets owned by the business are not sufficient to pay off the debts incurred by the business, the owners cannot be compelled to make up the deficit from their private resources. The point is that the business debts are not the owners' responsibility. They 'belong' to the company, which is regarded as a separate person in its own right.

The Companies Acts distinguish between:

(a) **Public limited companies** that are traded on an official stock market. (Such companies must include the letters 'plc ' in their names.)

(b) **Private limited companies** (which must include 'Ltd' or 'Limited' in their title) and whose shares are only transferable by direct contact and purchase from the shareholders (eg members of a family).

Public limited companies tend to be owned by a wide range of investors, whereas a private limited company, with no natural trading place for its shares, tends to be owned by a small number of shareholders.

Naturally the benefits of limited liability encourage companies to register as 'limited' or 'plc'. This protection attracts investors, secure in the knowledge that they will not be called upon to provide further capital to meet company debts. Limited liability can only exist where the company is a separate legal entity and it is these two fundamentals – limited liability and separate legal entity that distinguish companies from other forms of organisation.

Certain organisations may be limited by guarantee like a university or professional institute, or, rarely, a company may be unlimited, which does not give its members the protection of limited liability.

**Activity 1** **(10 minutes)**

Make the best match for the businesses listed below with the following business formats: (a) sole trader; (b) partnership; (c) private limited company; and (d) public limited company.

(i) Mass producer of cars
(ii) An inventor financed by two others setting-up a small factory
(iii) Three qualified accountants setting-up in private practice
(iv) Retailer with three employees

### 1.3 Size

The concept of size is problematic. It can be viewed in terms of:

(a) Numbers employed
(b) Volume of output
(c) Volume of sales
(d) Assets employed
(e) Profits earned
(f) Net worth in real terms.

There are both similarities and differences between large, medium and small businesses.

**Small businesses** – are usually owned and run by one person (a sole trader) or by a few people (partnership) and tend to sell their goods or services locally eg a plumber, a bicycle repair shop. They normally employ less than 50 people. Businesses of this type can include:

- small/medium-sized shops
- computer trainers
- solicitors and accountants.

**Medium-sized businesses** – normally employ between 50 and 250 people and operate either at local or national level. Examples include:

- manufacturers, eg clothing, furniture, household goods
- theatres
- insurance companies

**Large businesses** – normally have factories/offices and outlets in more than one city and often in more than one country. Typical examples of large businesses include:

- car manufacturers, eg Ford, Nissan
- retail food outlets, eg Tesco
- oil companies, eg Esso, BP
- finance companies/banks, eg Royal Bank of Scotland.

Most **national** businesses have household names, are easily recognised by their logos, are large in size, i.e. employ a workforce of more than 250 people and have branches/ factories in major towns/cities. Well-known national businesses include Royal Mail, Boots the chemist, Topshop, HMV and Specsavers.

**Multinational** businesses sell goods or provide services worldwide and operate in more than one country. Some well known multinationals include Ford, McDonalds, Shell and Esso.

---

**FOR DISCUSSION**

Size is an interesting issue – we see at the same time that Lloyds TSB take over Halifax Bank of Scotland, Carphone Warhouse planning (at the time of writing in Agusut 2009) to demerge into component parts. Investors and chief executives in the UK and the US seem to have a fascination with size – the same is not necessarily the case in (say) Germany – a point that might be of some significance.

---

Organisations grow large where economies of scale encourage the success of large firms in a market at the expense of small firms. In some markets, being large is essential. In others, small can be beautiful. Small and large organisations can coexist in a market by tackling different segments.

**Advantages of a large organisation** are as follows.

(a) A large-scale organisation should have access to sufficient **resources** to command a significant market share. This in turn will enable it to influence prices in the market so as to ensure continuing profitability.

(b) A large organisation can provide for **greater division of work** and **specialisation**. Specialisation, and the development of a wide range of products or customer services, should enable the organisation to attract continuing customer support and market shares. In contrast, a small or medium-sized business will require greater competence and versatility from its senior management, because they will not have the benefits of support from functional specialists, which are available to the top managers of large organisations.

(c) A large organisation with a wide variety of products or customer services should be able to offer an **attractive career to prospective employees**, and it is therefore likely to receive job application requests from very talented people. This in turn should enable the large organisation to recruit and develop high-quality personnel for future top management positions.

(d) Specialisation brings with it the ability to provide **expert services at a relatively low cost** to the customer. A large organisation is also able to make use of the advantages of efficient 'large-scale' equipment such as advanced computer systems or manufacturing equipment. For these (and other) reasons, large organisations are able to achieve **economies of scale** in the use of resources. Cheaper costs in turn mean either lower prices for customers or higher profits for the organisation.

(e) A large organisation is more likely to provide **continuity of goods or services,** management philosophy, customer relations and so on than a smaller organisation. A smaller organisation might be prone to sudden policy changes or changes of product when a new management team takes over.

The **disadvantages** of a large organisation are as follows.

(a) There is a tendency for the management **hierarchy** to develop too many levels. The more management levels there are, the greater the problem of communication between top and bottom, and the greater the problems of control and direction by management at the top.

(b) An organisation might become so widely **diversified** in the range of products or services it offers that it becomes difficult, if not impossible, for management to integrate all of the organisation under a common objective and within a single 'management philosophy' and culture.

(c) Top management might spend **too much time in maintenance** of the organisation (that is, with problems of administration) and lose sight of their primary tasks of setting objectives and planning for the future.

(d) There is a tendency of top management in large organisations to become 'ingrown and inbred, smug and self-satisfied'. The tendency towards '**group-think**' – an acceptance by all managers of a common attitude towards problems – might introduce an unconscious resistance to necessary changes and developments.

(e) The sheer size of an organisation may provide management with **problems of co-ordination, planning policy and effective control**. For example, a junior manager might find the organisation so large that he has relatively little influence. Decisions that he regards as important must be continually referred up the line to his superiors, for inter-departmental consultations. At the same time, the top management might find the organisation so large and complex, and changes in policy and procedures so difficult and time-consuming to implement, that they also feel unable to give direction to the organisation. The organisation is therefore a 'monster', which operates of its own accord, with neither senior nor junior managers able to manage it effectively.

(f) In a large organisation, many of the tasks of junior management are **routine and boring**. Even middle management might be frustrated by the restrictions on their authority, the impersonal nature of their organisation, the inability to earn a just reward for their special efforts owing to the standardisation of pay and promotion procedures and the lack of information about aspects of the organisation which should influence their work.

**Internal economies of scale** arise from the more effective use of available resources, and from increased specialisation, when production capacity is enlarged.

(a) **Specialisation of labour**. In a large undertaking, a highly skilled worker can be employed in a job, which makes full use of his skills. In a smaller undertaking, individuals must do a variety of tasks, none of which they may do very well ('Jack-of-all-trades – master of none').

(b) **Division of labour**. Because there is specialisation of labour there is also division of labour, ie work is divided between several specialists, each of whom contributes his share to the final product. A building will be constructed, for example, by labourers, bricklayers, plumbers, electricians, plasterers and so on. Switching between tasks wastes time, and division of labour avoids this waste.

(c) Large undertakings can make use of **larger and more specialised machinery**. If smaller undertakings tried to use similar machinery, the costs would be excessive because the machines would become obsolete before their physical life ends (ie their economic life would be shorter than their physical life). Obsolescence is caused by falling demand for the product made on the machine, or by the development of newer and better machines.

(d) **Dimensional economies** of scale refer to the relationship between the volume of output and the size of equipment (eg storage tanks) needed to hold or process the output. The cost of a container for 10,000 gallons of product will be much less than ten times the cost of a container for just 1,000 gallons.

(e) **Buying economies** may be available, reducing the cost of material purchases through bulk purchase discounts.

(f) **Indivisibility of operations**. There are operations which:

   (i) Must be carried out at the same cost, regardless of whether the business is small or large; these are fixed costs and average fixed costs always decline as production increases

   (ii) Vary a little, but not proportionately, with size (ie having 'semi-fixed' *costs)*

   (iii) Are not worth considering below a certain level of output (eg advertising campaigns)

(g) **Stockholding** becomes more efficient. The most economic quantities of inventory to hold increase with the scale of operations, but at a lower proportionate rate of increase.

*The advantages of small firms*

If large size can give economies of scale, why do small firms continue to prosper? In some industries and professions, small firms predominate (eg building, the legal profession) and in some, small and large firms co-exist (eg newsagents). The number of small firms in the UK has grown in recent years. The reasons for the survival of the small firm may be that there are problems with large size (**diseconomies of scale**).

(a) **Small firms** are more likely to operate in **competitive markets**, in which prices will tend to be lower and the most efficient firms will survive at the expense of the inefficient.

(b) They are more likely to be **risk takers**, investing 'venture capital' in projects that might yield high rewards. Innovation and entrepreneurial activity are important ingredients for economic recovery or growth.

(c) **Management-employee relations** are more likely to be co-operative, with direct personal contacts between managers at the top and all the employees.

(d) Small firms tend to **specialise**, and so can contribute efficiently towards the division of labour in an economy.

(e) The structure of a small firm may allow for greater **flexibility** (eg an employee or manager can switch from one task to another much more readily).

(f) Small firms often sell to a **local market**; large firms need wider markets, and may incur relatively higher costs of transport.

(g) Managerial economies can be obtained by hiring **expert consultants,** possibly at a cheaper cost than permanent management specialists.

(h) Some small firms act as **suppliers** or **sub-contractors** to larger firms.

(i) There may be **insufficient market demand** to justify large-scale production.

## 2 ECONOMIC ACTIVITY

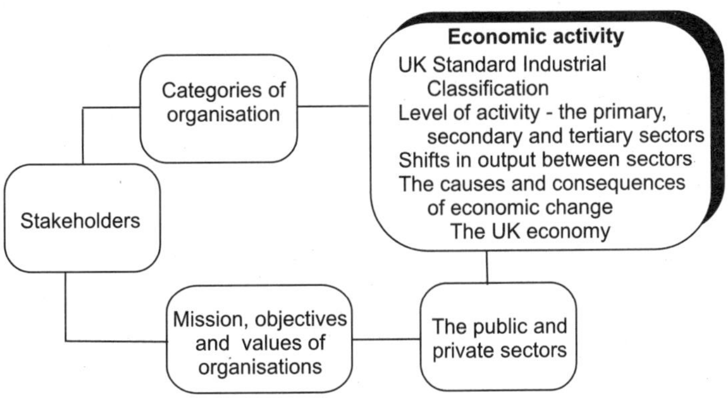


### 2.1 UK Standard Industrial Classification

The UK Standard Industrial Classification of Economic Activities (UK SIC(92)) is used to classify business establishments and other statistical units by the type of economic activities they are engaged in. The classification provides a framework and a common structure for the collection, tabulation, presentation and analysis of data and its use promotes uniformity. In particular, it underpins the collection by the Office for National Statistics (ONS) of all the UK's official statistics on business and industry. The UK SIC(92) is a hierarchical system with five levels of detail. At the highest level of aggregation are seventeen sections covering broad categories of industry, each denoted by a single letter from A to Q:

A Agriculture, hunting and forestry
B Fishing
C Mining and quarrying
D Manufacturing
E Electricity, gas and water supply
F Construction
G Wholesale and retail trade; repair of motor vehicles, motorcycles and personal and household goods

| | |
|---|---|
| H | Hotels and restaurants |
| I | Transport, storage and communication |
| J | Financial intermediation |
| K | Real estate, renting and business activities |
| L | Public administration and defence; compulsory social security |
| M | Education |
| N | Health and social work |
| O | Other community, social and personal service activities |
| P | Private households with employed persons |
| Q | Extra-territorial organisations and bodies |

Manufacturing, for example, is Section D. It has a subsection DB – *Manufacture of textiles and textile products (comprising divisions 17 and 18).* One of the lowest levels of aggregation is Subclass 17.51/1 — *Manufacture of woven carpets and rugs.*

### 2.2 Level of activity – the primary, secondary and tertiary sectors

The type of activity which individual businesses are involved in varies depending upon their product. There are three levels of economic activity:

1. *The primary sector* – this sector of industry consists of industries that produce raw materials, such as crops and minerals. Examples of this type of business activity would include oil extraction, wood felling or a coal mining company.
2. *The secondary sector* – this sector of industry consists of industries that use the raw material produced by the primary sector. For example, processing oil to produce petrol, chemicals, gas etc. Firms taking part in secondary production are either involved in manufacturing or in construction. They manufacture the finished article, or parts for further assembly and manufacture. They construct buildings such as houses and shops as well as building roads etc.
3. *The tertiary sector* – this sector of industry consists of distribution and service industries. They are involved in passing the goods from the producer to the consumer. Services include activities as diverse as banking, tourism, hairdressing, teaching, office cleaning, tax advice and the media. Tertiary industries involve passing the goods from the producer to the consumer.

All these activities can involve public or private sector organisations. For example, there are private sector colleges alongside local education authority colleges offering tuition for the examinations of professional bodies.

**Definition**

> The **Gross Domestic product** (GDP) is one way of measuring the 'size' of the economy. It is explained in more detail later in this section.

Table 1.1 below illustrates the share of the Gross Domestic Product (GDP) between the primary, secondary and tertiary sectors of the economy and shows some trends in these sectors.

| UNITED KINGDOM | % share of GDP in each sector | | | | | | |
|---|---|---|---|---|---|---|---|
| | **1969** | **1979** | **1989** | **1995** | **2000** | **2002** | **2004** |
| ***Primary sector*** | 4.3 | 6.7 | 4.4 | 4.4 | 4.1 | 3.9 | 2.9 |
| of which: | | | | | | | |
| Agriculture, forestry, fishing | 1.8 | 2.2 | 1.9 | 2.0 | 1.2 | 1.2 | 0.9 |
| Mining, oil and gas, quarrying | 2.5 | 4.5 | 2.5 | 2.4 | 2.9 | 2.7 | 2.0 |
| ***Secondary sector*** | 42.0 | 36.7 | 34.1 | 29.7 | 25.8 | 24.4 | 20.9 |
| of which: | | | | | | | |
| Manufacturing | 30.7 | 27.3 | 24.3 | 21.8 | 18.7 | 16.7 | 13.5 |
| Construction | 8.4 | 6.2 | 7.4 | 5.3 | 5.2 | 5.8 | 5.9 |
| Energy and water | 2.9 | 3.2 | 2.4 | 2.6 | 1.9 | 1.9 | 1.6 |
| ***Tertiary sector*** | 53.7 | 56.7 | 61.5 | 65.9 | 70.1 | 71.7 | 76.0 |
| of which: | | | | | | | |
| Distribution, hotels, catering | 13.3 | 12.7 | 14.1 | 14.0 | 15.7 | 16.1 | 14.6 |
| Transport and communications | 6.3 | 7.3 | 8.4 | 8.4 | 8.2 | 8.5 | 7.2 |
| Banking, finance, business | 8.6 | 11.0 | 18.5 | 21.1 | 28.2 | 24.5 | 28.9 |
| Public services | 14.1 | 14.2 | 16.9 | 18.6 | 17.4 | 22.6 | 17.6 |
| Others | 11.4 | 11.5 | 3.6 | 3.8 | 0.6 | | 7.6 |
| | 100.0 | 100.0 | 100.0 | 100.0 | 100.0 | 100.0 | 100.0 |

*Table 1.1: Distribution of UK national output*

A word of warning: Care should always be taken with national income statistics. Although they appear to be very exact they are prone to changes in collection methods and presentation.

***We will examine the primary sector first***

*The primary sector*

Britain's agricultural sector is small, but efficient. The industry has been damaged in recent years with various problems, such as BSE (Mad cow disease) and Foot and Mouth disease. Energy production is a large part of the UK economy. Oil and gas were discovered under the North Sea in the 1970s.

In the UK, over the long-term, the trend is one of decline in this sector when measured in terms of its share of GDP. Viewed against the process of economic growth, this declining share also reflects the rising level of output of other industries that are growing faster, as well as absolute decline in output in industries such as coal.

The beginning of North Sea oil and gas production in the 1970s interrupted this trend and increased the overall importance of the primary sector within the UK economy. By 1989, however, the shares of oil and gas within GDP had fallen to 56% of its 1979 share. Agriculture, forestry and fishing increased the share of GDP slightly from 1969 to 1979; the fall in shares from 2.2% in 1979 to 0.9% in 2004 reflects the long-term trend of declining importance for these industries. The relatively high share of 6.7% for the primary sector as a whole in 1979 mainly reflects the advent of North Sea oil. By 2004 this had dropped to 2.9% as oil production dropped.

***Next we consider the secondary sector***

*The secondary sector*

The history of manufacturing in Britain is unique because of Britain's role as the birthplace of the Industrial Revolution. Textiles, shipbuilding, iron, and steel emerged as important industries, and coal remained the most important industrial fuel. The structure of industry changed substantially in the last half of the 20th century. The coal mining and cotton textile industries declined. As coal production declined, oil production replaced it as a major industry.

Motor-vehicle production became a significant part of the industrial base but was subject to severe foreign competition. As incomes increased, consumer demand rose for durable goods such as cars and kitchen appliances. British industrial production also expanded into communications equipment, including fibre optics, computers, computer-controlled machine tools, and robots. Scotland is also a major producer of computers, employing about 40,000 people in the electronics industry, many of them working for overseas computer firms. Scotland and Northern Ireland are still noted for their production of whisky and textiles, especially linen from Northern Ireland and tweed from Scotland.

In the secondary sector of the economy, manufacturing has reduced by a large amount in recent years, however areas that are particularly strong are the pharmaceutical and chemical industries. GlaxoSmithKline is one of the world's largest drug companies. The ICI Group is one of the world's largest producers of speciality products and paints, employing over 45,000 people worldwide.

The secondary sector normally grows rapidly during the early stages of economic development. The data show how the UK has reached a later stage of decline in this sector. Most of the fall in GDP share from 42.0% in 1969 to 20.98% in 2004 is attributable to a decline in *manufacturing,* (eg cars, clothes), as opposed to *construction,* (eg house or road building) and *energy* (eg electricity generation). Manufactured goods are easy to transport and export (sell abroad). They are thus important in international trade.

The decline in the secondary sector has led to a reduction in employment bringing some severe unemployment in regions that have been heavily dependent on particular industries. Like most developed economies the secondary sector has become reduced, whilst service industries grow at a large rate. The service industry includes things such as tourism, finance etc.

***Finally we look at the tertiary sector***

*The tertiary sector*

This sector is made up mainly of goods distribution and service industries. It has become the predominant provider of employment and output in the UK economy in recent decades, growing from a 53% share in 1969 to a 72% share in 2002. This trend is shared in other wealthy countries such as the US. Even Germany and Japan are seeing a growing service sector.

The data shows that the main reason for the continuing growth during the 1980s and 1990s has been the rapid expansion in banking, finance, tourism and business activities, which expanded their GDP share from 8.6% to 28.2% between 1969 and 2000.

Britain is also one of the world's most popular travel destinations, and tourism is an essential part of the economy. In 2004 there were 27.8 million overseas visitors to the UK who spent £13 billion.

---

**FOR DISCUSSION**

Looking at the data set out in Table 1.1, how might you explain the changes between the three sectors in the economy since 1969?

---

***We shall now go on to explain some of the causes of the changes in the structure of the economy in recent times.***

### 2.3 Shifts in output between sectors

Within the primary sector, the most significant factor affecting the change in GDP shares over the period from 1969 has been the discovery and exploitation of North Sea oil, and later gas. In the earlier years, as well as benefiting from the peak in absolute output from the North Sea, this sector benefited from relatively high-energy prices compared with more recent years.

Britain's agricultural sector is small, but efficient. The industry has been damaged in recent years with various problems, such as BSE (Mad cow disease) and Foot and Mouth disease.

**Definitions**

1. **De-industrialisation**: often used to describe the long-term decline in the importance of manufacturing industry and the secondary sector in general.
2. **Trade surplus**: an excess of exports over imports.
3. **Trade deficit**: the deficit that occurs when imports are greater than exports.

Some argue that the decline of the secondary sector and the rise of the tertiary sector is an inevitable consequence of economic development. As in earlier stages of economic development, when the agricultural sector declined with the growth of the secondary sector, so the secondary sector has declined as demand has shifted, relatively, from goods to services. International comparisons offer some support for this explanation, since recent years have seen a decline in the share of employment accounted for by manufacturing in almost all advanced capitalist economies. However, the UK is unusual in that manufacturing employment reached its peak rather earlier (1955) than in many other countries, including the Federal Republic of Germany (1970), which faced major economic reconstruction following World War II. Some point out that Britain was the first country to industrialise, and during much of this century relative economic decline has been apparent in the UK, with many other industrialised countries overtaking the

UK in GDP per head. One of the causes might be increased productivity: it became possible to produce more with fewer people, freeing people for employment elsewhere.

Domestic output (ie goods or services produced in the UK) supplies both domestic demand and *exports*. A relative decline in manufacturing output may result from:

(a) People preferring goods made by overseas firms, which are imported
(b) UK businesses' inability to make enough goods to satisfy the demand
(c) The UK specialising in some goods and services as opposed to others

This explanation is borne out by the shift from a UK trade surplus in manufactured goods during the 1970s to significant deficits in manufactured goods from the 1980s to the present day. This may be the result of a shift of demand away from UK manufactured goods towards foreign manufactured goods coupled with a failure of UK manufacturing industries to meet demand.

Within the tertiary sector, the rising share of banking, finance and insurance reflects a number of factors.

(a) London has built on its reputation as one of the **leading financial centres** of the world, and in some areas (eg the foreign exchange markets) it is pre-eminent. The strong position of 'the City' (the London financial community) makes it a large exporter of financial services.

(b) **Increasing affluence and changing social factors** (eg increasing levels of owner-occupation of housing from the 1970s onwards) have increased domestic demand for financial products of various kinds (eg current accounts, mortgages and insurance products).

(c) The **abolition of exchange controls** (restrictions on how much money you could take out of the country) in 1979 and the deregulation of financial markets during the 1980s (for example, the Stock Exchange 'Big Bang' and the Building Societies Act of 1986) encouraged greater competition between banks, building societies and insurance companies.

More recently, the trade deficits in manufacturing have been offset by surpluses in oil exports, the service sector and in earnings from overseas assets. The problem then remains of how an overall balance of trade (on 'current account') is to be achieved as primary sector (oil) exports become less significant for the UK.

**Activity 2** **(10 minutes)**

Can the tertiary (service) sector take the place of the secondary sector (manufactured goods) in ensuring a healthy balance between imports and exports?

The UK, with its major world financial centre in the City of London, has been very successful in international trade in financial services. The UK's share of the world market in services (or 'invisibles') declined from 12% in 1978 to 8% in 1993 but increased to 11% in 2002.

## 2.4 The causes and consequences of economic change

**Definition**

> **Exchange rate**: the price of one currency in terms of another. If £1 can buy you $1.50 in US dollars, then the pound-dollar exchange rate is 1.50.

The economic structure of an economy may make it hard for the economy to adapt to future economic changes. For example:

(a) The discovery of North Sea oil and gas led to increased employment in these industries.

(b) Furthermore, it meant a rising exchange rate. This made UK manufactured exports too expensive for overseas customers to buy, whereas manufactured imports became much cheaper.

(c) Many firms failed and went out of business.

(d) With the oil and gas resources running down, the diminished manufacturing industry is poorly placed to take advantage of the new situation; it is unable to make up for the lost oil and gas output rapidly enough. Domestic manufactured goods have been replaced by imports, so the UK has to export something else or rebuild its factories.

> **Activity 3** **(10 minutes)**
>
> Describe what will happen when the oil supplies in the North Sea run out.

*World market conditions* may adversely affect an economy in which economic activity has become concentrated in particular sectors. Some poorer countries depend on exports from their primary sectors. Sri Lanka and Kenya, for example, export tea. If the price at which tea is traded on world markets begins to fall, the wealth of those economies will also fall. Issues of ethical trading practices have also been an issue for such countries. An economy may gain in the long run from having a widely based economic structure rather than one that is heavily reliant on particular sectors. You might note that both Sri Lanka and Kenya have attempted to diversify into tourism, a tertiary sector industry.

Technological progress brings about changes in economic structure, sometimes quite dynamically. Competition from overseas producers is also important. We discuss technology later.

**Definitions**

> - **Sunrise industries**: rising new industries, such as information technology and genetics. Their importance is increasing worldwide.
> - **Sunset industries**: gradually dying industries. In the Western economies they include heavy industries such as steel and shipbuilding, whose prices have been undercut for many years by more efficient producers in Korea and other countries in the Pacific.

The decline of industries can have the following consequences.

(a) Unemployment can be severe in the regions affected, particularly where there is heavy geographical concentration (as was the case with shipbuilding and coal mining) and if the industries on which a region is economically reliant are closed down rapidly.

(b) There may be knock-on effects for the rest of the region's businesses, as consumers' spending power is reduced and people begin to leave the area.

**Activity 4** **(10 minutes)**

Suggest some ways in which the government might be able to intervene in order to alleviate the effects of a decline in a particular industry.

Just as the run down of certain industries brings problems for the regions in which those industries are concentrated, so too the rapid expansion of certain sectors may present problems. In Britain during the last 25 years, the expansion of the banking, finance and insurance industries put strains on the economic infrastructure and brought continued high house price inflation in the South East region, where these industries are concentrated.

## 2.5 The UK economy

### How big is the UK economy?

The size of the UK economy can be illustrated in several ways. We will discuss output and labour statistics.

### Output

The 2010 first quarter gross domestic product (GDP) of £317.2billion (Office for National Statistics).

GDP is a commonly used measure and appears in a large number of official publications. It often forms the basis for comparisons over time and with other countries, using GDP per head of population.

The GDP figure published by the Office for National Statistics is itself an estimate and is based on subsidiary estimates of total output of goods and services; total incomes earned; and total value added. It is a gross measure because no allowance is made for the 'wearing out' of the capital goods used in production.

There are other measures that are used in connection with the size of an economy: in the UK these are based on the rules of the 1995 European system of accounts.

Gross national income (GNI) is equal to GDP adjusted for pay and property income either coming into the UK from other countries or going out to them.

GNI is adjusted to net national income by deducting an allowance for the capital consumption mentioned above.

GNI is also the basis of calculation of gross national product (GNP). The process of adjustment is rather technical and includes items such as military equipment and government licenses and fees.

### Labour statistics

In 2008, the population of the UK was 63.4 million. Of these people, just over 49 million were aged 16 and over, had finished their basic education and were therefore able to contribute to production. In fact, those in employment, self employment, training schemes and unpaid family work amounted to 29 million, while 2 million were registered as unemployed.

## 3 THE PUBLIC AND PRIVATE SECTORS

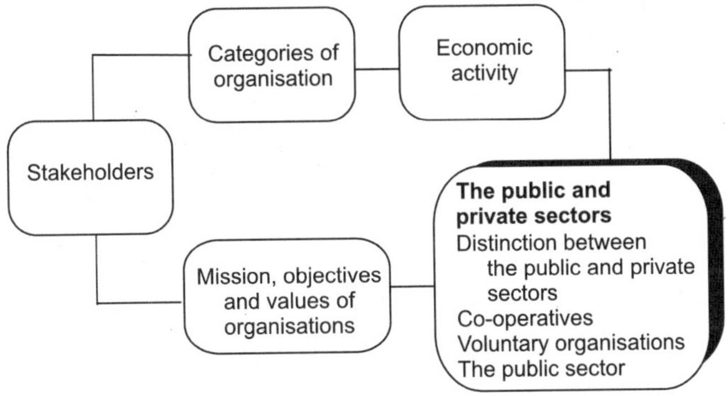


### 3.1 Distinction between the public and private sectors

The UK economy is a mix of private and public sector organisations. Private sector firms are owned by individuals, not by the state. These firms can be large or small, owned by one person or by thousands. By producing goods or services the majority of them intend to make a profit for their owners. Public sector organisations are run by the government for the benefit of the general public.

The main differences between the public and private sector may be summarised as:

1. **Private sector** organisations are usually set up for personal gain and are funded by shares issued, loans from banks, overdrafts etc.
2. **Public sector** organisations are usually set up in the interests of the community and are funded wholly or partly by the government from public funds and are answerable to a government department or the Treasury.

Classification by sector simply describes the organisation as being in the public sector (controlled by government and providing services for the public, the community and the nation) or in the private sector. Private sector organisations are not owned by the state or run by the state. They provide a huge variety of goods and services and include:

1. Organisations that **seek profit for their proprietors** by satisfying customers' requirements at a suitable price – they include:

   (a) Sole trader businesses (eg a local greengrocer)
   (b) Partnerships (eg a local firm of solicitors)
   (c) Private companies (not quoted on the stock market)
   (d) Public companies ('plcs', mostly quoted on the stock market)

***We have already discussed these earlier in the chapter***

2 Organisations with objectives other than purely profit – they include:

(a) Co-operatives and other mutual organisations such as building societies

(b) Voluntary organisations such as charities, which have specific charitable objectives, and other voluntary societies, clubs and associations

### 3.2 Co-operatives

**Definition**

> A **co-operative** is the result of a voluntary linking together of consumers, producers or retailers into a trading organisation, which is then used to represent its constituent members in the marketplace.

Co-operatives do not fall into conventional private or public enterprise categories and are not nationalised or state-owned. They are not legally constituted as private or public limited companies, although in the UK co-operative societies place legal restrictions on the size of individual shareholdings. Nevertheless, in common with limited liability companies, co-operatives pay back a proportion of the surplus generated during the year's trading to their members or subscribers. This return can take the form of dividends on profit, interest on shares held, or discounts on future purchases.

Co-operatives are established in the UK under the **Industrial and Provident Societies Acts** as corporate bodies with limited liability. There is a parallel with the limited company, in which the board of directors is elected by shareholders; members of the co-operative society elect a 'governing body' or management committee to which operational management must report. This governing body is responsible for policy, decision-making, and overall strategic management.

The co-operative is therefore 'quasi-democratic'. Its members can exercise a direct influence over its affairs through their voting rights and their response to the governing body's annual report.

*Different types of co-operative*

(a) **Wholesale or retail of goods** – The co-operative may be able to eliminate middlemen in the distribution chain and enjoy the economies of bulk buying. Such economies can then be passed on to the consumer via reduced or stabilised prices. In the UK, such a system would be operated by a **co-operative society**; obtaining their bulk supplies from the co-operative wholesale society (which they would own) for retail to the consumer.

(b) **Farming co-operatives** – Here, the scale of operation may permit the negotiation of contracts with buyers for the bulk supply of farm produce. Farming co-operatives also purchase seeds, fertilisers, fuel and feedstuffs in bulk, passing the savings on to the members, and may buy expensive farm machinery for use on a collective basis.

(c) **Producer co-operatives** – These are a thriving enterprise form, producing goods for sale in the market. They are particularly important in less developed countries and in the Third World, as their features include:

(i) provision of a simple enterprise form for self-help schemes

(ii) potential economies of operation and output volume

(iii) the scope to standardise products or services, allowing more effective marketing and distribution.

### 3.3 Voluntary organisations

**Definition**

> **Voluntary organisations** can be described as non-profit driven, non-statutory, autonomous and run by individuals who do not get paid for running the organisation.

The 'Social Economy' or 'Third Sector' are other terms used to refer to the voluntary sector. A perspective based on work carried out by the CBS Network (2002) defines the Third Sector as all constituted organisations, plus the family economy, as set apart from the statutory and private sectors, and as such voluntary organisations are predominant within it.

Voluntary organisations include large international charities, small community groups, arts and trade organisations, professional bodies and charitable trusts. They share many things in common.

(a) They are **non-profit making** organisations. Although raising the financial resources they need to operate is an important aspect of what they do, their objective is to achieve something beyond producing an income for shareholders.

(b) They are usually **dependent upon their members and supporters to survive**. Often the visible public face of such organisations is only a small part of a larger network or community of individuals.

(c) A key feature of voluntary organisations is that they are ultimately directed by **individuals who do not make their living** from their involvement in running the organisation.

*Charities*

The term charity or charity sector officially came into use in the 1600s when the first Act of Parliament was introduced to regulate groups of individuals involved in philanthropic work. To be a charity an organisation has to fulfill certain criteria:

(a) Its work must be recognised by UK law as being charitable. This means that its purpose must fit under one of the 'four heads' of charity (old-fashioned term for 'headings'). These are:

(i) The **relief of poverty** (There is no defined limit to the income of a person who can be helped under this heading. Assistance can be through the provision of goods, services or money direct to the client group or through the financial support of other organisations relieving poverty.)

(ii) The advancement of **education** (This is a broad definition, as well as schools and universities it includes youth organisations, sporting facilities, teaching aids, arts education etc.)

(iii) The advancement of **religion** (This category covers all monotheistic religions, not favouring one over another, assuming all religion to be for the good of society)

(iv) **Other purposes** beneficial to the community which do not fit under one of the other three heads. (This head covers 'public works, moral improvement, protection of lives or property of the community, preservation of public order, resettlement of offenders, servicemen, disaster funds, general promotion of industry, recreational and leisure facilities which are provided in the interests of social welfare' – The Non-Profit Sector (NFP) in the UK, CAF 1997)

(b) Its work must be for the **public benefit**. It must be of actual benefit and benefit the public as a whole or a significant section of it. It is for this reason that not all NFP organisations can be considered charities since this clause will automatically exclude any organisation that acts solely for the benefit of its membership, eg British Diabetic Association, a housing association etc. This means that the title 'charity' is awarded according to an organisation's work rather than its structure or legal classification and so a charity can take a variety of legal forms.

One of these forms is a company limited by guarantee (Charitable Corporation). This is an organisation that is incorporated, ie it has a defined legal identity and limited liability status. For example, Shelter is a charity and has a limited company for trading activities.

By taking up limited liability status, a charity limits the liability of its management or trustees in respect of any financial losses that it may sustain. The directors of the organisation (drawn from the membership/supporters), give a nominal guarantee, (usually of £1), and are not personally liable for any losses beyond that amount. A charitable company limited by guarantee is forbidden from distributing profits to its directors or members and so complies with the 'not for profit' classification. It must abide by both charity and company law with its directors acting as both company directors and charity trustees.

Some charitable organisations divide themselves into a number of associated parts, each with different legal status, ie a company limited by guarantee and an educational trust. In this way each part can benefit from different legal or tax benefits.

***We now look at ownership in the public sector.***

### 3.4 The public sector

It can be inferred from the general literature that public enterprises have three defining characteristics, they:

(a) are government owned and controlled

(b) are engaged in commercial (business) activities

(c) have socio-political goals alongside their primary economic goals.

Some provide services paid for by taxation. Others levy charges on users directly, although such charges may be reduced by subsidy. The *public sector* refers to *all* publicly-funded or publicly-owned bodies, even though they may not form part of the obvious apparatus of government.

---

**EXAMPLE: PUBLIC SECTOR ORGANISATIONS**

Service organisations owned by central government and/or local government include the following:

1 Civil Service agencies
2 The Crown Prosecution Service
3 Local authorities
4 Schools
5 Environmental protection agencies such as the National Rivers Authority
6 Job Centre Plus
7 The Diplomatic Service
8 The Armed Forces
9 Public libraries
10 The Fire Service

The British Broadcasting Corporation is still a state-owned ('nationalised') industry in the UK.

---

In theory, public sector organisations are run on behalf of the public and are accountable to Parliament.

Public sector organisations are features of all advanced Western economies. The United Kingdom spends a rather higher proportion of GDP on public expenditure than does the United States or Japan. In 2008 this was 43% of GDP. It spends a rather lower proportion than the Benelux countries and Scandinavia. It spends about the same proportion as Germany, France and Italy.

There was a marked variation from 34.1% in the south east of England to 62.7% in Northern Ireland.

---

**FOR DISCUSSION**

The creation of autonomous Executive Agencies, internal markets and compulsory competitive tendering has led to improved efficiency and a more 'business-like' approach by public sector organisations.

Discuss whether this is in fact true and whether the efficiency gains have led to improved services for the public.

---

### Political debate

The size of the public sector has become the subject of considerable political controversy. From the Second World War until the 1970s there was a broad political consensus over the welfare state and the mixed economy. There was then little fundamental disagreement over the extent of the public sector and the kind of services that the state should provide. The 1980s opened up differences in policies between those who supported increased state provision across a whole range of services, and those who advocated a drastic reduction in collective provision and the size of the public sector.

The debate today is not only about how public services should be delivered, but also about whether they should be supplied by the state at all. This fundamental question has affected virtually all public-sector organisations to some degree and has provoked considerable internal self-examination as well as external criticism.

Currently, a new consensus might see the state's role as an **enabler** rather than as a direct provider of services. This could lead to further reduction in provision of welfare, housing and education. A debate of particular interest to the current Government is related to the issue of state pensions and whether these should be provided by private insurance held by individuals.

**Activity 5** **(10 minutes)**

(a) Which publicly provided services have you used?

(b) What benefits do you think you have gained from using them?

(c) What do you expect to have gained in 40 years time?

(d) How might this change if the services are privatised?

(e) Find two examples of privatised services. Have they improved under private management?

## 4 MISSION, OBJECTIVES AND VALUES OF ORGANISATIONS

**Definition**

**Firm**: a wide term for any organisation that carries on a business. In spite of their many differences, we treat firms as single, consistent decision-taking units and, for the purposes of economic analysis, we ignore any differences in decision-making procedures and economic structures between them.

### 4.1 Mission and vision

An essential requirement for a meaningful strategic plan is the establishment of a set of goals and objectives for the organisation. The process of developing these can be shown as a progression or hierarchy of aims or purposes.

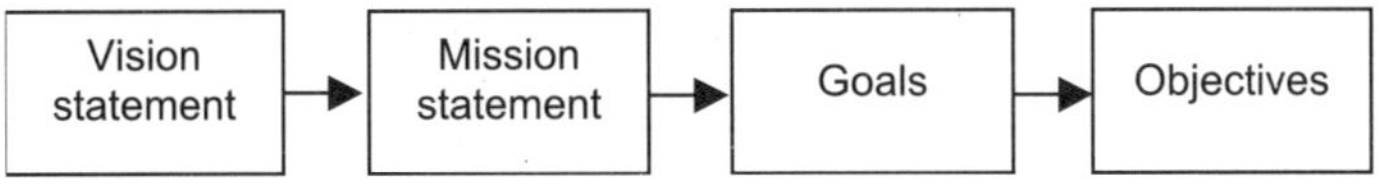


(a) **Vision statements** – are seen as documents that set out the **strategic intentions** of the organisation. They are about 'animating the dream'. A strategic vision can take many forms. Mercedes were guided by a vision of being the best in their field in terms of delivering quality products and services. Weight Watchers had a vision of building and exploiting its unique associations of dietary weight control and nutrition to gain a presence throughout the supermarket. Virgin had the vision 'to be the number 1 entertainment and service provider'. While a vision is meant to inspire, it is not very helpful in the shorter term. Many organisations now understand that their stakeholders need to know what the organisation stands for and why they should give it their loyalty. What is required is a 'road map' and this is often articulated in a mission statement. The difference between a mission and a vision is that the mission is about behaviour and actions for the present and immediate future; a vision is a sort of super-objective in that, like the Holy Grail, it may never be attained. Instead, it should provide continuous inspiration towards a desired end.

(b) **Mission statements** – should outline the specific role that the organisation plans to fulfil within society over the long-term and therefore limits the scope of its operations by implicitly excluding areas outside its stated mission.

(c) **Goals** – generally apply to shorter time frames than the more general mission statement but they are still non-specific and not quantified. They should interpret the mission statement into more understandable statements for the different groups of stakeholders, so that internal conflicts between stakeholders are minimised. Separate goals may be developed for customers, suppliers, employees and shareholders.

(d) **Values** – the goals or aims of the organisation will have an ideology based on beliefs, values and attitudes. This ideology is a means of control through shared beliefs and determines the culture of the organisation, providing a set of principles that govern the overall conduct of the organisation's operations, code of behaviour, the management of people and its dealings with other organisations. For example, a firm's moral principles might mean refusing an assignment if it believes the client will not benefit, even though this refusal means lost revenue. A sense of mission, or emotional bond, is where employees' personal values coincide with organisational values.

(e) **Objectives** – set out more specifically the goals of the organisation, the aims to be achieved and the desired end results.

### Corporate mission

**Definition**

> **Mission** 'describes the organisation's basic function in society, in terms of the products and services it produces for its clients' (*Mintzberg*).

Although hard to quantify, the idea of a *corporate mission* is taken seriously by many firms.

(a) Values and feelings are integral elements of consumers' buying decisions, as evidenced by advertising, branding and market research. Customers not only ask 'What do you sell?' but 'What do you stand for?'

(b) A respect for quantifiable information is part of the professional culture and training of the accountant; other people have different values and priorities.

(c) Studies into organisational behaviour suggest that employees are motivated by more than money. A sense of mission and values helps to motivate employees.

(d) Many firms take mission seriously in strategic management.

**Mission statements** are formal statements of an organisation's mission. They might be reproduced in a number of places (eg at the front of an organisation's annual report, on publicity material, in the chairman's office, in communal work areas and so on.) There is no standard format, but they should possess certain characteristics.

- Brevity – easy to understand and remember
- Flexibility – to accommodate change
- Distinctiveness – to make the firm stand out

---

### EXAMPLE: CORPORATE MISSION STATEMENTS

*GlaxoSmithKline (GSK)* mission is 'to improve the quality of human life by enabling people to do more, feel better and live longer'.

Low cost airline Easyjet's mission statement is:

'To provide our customers with safe, good value, point-to-point air services. To effect and to offer a consistent and reliable product and fares appealing to leisure and business markets on a range of European routes. To achieve this we will develop our people and establish lasting relationships with our suppliers.'

---

### Mission and planning

Although the mission statement might be seen a set of abstract principles, it can play an important role in the planning process.

(a) **Plans should outline the fulfilment of the organisation's mission.** To take the example of a religious organisation (the best example of a 'missionary organisation'), the mission of spreading the gospel might be embodied in plans to send individuals as missionaries to various parts of the world, plans for fund-raising activities, or even targets for the number of new converts.

(b) **Evaluation and screening**. Mission also acts as a yardstick by which plans are judged.

  (i) The mission of an ethical investment trust would preclude investing in tobacco firms.

  (ii) Mission helps to ensure consistency in decisions.

(c) **Implementation**. Mission also affects the implementation of a planned strategy, in the culture and business practices of the firm.

**Problems with mission**

(a) **Ignored in practice**. The inherent danger of mission is that it will not be implemented. *Official* goals often do not correspond with the end that seems to be pursued.

(b) **Public relations**. Sometimes, of course, mission is merely for public consumption, not for internal decision-making.

(c) **Post hoc**. Missions are sometimes produced to **rationalise** the organisation's existence to particular audiences. In other words, mission does not drive the organisation, but what the organisation actually does is assumed to be mission.

(d) **Full of generalisations**. 'Best', 'quality', 'major': is just a wish list.

### 4.2 Goals and objectives

From the vision and mission, **goals** are derived.

**Definition**

> *Mintzberg* (1997) defines **goals** as 'the intentions behind decisions or actions, the states of mind that drive individuals or collectives of individuals called organisations to do what they do.'

**Operational and non-operational goals**

**Operational goals** can be expressed as objectives. Here is an example.

(i) An operational goal: 'Cut costs'
(ii) The objective: 'Reduce budget by 5%'

**Non-operational goals** A university's goal might be to 'seek truth'. Not all goals can be measured.

Objectives are normally **quantified** statements of what the organisation actually intends to achieve over a period of time.

### Uses of objectives

(a) Objectives **orientate the activities** of the organisation towards the fulfilment of the organisation's mission, in theory if not always in practice.

(b) The mission of a **business,** whether stated or not, must include **profitability.**

(c) Objectives can also be used as standards **for measuring the performance** of the organisation and departments in it.

Many objectives are:

- Specific
- Measurable
- Attainable
- Results-oriented
- Time-bounded (SMART)

### Primary and secondary objectives

Some objectives are more important than others. In the hierarchy of objectives, there is a primary corporate objective and other secondary objectives, which should combine to ensure the achievement of the overall corporate objective.

(a) For example, if a company sets itself an objective of growth in profits, as its primary aim, it will then have to develop strategies by which this primary objective can be achieved. An objective must then be set for each individual strategy.

(b) Secondary objectives might then be concerned with sales growth, continual technological innovation, customer service, product quality, efficient resource management or reducing the company's reliance on debt capital.

To be successful the primary objectives of the business organisation may be seen as:

(a) to continue in existence – to survive;
(b) to maintain growth and development; and
(c) to make a profit

All three objectives are inextricably linked. If we accept survival as the ultimate objective then this involves the need for a steady and continuous profit and this is reliant on growth and development of the organisation's products or services.

### Corporate objectives

Corporate objectives concern the firm as a whole, for example:

- Profitability
- Market share
- Growth
- Cash-flow
- Return on capital employed
- Sales
- Customer satisfaction
- Customer satisfaction
- Quality
- Industrial relations
- Added value
- Earnings per share
- Risk
- Brand loyalty

### Unit objectives

**Unit objectives** are specific to individual units of an organisation.

(a) *Commercial*

  (i) Increase the number of customers by x% (an objective of a sales department)

  (ii) Reduce the number of rejects by 50% (an objective of a production department)

  (iii) Produce monthly reports more quickly, within five working days of the end of each month (an objective of the management accounting department)

(b) *Public sector*

  (i) Introduce x% more places at nursery schools (an objective of a borough education department)

  (ii) Respond more quickly to calls (an objective of a local police station, fire department or hospital ambulance service)

(c) *General*

  (i) Resources (eg cheaper raw materials, lower borrowing costs, 'top-quality college graduates')

  (ii) Market (eg market share, market standing)

  (iii) Employee development (eg training, promotion, safety)

  (iv) Innovation in products or processes

  (v) Productivity (the amount of output from resource inputs)

  (vi) Technology

  (vii) Level of service – a high level of service might be set as an objective, as this will enhance customer/user perceptions of the business.

---

### EXAMPLE: AMAZON

Amazon, the Internet retailer of books, compact discs and other items, enjoys a mainly positive perception among customers for its level of service. It made special arrangements with the Royal Mail to ensure delivery of pre-ordered and price discounted copies of the long awaited new 'Harry Potter' children's books on the date of publication to its UK customers.

---

### The nature of profit

To an economist, cost includes an amount for normal profit that is the reward for entrepreneurship. Normal profit is the opportunity cost of entrepreneurship, because it is the amount of profit that an entrepreneur could earn elsewhere, and so it is the profit that he must earn to persuade him to keep on with his investment in his current enterprise.

(a) *Accounting profits* consist of sales revenue minus the explicit costs of the business. Explicit costs are those, which are clearly stated and recorded eg, materials costs – prices paid to suppliers.

(b) *Economic profit* consists of sales revenue minus both the explicit costs and the implicit costs of the business. Implicit costs are benefits foregone by not using the factors of production in their next most profitable way. Normal profit is thus an implicit cost.

**Profit maximisation**

There is reasonable logic to support the idea that firms must seek to maximise profits, because competition from profit-maximising firms could force non profit-maximising firms out of business.

In order to maximise profits over time, the business will have to incur costs today in order to generate returns in the future. A profit-maximising firm will seek to make investments – in physical capital (eg machines), human capital (the employees), advertising and so on – and it would be wrong to think of profit maximisation as a 'short-term' motive.

**Return on capital employed (ROCE)**

The level of profit that a business earns does not relate profitability to the amount of funds (capital) employed in making those profits. An annual profit of £1 million may sound high for a small business, but if it is the profit earned by a larger company with many assets, it may in fact represent a low rate of 'return' in capital.

The most important measure of profitability is therefore the **return on capital employed (ROCE)** – sometimes called the **return on investment (ROI)**. The ROCE is calculated as profit **divided by** long-term capital employed, expressed as a percentage.

**Growth**

The *Ansoff* (1987) Growth Matrix is a tool that helps businesses decide their product and market growth strategy. It suggests that a business' attempts to grow depend on whether it markets new or existing products in new or existing markets.

| | **Existing products/services** | **New products/services** |
|---|---|---|
| **Existing markets** | Internal efficiency Expansion ie, increase in market penetration | Product/service development or innovation |
| **New markets** | Market development (sometimes called exploration) | Diversification |

*Figure 1.1: The Ansoff Growth Matrix*

The output from the *Ansoff* product/market matrix is a series of suggested growth strategies that set the direction for the business strategy. These are described below.

***Market penetration***

Market penetration is the name given to a growth strategy where the business focuses on selling existing products into existing markets. It has four main objectives:

(i) Maintain or increase the **market share** of current products – this can be achieved by a combination of competitive pricing strategies, advertising, sales promotion and perhaps more resources dedicated to personal selling

(ii) Secure **dominance** of growth markets

(iii) **Restructure a mature market** by driving out competitors; this would require a much more aggressive promotional campaign, supported by a pricing strategy designed to make the market unattractive for competitors

(iv) **Increase usage by existing customers** – for example, by introducing loyalty schemes

*Market development*

Market development is the name given to a growth strategy where the business seeks to sell its existing products into new markets. There are many possible ways of approaching this strategy, including:

(i) New geographical markets; for example exporting the product to a new country

(ii) New product dimensions or packaging: for example, supplying smaller sizes of ready-cook sauces to appeal to the single market

(iii) New distribution channels

(iv) Different pricing policies to attract different customers or create new market segments

*Product development*

Product development is the name given to a growth strategy where a business aims to introduce new products into existing markets. This strategy may require the development of new competencies and requires the business to develop modified products that can appeal to existing markets.

*Diversification*

Diversification is the name given to the growth strategy where a business markets new products in new markets. This is an inherently higher risk strategy because the business is moving into markets in which it has little or no experience.

**Trade-off between objectives**

When there are several key objectives, some might be achieved only **at the expense of others.** For example, a company's objective of achieving good profits and profit growth might have adverse consequences for the cash-flow of the business, or the quality of the firm's products.

There will be a trade-off between objectives when strategies are formulated, and a choice will have to be made. For example, there might be a choice between the following two options.

*Option A* 15% sales growth, 10% profit growth, a £2 million negative cash-flow and reduced product quality and customer satisfaction.

*Option B* 8% sales growth, 5% profit growth, a £500,000 surplus cash-flow, and maintenance of high product quality/customer satisfaction.

If the firm chose option B in preference to option A, it would be trading off sales growth and profit growth for better cash-flow, product quality and customer satisfaction. The long-term effect of reduced quality has not been considered.

---

**EXAMPLE**

A company's primary objective might be to increase its earnings per share from 30p to 50p in the next five years.

(a) **Strategies** for achieving the objective might be selected.

- Increase profitability in the next twelve months by cutting expenditure.
- Increase export sales over the next three years.
- Develop a successful new product for the domestic market within five years.

(b) **Secondary objectives** might then be re-assessed.

- Improve manpower productivity by 10% within twelve months.
- Improving customer service in export markets with the objective of doubling the number of overseas sales outlets in selected countries within the next three years.
- Investing more in product-market research and development, with the objective of bringing at least three new products to the market within five years.

---

**Objectives of not-for-profit organisations**

Objectives of organisations where profit is not the main objective are problematic for the following reasons.

(a) They more likely to have **multiple objectives** – a large teaching hospital may want to give the best quality care and treat as many patients as possible and train new doctors and research new techniques. Conflict is inevitable.

(b) It is more **difficult to measure objectives** – how do you measure whether a school is educating pupils well? Performance in exams? Percentage going on to university? Percentage getting jobs? Percentage staying out of prison once they leave?

(c) There may be a more equal balance of power between stakeholders – in a company, the shareholders hold ultimate power. If they do not use it, the directors generally get their way. In a school, the balance of power may be more even (or even undefined) between parents, governors, the headmaster and the local education authority.

(d) The people receiving the service are not necessarily those paying for it – the government and local NHS trusts determine a hospital's funding, not the patients. Consequently, there may be pressure to perform well in national league tables at the expense of other objectives.

### 4.3 Measuring objectives

**Definition**

> The **balanced scorecard** is 'a set of measures that gives top managers a fast but comprehensive view of the business. The balanced scorecard includes financial measures that tell the results of actions already taken. And it complements the financial measures with **operational** measures on customer satisfaction, internal processes, and the organisation's innovation and improvement activities.' *(Kaplan)*

It is acknowledged that businesses need to measure and control more than money flows into, around and out of the enterprise as well as, of course, overall profitability. 'Critical (or key) success factors' have been recognised for some time as non-financial aspects of an enterprise important in determining performance in the marketplace. There is considerable evidence that of those factors, the people resource is of considerable importance.

The limitations attached to traditional financial measures are said to be that they:

(a) Are backward looking and reflect yesterday's decisions

(b) Are unable to reflect contemporary value-creating actions upon which future financial success rests

(c) Reinforce short-term thinking

(d) Are sometimes of doubtful validity due to the manipulation of figures.

Measurements of control relating to non-financial aspects of operational practices and processes it is claimed should be given equal weight alongside the financial; in short what is needed is a 'balanced scorecard'.

The balanced scorecard allows managers to look at the business from four important perspectives:

1. **Financial perspective**: reflecting how the business looks to shareholders and typically would include familiar measures such as asset turnover and earnings per share.

2. **Customer perspective**: how the business looks to customers, indicated by market share and customer satisfaction, for example.

3. **Internal business processes**: pointing to what the organisation must excel at, response times and product quality for instance.

4. **Innovation and learning**: focusing on the ability to change and improve and will be reflected in employee attitudes and morale, organisational culture and so forth.

**Financial perspective**

'How do we appear to shareholders?' Financial performance indicators indicate 'whether the company's strategies, implementation, and execution are contributing to bottom-line management.'

**Customer perspective**

'How do customers see us?' Given that many company mission statements identify customer satisfaction as a key corporate goal, the balanced scorecard translates this into specific measures. Customer concerns fall into four categories.

(a) **Time** – lead time is the time it takes a firm to meet customer needs from receiving an order to delivering the product.

(b) **Quality** – measures not only include defect levels – although these should be minimised by Total Quality Management (TQM) – but accuracy in forecasting.

(c) **Performance** of the product. (How often does the photocopier break down?)

(d) **Service**. How long will it take a problem to be rectified? (If the photocopier breaks down, how long will it take the maintenance engineer to arrive?)

In order to view the firm's performance through customers' eyes, firms hire market researchers to assess how the firm performs using customer/user audits. Higher service and quality may cost more at the outset, but savings can be made in the long-term.

**Internal business processes**

The internal business perspective identifies the business processes that have the greatest impact on customer satisfaction, such as quality and employee skills.

(a) Companies should attempt to identify and measure their distinctive competences and the critical technologies they need to ensure continued leadership. Which processes should they excel at?

(b) To achieve these goals, performance measures must relate to employee behaviour, to tie in the strategic direction with employee action.

(c) An information system is necessary to enable executives to measure performance. An executive information system enables managers to drill down into lower level information.

**Innovation and learning**

The question is 'Can we continue to improve and create value?' While the customer and internal process perspectives identify the current parameters for competitive success, the company needs to learn and to innovate to satisfy future needs.

(a) How long does it take to develop new products?

(b) How quickly does the firm climb the experience curve to make new products?

(c) What percentage of revenue comes from new products?

(d) How many suggestions are made by staff and are acted upon?

(e) What are staff attitudes?

(f) The company can identify measures for training and long-term investment.

An example of a balanced scorecard might look like the following:

| | |
|---|---|
| **Financial** – How do we look to our shareholders?<br>• Return on capital employed<br>• Cash flow<br>• Project profitability<br>• Profit forecast reliability<br>• Sales backlog | **Process** – What must we excel at?<br>• Hours with customer on new work<br>• Tender success rate<br>• Rework<br>• Safety incident index<br>• Project performance index |
| **Customer** – How do our customers see us?<br>• Pricing index<br>• Customer ranking survey<br>• Customer satisfaction index<br>• Market share | **Innovation and Learning** – Can we continue to improve and create value?<br>• Percentage revenue from new projects<br>• Rate of improvement index<br>• Staff attitude survey<br>• Number of employee suggestions<br>• Revenue per employee |

*Figure 1.2: Example of a balanced scorecard*

In each perspective, sets of measures are chosen that both provide the appropriate balance as well as capturing the cause and effect relations inherent in a co-ordinated strategy. For example if Return on Capital Employed (ROCE) was the prime financial measure, then to increase that indicator would require retention and loyalty of customers so customer loyalty would be measured as the cause of high ROCE. Perhaps for the customers, the key determinant of their loyalty might be on time delivery: that would be the driver of customer loyalty. To achieve on time delivery, quality and cycle time would have to be improved, which in turn would require an increase in employee skills.

## 5 STAKEHOLDERS

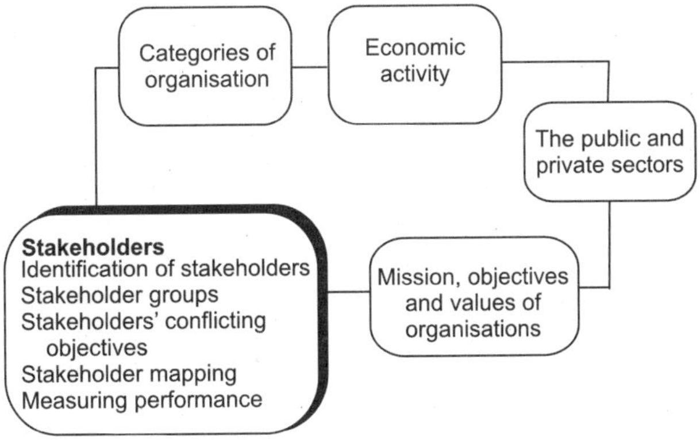


### 5.1 Identification of stakeholders

All enterprises, whether in the public or private sectors, whether they are profit or not-for-profit organisations, have stakeholders. Stakeholders are individuals or groups who have an interest in how the enterprise performs because it affects them in some way – that is they have a **stake** in the organisation. Traditionally, the owners of a business (for example, shareholders in a publicly listed company or the government in public service situations) were seen as the most important stakeholders, and meeting their requirements was the sole reason for the existence of the enterprise.

A more contemporary view is that there is a broader range of stakeholders, all of whose requirements must all be met in order for an enterprise to be considered successful.

A list of stakeholders is given below.

| Stakeholder groups | |
|---|---|
| Shareholders | Neighbours |
| Lenders (eg bank) | The immediate community |
| Intermediate (business) customers | The national society |
| Final (consumer) customers | The world society |
| Suppliers | Corporate management |
| Employees | The chief executive |
| Past employees | The board of directors |
| Retirees | Government and local government |
| Competitors | Special interest groups |

All organisations affect and are affected by different stakeholders. The aim of management with regard to stakeholders is to prioritise objectives so as to satisfy the majority of them for most of the time. Obviously, this involves choice and opportunity costs for every decision made.

Sometimes these are represented by **interest groups** (eg trade unions) and at other times their power is reflected in **commercial relationships** (eg suppliers).

The public is a 'stakeholder' to some degree and concerns might be represented by government action.

**There are three broad types of stakeholder in an organisation.**

(a) **Internal** stakeholders (employees, management)
(b) **Connected** stakeholders (shareholders, customers, suppliers, financiers)
(c) **External** stakeholders (the community, government, pressure groups)

**Internal stakeholders**

Because employees and management are so intimately connected with the company, their objectives are likely to have a strong and immediate influence on how it is run. They are interested in the organisation's continuation and growth. The organisation is a place where management and employees spend a great deal of their time and energy. It pays them. Management and employees have a special interest in the organisation's continued existence. This interest may not be held by shareholders. For example, if the organisation has surplus funds, the management might try and invest them in new projects whereas shareholders might prefer these funds to be returned to them, so that they can make up their own minds.

Employees have a major effect on the success of a business as it is they who are responsible for all aspects of work carried out therein. Many writers have stated that employees are the most important of all of the factors of production.

Employees when motivated, will usually be more productive, produce a better quality product/service, work as a team, provide ideas for improvement and guarantee that all objectives are met to the best of their ability.

Managers and employees also have individual interests and goals.

(a) Security of income
(b) Increases in income
(c) A safe and comfortable working environment
(d) A sense of community
(e) Interesting work
(f) Skills and career development
(g) A sense of doing something worthwhile

**Connected stakeholders**

There are several groups of connected stakeholders.

(a) **Shareholders/owners**. Their prime interest is a return on their investment, whether in the short- or long-term. As shareholders own the business, this is a commercial organisation's prime objective. Some shareholders are concerned with a corporation's ethical performance, hence the growth of investment funds designed to avoid certain companies. Shareholders are now being asked to take a more involved interest in a company's affairs.

(b) **Bankers** are also interested in a firm's overall condition, but from the point of view of the security of any loan they make. A bank is keen to minimise the risk of interest not being paid, or of its security being eroded. Banks provide finance in many different forms and may not require security for the advances they make. Overdrafts are often unsecured and are subject to higher interest rates in consequence. Mortgages are secured on real property while finance extended by debt factors (which are usually business units within banks) is secured on the customers' trading accounts receivable.

(c) **Customers** want products and services. Large customers have significant power over prices and procedures. They ultimately determine what is produced, what quality is needed, what price is charged and what development is needed. Failure to listen to customers will ultimately result in no sales and no market. The main ways that customers affect businesses is through feedback, complaints, suggestions, choosing whether or not to buy ('voting with their feet') and filling out questionnaires. Customers are likely to form a large proportion of debtors: debtors as a stakeholder group will expect to be treated ethically and not subjected to undue or illegal pressure.

(d) **Suppliers**, like other creditors, will expect to be paid and will be interested in future business.

**External stakeholders**

*External stakeholder groups* – the government, local authorities, pressure groups, the community at large, professional bodies – are likely to have quite diverse objectives and have a varying ability to ensure that the company meets them.

(a) Central government has a big role to play in the success of businesses through the passing of laws and policies it pursues. Its main roles include:

  (i) Passing laws to protect workers and customers
  (ii) Collecting taxes eg income tax, corporation tax, VAT
  (iii) Supporting businesses in socially or economically deprived areas
  (iv) Subsidising activities
  (v) Aiding exporters

The impact on businesses depends on whether they are putting more into or taking more out of the business concerned.

(a) **Local authorities** are interested, since companies can bring local employment. Also they can affect the local environment for instance by increasing road traffic.

(b) **Professional bodies** are interested to ensure that members who work for companies comply with professional ethics and standards.

(c) **Pressure groups** will have an interest in particular issues.

### 5.2 Stakeholder groups

| Stakeholder group | General concerns | Example |
|---|---|---|
| Shareholders | • A steady flow of income (dividends)<br>• Possible capital growth<br>• Continuation of business | If an organisation wishes to follow a strategy that will involve a large capital injection, the shareholders will be unhappy if the injection has an adverse effect on their income stream. |
| Managers | • Pay and status<br>• Job security<br>• Individual performance measures | If an organisation wishes to follow a strategy that results in a particular department being reduced in size or abolished, the manager of that department is likely to be hostile to the plans. |
| Employees | • Job security<br>• Pay and conditions<br>• Job satisfaction | If an organisation wishes to follow a strategy that results in workers being given more responsibility for monitoring quality, the employees may be unhappy unless this increased role is supported by an increase in wages. |
| Trade Unions | • The problems of the employees<br>• Taking an active part in the decision-making process | If an organisation wishes to follow a strategy that results in a manufacturing plant being closed, the union will be unhappy if it has not been consulted and if there is no scheme for helping the employees find alternative employment. |
| Customers | • Receiving goods and services of a reasonable quality<br>• Paying a reasonable price for those goods and services | If an organisation wishes to follow a strategy that increases the quality of a product at the same time as increasing the price, *existing* customers may not be willing to pay more for the product, while *new* customers are not attracted to a product that they will view as being of low quality. |

| Stakeholder group | General concerns | Example |
|---|---|---|
| Suppliers | • Being paid promptly for goods and services delivered<br>• Receiving regular repayments of any capital provided (eg, banks) | If an organisation wishes to follow a strategy that improves the working capital management by paying suppliers late, existing suppliers may decide to stop supplying the organisation leading to the increased cost of finding new suppliers. |
| Government and the general public | • The organisation is meeting relevant legal requirements<br>• The organisation does not harm the outside environment | If an organisation wishes to follow a strategy that relies on increased use of shops based in out-of-town retail centres, this will be affected by government attitudes towards increased road building and society's attitude towards this method of shopping. |

**EXAMPLE: SHISEIDO**

An example of the interests of one of the stakeholder groups, shareholders, is demonstrated in this article from the *Financial Times*.

Akira Gemma, head of Shiseido, one of the world's largest cosmetics companies, follows an un-Japanese, investor friendly strategy: setting rising targets for return on equity, stressing high standards of disclosure and planning a share buy back. About 24 per cent of its stock is held outside Japan and the company maintains investor relations offices in the US, UK and Switzerland.

The company is pushing for globalisation, aiming to be the world's number one cosmetics company and to generate a quarter of its sales outside Japan.

Shareholder's expectations are seen as very important by Gemma: 'I think that on the whole international shareholders seem to be somewhat more intent on getting information in line with global standards – return on assets and equity, efficiency of management of assets, and so on. They are also more persistent about questioning us about investments that do not seem to be paying their way.'

### 5.3 Stakeholders' conflicting objectives

Each stakeholder to some degree has a link of dependency to the organisation. Each will make demands on, and have expectations of, the organisation. These expectations may clash and conflict with the interest of other stakeholder groups. For instance, the rate of growth expectations of the managers of a family owned company might conflict with those of the family shareholders whose main interest may be in maintaining family control.

There will be occasions where the objective specified by the organisation is a formal statement of stakeholder expectations, for example:

(i) Return on capital employed expressing shareholders' expectations;
(ii) Pledges on non-pollution of environment expressing society's expectations.

Clearly, some stakeholder groups wield greater power than others. The government's legislative power is comprehensive, and rulings of the Competition Commission have a direct effect upon the objectives and strategies of companies affected.

Since stakeholder expectations are expressed through objectives and such expectations will vary over time; so we must expect objectives to change in response. It is important to an organisation to maintain an equitable and working balance among the claims of the various directly interested groups. Although management may seek to achieve a balance, a dominant stakeholder group can impose its demands at the expense of the others.

A typical example would occur when an organisation over-expands and its gearing ratio dictates that capital restructuring is necessary for survival. In these circumstances, the company's bankers will assume a dominant role and dictate the terms of the company's future with token regard to the interest of shareholders and employees.

**Activity 6** **(10 minutes)**

(a) Think about the different stakeholders in an organisation. List those whose interests may conflict. Try to use an organisation you know or work for. How can such conflicts be resolved?

(b) Using the list given above, categorise the stakeholders into internal, connected or external.

### 5.4 Stakeholder mapping

Stakeholders have very different degrees of power to control decisions that have effects on policies and institutions, and they have different degrees of 'potential' to contribute, or 'importance', to achieving a particular objective.

Since the stakeholder groups often have differing interests and some conflict is likely to occur, an organisation needs to analyse each group to evaluate:

(a) How much interest each group has in particular issues
(b) How much power that group has.

Stakeholders have very different degrees of power to control decisions that have effects on policies and institutions, and they have different degrees of 'potential' to contribute, or 'importance', to achieving a particular objective.

The process of stakeholder mapping involves asking the following questions:

(i) Who are they?
(ii) What do they want and what will they accept?
(iii) How satisfied are they?
(iv) How much power do they possess?
(v) What sort of power do they possess?
(vi) How compatible are their interests?
(vii) What conflicts exist?

These questions are critical in analysing stakeholders.

The stakeholder groups can be categorised in terms of their interest or aspirations against their level of influence or degree of power in order to decide how to respond to their concerns.

**Interest/aspirations**

| Power/influence | Low | High |
|---|---|---|
| Low | Minimal effort | Keep informed |
| High | Keep satisfied | Key players |

*Figure 1.3: Stakeholder mapping*

- **Key players** – strategy must be *acceptable* to them, at least. An example would be a major customer.
- Stakeholders in '**Keep satisfied**' segment must be treated with care. While often passive, they are capable of being key players. Large institutional shareholders might fall into this segment.
- Stakeholders in '**Keep informed**' segment do not have great ability to influence strategy, but their views can be important in influencing more powerful stakeholders, perhaps by lobbying. Community representatives and charities might fall into this segment.
- **Minimal effort** is expended on this segment.

Stakeholder mapping is used to assess the significance of stakeholders. This in turn has implications for the organisation.

### 5.5 Measuring performance

Under the stakeholder view of the business, stakeholders are the final judges of organisational performance. A successful business will be one that properly balances the requirements of all stakeholders. Senior managers must be able to ascertain the extent to which these requirements are being met. This involves determining what stakeholders require of the organisation, and measuring performance against those requirements.

Success measurements can only be determined once a business has identified its stakeholders, the requirements of each stakeholder group are known, and it is understood how stakeholders will judge whether their requirements have been met. Strategic planning is about how the organisation will satisfy the requirements of its stakeholders.

Success measurements are collected **outside** the organisation and they should be:

(a) **Exhaustive**, covering the full complement of stakeholder requirements, quantifiable,

(b) **Collected from stakeholders** themselves,

(c) **Reliable**, that is the measurement must accurately reflect the quantity it is designed to measure,

(d) **Repeatable**, so that if the quantity being measured remains unchanged over time data collected over time will reflect this, and

(e) **Revised** as stakeholder needs evolve.

While success measurements are likely to indicate how well the organisation has done in the past and how well it is doing now, organisations need information about how well they are likely to meet stakeholders' requirements in the future.

**Definition**

> **Key performance indicators** (KPIs) are measurements collected internally which help, in conjunction with broader information such as environmental, industry and competitor analysis, predict the future success of the business. They are collected within the business itself, but are related to the external success measurements.

Key performance indicators should also be:

(a) **derived from, and predictive of stakeholder requirements**, that is each KPI should directly relate to at least one success measure,

(b) **exhaustive**, that is, taken together a suite of KPIs should indicate how well stakeholders requirements have been met,

(c) **reliable** and **repeatable**,

(d) **timely**, so that organisations can respond to unsatisfactory data before stakeholder satisfaction is adversely affected,

(e) if possible represent an **aggregation of information** obtained from process measurements, and

(f) **revised** as stakeholder requirements change.

Organisations that understand what requirements their stakeholders have of them, and have measured how well they are doing against those requirements understand how well they are performing. Further, organisations that measure themselves internally in relation to stakeholder requirements are in a strong position to predict how successful they are likely to be in the future.

Measuring organisational performance indicates how well the vision and strategy of the organisation are being translated into outcomes. More than any other marker, looking at how an enterprise chooses to judge its own performance illuminates what matters to the organisation.

**Chapter roundup**

- Business formats include sole trader; partnership; private limited company; and public limited company.
- Economic activity can be analysed into primary, secondary and tertiary sectors. To simplify, the primary sector deals with raw materials, the secondary sector with making goods and the tertiary sector with services. The tertiary sector is likely to be the main engine of growth in the future.
- The firms in an economy pursue a number of goals. They are supposed to try to maximise profits over the long run, but there may be other objectives imposed by stakeholders other than shareholders. These might be represented by pressure groups. Most businesses like to grow.
- Goals or objectives are the intentions or decisions behind actions. Some goals are quantified. Quantified objectives (or operational goals) normally describe what an organisation hopes to achieve over a specific period and can be measured. They include indicators such as profitability and market share.

- There are internal, connected and external stakeholders. All stakeholders aim to influence the behaviour of the organisation. Sometimes, the stakeholder groups are in conflict with one another.

## Quick quiz

1. Give two examples of private-sector organisations.
2. Give two examples of public-sector organisations.
3. Name the three sectors of industry.
4. Which sectors of the economy can you identify?
5. Define mission.
6. Why is mission, as a set of values, relevant to an organisation?
7. List some of the objectives of a private-sector business.
8. What interests do shareholders have?
9. List three types of stakeholder.

## Answers to quick quiz

1. Sole trader (greengrocer), public limited company (Marks and Spencer plc).
2. Civil service agencies, the armed forces.
3. Primary, secondary, tertiary.
4. Public and private sectors.
5. *Mintzberg* defines an organisation's mission as its 'basic function in society, in terms of the products and services it produces for its clients'.
6. When the members of an organisation subscribe to common values, those values create a framework of control over what the organisation does and how it does it.
7. Profit maximisation, protection of the interests of stakeholders, provision of services.
8. Return on investment, dividends, capital growth, corporate survival, and ethical behaviour.
9. Internal, connected, external.

## Answers to activities

1

| | | |
|---|---|---|
| (i) | Mass producer of cars | (d) Public limited company |
| (ii) | An inventor financed by two others setting up a small factory | (c) Private limited company |
| (iii) | Three qualified accountants setting up in private practice | (b) Partnership |
| (iv) | Retailer with three employees | (a) Sole trader |

2 To a certain extent, the tertiary sector can take the place of the secondary sector in ensuring a healthy balance between imports and exports. However a major problem is that many services cannot, by their very nature, be traded internationally. This problem accounts for the

international market for manufactured goods being larger than the international market for services. The exception to this would be financial services, which have done very well in the international market.

3 When North Sea oil runs out, other forms of economic activity will make up the difference. Energy will be obtained from other sources.

4 The government could:

- Initiate training programmes in new skills
- Offer support for new employment opportunities in the affected areas
- Encourage geographical and occupational mobility of labour, making it easier for people to change where they live or the jobs they do
- Subsidise loss-making industries

5 (a) You may have used a number of public services. The most likely ones are the National Health Service and education.

(b) You may have gained the following benefits: from the Health Service – better health care, less serious illness and preventative care. From education – improved literacy and numeracy, greater knowledge and the skills and confidence to engage in lifelong learning.

(c) You may have said that in 40 years' time you expect these services to have enabled you to have a better and longer life.

(d) If health services were privatised, only wealthy people might then be able to afford certain kinds of medical treatment. If education were privatised, schools might not be available for all.

(e) 1 Transport – some transport has been privatised. There has been criticism of the fact that some less profitable routes have been axed. There have also been concerns expressed over issues of safety on the rail network and general standards of service on particular lines.

2 Education – some schools have 'opted out' and are now more selective about who they admit, resulting in restricted choice for some pupils.

6 (a) Shareholders may want as much profit as possible distributed as dividends. The government might want to see investment in industry instead, or higher tax revenues. Management and employees will probably want higher wages.

For private sector businesses, this conflict is usually resolved in the shareholders' interest. For other concerns, however, the matter is not as simple, especially for businesses with a public service element. Some decisions are subject to public enquiries (eg building new roads) and consultation. In other cases, conflicts of interest are managed by regulation.

(b) (i) Internal stakeholders – employees, past employees, retirees, corporate management, the chief executive, the board of directors

(ii) Connected stakeholders – shareholders, lenders, customers, suppliers, and competitors.

(iii) External stakeholders – neighbours, the immediate community, national and world society, central and local government, special interest groups.

# Chapter 2:
# RESPONSIBILITIES OF ORGANISATIONS

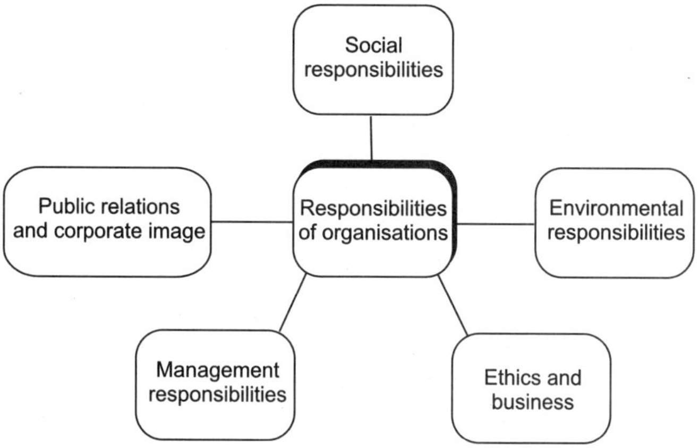


**Introduction**

Organisations are part of human society and, like people, are subject to rules that govern their conduct towards others. Some of these rules are law and enforced by legal sanction. Other rules fall into the realm of ethics or morality and are enforced only by the strength of society's approval or disapproval. Social responsibility and ethical issues relate to many aspects of the organisation – its environment, its culture and its management practice.

This chapter deals with the social responsibilities of organisations and the following two chapters continue by looking at the responsibilities towards consumers and then the responsibilities associated with employment.

It has been argued that business corporations have only one responsibility, and that is to make as much money as possible. Other writers, more recently, contend that organisations have social responsibilities to their various stakeholders and that they should establish codes of conduct to ensure that such responsibilities are properly fulfilled. Companies are coming under increasing pressure from many quarters for better environmental performance. Recent surveys have demonstrated that around three quarters of the population now apply environmental criteria in many purchase considerations.

Businesses are also being called to account for their actions towards the community as a whole. People expect a good example to be set.

**Your objectives**

In this chapter you will learn about:

(a) Social responsibility of organisations

(b) The stakeholder view of company objectives

(c) Environmental responsibilities

(d) How firms express their ethical codes

(e) How ethical behaviour can be enforced in organisations

(f) Why an organisation might attempt to build up a corporate image.

## 1 SOCIAL RESPONSIBILITIES

### 1.1 What is social responsibility?

The social responsibility of an organisation may be defined as the obligations that the organisation has towards the people and the environment in which the company operate. To that end, management's social responsibility is concerned with the way in which the enterprise interacts with the environment. The actions of an enterprise, and therefore, management, have social consequences that affect several groups, often referred to as the stakeholders. No organisation would ever admit to being socially **irresponsible**, and many organisations claim to act responsibly on social issues.

Social responsibility is expected from all types of organisation, be they businesses, governments, universities and colleges, churches or charities.

(a) **Local government** is expected to provide services to the local community, and to preserve or improve the character of that community, but at an acceptable cost to the council tax or business rate payers.

(b) **Universities and schools** are expected to produce students whose abilities and qualifications will prove beneficial to society. A currently popular view of education is that greater emphasis should be placed on vocational training for students.

(c) **Pollution control** is a particularly important example of social responsibility by industrial organisations, and some progress has been made in the development of commercial processes for re-cycling waste material. British Coal attempts to restore the environment by planting on old slag heaps.

Arguably, institutions such as hospitals and schools exist because health care and education are seen to be desirable social objectives by government at large, if they can be afforded.

However, where does this leave business? How far is it reasonable, or even appropriate, for businesses to exercise 'social responsibility' by giving to charities, voluntarily imposing strict environmental objectives on themselves and so on?

**Activity 1** **(10 minutes)**

What actions might businesses take to show 'responsibility'?

### 1.2 Stakeholder views

The stakeholder view of company objectives is that many groups of people have a stake in what the company does. Shareholders own the business, but there are suppliers, managers, workers and customers. A business depends on appropriate relationships with these groups. Each of these groups has its own objectives, so that a compromise or balance is required. Some of the pressures from various stakeholders are outlined below.

(a) **Shareholders** – one school of thought would argue that the management of a business has only one social responsibility, which is to maximise wealth for its shareholders. There are two reasons to support this argument.

  (i) If the shareholders own the business the assets of the company are, ultimately, the shareholders' property. Management has no moral right to dispose of business assets (such as cash) on non-business objectives, as this has the effect of reducing the return available to shareholders. The shareholders might, for example, disagree with management's choice of beneficiary. As many shareholders are large institutions like pension funds, then their own duties can be adversely affected by the use of organisational resources on activities that do not make a profit.

  (ii) A second justification for this view is that management's job is to maximise wealth, as this is the best way that society can benefit from a business's activities.

    (1) Maximising wealth has the effect of increasing the tax revenues available to the state to disburse on socially desirable objectives.

    (2) Maximising wealth for the few is sometimes held to have a 'trickle down' effect on the disadvantaged members of society.

    (3) Many company shares are owned by pension funds, whose ultimate beneficiaries may not be wealthy anyway.

  This argument rests on certain assumptions.

    (1) The first assumption is, in effect, the opposite of the stakeholder view. In other words, it is held that the rights of legal ownership are paramount over all other interests in a

business: while other stakeholders have an interest, they have few legal or moral rights over the wealth created.

(2) The second assumption is that a business's only relationship with the wider social environment is an economic one. After all, that is what businesses exist for, and any other activities are the role of the state.

This view might be regarded as an oversimplification, however, for the following reasons.

(1) In practice, organisations are rarely controlled effectively by shareholders. Most shareholders are passive investors.

(2) Large corporations can manipulate markets. Social responsibility, forced or voluntary, is a way of recognising this.

(3) Moreover, businesses do receive a lot of government support. The public pays for roads, infrastructure, education and health, all of which benefit businesses. Although businesses pay tax, the public ultimately pays, perhaps through higher prices.

(4) Strategic decisions by businesses always have wider social consequences. In other words, the firm produces two outputs:

- Its goods and services
- The social consequences of its activities (eg increased traffic, pollution, stress) which are inflicted on the wider population

(b) **Employees** – are internal stakeholders. Their relationship with the organisation is twofold. First, it is their labour which keeps the organisation in operational existence. Second, as citizens, they are members of the wider society in which the organisation exists. Employees value the certainty and regularity of wages, in other words they expect that the employing organisation will honour the contract of employment. To act with social responsibility also implies a concern and respect for workplace and work practices, which are healthy and safe, whether this relates to equipment, buildings, or hours worked.

An organisation's social responsibility towards its workers can also include the provision of a coherent career and training structure so that people can better themselves. It is believed that the level of workforce skills affects an economy's productivity, and so training is both beneficial for the trainee and for the country as a whole.

Other practices, which are examples of social responsibility, include adaptation to other pressures on employee's lifestyles. Workplace crèches, for example, are of great assistance to working women, but employers are unlikely to introduce them without any consequent commercial benefit: if the cost of labour turnover, for example, is higher than the cost of running workplace crèches and if labour turnover is reduced significantly by a workplace crèche, then the crèche can be financially justified.

The exercise of social responsibility towards the workforce is constrained by the law, by organised labour, and in some instances by the recognition that social responsibility can be of benefit in encouraging employee loyalty and skill.

(c) **Customers** – are stakeholders in that they pay for the organisation's output of goods and services. Here the situation is more complex. In some consumer goods sectors, public attitudes – with some direction from government and lobby groups – have made the environmental impact of an organisation's activities open to public comment. This has led suppliers to reduce CFCs in aerosol cans, and to introduce ranges of goods that are supposed to be friendly to the environment.

(d) **Suppliers** – in multinational corporations the exercise of social responsibility is distributed over several countries, but again, management will only let it override commercial objectives if it either is part of the inbuilt culture of the firm, or if the voice of public opinion in the market is strong. An example is the use of rainforest hardwoods: some consumer organisations are suggesting boycotting these products. A supplier may also make restrictions on the end-use of products a condition of sale. For example, a supplier of high-technology items may require that these are not re-exported to the enemies of the nation where the supplier is based.

(e) **Professional bodies** – control is exercised over certain members of management by their membership of professional bodies, which have standards of ethics and conduct

(f) **Neighbours** – every effort should be made to prevent any pollution of the environment, including noxious gases, noise and traffic disturbance to 'neighbours'.

(g) **Elected authorities** – society's elected political representatives are external stakeholders and can affect management in a number of ways:

  (i) by legislation as has already been mentioned,

  (ii) by influencing the climate of public opinion, or

  (iii) by trying to persuade commercial organisations to follow a particular line or policy. An example is business sponsorship of the arts in the UK.

**Activity 2** **(10 minutes)**

Think about the balance of consideration between the protection of the rights of employees and the rights of shareholders and former employees who become pensioners. Make a list of the possible conflicts of interest.

---

**FOR DISCUSSION**

Is there any justification for 'social responsibility' outside remedying the effects of a business's direct activities?

For example, should businesses give to charity or sponsor the arts? There are **several** reasons why they might – but what reasons are there why they *should?*

---

The arguments for and against social responsibility of business are complex ones. However, ultimately they can be traced to different assumptions about 'society' and the relationships between the individuals and organisations within it.

(a) If the stakeholder concept of a business is held, then 'the public' is the stakeholder in the business. A business only succeeds because it is part of a wider society. Giving to charity is one way of encouraging a relationship.

(b) Charitable donations and artistic sponsorship are a useful medium of public relations and can reflect well on the business. It can be regarded, then, as another form of promotion, which, like advertising, serves to enhance consumer awareness of the business and it's activities.

### 1.3 Objectives and responsibilities

*Ansoff* (1987) suggested that a company has a number of different levels of objectives.

(a) A **primary** objective, which is financial or economic, aimed at optimising the efficiency and effectiveness of the firm's 'total resource conversion process'.

(b) Social or **non-economic** objectives, which are **secondary** and modify management behaviour. These social objectives are the result of interaction among the individual objectives of the different groups of stakeholders.

(c) In addition to economic and non-economic objectives, there are two other factors exerting influence on management behaviour.

    (i) **Responsibilities** – these are obligations that a company undertakes, but which do not form a part of its internal guidance or control mechanism. Responsibilities would include charitable donations and contributions to the life of local communities.

    (ii) **Boundaries** – these are rules, which restrict management's freedom of action and include government legislation (on pollution levels, health and safety at work monopolies etc) and agreements with trade unions.

Many organisations pursue a variety of social and ethical objectives eg to provide job satisfaction for all employees, to make products that should last a certain number of years, to control pollution and to co-operate with the authorities in identifying and preventing health hazards in the products sold. The Body Shop has social objectives about the environment/ecology. Some companies actually issue their own code of conduct for their employees eg United Biscuits believe that their business ethics are not negotiable – 'a well founded reputation for scrupulous dealing is itself a priceless company asset and the most important single factor in our success is faithful adherence to our beliefs'.

At the turn of the century paternalistic owners of companies such as Cadbury's and Lever Brothers were very aware of their stakeholders and, despite their generosity towards their workforce, they still managed to make sufficient profit to keep the owners happy. They might argue that they would retain uneconomic products to preserve jobs, would avoid manufacturing 'anti-social' products and would be prepared to bear reductions in profitability for the social good.

## 2 ENVIRONMENTAL RESPONSIBILITIES

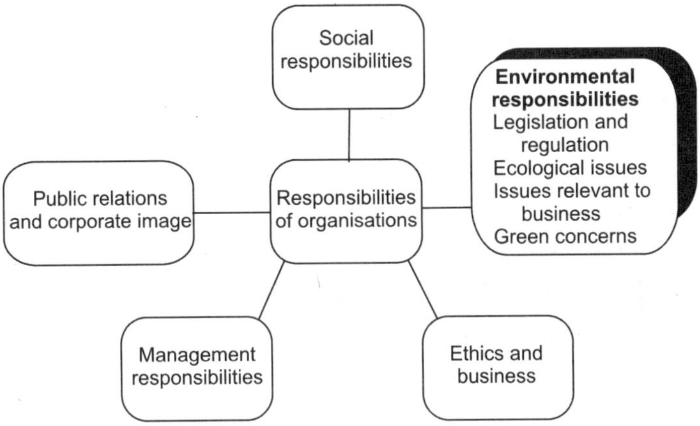


### 2.1 Legislation and regulation

Public concern with environmental pollution has resulted in government action.

(a) Some of this takes the form of tax incentives. For example, the UK government encouraged the use of lead-free petrol by levying a lower tax than on leaded petrol, before the withdrawal of leaded petrol from general sale on 1 January 2000. Vehicles that emit lower levels of carbon dioxide are charged less road vehicle tax. The government has also proposed taxing waste.

(b) The UK government has made a public commitment to cut carbon dioxide omissions.

The law on environmental protection is covered mainly in the *Environmental Protection Act 1997* (EPA) and the *Water Resources Act 2007.*

The EPA features the concept of integrated pollution control (IPC). Its aims are to:

(a) Prevent pollution happening, rather than to clear it up afterwards

(b) Ensure that business activities are conducted at minimal risk to human health and the environment

(c) Encourage the adoption of the most advanced technical solutions, offering the best practicable option for the environment as a whole

(d) Assess how much pollution the environment can sustain without damage

(e) Ensure that the polluter pays

The objectives of IPC are to:

(a) Minimise the release of pollutants and to neutralise the harmful effects of those that are released

(b) Develop an approach to pollution control that considers the environment as a whole

IPC, in part, overlaps with existing planning regulations. Under IPC, the chief regulatory bodies are:

(a) Her Majesty's Inspectorate of Pollution (HMIP) for air, water and land pollution by the most polluting *industrial* processes

(b) For pollution from other sources, the Environment Agency and local authorities

Note that the Act identifies certain *processes* as being polluting, and these are subject to control. Polluters must 'curb the creation and discharge of wastes by applying the best available techniques which do not entail excessive costs'. Hopefully, as technology improves, the standards will increase.

IPC is separate from the other aspects of planning. In practice, the government (in the person of the Secretary of State for the Environment) will:

(a) Identify those processes that require authorisation

(b) Set emission standards

(c) Allocate responsibilities between pollution inspectorate and other regulatory bodies

For certain processes, authorisation is required, and it is a criminal offence to carry out certain processes without authorisation. Enforcement is by means of an enforcement notice, supported by court injunctions.

Another air pollution Act is the Clean Air Act 1993, which consolidates earlier legislation (introduced after some spectacular London smogs of the 1950s).

**Waste**

The handling and disposal of waste has come under a number of EU directives, now incorporated in English Law.

Waste regulation is now organised separately from waste disposal. Waste management plans are meant to encourage firms to:

(a) Prevent or reduce waste production
(b) Develop products that do not harm the environment
(c) Develop appropriate techniques for disposing of dangerous substances
(d) Consider recycling
(e) Use waste as a source of energy

The overarching principle is that waste must not be treated, disposed of, or kept in a manner likely to pollute the environment or harm human health. This is enforced through a licensing system and businesses must pay Landfill Tax on hazardous waste. Furthermore, to prevent toxic waste from being simply 'dumped' on poorer countries, there are controls over the import or export of waste.

**Activity 3** **(30 minutes)**

Imagine that you work for a firm of chartered accountants that up until now has not really had a coherent waste management plan. Prepare a memorandum for the managing director outlining the benefits of recycling where possible. List some common items in daily use that could be used more than once. Also, mention some items that could be utilised that are made from recycled materials.

**Water**

The Water Resources Act 1991 and the Water Industry Act 1999 were brought in when the UK water industry was privatised. There are a number of offences relating to discharges into 'controlled waters'.

## 2.2 The role of the Environment Agency

**Definition**

> The role of an environmental agency is to protect the environment and promote sustainable development.

### 2.2.1 The goal of the Environment Agency

The **Environment Agency** of England and Wales and the Scottish Environment Protection Agency were created in 1996.

The stated mission of the newly created agencies was '*to protect or enhance the environment, taken as a whole*' so as to promote '*the objective of achieving sustainable development*'.

## 2.3 The responsibilities of the environment agency

### 2.3.1 Flood risk management

The agency is the main body responsible for creating and maintaining flood defences and providing flood warning systems. Control of water levels is usually by systems of sluices, weirs and locks. The agency issues regular flood warnings and maintains maps of areas liable to flooding.

### 2.3.2 Waste regulation

The agency is the regulatory authority for all waste management activities including the licensing of sites such as landfill and incineration facilities. It also grants licenses for handling special waste such as radioactive, chemical or medical materials. The agency monitors waste management sites and any individuals or companies found to have caused pollution or have infringed their licence conditions can be prosecuted and potentially have waste handling licenses revoked by the Courts.

### 2.3.3 Pollution control

Under the provisions of a series of Acts of Parliament, the Agency is the main regulator of discharges to the aquatic environment, to air and to land. It does this through the issue of formal consents to discharge or, in the case of large, complex or potentially damaging industries, by means of a permit. Failure to comply with such a consent or permit or making a discharge without the benefit of a consent or permit can lead to criminal prosecution. Under recent legislation changes enforcement action regarding a pollution event can, through the Magistrates courts system, result in a fine of up to £50,000 or five years imprisonment, or unlimited fines and up to five years' imprisonment through the Crown courts.

### 2.3.4 Air quality management

The Agency regulates the release of air pollutants into the atmosphere from large, complex industrial processes. This will soon include emissions from some large-scale agricultural activities, but air pollutant releases from many agricultural activities will continue to be unregulated.

Emissions from major sources of pollution, such as transport, are subject to various measures at the European, national and local level. Local authorities control air pollution from smaller industrial processes.

The Agency works with local authorities, the Highways Agency and others to implement the UK government's air quality strategy in England and Wales as mandated in the Environment Act 1995.

***Different ecological issues have varied impacts on different types of business.***

## 2.4 Ecological issues

The effects of ecological concerns on businesses can be either direct or indirect.

*Direct impacts:*

(a) Can affect costs or the availability of resources. For example, companies may be prohibited from mining in areas of natural beauty or special scientific interest.

(b) Can affect consumer demand. Shell became concerned by a consumer boycott in Germany over its plans to sink a disused oil platform in the North Sea.

(c) Affect power balances between competitors in a market. Environmental damage may place some competitors at a disadvantage because of the additional operating costs required to clean up the product or processes.

Legislative change may affect the framework within which businesses operate, as we have seen.

*Indirect impacts* may manifest themselves in, for example, pressure from customers or staff as a consequence of concern over ecological problems.

***We now look at some examples of how various environmental issues are relevant to business.***

## 2.5 Issues relevant to business

Among the ecological issues that are likely to be seen as relevant to businesses are the following.

### Resource depletion

Resource depletion may influence business operations through impacts on the availability of raw materials through damage to soil, water, trees, plant-life, energy availability, mineral wealth, animal and marine species.

### Genetic diversity

Genetic diversity is relevant to pharmaceutical firms, firms in biotechnology and the agriculture and food industries. The development of many new strains of plants, new breeds of animals, and new types of medicines can depend on the availability of wild species from which genetic resources can be drawn. In developing high-yield and disease-resistant plants, for example, wild species are a critical resource. Opposition to genetically modified food is growing, because of uncertainties about its long-term effect on people and animals. Production of organically-produced foods is thus becoming more profitable and consumers are willing to pay a premium price.

### Pollution concerns

Pollution concerns are at the centre of most worries about the environment.

(a) Businesses are under pressure to curtail the impacts of their activities on the **water table**, the seas and the oceans. Concern over the quality of drinking water has generated a massive increase in the size of the bottled water market in the UK. In 2007, more than half the UK population, that's 26 million adults, drank over two billion litres of bottled water. However, some commentators have argued that the success of bottled water in the UK is simply a triumph of 'marketing'.

(b) The **quality of air** has been much discussed, as a result of the effect of motor car exhausts, and the general impact of road vehicles. This issue may well have a bearing upon distribution policies.

(c) Concerns about **the pollution of land**, through landfill policies and the long-term damage wrought by industry upon the land it occupies, are all likely to require some policy changes over the next few years.

(d) **Noise pollution** is also likely to become more important, and this can have far reaching impacts on the operation of all manner of businesses.

In order to take action to remedy these problems, the *polluter pays principle* was adopted by the OECD in the early 1970s, and it now has broad acceptance.

**Definition**

> **Polluter pays principle**: aims to relate the damage done by pollution involved in the production of goods and services to the prices of those goods. The intention is to deter potential polluters by making it uneconomic to produce goods and services that also create pollution. This principle has been broadly accepted and has been a major factor in reaction to major pollution incidents, such as large-scale oil and chemical spills.

---

**FOR DISCUSSION**

How practical is the proposal to make the polluter pay?

---

### Acid rain

Acid rain is linked to damage to forests throughout northern Europe, and acidification of water supplies and fish-bearing lakes and rivers. It has generated massive bills, but it is not always possible to establish direct culpability, so the polluter pays principle has not enabled Swedish foresters to claim from British industrialists, or Russian power stations. So large are the bills involved, and so clear are the impacts on the natural environment and agri-systems, that political pressures to constrain the effects of industrial production have increased enormously.

### Ozone depletion

Similar alarms have been expressed about ozone depletion. Alternatives to CFCs have been developed to act as solvents in the electronics industry and coolants in refrigerators. The use of CFCs for blowing polystyrene foam used as insulation by the building industry has been banned in some countries and is being phased out in many others.

### Waste

Waste is causing just as much alarm, whether it is nuclear waste from power stations or industrial or domestic waste in landfill sites. The handling of waste is increasingly becoming the target of legislation by national governments. It is also the subject of new international agreements, arrived at by governments concerned, for example, about the effects of waste dumping on the marine life and on the beaches of many different countries. The new waste management regulations were discussed earlier.

**Activity 4** **(20 minutes)**

What issues are raised by the following information?

There is growing pressure on local authorities to pay recycling credits to third parties involved in local recycling schemes. A few years ago, a report by MEL Research for the Department of the Environment found that many waste disposal authorities are not paying voluntary groups for collecting paper, cans and glass for recycling, even though they have the power to do so. The then environment minister Robert Atkins hinted that he might make the payment mandatory if the authorities did not catch up. 'At present, in addition to some authorities not paying at all, others delay payment for months or impose an administration fee that virtually cancels any payment out,' said Ray Georgeso, for Waste Watch. Only a small amendment to the Environmental Protection Act 1990 would be required to make the scheme mandatory, and lobbyists hope that proposed legislation for an Environment Agency will be able to carry through the alteration.

### Climatic change

Climatic change, involving the effects of excess carbon dioxide in the atmosphere, is still debatable in terms of its actual effects in producing 'unnatural' weather. Potentially, the consequences could be profound, with average world temperatures increasing and sea levels rising. If this happened there would be disastrous effects on agriculture and flooding of low-lying areas. Great changes would be necessary, including, for example, new types of agricultural practices and different areas of tourism, as well as modification to the production processes and consumption patterns that have been identified as contributory factors. Laws would have to be enacted in a wide range of business and marketing-related areas to enforce such restrictions as were thought appropriate.

The Kyoto Treaty of 1997 was an attempt to control pollution of the environment by emission of 'greenhouse gases', particularly carbon dioxide, which have been linked to climate change.

The Treaty implements the United Nations Framework Convention for Climate Change and legally binds industrialised nations to reduce emissions by an average of 5.2% below 1990 levels. The USA withdrew from the Treaty in March 2001. Although, as of January 2009, 183 nations have ratified a scaled-down version of the treaty, President Bush stated that the USA would never sign it. President Obama has, as at August 2009, taken no action with the Senate that would change the position of the USA.

The Kyoto Treaty assigns 'carbon credits' to countries based on existing economic and environmental factors, which countries can then exchange with other countries. Some countries might end up increasing overall emissions, and the system is open to abuse.

Some (such as *Sarewitz* (2000), in '*Breaking the Global-Warming Gridlock*') argue that there should be greater emphasis on improvements to infrastructure and land use patterns rather than carbon emissions. Such improvements would make us better prepared for future climatic changes.

---

**FOR DISCUSSION**

The publicity for Al Gore's 2006 film *An Inconvenient Truth* stated that:

'Humanity is sitting on a ticking time bomb. If the vast majority of the world's scientists are right, we have just ten years to avert a major catastrophe that could send our entire planet into a tail-spin of epic destruction involving extreme weather, floods, droughts, epidemics and killer heat waves beyond anything we have ever experienced.'

Hollywood hype or an inconvenient truth – what do you think?

---

**Energy resources**

Concerns about energy resources and about the environmental impacts of energy usage at the moment are related to the concern over climatic change. Some of the energy sources currently used are yielding far less of their potential than seems possible – coal, for example, typically gives up only 40% of its potential into electricity. Energy-saving programmes are underway in most of the countries of the developed world, involving the development of more efficient plant and projects such as combined heat and power systems serving neighbourhoods or industrial plants. New energy efficient products are also being developed. Possible legislation that would penalise the use of certain scarce, potentially wasteful or dangerous materials – for instance, a 'carbon tax' – may well discourage the demand for such products. This may also lead to changes in the ways in which buildings, cars and electrical devices are designed.

### 2.6 Green concerns

Green issues have varying impacts on the different sectors of industry.

#### The primary sector

Many industries in the primary sector of the economy, such as mining, are involved directly with the physical environment. Primary industries are under constant scrutiny with regard to environmental legislation, and are the target of international concerns about the destruction of natural ecosystems and wildlife habitats. Concerns here relate to the following.

(a) Deforestation

(b) Threats to wild creatures

(c) Replacing a natural habitat containing a diversity of species with a monoculture where only one strain is bred

(d) Pollution

(e) Health and safety of produce

(f) Poor working conditions and wages

Green policies here would aim to promote efficient and effective use of finite resources by diversification of supply and recycling where appropriate, and developing alternatives to the materials that are being used up.

#### The secondary sector

In the secondary sector of the economy, building and construction are relevant. Recently there has been significant opposition to the building of new roads.

#### Consumer goods

Manufacturers here may be seen as:

(a) Damaging the environment or social institutions to meet consumer demand
(b) Producing 'dirty' products
(c) Using 'dirty' processes
(d) Using up scarce raw materials (eg rare woods)

Some manufacturers already make products that contribute to environmental improvements (biodegradable packaging, for example), while larger manufacturers are under pressure to act in a socially responsible manner.

(a) Manufacturers of washing machines and dishwashers have brought out models that use less water

(b) Car manufacturers are producing models that have a high degree of recyclability and durability

(c) Detergent manufacturers are making products that are kinder to animal species, or that perform more effectively with smaller amounts

#### Industrial and business-to-business marketers

Industrial and business-to-business marketers are finding themselves having to fit in with the policies of customers who are producing green products.

### The tertiary sector

*Retailing*

In retailing the green consumer is dealing directly with the enterprise. The enterprise acts as a 'filter', deciding which products will actually reach the customer.

*Service providers*

Service providers have traditionally thought that green issues are less relevant to them than to other types of business enterprise. Although service enterprises typically do have less environmental impact than other types of business, they still consume resources and generate waste. Such businesses still face the same decisions in their choice of suppliers, their investments and their contribution to the welfare of staff and customers. In fact, the very proliferation of green marketing practices is creating a growing demand for business services such as environmental auditing, green training, waste management and pollution control specialists.

### Small businesses

*Small businesses* face a different scale of environmental challenge than large-scale enterprises. The latter produce much larger environmental impacts by consuming large amounts of raw materials and producing large volumes of waste.

Despite this difference, green issues are becoming more significant for small businesses for the following reasons.

(a) Small companies may be able to develop products for green 'niches' more effectively than large enterprises, and can take advantage of flexibility to create green processes and systems.

(b) Many small businesses are using traditional methods of manufacture, which are often greener than more modern processes, using less energy and fewer non-renewable resources. Demand for such products is increasing.

However, in areas where the demand for green products is increasing, it may be difficult for small companies to compete with larger companies (with their greater command of power and resources).

---

### FOR DISCUSSION

In the West, 'big business' is often blamed for environmental malpractice. The state is seen as the only protector of the environment.

However, Russia and other countries of the former Soviet Union have seen environmental pollution on a catastrophic scale, even though all the industries were owned by the state.

---

**Activity 5** **(45 minutes)**

Assuming the role of press officer of a local chamber of commerce, draft a 200-word statement about environmental concerns in your home district.

## 3 ETHICS AND BUSINESS

***Ethics is about the codes of moral principles that people follow with respect to what is right or wrong. Ethical principles are not necessarily enforced by law, although the law can incorporate moral judgements (murder is 'wrong' ethically, and is also punishable legally).***

### 3.1 Ethical practice

Ethics in organisations relates to issues of social responsibility and issues of business practice. These ethics exist at three levels:

(a) At the *macro* level there are issues about the role of business in the national and international organisation of society eg, free enterprise and centrally planned economies.

(b) At the *corporate* level the issue is focused on the ethical issues facing organisations when formulating and implementing strategies.

(c) At the *individual* level the issue concerns the behaviour and actions of individuals within organisations.

Some companies have a voluntary code of conduct. A code is a statement of policies, principles or rules that guide behaviour. Codes of ethics do not only apply to organisations but should guide the behaviour of people in everyday life. Most of us operate with a more or less well defined set of ethical values, principles or rules of thumb that guide decision-making. They are seldom spelled out explicitly in a list but if you had to make a list it would probably include:

- obey the law
- be fair
- avoid harming others
- prevent harm to others
- respect the rights of others
- help those in need
- do not lie or cheat

Simply stating a code of conduct (or ethics) is not enough. The organisation should appoint an ethics committee, consisting of internal and external directors, to institutionalise ethical behaviour.

For ethical codes to be effective, provisions must be made for their enforcement. Unethical managers should be held responsible for their actions. This means that privileges and benefits should be withdrawn and sanctions should be applied. Although the enforcement of ethical codes may not be easy, the mere existence of such codes can increase ethical behaviour by clarifying expectations. When integrated into the day-to-day operations of an organisation, such codes can help prevent damaging ethical lapses, while tapping into powerful human impulses for moral thought and action. Thus an ethical framework becomes no longer a burdensome constraint within which the organisation must operate, but the governing ethos.

### 3.2 Business ethics

Ethical codes are rooted in a wider value system, as to what is right or wrong. Is killing always wrong? What about killing in self-defence? For example, there are conflicting views and continuing debates about such questions as:

(a) Criteria for distribution of profit

(b) The relative pay and rewards for all employees – from directors to junior staff

(c) Decisions about priorities, for example in respect of public expenditure

(d) Loan charges, ie payment of interest to lenders of money

(e) The sale of harmful products, eg tobacco

People who work for organisations bring their own values into work with them. These can be personal (eg deriving from a person's upbringing, religious or non-religious beliefs, political opinions, personality) and professional (eg code of ethics, medical ethics). The way the organisation behaves also has an ethical dimension.

Some organisation specialists suggest that ethical decisions are becoming more important as penalties (in the US at least) for companies that break the law become tougher. (This might be contrasted with UK, where a fraudster whose deception ran into millions received a sentence of community service.)

(a) A **compliance-based approach** is primarily designed to ensure that the company acts within the letter of the law, and that violations are prevented, detected and punished. Some organisations, faced with the legal consequences of 'unethical behaviour' are attempting to define how the idea of **social responsibility** affects business. This gives a wider approach than mere adherence to the letter of the law, and avoiding problems such as bribery (discussed later).

(b) This **integrity-based approach** takes a wider view, based on promoting ethical behaviour in the business by building it into the very assumptions with which people go about their work.

Figure 2.1 indicates some of the differences between the two approaches.

| Area | Compliance | Integrity |
|---|---|---|
| Ethos | Knuckle under to external standards | Choose ethical standards |
| Objective | Keep to the law | Enable legal and responsible conduct |
| Originators | Lawyers | Management, with lawyers, HR specialists etc. |

| Area | Compliance | Integrity |
|---|---|---|
| Methods (both include education, and audits, controls, penalties) | Reduced employee discretion | Leadership, organisation systems |
| Behavioural assumptions | People are solitary self-interested beings | People are social beings with values |
| Standards | The law | Company values, aspirations (including law) |
| Staffing | Lawyers | Managers and lawyers |
| Education | The law, compliance system | Values, the law, compliance systems |
| Activities | Develop standards, train and communicate, handle reports of misconduct, investigate, enforce, oversee compliance | Integrate values into company systems, provide guidance and consultation, identify and resolve problems, oversee compliance |

*Figure 2.1: Compliance v integrity based approaches to ethics*

In other words, an integrity-based approach incorporates issues of ethics in corporate procedure and systems.

**Activity 6** **(5 minutes)**

A business may be strictly operated on principles that strive to be:

(a) Moral and legal
(b) Immoral and legal
(c) Moral but illegal
(d) Immoral and illegal

Try to list one example of current business practice that would fit each heading.

An example of the difference between the legality and ethicality of a practice is the sale in some countries of defective products without appropriate warnings. Companies trading internationally often discover that conduct that infringes recognised standards of human rights and decency is legal in some jurisdictions.

The compliance approach also over-emphasises the threat of detection and punishment in order to channel appropriate behaviour. Arguably, some employers view compliance programmes as an 'insurance policy' for senior management, who can cover the tracks of their arbitrary management practices. After all, some performance targets are impossible to achieve without cutting corners: managers can escape responsibility by blaming the employee for not following the compliance programme, when to do so would have meant a failure to reach target.

Furthermore, mere compliance with the law is no guide to behaviour that sets an example and is above reproach.

Many modern companies are publishing the terms under which they choose to operate as a 'code of ethics', although this may also be published under different titles (such as a code of conduct, principles of conduct, guidelines, operating principles, company objectives or a staff handbook).

**Activity 7** **(40 minutes)**

Conduct a brief survey of newspapers or business journals. Try to find some examples of companies who specifically state their code of practice or ethical stance on business issues.

***There are differing views about the extent to which external environmental constraints modify business objectives and form boundaries to the exercise of management discretion. Below we identify some ethical problems that managers face.***

### 3.3 Ethical problems facing managers

Managers have a duty (in most enterprises) to aim for profit. At the same time, modern ethical standards impose a duty to guard, preserve and enhance the value of the enterprise for the good of all touched by it, including the general public. Large organisations tend to be more often held to account over this than small ones. The types of ethical problem a manager may meet with in practice are very numerous. A few of them are suggested in the following paragraphs.

In the area of products and production, managers have a responsibility to ensure that the public and their own employees are protected from danger. Attempts to increase profitability by cutting costs may lead to dangerous working conditions or to inadequate safety standards in products. In the United States, product liability litigation is so common that this legal threat may be a more effective deterrent than general ethical standards. The Consumer Protection Act 2007 and EU legislation generally is beginning to ensure that ethical standards are similarly 'enforced' in the UK.

---

**EXAMPLE: DEVELOPMENT RISK**

The pharmaceutical industry is one where the problem of product liability is particularly acute. On the one hand managers may be influenced by a genuine desire to benefit the community by developing new drugs that at the same time will lead to profits; on the other hand, they must not skimp their research on possible side-effects in rushing to launch the new product. In the UK, the Consumer Protection Act 2007 attempts to recognise this dilemma. Drugs companies are not held liable for side-effects that could not have been foreseen by scientific knowledge, as it existed, at the time the drug was developed – the 'development risk' defence.

---

Ethical issues also arise in the area of corporate governance and finance. An example is provided by the various allegations made against the Maxwell empire and some accusations that companies are over zealous in their use of creative accounting techniques.

Another ethical problem concerns **payments by companies to officials** (particularly officials in foreign countries) who have power to help or hinder the payers' operations. There are fine distinctions in this area.

(a) **Extortion**. In some countries officials have been known to threaten companies with the complete closure of their local operations unless suitable payments are made.

(b) **Bribery**. This refers to payments for services to which a company is not legally entitled. There are some fine distinctions to be drawn; for example, some managers regard political contributions as bribery.

(c) **Grease money**. Multinational companies are sometimes unable to obtain services to which they are legally entitled because of deliberate stalling by local officials. Cash payments to the right people may then be enough to oil the machinery of bureaucracy.

(d) **Gifts**. In some cultures (such as Japan) gifts are regarded as an essential part of civilised negotiation, even in circumstances where to Western eyes they might appear ethically dubious. Managers operating in such a culture may feel at liberty to adopt the local customs.

A difficult area for managers concerns the extent to which an organisation's activities may appear to give support to **undesirable political policies**. The boycotting of goods and services from South Africa, when it was run by the apartheid regime, is an example.

Business ethics are also relevant to competitive behaviour. This is because a market can only be 'free' if competition is, in some basic respects, fair. There is a distinction between competing aggressively and competing unethically. The dispute between British Airways and Virgin centred around issues of business ethics, and *allegations* of:

(a) The theft of information

(b) The planting of inaccurate and derogatory stories in the press

(c) The refusal of normal aircraft service to Virgin (when it was offered to other airlines)

(d) An unfair price war

---

**FOR DISCUSSION**

Look at the following scenarios. Which would you say merely involve aggressive competition and which would you say involve unethical practices?

(a) The Widget Company buy up advertising space so that they can place their advertisements directly opposite those of their main competitor Widgets Incorporated. They intend to match whatever statements are made by Widgets with better ones of their own.

(b) A company is very worried as it feels that they are losing a competitive battle with a rival. They decide to hire a private detective to follow the Chairman of their rival company in order to gather information about his private life, which they will then use to instigate a smear campaign against him. They hope that the resulting publicity will lead to his resignation and produce turmoil in the management structure.

(c) The Sweetness Sugar Company engages a team of scientists to discover possible risks associated with the use of artificial sweeteners in place of sugar. A discovery is made that doses of artificial sweetener several thousand times more than any person would be subjected to may cause cancer in rats. The sugar company publish this information and makes it the basis of a major advertising campaign to convert people back to using sugar.

---

***Next we examine some examples of management responsibility.***

## 4 MANAGEMENT RESPONSIBILITIES

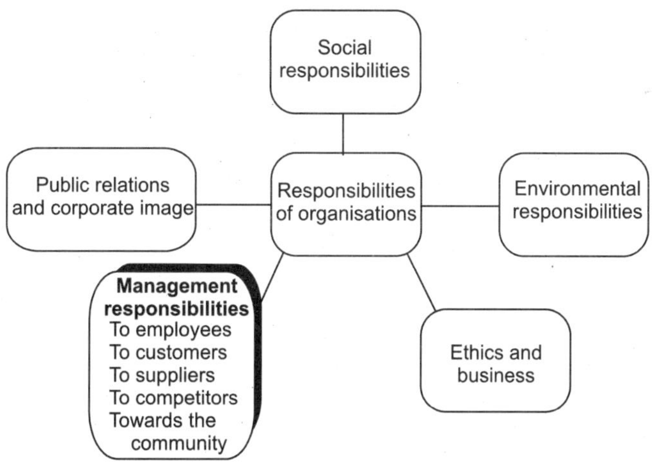


***We looked at the stakeholder view of corporate objectives at the beginning of this chapter and at some of the pressures from various groups.***

The stakeholder view suggests that management is responsible not only to the organisation's owners (shareholders), but also has responsibilities to:

(a) Employees
(b) Customers
(c) Suppliers
(d) Competitors
(e) The local community
(f) The general public (and government)

***We start with looking at responsibilities to employees.***

### 4.1 Responsibilities to employees

An organisation's broad responsibilities to its employees may be similar to the following example.

## EXAMPLE: UNITED BISCUITS AND ITS EMPLOYEES

The following is drawn from a code used by United Biscuits.

'To achieve the dynamic morale and team spirit based on mutual confidence without which a business cannot be successful, people have to be cared for during their working lives and in retirement. In return we expect, from all our staff, loyalty and commitment to the company. We respect the rights and innate worth of the individual. In addition to being financially rewarding, working life should provide as much job satisfaction as possible. The company encourages all employees to be trained and developed to achieve their full potential.

United Biscuits takes a responsible attitude towards employment legislation requirements and codes of practice, union activities and communications with staff. We place the highest priority on promoting and preserving the health and safety of employees. Employees, for their part, have a clear duty to take every reasonable precaution to avoid injury to themselves, their colleagues and members of the public.'

---

General principles have to be converted into practice, and should take the form of good pay and working conditions, and good training and development schemes. They should also extend into:

(a) Recruitment policy, and
(b) Redundancy and retirement policies

**Recruitment** of new staff should be done as carefully as possible, because if an organisation recruits an individual who turns out to be bad at the job, the company has to sack them. Dismissals are inevitable in any large organisation, but careful recruitment methods should manage to keep such demoralising incidents down to a small number.

Staff who are about to retire, after years of service with the organisation, should be provided for in their **retirement**.

(a) The organisation might have a good pension scheme.
(b) One of the problems for retired people is learning what to do with their leisure time. Some organisations provide training courses and discussion groups for employees who are coming up for retirement, to help them to plan their future time constructively.

Dealing with **redundancies** is a more difficult problem. Even for organisations that show an ethical sense of responsibility towards their employees, there may be occasions when parts of the business have to be closed down, and jobs lost. In such a situation, the organisation:

(a) Should try to redeploy as many staff as possible, without making them redundant, and
(b) Where necessary, should provide retraining to give staff the skills to do a new job

For those staff who are made redundant, the organisation should take steps to help them to get a job elsewhere. Measures could include:

(a) Counselling individuals to give them suggestions about what they might try to do

(b) Providing retraining, or funds for training, in other skills that the employees could use in other organisations and industries.

(c) Arranging 'job fairs', by inviting other employers to come and display the jobs that they have on offer, and to discuss job opportunities with redundant employees

(d) Providing good redundancy payments, which employees might be able to use to set up in business themselves, or which at least should tide them over until they find employment again

***Next we consider responsibilities towards the customers of a business.***

### 4.2 Responsibilities to customers

Ethical responsibilities towards customers are mainly those of providing a product or service of a quality that customers expect, and of dealing honestly and fairly with customers.

The guidelines of United Biscuits plc again provide a good example of how these responsibilities might be expressed.

---

**EXAMPLE: UNITED BISCUITS AND ITS CUSTOMERS**

'UB's reputation for integrity is the foundation on which the mutual trust between the company and its customers is based. That relationship is the key to our trading success.

Both employees and customers need to know that products sold by any of our operating companies will always meet their highest expectations. The integrity of our products is sacrosanct and implicit in the commitment is an absolute and uncompromising dedication to quality. We will never compromise on recipes or specification of products in order to save costs. Quality improvement must always be our goal.

No employee may give money or any gift of significant value to a customer if it could reasonably be viewed as being done to gain a business advantage. Winning an order by violating this policy or by providing free or extra services, or unauthorised contract terms, is contrary to our trading policy.'

---

***Suppliers are another important group towards whom a business may be thought to have responsibilities.***

### 4.3 Responsibilities to suppliers

The responsibilities of an organisation towards its suppliers are expressed mainly in terms of trading relationships.

(a) The organisation's size could give it considerable power as a buyer. One ethical guideline might be that the organisation should not use its power unscrupulously (eg to force the supplier to lower his prices under threat of withdrawing business).

(b) Suppliers might rely on getting prompt payment in accordance with the terms of trade negotiated with its customers. Another ethical guideline is that an organisation should not delay payments to suppliers beyond the agreed credit period.

(c) All information obtained from suppliers and potential suppliers should be kept confidential.

(d) All suppliers should be treated fairly, and this means:

   (i) Giving potential new suppliers a chance to win some business, and also

   (ii) Maintaining long-standing relationships that have been built up over the years with some suppliers. Long-established suppliers should not be replaced unless there is a significant commercial advantage for the organisation from such a move.

***Organisations also have some responsibilities towards competitors.***

### 4.4 Responsibilities to competitors

Some ethical responsibilities should exist towards competitors. United Biscuits again provides a good example.

---

### EXAMPLE: UNITED BISCUITS AND ITS COMPETITORS

'We compete vigorously, energetically, untiringly but we also compete ethically and honestly. Our competitive success is founded on excellence – of product and service. We have no need to disparage our competitors either directly or by implication or innuendo....

No-one may attempt improperly to acquire a competitor's trade secrets or other proprietary or confidential information. 'Improper' means are activities such as industrial espionage, hiring competitors' employees to get confidential information, urging competitive personnel or customers to disclose confidential information, or any other approach which is not completely open and above board.'

---

Responsibilities regarding competition are by no means solely directed by ethics however: there is also a great deal of law surrounding the conduct of fair trading, monopolies, mergers, anti-competitive practices, abuses of a dominant market position and restrictive trade practices.

***Finally, we consider responsibilities towards the wider community.***

### 4.5 Responsibilities towards the community

An organisation is a part of the community that it serves, and it should be responsible for:

(a) Upholding the social and ethical values of the community

(b) Contributing towards the well-being of the community, eg by sponsoring local events and charities, or providing facilities for the community to use (eg sports fields)

(c) Responding constructively to complaints from local residents or politicians (eg about problems for local traffic caused by the organisation's delivery vehicles)

---

## EXAMPLE: ANGLO AMERICAN

Anglo American is one of the world's leading international mining companies, employing 105,000 permanent staff worldwide. Most of its operations are in the primary sector, for example, extracting materials through mining and quarrying. Anglo American tries to operate in a way that promotes sustainable development through having a positive effect on different types of 'capital':

- social – increasing the life chances of people in local communities
- natural – reducing energy use and the impact of operations on nature
- manufactured – providing infrastructure; coping with waste
- human – supporting education and investing in skills
- financial – concentrating on the whole financial performance, not just returns to shareholders

**Sustainable development**

Sustainable development means not depleting stocks of these types of capital, but passing on at least as much as our generation started with. It shows respect for everyone who shares the planet now or in the future and respect for nature itself. As a major supplier of raw materials, Anglo American tries to balance its use of natural capital (e.g. ore deposits or water used in processing) by increasing human and social capital. To help, it has created a set of principles to meet targets of sustainable development.

**In practice**

When Anglo American carries out its mining operations, it tries to have a positive effect on three areas:

(1) In the area where the mine is located, it carries out operations with care and tries to improve the life chances of local people.

(2) In the area immediately surrounding the mine, it is active in conservation and improvement.

(3) In the wider region around the mine, it contributes financially to local communities and helps to generate new businesses and other economic opportunities.

**Pressures**

There are pressures to be environmentally responsible from both within and outside the business. Internally, the Board decides how best to work with local communities and mine sensitively. Shareholders are also internal. As the owners of the company they want the business to do well, but to do so, Anglo American must be welcome in the communities where it works or wants to work in the future. By showing that it behaves responsibly, the business is also able to attract the best staff.

Externally, pressures come from legislation designed to protect the environment and from national and international standards and regulations. Customers and other external bodies, like NGOs, also demand high standards of performance.

**Benefits**

Acting responsibly gains the trust of communities, respect from governments and the public, and loyalty from customers. It also gives the company an advantage when recruiting new staff. All stakeholders benefit and Anglo American has created a tool (the Socio-Economic Assessment Toolbox or SEAT) to ensure that it consults widely and regularly with local people and measures the impact of its activities in the areas where it operates. It can be used to improve performance

**Conclusion**

As a major mining company, Anglo American recognises that it has social and environmental responsibilities in the areas in which it operates and that these are fundamental to its business. It has built itself a strong reputation in terms of sustainable operations and through its policies that are carried all the way through the company.

Source: *www.TheTimes100.co.uk*

Contrast the report from the Times100 website with the criticisms of Anglo American on Wikipedia in August 2009:

'In 1977, the company demanded the paper it owned, Rand Daily Mail, tone down its equal-rights support after exposing the murder of South African activist Steve Biko amid the subsequent government backlash. In August 2007, the British charity, War on Want, published a report accusing Anglo American of profiting from the abuse of people in the developing countries in which the company operates. According to the charity, "in the Philippines and South Africa, local communities threatened with Anglo American mines have faced severe repression in their fight to stay on their land, while in Ghana and Mali, local communities see little of the huge profits being made by AngloGold Ashanti but suffer from fear and intimidation and from the damaging impact of its mines on their environment, health and livelihoods".

'Anglo American was also accused in 2007 of damaging environmental practices: in order to complete its planned Alaskan Pebble Mine in collaboration with Northern Dynasty Minerals, the global mining giant may build a massive dam at the headwaters of the world's largest sockeye salmon fishery, which it would risk obliterating. Opponents are also pointing to the use of cyanide, heavy metals, and acid mine drainage which can all have potentially devastating effects on the pristine environment of the Bristol Bay area.

'Nunamta Aulukestai (Caretakers of Our Land) and the Renewable Resources Coalition commissioned a report regarding Anglo American and their current and past subsidiaries. The report is written by Philip Mattera, a corporate reporter. The report, released in July 2008, criticizes Anglo American for community, worker safety, public health, and environmental problems at their mining operations in South Africa, Zimbabwe, Ghana, Mali, Ireland, and the United States (Nevada) and notes the difference between Anglo's stated corporate goals and their actual corporate performance.'

Source: *www.Wikipedia.org* (August 2009)

**Activity 8** **(40 minutes)**

The Heritage Carpet Company is a London-based retailer that imports carpets from Turkey, Iran and India. The company was founded by two Europeans who travelled independently through these countries in the 1970s. The company is the sole customer for carpets made in a number of villages in each of the source countries. The carpets are hand woven. Indeed, they are so finely woven that the process requires that children be used to do the weaving, as their small fingers are required for the task. The company believes that it is preserving a 'craft', and the directors believe that this is a justifiable social objective.

Recently a UK television company reported unfavourably on child exploitation in the carpet weaving industry. There were reports of children working twelve-hour shifts in poorly lit sheds and cramped conditions, with consequent deterioration in eyesight, muscular disorders and a complete lack of education. The examples cited bear no relation to the Heritage Carpet Company's suppliers, although children are used in the labour force, but there has been a spate of media attention. The regions in which the Heritage Carpet Company's supplier villages are found are soon expected to enjoy rapid economic growth.

Explain the issues that are raised for the Heritage Carpet Company.

## 5 PUBLIC RELATIONS AND CORPORATE IMAGE

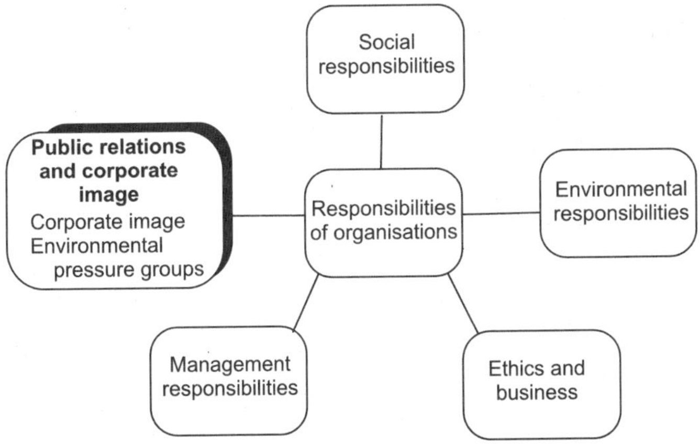


### 5.1 Corporate image

Corporate image describes the public attitude towards a company, or the image of the company in the mind of the general public and, perhaps more specifically, in the minds of potential customers. It is possible to promote a desired corporate image through a combination of public relations, advertising and the experience and attitudes built up by customers over the years. (For example, the favourable corporate image of Marks and Spencer grew up over many years, without the need for substantial PR or advertising.)

There are various reasons why an organisation might attempt to build up a corporate image.

(a) The organisation may want to strengthen customer loyalty, and so a corporate image of good quality products and services, and concern for the customer's interests, could be fostered.

(b) Rather than strengthen customer loyalty, a corporate image might be developed to create customer awareness. Some companies have faced the problem that customers do not know what they are and have never heard of them. A corporate image is then needed to give the company a public identity (eg Racal plc spent large sums advertising itself as one of the largest companies no one had ever heard of).

(c) Corporate image can strengthen an employee's attachment to the company for which he or she work, because of corporate identity. People may want to work for a company because of its image in the mind of the public ('prestige' jobs) or because the company has a 'get-ahead' image.

(d) Some companies may wish to develop a corporate image of social responsibility, in order to avoid unfavourable legislation, to prevent adverse publicity or to prevent pressure from stakeholder groups. Examples of this motive are:

    (i) The attempt by oil companies to establish an image of caring for the environment and for the future needs of society

    (ii) The attempt by British Nuclear Fuels to promote an image of deepest concern for the environment

    (iii) The attempt by fur traders to counter the adverse publicity built up against them by the efforts of animal rights activists, and

    (iv) The efforts of independent TV companies to promote an image of 'quality' programme-makers, to strengthen their chances of winning a bid for franchises

(e) Some companies may wish to have a favourable corporate image that they can subsequently use to win public and political support

(f) A good corporate image has a variety of benefits for management, in addition to strengthening customer loyalty. An image of a sound, well-established company might encourage investors to put more money into the business, and suppliers to grant longer credit.

Market research by MORI has shown that:

(a) Two out of every three people in the UK believe that a company that has a good reputation would not sell poor quality products (this suggests that customers would be more willing to try a new product if it is promoted by a well-known corporate name than if it is made by an unknown company), and

(b) Nine times out of ten, the better known a company is, the more highly it is regarded

**Activity 9** **(15 minutes)**

A company manufacturing baby food, in a very competitive market, has received in private, a disturbing phone call. Some cartons of its product have been tampered with, and contain shards of broken glass. The affected cartons are already for sale in chemists and supermarkets. What would be the most ethical approach to deal with this problem? Which of the following do you think would be in the best interests of the company?

(a) Withdraw all goods from sale.

(b) Take out warning advertisements in newspapers.

(c) Assume a hoax, but offer substantial compensation to people whose children were affected, in return for their silence if the threats turn out to be true.

Give reasons for your answer.

### 5.2 Environmental pressure groups

Environmental pressure groups have typically exerted pressure through three main types of activity.

(a) **Information-based activity** – gathering and providing information, mounting political lobbies and publicity campaigns.

(b) **Direct action** – varying from peaceful protests and the semi-legal activities of organisations such as Greenpeace and Friends of the Earth through to the environmental terrorism of more extreme organisations.

(c) **Partnership and consultancy** – groups here aim to work with businesses to pool resources and to help them to improve environmental performance.

**Employees** are increasing pressure on the businesses in which they work partly for their own safety, and partly in order to improve the public image of the company.

**Legislation** is increasing almost by the day. Growing pressure from the green or green-influenced vote has led to mainstream political parties taking these issues into their programmes. Most countries now have laws to cover land-use planning, smoke emissions, water pollution and the destruction of animals and natural habitats.

**Media pressure** focuses on large-scale disasters and more technical issues, such as global warming. Newspaper and television reports have generated very widespread public awareness of the issues concerned.

### Chapter roundup

- Companies have social responsibilities towards those they affect, either directly or indirectly.
- The stakeholder view holds that there are many groups in society with an interest in the organisation's activities. Some firms have objectives for these interests. Some argue, however, that a business's only objective should be to make money: the state, representing the public interest, can levy taxes to spend on socially desirable projects or can regulate organisational activities.
- There is increasing public concern about potential danger to the environment. This can be seen by growing membership of voluntary organisations.
- Firms have to ensure that they obey the law: but they also face ethical concerns, because their reputations depend on a good image.
- Inside the organisation a compliance-based approach highlights conformity with the law. An integrity-based approach suggests a wider remit, incorporating ethics in the organisation's values and culture.
- Organisations sometimes issue codes of conduct to employees. Many employees are bound by professional codes of conduct.

### Quick quiz

1 List some stakeholders management is responsible to.

2 List some ways in which a business can demonstrate its responsibility to employees.

3 List three types of direct ecological impact on a business.

4 Give examples of indirect pressure that a business could experience.

5 What is the basic idea behind the 'polluter pays' principle?

6 List some of the environmental concerns most relevant to the primary sector of industry.

7 List some of the environmental concerns most relevant to the tertiary sector.

8 Distinguish between responsibilities and boundaries. What ethical problems face management?

9 To whom might management have responsibilities, and what are some of these responsibilities?

10 What might shareholders argue is the main responsibility of an organisation?

11 Why is it good PR for a business to show it has social responsibility?

12 What factors contribute to a 'good' corporate image?

13 What is the role of the PR department?

## Answers to quick quiz

1. Stakeholders could include shareholders, employees, customers, suppliers, competitors, the local community, the general public and government.
2. Good pay and working conditions, good training and advancement opportunities, good retirement packages, social aspects.
3. Costs, availability of resources, consumer demand, competition, legislation.
4. Customer pressure, staff pressure.
5. The intention is to deter potential polluters by making it uneconomic to produce goods and services that also create pollution.
6. The physical environment is the main concern.
7. Consumption of resources, production of waste, choice of suppliers, investments, welfare of staff and customers.
8. Responsibility is something you are likely to be called into account for if you fail to exercise it. A boundary is a limit beyond which you cannot go. In business terms, responsibilities are things you ought to do, boundaries are rules that must not be broken, or limits that you are obliged to remain within. For example, a haulage firm should instruct its drivers to drive carefully and be considerate to other road users, but they are not obliged to do so. However, all lorries must be fitted by law with a tacograph and drivers must only drive within their permitted hours.
9. Management has responsibilities to almost anyone who comes into contact with the business. For example, responsibilities to employees for their safety and welfare, responsibility to customers under consumer safety legislation, responsibility to shareholders to protect their interests, legal responsibilities of corporate governance and financial dealings, responsibility to the general public – pollution, image, advertising etc.
10. Shareholders might argue that the main responsibility of management is to make a profit.
11. It can enhance the corporate image of the company. This can lead to increased sales, customer loyalty, employee loyalty and desirable shares.
12. Factors that could contribute to a 'good' corporate image include, being a responsible employer, dealing fairly with suppliers and customers, good quality products leading to few customer complaints, clear statements of company policy, avoidance of unethical investments or trading practices.
13. The role of the public relations department is to maintain the good image of the company at all times. Sometimes, when a company is new or is not well known, an image needs to be created. The role when the company has transgressed is of damage limitation.

## Answers to activities

1 To assist you we can give you some examples. Should the company support the Prince's Trust? This helps young people to start up enterprises. Co-operative Retail Services publishes a social report to its shareholding members who number over a million. A number of firms publish reports for their employees. Some companies set aside a percentage of their profits for selected charities.

2 Conflicts of interest largely relate to distributing the profits of the firm, the size of the pension fund and shareholders' returns

3 Benefits of recycling: savings on refuse collection, expenditure on office stationery and equipment, environmental 'knock on' effects eg less paper used, fewer trees felled. Items that could easily be recycled include: paper clips (can be used several times), envelopes (can be re-used), spare copies of documents (can be cut up and used for rough memo paper), card dividers (can be re-labelled and used again). Items that could be made from re-cycled materials: paper for printing/photocopying, files, dividers, office equipment can be made from recycled plastics, wooden furniture can be made from easily renewable sources (eg pine instead of mahogany).

4 First, there is a market for old newspapers. In fact, there have been reports of old newspapers being stolen. This is because there is currently undercapacity in the paper-making industry, and demand for paper is strong. Second, government policy is moving towards compulsory recycling (as is the case in Germany). Finally we note the role of lobbyists.

5 You should have considered the following factors.

(a) Is yours a rural or urban area?

(b) What industries are important: manufacturing, service, extraction?

(c) How is public health?

6 (a) A company that promotes itself as acting morally and legally is the Body Shop.

(b) An activity that could be classed as immoral and legal could be selling arms to brutal military dictators.

(c) An activity that could be seen as moral but illegal would be the publishing of stolen, but revelatory, documents about government mismanagement, eg a 'leak' of secret information.

(d) An activity that could be classed as immoral and illegal would be the drugs trade.

7 Companies that appear to have clear ethical codes and promote these widely include the Body Shop, The Co-operative Bank (advertises the fact that it does not invest in arms dealers etc), Daewoo (which has clear codes about customer care), and Café Direct (which imports coffee from third world countries in order to assist their economic development). There are also a number of insurance and unit trust companies that specialise in ethical investments.

8 Many issues are raised in this situation. This is a case partly about boundary management and partly about enlightened self-interest and business ethics. The adverse publicity, although not about the Heritage Carpet Company's own suppliers, could rebound badly — potential customers might be put off. Economic growth in the area may also mean that parents will soon prefer to send their children to school than to work. The Heritage Carpet Company, as well as promoting itself as preserving a craft, could reinvest some of its profits in the villages (eg by funding a school), or by enforcing limits on the hours children work. It could also pay a decent wage. It could advertise this in a 'code of ethics', so that customers are reassured that the children are not simply being exploited. Alternatively, it could not import child-made carpets at all. (This policy, however, would be unlikely to help communities in which child labour is an economic necessity.)

9 This is similar to a case in the US. The affected company withdrew all its products for sale, and better security procedures were installed at the factory. An advertising campaign was instituted to reach people who had purchased the product. This draconian approach earned the company public goodwill. You might also find it interesting to compare the actions taken by various businesses over the uncertainties about BSE ('mad cow disease').

# Chapter 3:
# CONSUMER PROTECTION

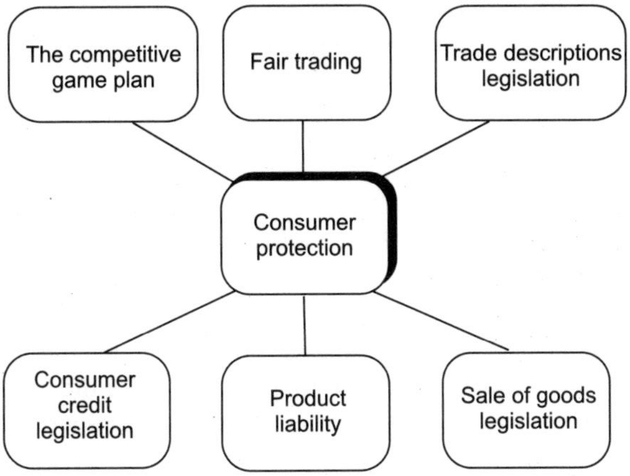


## Introduction

This chapter concentrates on the ways in which the law protects individual citizens and consumers from unfair trading practice. It explains the types of independent advice available to those seeking redress against unfair practices. It also examines remedies for faulty or defective goods.

## Your objectives

In this chapter you will learn about:

(a) The arguments for consumer protection

(b) The role of the Office of Fair Trading

(c) What is meant by 'false trade description' and 'misleading prices'

(d) The remedies available against retailers for defective goods

(e) Manufacturers' liability for defective products

# 1 THE COMPETITIVE GAME PLAN

Individuals with complaints against businesses mainly rely upon legislation, voluntary undertakings such as the **codes of practice** published by banks and building societies, or **charters** (guaranteeing standards of service) in public transport, health and local government services.

Official institutions financed by government exist to act as 'watchdogs' on behalf of consumers. Examples are the Users Consultative Committees appointed to represent the public and act as informed judges of the performance of utilities such as gas and electricity. Community Health Councils perform a similar role for the NHS.

In addition to the official complaints agencies, the voluntary sector provides advisory assistance for individuals. Examples are the Citizens Advice Bureaux, and local law centres with a network of branches throughout the country. Both may be staffed by solicitors or other legally trained staff.

Individuals can also help themselves by subscribing to membership of the Consumer's Association to receive regular reports evaluating and comparing the whole range of products and services on offer to the public. There are also regular TV and radio programmes and press features devoted to consumer protection.

In a complex mixed economy, individuals need basic protection against unfair business practice. This is provided through legislation such as the Trades Descriptions Act. But it is not always necessary to resort to legal action – particular individual complaints may best be handled by agreed voluntary methods such as the Ombudsman services provided by banks. The essential point is that unscrupulous behaviour by organisations, public or private, large or small, can be challenged by individuals through legal action or by using voluntary procedures.

**Activity 1** **(15 minutes)**

It is Monday morning. You have had the most horrendous weekend. Your neighbour had a party on Saturday night that went on until midday Sunday. The music was blasting out and people parked cars all over your front lawn. When you went round to complain no-one heard your knocking and the door remained firmly shut. Finally, the party guests left and peace and quiet were restored. You decided to put a Brahms concerto on to play. You had been desperate to try your new CD player all weekend! You insert the disc only to hear a terrible grinding noise and see a lot of blue sparks coming from the back of the CD player. You give up in disgust. To cap it all you have just opened your morning post. Amongst the circulars and a letter from your Aunty Agatha you discover your bank statement. You appear to be overdrawn by £499, yet you paid in a cheque for £1,000 a week ago. The bank does not appear to have credited it to your account!

In your opinion, what would be the best way to deal with all the problems you have had over the weekend? Do you need to hire a solicitor or can you manage on your own?

***The Enterprise Act 2002 is a good starting point in any discussion of consumer protection.***

## 2 FAIR TRADING

### 2.1 The Office of Fair Trading

The legal powers of the Office of Fair Trading (OFT) derive from The Fair Trading Act 1973 (FTA) and the Enterprise Act 2002. The OFT promotes Codes of Practice.

The Office of Fair Trading (OFT) as an independent statutory body with a Board, giving them a greater role in ensuring that markets work well to the benefit of all. The OFT board consists of a chairman (Philip Collins) and six other members, appointed by the Secretary of State. The tenure of OFT members (including the Chairman) is determined by the Secretary of State although terms of office may not exceed five years.

The OFT's job is to make markets work well for consumers. Markets work well when businesses are in open, fair and vigorous competition with each other for the consumer's custom. They ensure that consumers have as much choice as possible across all the different sectors of the marketplace.

As an independent professional organisation, the OFT plays a leading role in promoting and protecting consumer interests throughout the UK, while ensuring that businesses are fair and competitive. To carry out this work they are granted powers under consumer and competition legislation.

They have three main operational areas:

(1) **Competition Enforcement** (CE) – The CE division plays a key role:

- enforcing current legislation including The Competition Act 1998
- stopping cartels and other damaging anti-competitive agreements
- stopping any abuse of a dominant market position
- promoting a strong competitive culture across a wide range of markets
- informing business, through a widespread education programme, about changes in legislation
- working with the European Commission on EC cases

(2) **Consumer Regulation Enforcement** (CRE) – The CRE team:

- ensures that consumer legislation and regulations are properly enforced
- takes action against unfair traders
- encourages codes of practice and standards
- offers a range of information to help consumers understand their rights and make good choices
- liaises closely with other regulatory bodies that also have enforcement powers.

(3) **Markets and Policies Initiatives** (MPI) – there are three main areas of activity within MPI.

- economic and statistical advice and financial analysis
- market investigations and competition
- relations with stakeholders, including government departments and public enquiries.

Each branch works closely with the other two, and often in project teams involving colleagues across the OFT.

***The UK's approach is to encourage industries to regulate themselves.***

## 2.2 Codes of practice

**Definition**

1 **Code of practice**: lays out a set of procedures and policies that a firm will follow. For example: 'we will always give you two weeks notice of withdrawal of overdraft facilities'. Adherence to the code is sometimes necessary for membership of certain trade associations.

2 **Ombudsman**: used to describe the provision of a final independent appeal that a dissatisfied customer may make against what he or she believes to be unfair or incompetent treatment. (The term is Swedish. The term ombudsperson is now sometimes used.) Some Ombudsmen are provided with government support. In the private sector, banks, building societies and insurance companies may support Ombudsmen on a voluntary basis.

Many codes of practice exist, including the Code of Banking Practice. Some provide for the existence of an Ombudsman. Codes of practice can be classified into four groups:

(a) Codes carrying the OFT's endorsement
(b) Enforceable codes
(c) Statutory codes
(d) Other codes of practice with limited status

These are described briefly below.

### Codes of practice carrying the OFT's endorsement

The OFT is responsible under the Enterprise Act for promoting codes of practice amongst traders. After negotiations between the OFT and the relevant trade association a list of rules of conduct is drawn up, in order:

(a) To promote a high standard of trade practice, and
(b) To protect the consumer's interests

**Activity 2** **(2 hours)**

Carry out an investigation to find out what codes of practice exist to fulfil the functions identified above. You could work in groups, with each group looking at a different trade or industry.

The weakness inherent in any system of voluntary codes is that they do not bind traders who are not members of an appropriate association. Even disciplinary action by a trade association may be of questionable value since there is the obvious question of bias towards its members. However, the existence of codes can help the consumer to derive reasonable expectations as to acceptable levels of service and facilities.

### Enforceable codes of practice

**Definition**

> **Enforceable code of practice**: a code of practice that is enforceable by means of sanctions falling short of legal proceedings. It will set down codes of conduct that can be enforced against people engaged in a certain trade or business, even though they are not members of the relevant trade body.

---

**EXAMPLE: BRITISH CODE OF ADVERTISING PRACTICE**

The British Code of Advertising Practice is an enforceable code of practice. It was developed and promoted by the Advertising Standards Authority (ASA), an independent body. Under the code, advertisements must be 'legal, decent, honest and truthful'. It contains provisions relating to specific products, for example weight control and mail order advertisements. Complaints are invited from members of the public, and the ASA will carry out investigations and publish the results, issuing warnings to offenders where appropriate.

---

> **Activity 3** **(20 minutes)**
>
> What do you think is meant by 'legal, decent, honest and truthful'? Do you think all advertisements satisfy this requirement? What are the difficulties in enforcing this?

### Statutory codes of practice

Codes that are drawn up with the involvement of government departments and the approval of the relevant minister may be given full or partial legal status. Such codes are increasingly common if people feel that other types of code of practice are ineffective. Examples includes the Highway Code (which may be relied upon in legal proceedings to establish liability), the Sex Discrimination Code of Practice (which may be taken into account by Industrial Tribunals) and the Code of Practice on Picketing in the case of strikes.

### Other codes of practice

Because of the aura of respectability imparted to a trade that has an association and a code of practice, many commercial areas have acquired codes of practice that have no legal status at all and afford neither legal nor practical assistance.

*The Banking Code*

An example of a code of practice is the Banking Code, which was prepared by the British Bankers' Association, The Building Societies Association and the Association for

Payment Clearing Services. It is a voluntary code and sets out the standards of good banking practice to be observed by UK banks and building societies in their dealings with personal customers.

Part of the Banking Code 2008 is given below.

*Fairness commitment*

We promise we will treat you fairly and reasonably when providing you with products and services covered in this Code.

We will keep this promise by meeting all of the key commitments shown below.

- We will make sure that our advertising and promotional literature is clear and not misleading and that you are given clear information about our products and services.
- We will give you clear information about accounts and services, how they work, their terms and conditions and the interest rates which may apply.
- We will help you use your account or service by sending you regular statements (where appropriate) and we will keep you informed about changes to the interest rates, charges or terms and conditions.
- We will help you to switch your current account between financial institutions that subscribe to this Code.
- We will lend responsibly.
- We will deal quickly and sympathetically with things that go wrong and consider all cases of financial difficulty sympathetically and positively.
- We will treat all your personal information as private and confidential, and provide secure and reliable banking and payment systems.
- We will publicise this Code, have copies available and make sure that our staff are trained to put it into practice.

---

**FOR DISCUSSION**

Do you think the Banking Code is too general? Why is it general? As a customer of a bank or building society, what would you like to see included in the Banking Code?

---

***We now examine legislation relating to trade descriptions.***

## 3 TRADE DESCRIPTIONS LEGISLATION

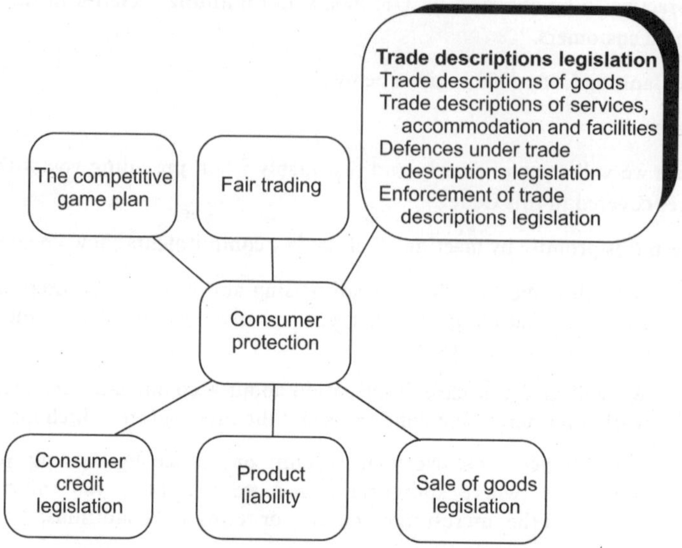


***The law relating to trade descriptions is contained in the Trade Descriptions Act 1968 (TDA) and in the Consumer Protection Act 1987 (CPA).***

### 3.1 Trade descriptions of goods

**Definition**

**Trade description**: any indication, direct or indirect, of any of the following:

(a) Quantity, size or gauge of goods

(b) Method of manufacture, production, processing or reconditioning

(c) Composition (in the case of *British Gas Corpn v Lubbock 1974* a gas board brochure giving details of cookers stated that 'ignition is by hand-held battery torch supplied with the cooker'. A cooker was sold without a torch. The court held that this was a trade description relating to composition of goods

(d) Fitness for purpose, strength, performance, behaviour or accuracy

(e) Any physical characteristics not included in the preceding paragraphs

(f) Testing by any person and the results of testing

(g) Approval by any person or conformity with a type approved by any person. For example, this would cover a statement that the item had qualified for the 'kite mark' of the British Standards Institute

(h) Place or date of manufacture, production, processing or reconditioning

(i) Person by whom manufactured, produced, processed or reconditioned

(j) Other history, including previous ownership or use. For example, this would cover the kind of claim often made by car dealers, 'only one previous owner' or 'one lady owner'

There are three principal offences created by the trade description legislation:

(a) Applying a false trade description to goods and supplying or offering to supply any such goods (a strict liability offence)

(b) Making false statements relating to services, accommodation or facilities

(c) Making misleading statements as to the price of goods

Private individuals are not within the scope of the Act; these activities only constitute an offence if they occur **in the course of a trade or business.**

False trade descriptions need not necessarily be made by the seller: a buyer can commit the offence.

---

**EXAMPLE: FALSE TRADE DESCRIPTION**

*Fletcher v Budgen 1974*

A car dealer bought an old car from a private seller, stating that it was only fit to be scrapped. The dealer paid the seller £2 for the car. Later the seller saw the car on the garage forecourt – it had been repaired and was for sale for £135. The court held that the dealer was guilty of an offence.

---

A false statement might be made deliberately, recklessly or entirely innocently – the offence is the same. Furthermore, a statement that is misleading – that is, not false to a material degree – may still be caught by the TDA.

---

**EXAMPLE: MISLEADING STATEMENT**

*Dixons Ltd v Barnett 1988*

Dixons correctly described a telescope for sale as having a magnification of 455 times, but did not add that at that level of magnification the image was simply a blur.

The court held that an offence had been committed under s1 TDA.

---

**Odometer readings**

The motor trade has featured in a number of cases under the TDA, particularly in respect of the mileage and condition of used cars.

---

**EXAMPLE: USE OF DISCLAIMER**

*Norman v Bennett 1974*

A purchaser looked at a second-hand car in a salesroom. The odometer reading was 23,000 miles, although the car had covered 68,000 miles. The purchaser agreed to buy the car, accepting a salesman's explanation that it was a director's car (regarded as a sufficient explanation for a low recorded mileage). He signed an agreement that included the words 'speedometer reading not guaranteed'.

The court held that a disclaimer as to the accuracy of the clock (mileometer or odometer) given equal prominence as the figure on the clock is a valid defence. But the disclaimer must be reasonable under the Unfair Contract Terms Act 1977 and its terms must be as 'bold, precise and compelling' as the claim itself.

---

A supplier who has **deliberately** made a false statement cannot issue a disclaimer in relation to it.

***As the service sector of the economy grows, descriptions of services will become increasingly relevant.***

### 3.2 Trade descriptions of services, accommodation and facilities

With regard to **services, accommodation or facilities,** it is an offence to make false statements deliberately or recklessly. The statement in question must be false 'to a material degree'. An element of knowledge or recklessness is required. Knowledge requires proof that the defendant knew his or her statement to be false (usually ascertained by their admission or by documentary evidence). Recklessness covers statements made regardless of whether they are true or false. The situation here differs from the situation with regard to goods: false statements with regard to goods are normally an offence whether or not they were made deliberately and/or recklessly.

Statements include such things as information in a travel brochure, wherever communicated to a reader.

---

**EXAMPLE: WHEN IS A STATEMENT FALSE?**

*Wings Ltd v Ellis 1985*

The appellant, a tour operator, had distributed a travel brochure for the 1981/82 winter season. The tour operator then discovered that the brochure contained a statement (which concerned air conditioning in a hotel in Sri Lanka) that was false to a material degree. The mistake was discovered and steps taken to rectify it in May 1981. W had booked a holiday from an unamended brochure; at the time of booking the tour operators were aware that the statement was false.

The court held: 'the brochure was inaccurate, the respondent knew that it was inaccurate and W was misled'.

---

**Activity 4** **(10 minutes)**

Examine the following situations. For each, decide whether or not a false trade description has been applied.

(a) Mr and Mrs Gullible have booked a weekend break in the Salty Towers hotel. The brochure describes it as 'A friendly beachside hotel with large and comfortable rooms. All rooms with sea view. Swimming facilities and sauna available.' When they arrive they find that the receptionist is aloof and curt, the hotel is indeed next to the beach but the sand itself is at the bottom of a 100 foot cliff, the bed in the room is so soft it is like sleeping on a marshmallow and it turns out that the swimming pool and sauna are not in the hotel but are available at the leisure centre across the road.

(b) A lager pump in the student's union bar is labelled 'probably the best lager in the world'.

(c) A car is described as in 'immaculate' condition. It is in fact very clean and well polished. Mrs Dim buys it but then finds out that although it looks fantastic it does not drive more than ten miles without overheating.

**Falsity** is judged as at the time the statement was made, as where a holiday brochure indicates a hotel is fully built when in fact the picture of it is just an artist's impression: *Yugotours Ltd v Wadsley 1988*. But if the statement was true when it was made, subsequent events do not then render it false.

---

**EXAMPLE: WHEN IS A FALSE STATEMENT TRUE?**

*Sunair Holidays v Dodd 1970*

Travel agents described accommodation in a resort as 'all twin-bedded rooms with private bath, shower, WC and terrace'. Two couples booked holidays with them on this basis, but on arrival were given rooms without terraces.

The court held that no offence had been committed. The accommodation existed when the statement was made and the statement was true. Nothing that occurred subsequently affected the accuracy of the statement when made.

---

Recklessness will be established even though the falsity was due to lack of thought rather than actual dishonesty.

---

**EXAMPLE: RECKLESSNESS**

*MFI Warehouses Ltd v Natrass 1973*

A mail order company advertised goods as 'on fourteen days free approval' and 'carriage free'. The offer was intended to cover only certain goods in an advertisement but appeared to cover them all.

The court held that the company had been reckless; the chairman had given insufficient care to the advertisement.

---

The TDA also covers 'services, accommodation and facilities' and includes when they are provided, how they are provided and who provides them. Furthermore, the Act also covers whether the amenities have been inspected.

Services include professional services such as those of an architect: *R v Breeze 1973*. However, a description as to the nature of a sale (for instance, advertising a seasonal sale as a 'Closing Down Sale') is not applied to 'facilities' and hence is not covered.

**Activity 5** **(5 minutes)**

Sid Gasman tells Mr Swallow that he will give his gas central heating boiler 'a complete going over'.

Cal Gasman's invoice to Mr Zapp states that the fee charged is in respect of 'a complete service' of his gas central heating boiler.

In both cases, only a filter is changed. Has either Sid or Cal committed an offence?

### Misleading prices

With regard to the **price** of goods, services, accommodation or facilities, the Consumer Protection Act 1987 Part III makes it an offence to make misleading statements to consumers in the course of business. This covers the provision of goods, services, accommodation or facilities. Such misleading indications might be that the price:

(a) Is less than it really is

(b) Depends on facts that are not in fact the case

(c) Covers matters for which an additional charge will actually be made

(d) Is expected to rise, fall or stay the same, when in fact the trader has no such expectation

There are other ways in which a price description may be misleading. For example, it may be an offence to indicate a price that fails to state that VAT will be added.

It is not only the person offering goods or services to the public who may commit the offence: it also extends to agents, advertisers and publishers who have not shown due diligence.

### The prices code

A code of practice has been issued giving practical advice to retailers as to what exactly constitutes a misleading price indication. It mainly deals with some difficult issues such as price comparisons and seasonal sales. It is not automatically a criminal offence to contravene the code.

***Anybody accused has a right to defend themselves.***

### 3.3 Defences under trade descriptions legislation

A person or firm accused of breaching the TDA can put forward the following defences.

(a) That the commission of the offence was due to:

(i) A mistake, or
(ii) Reliance on information supplied to the defendant, or
(iii) The act or default of another person, or
(iv) An accident or some other cause beyond his or her control, and

(b) That he or she took all reasonable *precautions* and exercised all due diligence to avoid the commission of such an offence by him or herself (or any person under his or her control). Such precautions must be more than a token gesture.

The defence will fail unless *both* points in the previous paragraph can be proved.

---

**FOR DISCUSSION**

Do you think the defences are fair to the customer, or give the supplier an easy let-out?

---

The person supplying the goods (the retailer) has a defence if they can show that they did not know and could not reasonably have found out:

(a) That the goods did not conform to the description, or
(b) That the description had been applied to the goods

***Enforcement is often a problem.***

### 3.4 Enforcement of trade descriptions legislation

It is the duty of local weights and measures authorities to enforce the law on trade descriptions; most authorities have appointed *trading standards officers* at district and borough council level to do so. It is not easy for the consumer to get any compensation, as offences are criminal offences. However, it is still possible to ask the court to award a criminal compensation order.

***The Sale of Goods Act 1979 gives an alternative route to victims who may wish to sue for damages.***

# 4 SALE OF GOODS LEGISLATION

## 4.1 Sale of goods to consumers

A sale of goods is a transaction whereby a customer obtains ownership of goods in return for the price. Any sale like this is governed by the *Sale of Goods Act 1979* (SGA) (as amended by the *Sale and Supply of Goods Act 1994* and the *Supply of Goods to Consumers Regulations 2002*). This act is contained within civil law, which means that a customer could use it to assist them in a case if they had to sue.

The SGA gives a customer certain rights against a business who is selling them goods.

## 4.2 Implied terms of the Sale of Goods Act

**Definitions**

1. **Implied terms**: terms that are automatically part of a contract whether the parties mention them or not. The implied terms of the SGA cannot be removed from a consumer contract.
2. ***Caveat emptor***: let the buyer beware. There is a duty on customers to be careful in their purchases.

The SGA implies certain terms into any contract of sale between a consumer and a business. They give the consumer the right to expect certain things from the seller and the goods.

There is an implied term that the seller has the right to sell the customer the goods; ie that the goods are not stolen or do not belong to anyone else who would object to the sale. There is also an expectation that the goods are not being sold in breach of anyone else's copyright or trademark.

Goods must be as described. The Trade Descriptions Act already creates *criminal* offences in this area. The SGA gives the customer the right to sue for damages (usually the return of the purchase price) if goods are not as described.

## EXAMPLE: GOODS NOT AS DESCRIBED

*Beale v Taylor 1967*

A car was advertised as a '1961 Triumph Herald 1200'. The buyer purchased the car but later found that in fact only the front half was a Triumph Herald 1200. This had been welded to the back half of a Triumph Herald 948. The car was in fact unroadworthy. The buyer sued for damages.

The buyer got his money back because the car was not as described.

---

It is important to note, however, that customers are expected to use some 'common sense' when making purchases. They should check anything they are unsure of and ask questions if necessary. If goods are also to be used for a specific purpose it would be sensible to check with the seller that they are suitable for this. The law uses a rule of *caveat emptor*, which gives the customer some responsibility for their own purchases.

---

## FOR DISCUSSION

There is a suggestion often made that 'the customer is always right'. Do you think that this is always the case?

---

### Satisfactory quality

Any goods supplied must be of 'satisfactory' quality. 'Satisfactory' could take into account the following factors:

(a) Fitness for the purpose for which goods of the kind are commonly supplied
(b) Appearance and finish
(c) Freedom from minor defects
(d) Safety
(e) durability

Generally, 'satisfactory' means that the goods meet the standard that a reasonable person would expect, taking into account descriptions of the goods, the price and anything else relevant in the circumstances.

You cannot return something simply because you do not like it after all, the colour is not as nice as you thought or it does not fit. You should have checked these things out yourself before buying – *caveat emptor*. However, some shops will exchange or refund for the above reasons. This is done as a goodwill gesture on their part – they are not *obliged* to do so.

### EXAMPLES: PURPOSE AND QUALITY

*Grant v Australian Knitting Mills 1936*

Dr Grant purchased some long woollen underpants. After wearing them he contracted dermatitis and had to spend some considerable time in hospital for treatment. He sued the retailer claiming the goods were not fit for their purpose. It emerged during the course of the trial that some chemicals used in the production process had not been properly removed from the pants and that it was this that caused the dermatitis.

The court held that the pants were clearly not fit for their purpose (ie wearing next to the skin). Dr Grant was awarded damages.

*Wren v Holt 1903*

Some beer was sold to a customer that contained arsenic.

The court held that the beer was clearly not of satisfactory quality.

*Priest v Last 1903*

A customer purchased a rubber hot water bottle and specifically asked if it would withstand boiling water. He was told by the seller that it would not, but that it would take very hot water. When the water bottle was used it burst and caused injury to the customer's wife. The customer sued.

The court held that the hot water bottle was not fit for the purpose. The customer had specifically stated what he wanted and had relied on the advice given by the shop assistant. He was awarded damages.

**Activity 6** **(15 minutes)**

(a) What could the customer expect from goods labelled 'shop soiled', 'second' or 'special purchase'?

(b) What can the customer expect if he or she buys second-hand goods?

Finally, the SGA states that where goods are sold by looking at a sample, when the actual purchase arrives it should be the same as the sample looked at when ordering.

***We now look at how a customer can act when goods are unsatisfactory.***

### 4.3 Action when goods are not 'satisfactory'

Usually, the easiest thing for the customer to do is to return the goods to the seller. The implied terms give rights against the seller of the goods directly. Customers are under no obligation to accept an offer to have goods returned to the manufacturer, or to have them repaired.

Breach of the implied terms gives the customer the right to reject the goods and claim compensation. This compensation would usually take the form of the return of the purchase price, but if a customer suffered other losses as a result of the goods or was injured by them they might want to claim more.

For a normal type of complaint, eg the heel drops off your new shoes after one day's wear, you should go back to the seller and ask for your money back. It is always a wise precaution to keep receipts or other proof of payment so that you can show when and where you purchased goods. State your case calmly and clearly and say what you would like to be done.

If the shop refuses to help you, and your case is justified, then you may wish to enlist the help of your local Trading Standards Officer. Often, a call from them can do the trick.

If your case is potentially more serious, or the shop refuses to co-operate, you may have to sue in the County Court. For most transactions you would use the small claims procedure, which is simple and quick. Your local court will instruct you on the procedure for this.

**Activity 7** **(20 minutes)**

Working in pairs, perform a role play of the following situation adopting the roles of Mr Bloggs and the shop assistant.

Mr Bloggs has purchased a pair of shoes from 'Super Shoes'. He had asked for a pair of work boots, telling the assistant he worked on a building site. When the assistant brought him out a pair he was concerned at their lightweight appearance but was told 'Don't worry – these are a new design. They have been developed using new technology and have been made to withstand all sorts of tough conditions.' Mr Bloggs purchased the shoes.

Mr Bloggs wore the shoes for one week. The sole has dropped off one of them. He has taken them back to the shop and wants a refund. The shop does not want to refund the money.

**Supply of Goods and Services Act 1982**

The Supply of Goods and Services Act 1982 applies to certain contracts which do not fall within the definition of sale of goods even though they do involve a transfer of ownership. The types of transaction which are covered by the Act include the following.

(a) **Contracts of exchange or barter**. These are not contracts of sale of goods because there is no money consideration involved.

(b) **Contracts of repair**. Although some goods are supplied (eg spare parts) the substance of the contract is the provision of services (see below).

(c) **Contracts of hire**. These are not contracts for sale of goods because they contain no provision for ownership to pass to the hirer;

(d) **Collateral contracts to the sale of goods**. For example, where a person buys a car and receives a free set of seat-covers as part of a special deal, the purchase of the car is governed by the Sale of Goods Act 1979 but the seat-covers, for which consideration was given by buying the car, are part of a collateral contract governed by the Supply of Goods and Services Act 1982.

If the main purpose of a contract is, for example, the provision of skilled labour, whilst an ancillary object is the transfer of ownership of goods, the contract is one governed by the 1982 Act. This means that an accountant's contract to prepare a report or an artist's commission to paint a portrait, for example, are covered by the 1982 Act.

***We now look at product liability legislation.***

## 5 PRODUCT LIABILITY

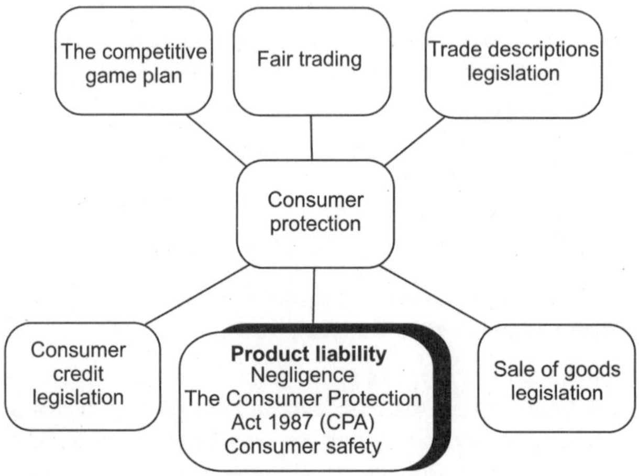


### 5.1 Negligence

In the past, if you bought a product and there was something wrong with it which caused you harm of some sort, you had to prove that the manufacturer was negligent in some way, and that the manufacturer owed you a duty of care.

**Definition**

> **Negligence**: to succeed in an action for negligence, the plaintiff (the person taking the matter to court) must show three things:
>
> (a) The existence of a duty of care by the defendant
>
> (b) A breach of that duty by the defendant
>
> (c) Injury or damage (or in some cases financial loss) suffered by the plaintiff as a foreseeable consequence of the breach of the duty of care

**Duty of care**

A manufacturer's liability for physical damage or injury to users of his or her products has been well established since the case of *Donoghue v Stevenson 1932*. In this celebrated case, the House of Lords ruled that a person might owe a duty of care to another with whom he had no contractual relationship at all.

### EXAMPLE: DUTY OF CARE

*Donoghue v Stevenson 1932*

A purchased from a retailer a bottle of ginger beer for consumption by A's companion B. The bottle was opaque, so that its contents were not visible. As B poured the ginger beer, the remains of a decomposed snail fell into her glass from the bottle. B became seriously ill. She sued C, the manufacturer, who argued that, as there was no contract between B and him, he owed her no duty of care and so was not liable.

The court held that C was liable to B. Every person owes a duty of care to his 'neighbour', to 'persons so closely and directly affected by any act that I ought reasonably to have them in contemplation as being so affected'.

---

In other words, normally there would be two contracts: one between the manufacturer and the retailer and one between the retailer and the consumer. The case suggested that despite the absence of a contract between the manufacturer and the consumer, the manufacturer had responsibilities to the consumer.

The law of negligence applies in product liability cases such as *Donoghue v Stevenson* itself where physical injury or damage results from a failure to take proper precautions. However, if the consumer/user has a reasonable opportunity of avoiding the injury by or by taking routine precautions, the consumer should take it.

#### Breach of duty of care

The standard of care when a duty of care exists is that which is reasonable. This requires that the person concerned should do what a reasonable person 'guided upon those considerations that ordinarily regulate the conduct of human affairs' would do, and abstain from doing what a reasonable person would not.

**Activity 8** **(30 minutes)**

Investigate the case of *Bolton v Stone*. Try the internet or a basic law textbook. Were the defendants held to have acted in a reasonable manner or not?

#### Consequential harm

In deciding whether a claim should be allowed, the court will consider whether:

(a) The breach of duty of care gave rise to the harm (fact), and
(b) The harm was not too remote from the breach (law)

#### Economic loss

The cases above relate to instances of damage to person or property. The question of liability for purely economic loss is still uncertain in its scope. Economic loss usually arises in the form of profits that a business would have generated had it not been for the act complained of. Generally, if financial loss is attached in some way to physical damage it can be claimed, but loss of pure profits is rarely recoverable.

**Activity 9** **(5 minutes)**

I am holding a car boot sale and I have various items for sale. You knock an ornament off my table that is priced at £1. It smashes into a thousand pieces. You say it was an accident. I say you were careless and should not have touched it and insist on taking your name and address when you refuse to pay me.

You have now been served with a writ in which I am claiming damages of £5.3m. The basis of my case is that had I sold the ornament and made the £1 profit I would have bought a lottery ticket. I would have used my normal weekly numbers, which this week happened to come up. I am now claiming the winnings I would have collected had I been able to buy that ticket. What are my chances of success against you?

***One of the consequences of the law is that consumers are protected even further. EU law is incorporated in the Consumer Protection Act.***

### 5.2 Consumer Protection Act 1987 (CPA)

Under the Consumer Protection Act 1987 (CPA) the consumer no longer has to prove negligence. In other words the Act imposes what is called *strict civil liability*, and this liability cannot be excluded by any disclaimer.

**Strict product liability**

The consumer can bring claims for losses caused by defects in a product against any of the following:

(a) The **manufacturer** of the end-product

(b) The **manufacturer of a defective component** (unless the instructions or design specifications supplied by the manufacturer of the end-product were to blame)

(c) The **importer** of the product into the EU (anybody responsible outside the EU may be much more difficult to find)

(d) An '**own-brander**'

(e) A **supplier**, who is usually a retailer

In practice, a supplier or retailer only become liable if they will not disclose the identity of the importer or manufacturer.

The **consumer** has to prove that:

(a) The product contained a defect
(b) He or she suffered damage
(c) The damage resulted from the defect, and
(d) It was the fault of the producer or some other person listed above

**Product**

This legislation covers all products, including component parts and raw materials. 'Product' is defined as 'any goods or electricity'; goods include substances (natural or artificial in solid, liquid or gaseous form), growing crops, things comprised in land by virtue of being attached to it, ships, aircraft and vehicles. It does not include primary (non-processed) agricultural products.

### 'Defective' product

A product will be found to be unsafe where it is not as safe as it is reasonable to expect it to be. This standard of relative safety requires a court to take into account all circumstances surrounding the product – the way it is advertised, the time at which it was supplied, its anticipated normal use, the provision of instructions for use, even its likely misuse – in establishing the standard required. The court should also consider the benefit to society and the cost of making the product safer.

### Scope of the Act

Consumers and other users (such as the recipient of an electric iron received as a gift), but not business users, can claim compensation for **death, personal injury or damage to other property** (not to the product itself, nor for economic loss caused by the product not working). There is unlimited liability, but the following limitations apply.

(a) A claim must be brought within three years of the fault becoming apparent.

(b) No claim may be brought more than ten years after the original supply.

(c) Where the claim is for damage to property, it must not be business property that is damaged and the amount of the damage must be more than £275.

### Defences

The defendant in a case under this Act has six possible defences.

(a) The product complied with mandatory statutory or EU standards.

(b) The product was not at any time supplied to another.

(c) The product was not supplied in the course of a business.

(d) The defect did not exist in the product when originally supplied.

(e) 'Development risk' – the state of knowledge at the time of manufacture and supply was such that no manufacturer could have been expected to detect the fault. The inclusion of this defence in the Act means that many victims of drugs that had damaging side-effects may be left without a remedy. The defence was kept so as not to discourage medical research. As the Act is new, it is not certain how far reaching this might be.

(f) The defect was wholly attributable to the design of a *subsequent* product into which the product in question was incorporated.

The Act is a significant step towards protection against unsafe goods. Producers and other distributors now have to ensure that they are protected by insurance in their business contracts; careful record-keeping is also required so that the other people in the distribution chain are adequately identified.

**Activity 10** **(5 minutes)**

What you think is the significance of the development risk defence?

***Strict civil liability is a separate issue from that of consumer safety, and adherence of products to safety regulations.***

### 5.3 Consumer safety

It is a criminal offence to supply consumer goods that fail to comply with a **general safety requirement** under Part II of the Consumer Safety Act. This requires that goods must be reasonably safe, bearing in mind the manner in which, and the purposes for which, they are marketed, any instructions or warnings provided with them, any published safety standards and the existence of any means by which it would have been reasonable to make the product safer.

The general safety requirement applies to all consumer goods, except for a defined list of items, each of which is either covered by its own more specific legislation (thus food falls under the Food Safety Act 1990) or falls into a special category (eg tobacco, which 'could raise particular problems').

The Department of Trade and Industry is empowered to make safety regulations under the Act. Contravention of such regulations is a criminal offence. Examples include the following.

(a) Cooking Utensils (Safety) Regulations 1972/1957. These govern the proportion of lead permitted in kitchen utensils used for cooking food.

(b) Electrical Equipment (Safety) Regulations 1975/1366. These require that various items of electrical equipment shall comply with appropriate British Standards.

(c) Pencil and Graphic Instruments Safety Regulations 1974/226. These control the maximum amounts of arsenic, cadmium, chromium, mercury, antimony, lead and barium permitted in pencils, pens, brushes, crayons and chalk.

The general safety requirement and the safety regulations are again enforced by trading standards officers, who have a system of notices that are served on offenders.

Product Safety Regulations 1994 impose additional safety requirements. They are relevant to all suppliers of consumer products, and impose a general safety requirement on all products to be placed on the market by producers or to be sold, offered for sale or possessed by distributors. The two safety requirements (ie the new regulations and Part II CPA 1987) are not identical. The key provision of the 1994 regulations states that no products should be placed on the market unless it is a 'safe product'. This is a product which, under normal or reasonably foreseeable conditions of use, presents no, or minimal, risk. This must be consistent with a high degree of protection for user's health and safety. Four factors will be taken into account.

(a) The characteristics of the product, eg packaging and instructions for assembly

(b) The effect of the product on other products

(c) The presentation of the product, eg labelling and instructions for use

(d) The categories of consumer (eg children) at serious risk

---

**FOR DISCUSSION**

Why is it necessary to enforce such a strict regulatory framework on business?

---

## 6 CONSUMER CREDIT LEGISLATION

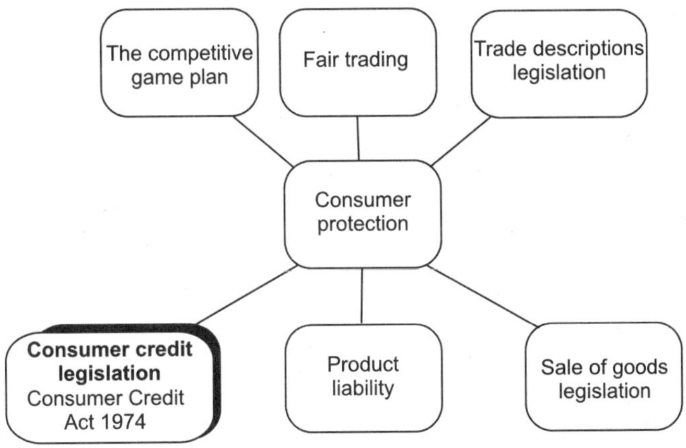


### 6.1 Consumer Credit Act 1974

The Consumer Credit Act 1974 (as amended in 2006) was passed to protect consumers by introducing a new concept – that of 'truth in lending'. The Act applies to loans or other forms of credit offered to individuals, and not to companies. As an example of its scope, the lender must inform the borrower of all charges connected with the loan, and the rate of interest must be calculated and quoted in a similar way. (These are the two requirements for the quotation of the Total Charge for Credit and the Annual Percentage Rate).

The Act was meant to deal with the problems of inaccurate advertising, canvassing and the charging of extortionate rates of interest by lenders. The Act is a complex piece of legislation and seeks to regulate various types of transaction, including:

(a) Hire purchase agreements
(b) Conditional sale transactions
(c) Credit sales, and
(d) Personal loans

The main provisions of the Act address the following areas:

(a) Licensing of businesses that provide credit, lend money or hire out goods

(b) Advertising for credit and the provision of quotations

(c) Canvassing, involving attempts to persuade an individual to sign an agreement for credit facilities when not previously requested to do so in writing or away from the canvasser's trade premises

(d) Regulated agreements – the form and contents of credit agreements is prescribed by the Act, and there are rules as to provision of copies

(e) Debtor-credit-supplier agreements, for example credit card schemes

(f) Charges for credit, which must be advised to the borrower

**Activity 11** **(15 minutes)**

Examine some credit advertisements in newspapers. You will see that some offer 'secured' loans and some offer 'unsecured' loans. What is the difference?

**Chapter roundup**

- The OFT is involved in consumer protection, in monitoring business practices and enforcing the law.
- Many industries have drawn up codes of practice to improve their standing and procedures. Not all are enforceable at law.
- The law on product liability has changed. A consumer who suffers from a product no longer has to prove that the manufacturer was negligent.
- Trade descriptions legislation controls the claims that may be made about goods and services.
- The Sale of Goods Act gives consumers the right to redress when goods do not meet normal expectations.

## Quick quiz

1 What is the Office of Fair Trading?

2 Outline what an 'ombudsman' does.

3 What are codes of practice designed to achieve?

4 What is the problem with a voluntary code of practice?

5 List the three principal offences created by trades descriptions legislation.

6 Explain the term 'false description'.

7 Give some examples of false descriptions.

8 What defences are available to an accusation of false description?

9 Does the Sale of Goods Act I979 involve civil or criminal law?

10 What are the four main areas covered in respect to goods?

11 What does *caveat emptor* mean?

12 What is product liability?

13 What three things must be proved in order to prove negligence?

14 How does the Consumer Protection Act I987 make claiming damages easier?

15 What does the term 'defective' mean?

16 Can business users of a product claim under the CPA?

17 List the six defences to an action taken under the CPA.

18 What is the development risk defence?

19 List some goods covered by safety regulations.

20 Who enforces safety requirements and regulations?

21 What legislation seeks to protect and individual who is taking out a personal loan?

## Answers to quick quiz

1 The OFT is a government department that generally monitors commercial activities affecting consumers and makes proposals and regulations to control unfair practices.

2 An Ombudsman is the person who provides an avenue of appeal for dissatisfied customers who have not obtained satisfaction from a particular business. Some are supported by government and some are provided voluntarily by organisations.

3 Codes of practice are designed to promote a high standard of trade practice and to protect the consumer's interests.

4 It is not enforceable, merely voluntary.

5 Applying a false trade description to goods, making false statements as to services, being misleading as to price.

6 A false trade description is a description made of goods or services that is untrue or misleading.

7 Some examples of false trade descriptions could be; stating a price without saying that VAT has to be added, stating that certain facilities will be available when they are not, stating that a particular product is 'endorsed' by a celebrity when they have never heard of it.

8 Mistake; reliance on information supplied; act or default of another person; accident or cause beyond their control.

9 Civil law.

10 Title, description, satisfactory quality, bulk corresponds to sample.

11 Buyer beware.

12 The manufacturer's responsibility to a consumer injured by their product.

13 Duty of care, breach of duty, damage resulting.

14 There is no need to prove negligence.

15 Defective means not as safe as it is reasonable to expect.

16 No. The Act only covers consumers.

17 Product complied with EU standards, product was not supplied to another, not supplied in the course of business, no defect when product supplied, development risk defence.

18 The state of knowledge at the time of manufacture would not have allowed for detection of the fault.

19 Cooking utensils, electrical equipment, pencils.

20 Trading Standards Officers.

21 Consumer Credit Act 1974.

## Answers to activities

1 You can probably sort out the majority of your problems yourself. If you do decide that you need help there are other potentially more useful sources available than solicitors and courts.

*Noisy neighbours*: try a diplomatic complaint. Most people are reasonable and will not want to have an argument. However, if problems persist you could contact your local council, who have environmental officers responsible for enforcing laws on noise pollution. They could approach the neighbours for you and prosecute if necessary. As a last resort, you could sue your neighbours for private nuisance, but this will cost you a lot of time, money and effort. It may not be worth it. In a recent case where a neighbour sued over a pig being kept in a residential area the costs of the case amounted to some £20,000 and the loser had to pay these plus £15,000 damages.

*Faulty CD player:* take it back to the shop and ask for a refund. The Sale of Goods Act 1979 says that the player should be fit for its purpose. It clearly is not, so you are entitled to a refund. Take your receipt with you.

*Bank statement:* something has obviously gone wrong. Telephone the bank and query the missing money. If they deny receiving the cheques, take your paying-in slip in to prove it. If you still get no help, contact the Banking Ombudsman for assistance.

2 There are codes of practice for many different trades and industries, including the motor trade, shoes, funeral services, dry cleaning, and estate and travel agents. There are about twenty in all. These codes are purely voluntary in that they are not enforced by the courts, but the OFT monitors their operation and the trade associations themselves try to ensure that the standards are adhered to by their members. Common features in these codes would be an agreement not to limit legal liability except in special, stated circumstances (and obviously within the limits of the Unfair Contract Terms Act 1977), a set standard of care, a disciplinary procedure for members and agreed procedures for the settlement of disputes, such as arbitration.

3 Adverts are not always legal, decent, honest and truthful. There are many complaints made each year about advertisements that have given offence. The problem with enforcement is that people have different interpretations of what is 'legal, decent, honest and truthful'.

4 (a) While the advert may have been misleading it cannot really be said to be untrue. Also, some of the statements made would depend on an individual's view of what is 'friendly' or 'comfortable'. The swimming pool and sauna are available – the advert did not say they were on the premises. However, if there was an implication that they were available as part of the price then this should be the case.

(b) The notice says that the lager is 'probably' the best in the world. It doesn't say it is. The statement is meaningless and again would depend on the opinion of the drinker. Merely an advertising gimmick that would not mislead most people.

(c) This would be a false trade description. A reasonable person would take the statement to include the mechanics of the car as well as its appearance. See the case of *Robertson v Dicicco 1972* where the description of a 'beautiful car' was taken to include the mechanics and the appearance.

5 In Sid's case, it is debatable whether the statement could be said to have been made 'in the course of service'. It is a statement of intent or a promise; it would be difficult to prove it was made 'deliberately or recklessly'. Cal, on the other hand, made the false statement of fact after the work had (or rather, had not) been done; the invoice words are hence capable of being construed as 'being made in the course of service' and, provided they were made carelessly or deliberately, knowing them to be false, an offence has been committed.

'The section specifically refers to the reckless making of a statement that is false. That means that if at the end of the contract a person giving the service recklessly makes a false statement as to what he or she has done, the matter may well fall within s14, but if, before the contract has been worked out, the person who provides the service makes a promise as to what he or she will do, and that promise does not relate to an existing fact, nobody can say at the date when that statement is made that it is either true or false': *Becket v Cohen 1973.*

6 (a) Goods labelled 'shop soiled' should still be of satisfactory quality, although the customer would not be entitled to complain about any faults that were pointed out at the time of sale. For example, a refrigerator could be labelled 'shop soiled' because it has a scratched door. The customer could not complain about the scratches but they could complain if the refrigerator does not keep food cold. The same would apply to goods marked 'seconds'. They are clearly not going to be as good as perfect goods. 'Special Purchase' goods should be perfect, but they are obviously not as expensive as some goods so the quality may not be as good. They should still be both 'satisfactory' and 'fit for their normal purpose'.

(b) The customer knows that they are not likely to get perfection. However, the goods must be reasonably adequate bearing in mind all the circumstances.

7 In your role play, Mr Bloggs should state his case clearly and calmly. He will probably want to argue that the goods are not fit for their purpose. He relied on the assistant's advice, and it was wrong. He should ask for a full refund. When the assistant refuses this he should re-state his case and explain why the law backs him up. He should not get involved in a slanging match with the assistant. If he cannot talk the assistant round he should state that he is going to refer the matter to the local Trading Standards Office and also write to the shop's head office to complain. It often works wonders if you ask to speak to the manager of the shop!

8 In this case Mrs Bolton was hit on the head by a cricket ball that was hit out of a cricket ground. She sued, claiming that the cricket club were negligent in allowing balls to fly out of the ground. The club were able to prove that this type of incident had only happened six to ten times during the past 35 years and nobody had previously been injured. They had a high fence and had taken every precaution to avoid accidents. The court held that they were not negligent and had acted reasonably in the circumstances. Mrs Bolton's injuries had been caused by a 'freak' accident.

9 It is extremely unlikely that I would win my claim. I may get back the £1 that is attached to physical damage to the ornament. The difficulty in claiming the £5.3 million is that of proof. How can I prove that I would have bought a ticket, that I would have used those numbers etc? Also, the damage is too remote – it is not closely connected enough to the incident to flow from it. You could not have known my intentions.

10 This 'state of the art' or 'development risk' defence challenges directly the concept of strict liability for defective products. Because the Act is relatively new, it is not clear what attitudes the courts will adopt towards the state of the art defence. A practical approach might look to a producer to make his or her product as safe as possible, taking into account reasonable constraints on cost, an assessment of market expectations and the existence of safe alternatives to the product. A stricter approach might assume that the producer should be aware of all available information relating to the product, regardless of cost and circumstances.

11 A 'secured loan' attaches to an asset which the borrower already has. For example, a house. If the loan is not repaid as agreed then the lender can take possession of the specified property in order to sell it to realise the amount owed. An unsecured loan only gives the lender the remedy of suing for the outstanding payments. They cannot take possession of any property automatically.

# Chapter 4:
# PEOPLE IN THE WORKPLACE

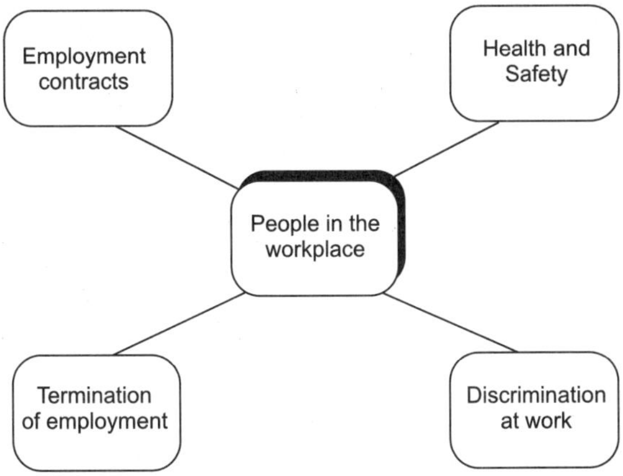


**Introduction**

The management of people is a crucial factor in the success of any business. Investment in selection and training increases and improves the skills of employees and enhances their value to the organisation. There are a number of matters that are common to all organisations – namely, the statutory rights of employees. Evidence from cases heard by Industrial Tribunals reveal that many firms are not familiar with the concept and law of employee rights, and their failure to understand this has proved costly in terms of financial compensation, legal defence and damaging publicity. Instances of sexual and racial discrimination are regularly reported.

Employee relations can prove one of the most potentially dangerous areas of the operating environment. Everyone responsible for staff should know that employees have rights that are incorporated in legal or other procedures.

**Your objectives**

In this chapter you will learn about:

(a) The importance of contracts of employment

(b) The concept of unfair treatment of the employee and the role of industrial tribunals

(c) Discrimination law

(d) Redundancy procedures

# 1 EMPLOYMENT CONTRACTS

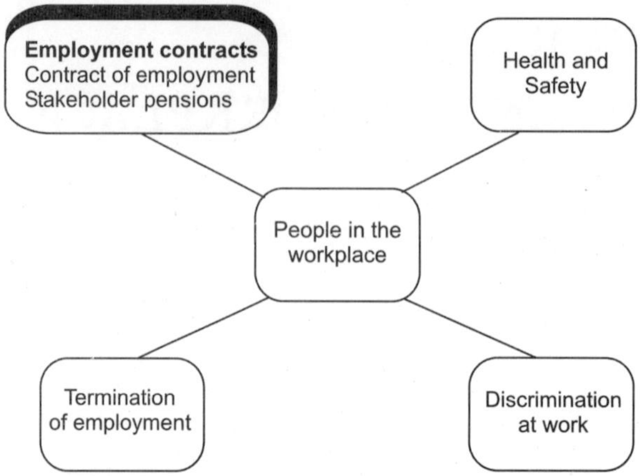


## 1.1 Contract of employment

Normally, the **contract of employment** will be a written document, and will contain details of the terms and conditions of the employment and various employment particulars. If the contract was not in writing, or did not contain the pertinent information, an employee is entitled within two months of starting work to receive a written **statement of particulars**. The statement must contain, or refer to, other documents that contain the information below.

(a) The names of **employer** and **employee**

(b) The **date** on which employment began (important if it becomes necessary to decide what period of notice should be given)

(c) Whether any service with a previous employer forms part of the employee's **continuous period** of employment (important if the employee wished to claim for redundancy or unfair dismissal)

(d) **Pay** (scale or rate and intervals at which paid)

(e) **Hours of work** (including any specified 'normal working hours')

(f) Any **holiday** and **holiday pay** entitlement (including any right to accrued holiday pay on termination of employment)

(g) **Sick leave** and **sick pay** entitlement (if any)

(h) **Pensions** and **pension schemes** (unless statutory)

(i) Length of **notice** of termination to be given on either side (or the expiry date if employed for a fixed term)

(j) The **title** of the job that the employee is employed to do

Whenever any change is made in any term contained in the written particulars, the employer must, within one month, provide a written statement of the change. If a change is made by collective agreement between the employer and a trade union, the terms of employment of the individual employee are effectively changed without his consent. If such change is possible, the statement must say so.

**Activity 1** **(30 minutes)**

Draft a letter of appointment for a new member of staff at your college and include terms and conditions of the appointment. Base the offer on the information in this chapter.

Employment particulars can be given by instalments, during the two months period. A 'principal statement', which must include items (a) to (f) above and the title of the job, must be provided, but other particulars may be given by way of separate documents.

The written particulars must also contain details of disciplinary procedures and grievance procedures, or refer to where they can be found. If they are in a separate booklet, each employee must be given a copy. Employers with fewer than twenty employees do not need to provide particulars of disciplinary procedures, but employees must still be told of grievance procedures. Failure by an employee to initiate an established grievance procedure may, in the event of unfair dismissal, amount to contributory fault leading to a reduction in any award.

A few other facts are of relevance.

(a) If there is no express agreement in the contract as to how much, the employee is entitled to a 'reasonable' pay, decided on the particular facts by the court. The Government has recently announced the introduction of a statutory minimum wage.

(b) If the written particulars do not contain terms as to payment during illness, the employee may go to a tribunal to determine whether it was agreed; it is generally presumed to be payable but not necessarily from the employer's own funds.

(c) An employee is entitled to receive an *itemised pay slip* at or before payment of wages or salary. This will show both gross and net pay. It will also show all deductions (ie tax, national insurance contributions etc) made and the method of calculation of different parts of net pay if these are made in different ways.

### 1.2 Stakeholder pensions

The stakeholder pension is a private sector initiative designed to provide a secondary pension for people outside the net of established additional schemes. It is a response to a crisis that has been gathering momentum for some considerable time. It stems from profound shifts in demographic patterns. In the UK and in other developed countries, fewer people are being born, and improvements in health care and general living conditions mean that people are living longer. These trends, taken collectively, suggest the number of retired people will grow while the working population will diminish. So the capacity of working people to fund pension requirements will be reduced. This fact has serious implications for the viability of pay-as-you-go pension systems, in which today's pensions are paid by the contributions of today's workers.

These demographic changes will not impact on the UK as painfully as threatens to be the case in, for example, Germany and France. This is because we have in this country a highly developed and well-funded framework of secondary pension provision. This being said, there remain significant gaps in pension provision, and these are a matter of real concern to the government.

The fact that people with no second pension will have to rely on the basic state pension is unsatisfactory for two reasons.

(a) Even the full state pension is only available to those with a complete NI contribution record.

(b) Because of the break of the link between the state pension and average earnings, the value of the basic state pension is continuing to decline; the OFT has estimated that, by 2030, it will be worth only 9 per cent of average earnings.

To address this major deficit, the Labour Government has proposed the creation of a new type of pension scheme, which it has chosen to call the stakeholder pension, and which is intended to meet the needs of those groups in society who are currently outside the secondary pensions net.

Stakeholder pensions have been available since April 2001 to make it easier for people to save more money for their own retirement. From October 2001, employers have had to offer their employees access to a stakeholder pension scheme unless they offer a suitable alternative pension scheme. This will involve the designation by the employer of their chosen stakeholder provider and failure to comply with this requirement risks the employer facing a fine from the Occupational Pensions Regulatory Authority (OPRA). Those employers with fewer than five employees will be exempt from the requirement to offer access to a stakeholder pension, although they may offer access if they wish.

Employers with at least five employees must offer access to a stakeholder pension earning limit to their 'relevant' employees. The full definition of relevant employees is outlined in the legislation but in practice, for most employers, relevant employees will be:

(a) Any employee who earns at or above the lower earnings limit (£82 per week in 2005/6)

(b) Any employee who is not a member of an occupational pension scheme.

Directors should be included in the total number of employees, if they count as employees for other purposes. Part-time employees must also be included in the number of total employees. The employer has to offer access to the stakeholder scheme to all relevant employees within three months of their joining his/her service.

Employers need only provide employees with access to a stakeholder pension. They do not have to make contributions to the scheme. But they may make contributions if they wish and any contributions they do make will attract corporation tax (or income tax) relief.

An employer who already offers either an occupational scheme or a group personal pension may be exempt if the arrangement meets certain criteria. It is the employer who is exempt and not the scheme.

## 2 HEALTH AND SAFETY

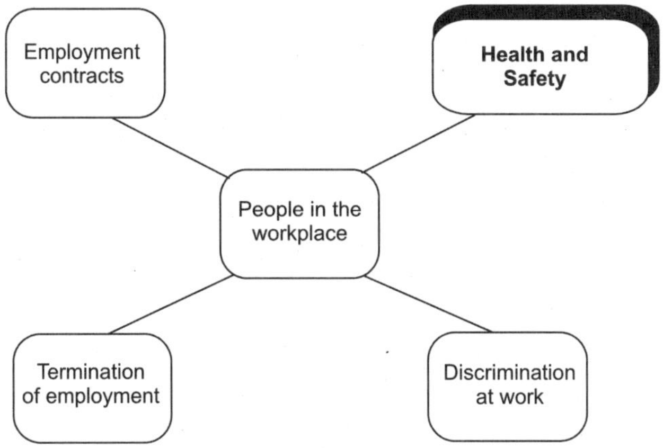


Health and safety in the work place is regulated by both UK and EU law. Apart from humanitarian concerns about employee well-being, employers are liable to be sued if unsafe practice leads to injury or worse.

Health and safety is not only relevant to factories with potentially dangerous equipment, or building sites. It is also relevant to the *office*. (Many accidents are caused when people stand on 'swivel chairs'.)

The legal issues on health are governed by:

(a) The Health and Safety at Work Act 1974

(b) Regulations issued in 1992 and 1999, relating to the management of health and safety, and health and safety in the workplace (health and safety regulations)

Other specific regulations relate to fire.

In brief, the employer's duties are these.

(a) All systems (work practices) must be safe.

(b) The work environment must be safe and healthy (well-lit, warm, ventilated and hygienic).

(c) All plant and equipment must be kept up to the necessary standard (with guards on machines and so on).

In addition, information, instruction, training and supervision should be directed towards safe working practices, and the safety policy should be clearly communicated to all staff.

Implementation of the **EU directives** as (legally enforceable) regulations means that employers have the following additional general duties (as summarised in the *Administrator*, September 1992).

(a) They must carry out risk assessment, generally in writing, of all work hazards. Assessment should be continuous.

(b) They must introduce controls to reduce risks.

(c) They must assess the risks to anyone else affected by their work activities.

(d) They must share hazard and risk information with other employers, including those on adjoining premises, other site occupiers and all subcontractors coming onto the premises.

(e) They should revise safety policies in the light of the above, or initiate safety policies if none were in place previously.

(f) They must identify employees who are especially at risk.

(g) They must provide fresh and appropriate training in safety matters.

(h) They must provide information to employees (including temporary staff) about health and safety.

(i) They must employ competent safety and health advisers.

Under the Health and Safety and Work Act, the employee also has a duty:

(a) To take reasonable care of himself/herself and others

(b) To allow the employer to carry out his or her duties (including enforcing safety rules)

(c) Not to interfere intentionally or recklessly with any machinery or equipment

Employees must inform their employer of any situation that may be a danger (although this does not reduce the employer's responsibilities in any way because his or her risk assessment programme should have spotted the hazard in any case). Employees must use all equipment properly, in accordance with instructions.

Other more detailed regulations cover areas such as equipment handling and VDUs.

---

**FOR DISCUSSION**

Do you think employers should go further than obeying the letter of the law and instead take a more active approach in promoting employee health, for example by prohibiting smoking at work, providing health check-ups or providing counselling?

---

***We now look at workplace health, safety and welfare regulations.***

**Health and safety regulations**

The Workplace (Health, Safety and Welfare) Regulations 1992 implemented the European *Workplace Directive* covering matters that have been statutory requirements for many years in the UK under legislation such as the *Offices, Shops and Railway Premises Act 1963*, although in some cases the requirements have been more clearly defined. The following provisions are made.

(a) **Equipment**. All equipment should be properly maintained.

(b) **Ventilation**. Air should be fresh or purified.

(c) **Temperature**. The temperature must be 'reasonable' inside buildings during working hours. This means not less than 16°C where people are sitting down, or 13°C if they move about to do their work. A thermometer should be provided.

(d) **Lighting** should be suitable and sufficient, and natural, if practicable. Windows should be clean and unobstructed.

(e) **Cleaning and decoration**. Floors, walls, ceilings, furniture, furnishings and fittings must be kept clean. Floors should be cleaned weekly. Rubbish should not be allowed to accumulate.

(f) **Room dimensions and space**. Each person should have at least 11 cubic metres of space, ignoring any parts of rooms more than 3.1 metres above the floor or with a headroom of less than 2.0 metres.

(g) **Floors** must be properly constructed and maintained (without holes, not slippery, properly drained and so on).

(h) **Falls or falling objects**. These should be prevented by erecting effective physical safeguards (fences, safety nets, ground rails and so on).

(i) **Glazing**. Windows should be made of safe materials and if they are openable it should be possible to do this safely.

(j) **Traffic routes**. These should have regard to the safety of pedestrians and vehicles alike.

(k) **Doors and gates**. These should be suitably constructed and fitted with any necessary safety devices (especially sliding doors and powered doors, and doors opening in either direction).

(l) **Escalators and travelators** should function safely and have readily accessible emergency stop devices.

(m) **Sanitary conveniences** and washing facilities must be suitable and sufficient. This means that they should be properly ventilated and lit, properly cleaned and separate for men and women. 'Sufficient' means that undue delay is avoided!

(n) **Drinking water**. An adequate supply should be available with suitable drinking vessels.

(o) **Clothing**. There should be suitable accommodation for outdoor clothing, which should be able to dry out if wet. Facilities for changing clothing should be available where appropriate.

(p) **Rest facilities and eating facilities**. These must be provided unless the employees' workstations are suitable for rest or eating, as is normally the case for offices.

The *Management of Health and Safety at Work Regulations 1999* extend the 1992 regulations in some respects, and covers the following issues.

- **Risk assessments** to be undertaken by employers
- **Health and safety** arrangements
- Health **surveillance**
- Health and safety **assistance**
- Procedures for **danger areas**
- Contacts with **external services**
- **Information** for employees
- **Co-operation** between employers sharing a workplace
- Working in '**host**' premises
- Taking account of **employee capabilities**
- **Employee duties**
- **Temporary workers, expectant mothers** and **young** people

- **Liability** and **exclusion** of civil liability
- Premises and activities **outside Great Britain**

**Activity 2** **(1 hour)**

You have recently been appointed as assistant to the Health and Safety Officer for Thermo plc, a manufacturer of thermal underwear. The premises house the production areas of the factory, the office staff and the executive offices. There is a wide variety of different working environments and equipment and this creates quite a health and safety priority.

Lately, your boss has noticed that people seem to have become somewhat careless about health and safety issues. They have adopted an attitude of 'it's not my problem – we have a Heath and Safety Officer to think about it'. People are not taking responsibility for their own well-being and safety.

The occupational nurse also works within your department and she is concerned about the general health and fitness levels of the workforce. A number of workers are heavy smokers and the canteen does a roaring trade in chips and fry-ups. She has also noticed that a number of the executives have very high pressure jobs and she is worried about their stress levels.

You have been asked to outline some ideas on how to introduce effective training for health and safety in the various parts of the firm. You have also been asked to jot down some ideas for a health-promotion campaign that the occupational nurse could run. Your main brief is to make people want to participate in the activities rather than attend because their boss says they must.

## 3 DISCRIMINATION AT WORK

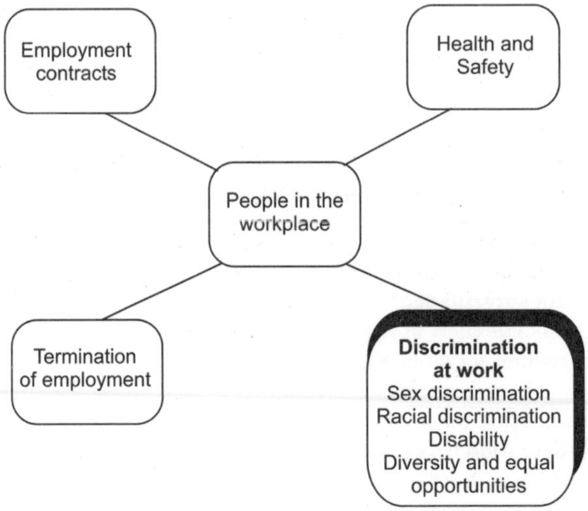

***One area of employment law that has given rise to several pieces of legislation in the last twenty-five years is the issue of equal opportunities and discrimination at work. This may be on the grounds of sex, marital status, race or disability.***

### 3.1 Sex discrimination

Sex discrimination is governed by the Sex Discrimination Act and Equal Pay Act. These are policed by the Equal Opportunities Commission.

**Equal Pay Act 1970**

Under this Act, contractual employment terms given to a man or woman should be at least as favourable as those given to an employee of the opposite sex. This has been held to mean that where, say, a woman does work 'of equal value' to a male colleague, she is entitled to equal pay. The Act covers other terms such as sick pay, holiday pay and working hours, and it applies to all forms of full-time and part-time work.

---

**EXAMPLE: EQUAL PAY FOR WORK OF EQUAL VALUE**

*Hayward v Cammell Laird Shipbuilders 1986*

The House of Lords upheld the claim of a canteen cook to equal pay with painters, joiners and thermal insulation engineers employed in the same shipyard on the ground that her work was of equal value. This very important decision was based on a report by an independent expert who compared the jobs under five headings (physical demands, environmental demands, planning and decision-making demands, skill and knowledge demands and responsibility demands). Under each heading the demands were ranked as low, moderate or high.

Overall the applicant was considered to be employed on work of equal value. Hayward's application was the first successful claim for equal pay for work of equal value. It is interesting to note that the claim succeeded even though the applicant had better fringe benefits (eg paid meal breaks, extra holidays) than the workers with whom her work was compared.

The right to equal pay applies to:

(a) employees in the United Kingdom whether or not they are British and regardless of the law governing their employment contract, and

(b) men as well as to women

---

**FOR DISCUSSION**

Should there be any exceptions to sex discrimination legislation? Do you think it is right that anti-discrimination legislation has now been extended to include sexual orientation?

---

Under the Act, an equality clause is implied into every person's contract of employment that, where the person is employed on similar or equivalently rated work to that of a person of the opposite sex, or on work of equal value to that of a person in the same employment, the right to equal pay is assumed.

Furthermore, the *employer* has to show that the reason for any difference is a genuine material factor *other* than sex. Examples of differences are these:

(a) Greater length of service is a material factor.

(b) Working at different times of day is not a material factor.

(c) A distinction in hourly pay between workers in London and those based in (the cheaper area of) Nottingham is based on a material factor.

**Sex Discrimination Acts 1975 and 1986**

This legislation prohibits discrimination on the grounds of sex against any employee, male or female, in the recruitment, promotion, training, benefits or dismissal of employees. A Code of Practice drawn up in April 1985 recommends that:

(a) Employers should have a clearly stated equal opportunities policy, regularly monitored, and

(b) Advertisements should be worded to encourage applicants of both sexes.

Companies with a compulsory retirement age must abolish different retirement ages for men and women. The Act does not, however, affect the payment of company or State pensions.

There are two forms of discrimination that can be distinguished.

(a) *Direct discrimination* occurs where an employer or prospective employer treats an employee or job applicant less favourably than another on grounds of sex.

(b) *Indirect discrimination* occurs in cases such as the imposition of a qualification for promotion with which fewer people of one sex than the other could comply.

---

**EXAMPLE: INDIRECT DISCRIMINATION**

*Price v Civil Service Commission 1978*

The Civil Service Commission imposed a maximum age limit of 28 for appointment to the civil service grade of Executive Officer. A woman argued that this was indirectly discriminating against women since women in their twenties are often prevented by care of children from taking up employment.

The court held that the imposition of an age limit was indirect discrimination.

---

In some jobs, however, it is accepted that male or female sex is a 'genuine occupational qualification' (GOQ). An advertisement for a job abroad in a country whose laws and customs might make it difficult for a woman to perform her duties would be acceptable. Decency may require a male attendant in a male lavatory or sports facilities. Some occupations, such as ministers of religion and police and prison officers, are exempt from the statutory rules.

The *Equal Opportunities Commission* (EOC) oversees the working of safeguards for equality of men and women. It promotes test cases in the courts and makes recommendations for changes in the law. It may issue codes of practice and conduct investigations.

### Discrimination on the grounds of marital status

The Sex Discrimination Acts make it unlawful to discriminate against married people in any way, for example if an employer believes that a single man will be able to devote more time to a job than a married man. Since the Civil Partnership Act 2004 came into force on 5 December 2005, the same protection is afforded to those in a civil partnership as those who are married. Oddly, however, there is no provision preventing discrimination against single people.

In recent years there have been many developments in Europe to promote equality. The Equal Pay and Equal Treatment Directives have mainly been incorporated into UK legislation. Directives have also addressed the rights of pregnant workers, and the Amsterdam Treaty now addresses issues of sexual orientation.

### Discrimination on the grounds of sexual orientation

The **Employment Equality (Sexual Orientation) Regulations 2003** apply to discrimination on grounds of orientation towards persons of the same sex, the opposite sex or persons of both the same and the opposite sex. They also cover discrimination on grounds of perceived as well as actual sexual orientation, that is assuming, whether correctly or not, that someone is of a particular sexual orientation and acting on the basis of that assumption. In addition they cover association, that is discrimination on the grounds of the sexual orientation of the people with whom the victim associates, such as their friends or family. For example if A is the victim of discrimination because his brother B is homosexual, then A will be able to act under the Regulations.

The Regulations seek to outlaw:

- **Direct discrimination**, ie treating people less favourably than others on grounds of sexual orientation
- **Indirect discrimination**, which includes applying an unjustified provision, criterion or practice which would disadvantage people of a particular sexual orientation, religion or belief
- **Harassment**, which is unwanted conduct that has the effect of violating people's dignity or that creates an intimidating, hostile, degrading, humiliating or offensive environment
- **Victimisation**, which is treating people less favourably because they have taken some kind of action under the Regulations, for example complained of some form of discrimination or given evidence in a hearing at a tribunal.

The Regulations apply at all stages of the employment relationship: during recruitment, during the period of employment (for example on issues such as pay and promotion) and on dismissal, and in some circumstances after the employment has finished, for example in the giving of a reference.

The Regulations provide protection to all workers in all employers or businesses regardless of their size, in both the public and the private sector. They also apply to office holders, such as the clergy and the holders of judicial offices. They cannot be relied upon by people who hold elected office.

***Discrimination on grounds of race, colour or ethnic origin is also prohibited.***

### 3.2 Racial discrimination

Discrimination on the grounds of race is prohibited by the *Race Relations Act 1976*, which also set up the *Commission for Racial Equality (CRE)*. It is an offence to discriminate against an employee on account of his or her colour, race, ethnic or national origin. Discrimination consists of treating an employee less favourably than the employer treats other employees. The Act's provisions are similar to the Sex Discrimination Act 1975, although there are fewer grounds to justify discrimination, being:

(a) Authenticity in entertainment, art or photography: a black man to play Othello for instance

(b) Personal services: recruiting a Bangladeshi housing officer in a Bangladeshi area, for example

(c) Maintaining ethnic authenticity in a bar or restaurant: such as Chinese waiters in a Chinese restaurant

The Act covers discrimination in advertising for engaging or dismissing an employee, or in conditions of employment (such as opportunities for training and promotion). The CRE published a code of practice in 1983 that, among other points, advised employers to make periodic analysis of the racial composition of their workforce and of the decisions taken on recruitment, training and promotion. It is argued that only if such matters are kept under systematic and active review will covert racial discrimination be disclosed so that remedial measures may be taken.

An individual employee may apply to an industrial tribunal if he or she considers that his or her rights have been infringed by discrimination. There have been many awards of high compensation in recent years. Many organisations aim to go further than the strict letter of the law by having an equal opportunities policy.

**Activity 3** **(10 minutes)**

What value could there be for a firm to maintain records of the ethnic origin of employees? What other information would be useful to help a firm to obtain a good profile of its employee base?

### 3.3 Disability

The Disability Discrimination Act (DDA) 1995 aimed to end the discrimination that many disabled people faced. This Act has been significantly extended, by the Disability Discrimination Act 2005. It now gives disabled people rights in the areas of:

- employment
- education
- access to goods, facilities and services

- buying or renting land or property, including making it easier for disabled people to rent property and for tenants to make disability-related adaptations

The Act now requires public bodies to promote equality of opportunity for disabled people. It also allows the government to set minimum standards so that disabled people can use public transport easily.

## 3.4 Diversity and equal opportunities

**Definition**

> **'Equal opportunities'** is a generic term describing the belief that there should be an equal chance for all workers to apply and be selected for jobs, to be trained and promoted in employment and to have that employment terminated fairly.

Employers should only discriminate according to ability, experience and potential. All employment decisions should be based solely on a person's ability to do the job in question, no consideration should be taken of a person's sex, age, racial origin, disability or marital status.

A number of employers label themselves as equal opportunity employers, establishing their own particular kind of equal opportunity policy. While some protection is afforded by employment legislation, the majority of everyday cases must rely on good practice to prevail.

**Definition**

> **Diversity** can be defined as 'all the ways in which we are different and similar along an infinite number of lines.' It refers to a broad range of characteristics including: gender, age, race, disability, cultural background, sexual orientation, education, religious belief, class and family responsibilities.

Four distinct dimensions characterise the many facets of differences and similarities of diverse employees. These four dimensions are:

(a) **Personality dimensions**: The unique characteristics of each individual that directly impact communication with others, which may include, patient or impatient, doer or thinker, assertive or non-assertive, listener or talker, flexible or inflexible, rational or emotional.

(b) **Internal dimensions**: Diversity characteristics that for the most part are not within a person's control, but shape expectations, assumptions and opportunities such as, age, gender, ethnicity, race, physical ability and sexual orientation.

(c) **External dimensions**: Social factors and life experiences that are more under a person's control and also exert a significant impact on behaviour and attitude. Examples of these include religion, marital status, parental status, educational background, income, appearance, geographic location, and work experience.

(d) **Organisational dimensions**: Characteristics of a person's experience within an organisation that impact on assumptions, expectations, and opportunities. This may include functional level or classification, management status, department/division/unit and work group, union affiliation, work location, seniority, work content or field.

From the employer's point of view, an organisation's work force is representative when it reflects or exceeds the demographic composition of the external work force. A representative work force reflects or exceeds the current proportions of women, visible minorities and persons with disabilities in each occupation as are known to be available in the external work force and from which the employer may reasonably be expected to draw from.

A representative work force is a good indication that an employer is not limiting access to the skills and talents of workers by discriminating on the basis of sex, race, colour or disability. A non-representative work force signals the need for evaluation and action, so that whatever is blocking or discouraging certain groups from employment and advancement may be corrected.

Some organisations set themselves goals on the representation of certain groups eg, there is an under representation of certain ethnic groups within the police force. To address this type of problem, a diversity assessment will show how an organisation's systems may provide supports or may act as barriers to diversity.

A diversity assessment is a structured process to gather information about the experience of current employees and, if desired, former employees using focus groups of current employees, personal interviews with senior managers, and telephone interviews of employees who have left the organisation.

The three general approaches for implementing diversity in an organisation are:

(a) **Affirmative action** – an approach with a goal to gain representation and upward mobility for ethnic minorities and women. It is focused on special efforts for targeted groups who are under-utilised. It opens up the doors of the organisation to establish the base for diversity.

(b) **Valuing diversity** – an approach with a goal to improve the quality of relationships between people. It is focused on understanding the cultural similarities and differences within an organisation. There is strong research evidence (*Meredith Belbin's* 1981 studies on team effectiveness) to support the view that groups that have a diverse mix of experiences, skills, knowledge and working approaches are generally more creative and productive than groups with a more uniform profile. Diversity is therefore a valuable organisational asset, and needs to be perceived as such.

(c) **Managing diversity** – an approach with a goal to improve the full use of all human resources in the organisation. The process is focused on creating a diversity friendly management system. It opens up the whole system to change and questions the policies and practices of the organisation in light of the current diverse environment.

# 4 TERMINATION OF EMPLOYMENT

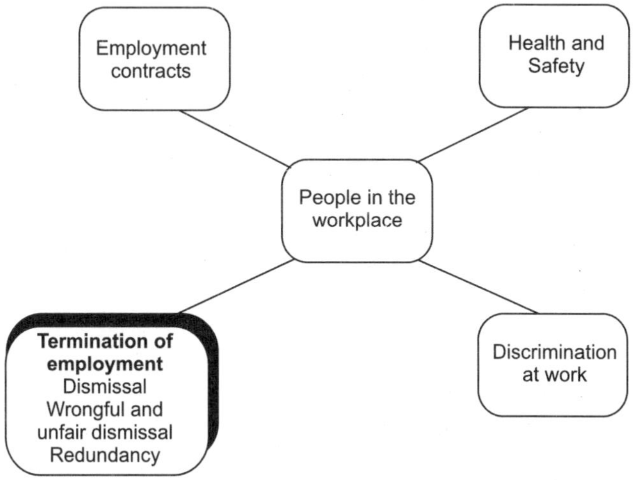


An employment contract is terminated by breach where there is:

(a) Summary dismissal
(b) Constructive dismissal
(c) Inability on the employer's behalf to continue
(d) Repudiation of the contract by the employee

## 4.1 Dismissal

### Summary dismissal

Summary dismissal occurs where the employer dismisses the employee without notice. This may be done if the employee has committed a serious breach of contract. Summary dismissal in these circumstances does not incur any liability for the employer. If, however, the employer has no sufficient justification for a summary dismissal, the employer is liable for breach of contract and the employee may claim a remedy for wrongful dismissal (see below). Whether the employee's conduct justifies summary dismissal varies according to the circumstances of the case.

### Constructive dismissal

Constructive dismissal occurs where the employer, although willing to continue the employment, repudiates some essential term of the contract, (for example by the unilateral imposition of a complete change in the employee's duties) or makes it very difficult for the employee to remain in post, and the employee resigns. The employer is liable for breach of contract. For example, an employer who constantly sexually harassed staff could be accused of constructive dismissal if those staff felt that the only way to resolve the problem was to leave the job.

### Employer's inability to continue employment

The employer may become unable to continue to employ the employee, for example if the firm is wound-up and ceases trading.

**Repudiation of the contract by the employee**

If the employee resigns or goes on strike or fails to perform the contract and to observe its conditions, that is breach of contract on their part, and the employer may dismiss them for that reason.

***Summary dismissal and constructive dismissal are both examples of dismissal without proper notice. A dismissal with proper notice is generally held to be lawful, unless it is shown to be wrongful or unfair.***

### 4.2 Wrongful and unfair dismissal

(a) Wrongful dismissal is a common law concept, arising in specific circumstances, which gives the employee an action for breach of contract.

(b) Unfair dismissal is a concept introduced by employment protection legislation. As a rule, every employee has the right not to be unfairly dismissed.

**Definitions**

Where the employer has summarily dismissed an employee without notice, or with less notice than the period outlined in the contract (as where the employer becomes insolvent), there may be a claim for damages for **wrongful dismissal**. However, a claim will not succeed where the employer can show justification (eg breach of contract).

**Unfair dismissal** is a concept that was created by industrial relations legislation about twenty years ago. It is now an extremely important element of employment protection legislation.

Whereas the remedies available following a successful action for wrongful dismissal are limited to damages equivalent to the earnings if proper notice had been given, the unfair dismissal legislation seeks to widen the scope of protection and increase the range of remedies available to an employee who has been unfairly dismissed.

**Activity 4** **(10 minutes)**

List some reasons for dismissal that are automatically considered to be unfair.

**Remedies for unfair dismissal: application to a tribunal**

An employee who alleges **unfair dismissal** must normally present their complaint to an **employment tribunal** within three months of the effective date of termination.

The employment tribunal might decide the following remedy for unfair dismissal.

(a) **Reinstatement**. If unfair dismissal is established, the tribunal first considers the possibility of making an order for reinstatement, which is return to the same job without any break of continuity.

(b) **Re-engagement**. The tribunal may alternatively order re-engagement. The employee is given new employment with the employer (or their successor or associate) on terms specified in the order. The new employment must be comparable with the old, or otherwise suitable.

(c) **Compensation**. If the tribunal does not order reinstatement or re-engagement, or if the employer does not comply with such an order, the tribunal may award compensation.

  (i) A basic award is calculated as follows. Those aged between 41 and 65 receive one-and-a-half weeks' pay (up to a maximum gross wage per week, which is determined each year) for each year of service up to a maximum of twenty years. In other age groups the same provisions apply, except that the 22 to 40 age group receive one week's pay per year and the under-22 age group receive half a week's pay. If the employee is also entitled to redundancy pay, the lesser is set off against the greater amount.

  (ii) A compensatory award (taking account of the basic award) for any additional loss (earnings, expenses, benefits) on common law principles of damages for breach of contract.

  (iii) If the employer does not comply with an order for reinstatement or re-engagement, and does not show that it was impracticable to do so, a punitive additional award is payable.

  (iv) There is an overall limit on the amount that may be awarded, which is raised from time to time to keep it in line with average earnings. In line with a recent European Court judgement, there is no upper limit on the awards that may be made in sex discrimination or race discrimination cases.

***Redundancy is a special case. Here it is the job that is ended, rather than the individual's occupation of the post.***

## 4.3 Redundancy

To qualify for redundancy pay, the following conditions apply.

(a) The employer has ceased, or intends to cease, to carry on the business in which the employee has been employed, or

(b) The employer has ceased to carry out the business in the place where the employee was employed, or

(c) The requirements of the business for employees to carry out work of a particular kind have ceased or diminished (or are expected to)

In order to obtain a redundancy payment:

(a) The employee must be under the normal retirement age for the business, or under 65 if no retirement age is specified, and

(b) Must have been continuously employed for at least two years, and

(c) Must have been dismissed (or laid off or put on short time), and

(d) The reason for dismissal must be redundancy

Redundancy pay is calculated on the same scale as that specified for unfair dismissal compensations. Note that if the employee unreasonably refuses an offer of alternative employment with the employer, they lose their redundancy pay.

**Activity 5** **(5 minutes)**

Bert is 45 years old. He has worked for your company for the past ten years. Unfortunately you have no alternative but to make him redundant. Calculate how many weeks' pay he should get as redundancy pay.

### Resignation

An employee is not entitled to redundancy pay if he or she resigns voluntarily.

### Misconduct of the employee

An employee who is dismissed for misconduct is not entitled to redundancy pay.

### Consultation with trade unions

In the event of planned redundancies, it is the employer's duty to consult any trade union that is independent and recognised (in collective bargaining) by them as representative of employees. The consultation must begin not later than the beginning of the appropriate period, which is:

(a) 90 days before the first dismissal, if 100 or more employees are to be dismissed at any one establishment

(b) 30 days before the first dismissal of 10 to 99 employees

(c) At the earliest opportunity before even one (but not more than nine) employees are to be dismissed for redundancy

These rules are applied to the total number involved and cannot be evaded by making essential dismissals in small instalments.

### Consultation with employees

The ACAS Code of Practice recommends that employees should be consulted where plans are made for their redundancy, even if such consultation will make no difference (as when a company is insolvent).

## Chapter roundup

- Most employers are required to give employees a statement of prescribed particulars relating to their employment within eight weeks of commencement, unless the employee already has a written contract of employment covering these particulars.
- The employer has an implied duty to take reasonable care of his or her employees; the employer must select proper staff, materials and provide a safe system of working. The employee has a duty to exercise care and skill in performance of his or her duties.
- Breach of the employment contract occurs where there is summary dismissal, constructive dismissal, inability on the employer's side to continue employment, or repudiation of the contract by the employee.
- If an employee is dismissed with shorter notice than the statutory or contractual requirements, or without notice when summary dismissal is unjustified, the employer can be sued by them for damages for wrongful dismissal.
- Dismissal is *automatically unfair* if it is on the grounds of trade union membership or activities, refusal to join a trade union, pregnancy, redundancy when others are retained, a criminal conviction that is 'spent' under the Rehabilitation of Offenders Act 1974, the employee taking steps to avert danger to health and safety at work, race or sex.
- Dismissal is caused by redundancy when the employer has ceased to carry on the business in which the employee has been employed or the business no longer needs employees to carry on that work. Dismissal is presumed by the courts to have been for redundancy unless otherwise demonstrated.
- The only effective remedy available to a wrongfully dismissed employee is a claim for damages based on loss of earnings.
- Remedies for unfair dismissal include reinstatement, re-engagement and compensation.
- To obtain a redundancy payment, the employee must be under retirement age, must have been continuously employed for at least two years, must have been dismissed, laid off or put on short-time and must have been dismissed for redundancy.
- The employer planning redundancies has a duty to consult any independent trade union that is recognised for collective bargaining as the representative of the employees. Certain consultation procedures are laid down.

## Quick quiz

1 When should an employee be issued with a written statement of particulars?

2 Do terms and conditions of employment all have to be contained in the same document?

3 Distinguish between wrongful dismissal and unfair dismissal.

4 How is health and safety in the workplace regulated?

5 What are the employer's duties regarding health and safety?

6 What are the employee's duties regarding health and safety?

7 Define 'discrimination'.

8 List two types of dismissal.

9 What remedies may be available for unfair dismissal?

10 What is redundancy?

11 What does the ACAS Code of Practice recommend when redundancies are inevitable?

## Answers to quick quiz

1 Within two months of commencing work.

2 No. An employee can be referred to a variety of documents.

3 Wrongful dismissal is when the dismissal procedure has been carried out incorrectly eg the correct notice has not been given. Unfair dismissal is when the reason for the dismissal is wrong.

4 By UK and EU law.

5 All systems must be safe, the work environment must be safe and healthy, all plant and equipment must be kept up to the necessary standard.

6 The employee should take reasonable care of himself/herself and others, must allow the employer to carry out his or her duties and must not interfere with any machinery or equipment.

7 Discrimination means treating a particular person or group less favourably than another.

8 Summary dismissal, constructive dismissal.

9 Reinstatement, re-engagement, compensation.

10 Redundancy is where a particular job or job function is no longer required.

11 Consultation with employees and/or unions.

## Answers to activities

1 Try to study examples of contracts of employment from family or friends, or even your tutor. See section 1 to remind yourself of the required content.

2 You could do the following: establish a health and safety consultative committee. Review communications and training procedures. Start a health and safety campaign – ask all departmental managers to have a meeting with their staff, put up posters everywhere to make people think about the issues. Start a staff suggestion scheme for ways to improve safety. The nurse could also have a health and fitness campaign. Use it as publicity for the firm, eg the accounts department doing a fun run for

charity. Get the staff association to suggest some social events that could be sporty or informative. Ask staff to suggest things they would like help with, such as a quit smoking support group, weight watchers. Offer staff a free health MOT. Start some sports teams. Get some celebrity chefs to come and do a healthy lunch session, get the canteen to vary their menu and not offer chips every day. Provide free bowls of fruit in staff rest rooms.

3 Keeping this type of record can allow a firm to see if a particular ethnic group is under-represented bearing in mind the local population patterns. If so, the firm can investigate the cause. Other areas to look at would be the sex distribution of the workforce – are there any particular trends, how many women are managers, do men work part-time? Age is also relevant – is it an ageing workforce or a young one, or is there a good mix?

4 Some examples of dismissal that would automatically be considered unfair include dismissal purely on grounds of pregnancy, dismissal for participating in union activities or for joining a union, dismissal for taking steps to avert dangers to health and safety at work, and dismissal on grounds of racial discrimination.

5 Bert would receive 1.5 weeks' pay for each year of service = 15 weeks' money.

Part B

# Economic, Social and Global Environment

# Chapter 5:

# RESOURCE ISSUES AND ECONOMIC SYSTEMS

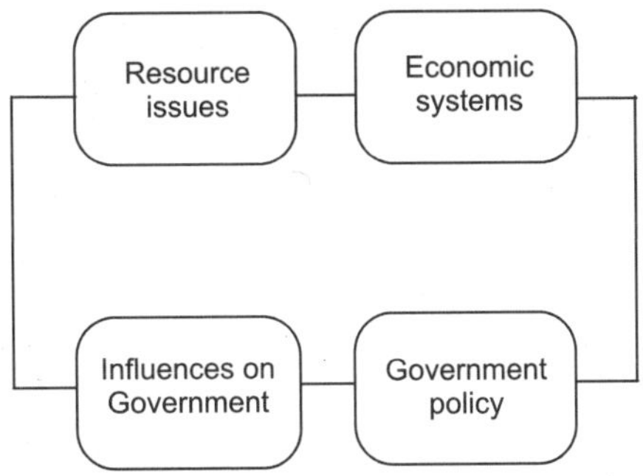


## Introduction

The crux of the economic problem is unlimited wants versus limited resources. We deal first in this chapter with the central problem of resource scarcity faced by all economies and how this forces societies to make choices about the allocation of them.

The study of economics is fundamentally a study of how nations decide to spread or allocate their resources in the best possible way to maximise the production of goods and services in order to achieve the greatest possible satisfaction of wants.

All societies are faced with the problem of scarcity but they differ in the way that they tackle it. One important difference between societies is the degree of government control of the economy. At one extreme lies the completely free market economy and at the other extreme lies the completely planned or command economy. In practice all economies are a mixture of both with different types and levels of government intervention through its overall economic policy and through legislation to regulate business activities.

## Your objectives

In this chapter you will learn about:

(a) The factors of production

(b) The problem of scarcity of resources

(c) Centrally planned and market economies

(d) Public and private sector initiatives

(e) Fiscal and monetary policy in the UK

(f) Industrial policy in the UK

(g) Social and welfare policy in the UK

(h) Interest groups

## 1 RESOURCE ISSUES

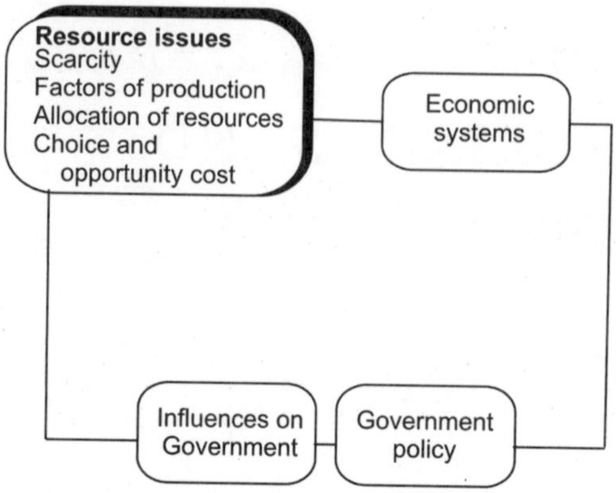


### 1.1 Scarcity

**Definition**

> **Scarcity** is the excess of human wants over what can actually be produced to fulfil these wants

Economics is concerned with the economic system through which societies attempt to meet people's material needs and wants through the production of goods and services. Goods are tangible, as are cars or shoes. Services are intangible eg, education or haircuts. Production itself is the process of transforming inputs of resources like labour power and raw materials into goods and services. The final goal of production is consumption – individuals satisfy their material needs and wants by using up or 'consuming' goods and services. Their capacity to do so is constrained by their income, so the size of a household's income is usually taken as an indicator of its material living standards or economic welfare.

Most people, when asked whether they would like more money, would say 'yes'. This applies not only to poor people but also to most wealthy people as well. The point is that human wants are virtually insatiable; so even the wealthiest individual will get positive satisfaction from another villa on the Mediterranean, a personal chef or gardener, but unfortunately the means of fulfilling these wants are limited.

All states have to deal with the problem *of scarcity.* There are never enough resources to satisfy all the needs of society. The factors of production are limited; every country has to make decisions about how to make the best use of the resources it has. This dilemma is known as the economic problem: finite resources and infinite wants.

In poor countries – euphemistically called developing or less developed countries by economists – there may be a problem of absolute scarcity where the country is unable to produce enough to satisfy even the basic needs of food and shelter. Living standards in many less developed countries are abysmal for much of the population with low levels of literacy, short life expectancy and near-zero ownership of consumer goods like cars and washing machines – things that are almost taken for granted in rich countries.

In developed countries, by contrast, the problem is largely one of *relative* scarcity. While they have significant pockets of poverty, these are the outcome of an uneven distribution of the national income. Average income per head is generally far above subsistence level enabling people to enjoy unprecedented levels of consumption of 'luxury' goods and services.

### 1.2 Factors of production

All societies have available quantities of productive resources or what economists call factors of production. Traditionally, these factors are classified into three main groups:

(a) **Labour** – includes all types of physical and mental power of human beings. Labour as a factor of production is clearly very diverse or heterogeneous. It ranges from the raw labour power of an unskilled manual worker to the highly specific services provided by a musician, accountant or surgeon.

(b) **Land and natural resources** – countries are differently endowed with land of varying quality for farming and other uses and also with natural resources like oil, coal and other mineral deposits, water, fish from the sea, the climate and terrain.

(c) **Capital** – we mean here the economy's stock of physical assets such as machinery and plant installed in manufacturing firms, the premises and offices of all types of business and also the social infrastructure of roads and sewers commonly provided by the government.

The distinguishing feature of a capital good like a machine is that it is not produced for its own sake to satisfy the wants of consumers but to assist in further production. Thus, the application of capital increases the efficiency and productivity of labour and land and is a potent source of economic growth. The productivity of capital is also limited by the state of technology. Physical capital is accumulated over time by investment – the diversion of part of the economy's resources into the production of capital goods rather than final consumer goods.

In order to produce goods and services, factors of production have to be combined and an essential role here is provided by **entrepreneurship** in which the owners of an enterprise put up the financial risk capital and undertake the overall co-ordination of factors. Also, the efficiency with which factors are used depends very much on the technology deployed. Technology means the application of knowledge or science to production.

Experience in production usually leads to greater efficiency in organisation and management, while over time firms progressively introduce more advanced technology and production methods. The result is increased productivity – a greater output of goods and services from given inputs of resources. Modem economies typically grow over time, increasing their output and income per head of population. They do this through a combination of investment in human and physical capital and by the application of advances in organisational methods, management skills and technology.

### 1.3 The allocation of resources

Scarcity means that decisions have to be taken about the allocation of resources among competing claims. There are three aspects to this core problem:

(a) **What goods and services will be produced** with the available resources? In a market economy, this will depend on what consumers want to buy, and what they will pay for each product or service. The decisions about what will be produced relate to demand and supply. (Satisfied demand is **consumption**; the actual supply of goods and services is referred to as **production**.) At the broadest level societies must choose between production of, say, capital goods and consumer goods. More investment in machines and education may increase productivity and income in the future but only at the sacrifice of present consumption. Then there is the question of which specific goods and what quantities of them to produce from all the thousands of different goods which can be produced. Do we train more doctors or build more bridges? Do people want more meat or more digital cameras?

(b) **How will these goods and services be produced?** Having decided what to produce it is then necessary to choose the most appropriate and efficient production methods and technology. The producers or suppliers of goods and services might be small companies, large companies, monopolies, state-owned enterprises or the government itself. The choice about who will produce the goods and services, and what mix of resources the producers will use, will depend on the costs of resources and the efficiencies of resource utilisation.

(c) **To whom will the goods and services be distributed?** Finally, there must be mechanisms for deciding *who* is to get what is produced. This is the problem of distribution of income among households and among various social classes and groups such as workers, landowners and capitalists, the employed and unemployed, the sick, large families and pensioners. Some goods and services are provided free by the state (for example, in the UK, some health care and education) but others have to be paid for.

### 1.4 Choice and opportunity cost

The concept of opportunity cost emphasises the problem of choice by measuring the cost of obtaining a quantity of one commodity in terms of the quantity of other commodities that could have been obtained instead. For example, think of the choices you are faced with – what to buy, what to wear, what to eat, how much time to spend studying or whether to go out. For each of these choices to do something you are rejecting doing some alternative.

Now consider the same problem at the level of a whole society. If the government elects to build more roads and finds the money by cutting down on building hospitals then the cost of the new roads can be expressed as so many hospitals per mile of road or in terms of the hospitals foregone.

At any time, the economy has available only limited quantities of resources, which determine its productive capacity. We can imagine a nation devoting all of its resources to producing just two goods – food and furniture. The maximum possible combination of food and furniture that can be produced in a week is:

| Production possibilities | Units of food (thousands) | Units of furniture (thousands) |
|---|---|---|
| A | 20 | 0 |
| B | 19 | 6 |
| C | 17 | 10 |
| D | 14 | 13.5 |
| E | 10 | 16.5 |
| F | 6 | 18 |
| G | 0 | 19 |

***This is of course an enormous simplification when we consider the complex economies of the real world.***

If all its resources were used to produce food, it could produce twenty thousand units a week. Similarly, if only furniture was produced the greatest possible output might be nineteen thousand units a week. If the nation chose to produce more of one good it would have to sacrifice the production of some of the other. These values fix the extreme points on what is termed the economy's production frontier or production possibilities curve drawn in Figure 5.1.

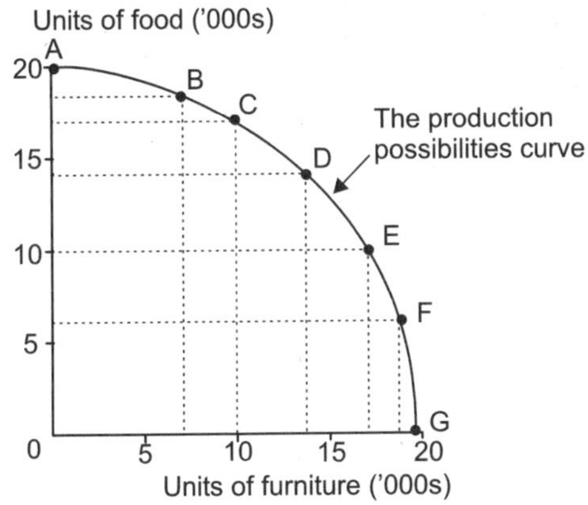


*Figure 5.1: The production possibilities curve or production frontier*

The slope of the production possibilities curve measures the opportunity cost of food and furniture. The curve shows the maximum output of one good, given the output of the other. Turning out more furniture, therefore, has a real cost in terms of the sacrifice of food that could have been produced instead. Economists argue that practically every good or service has a positive opportunity cost – production of one commodity involves foregoing output of something else.

If the economy is inside the boundary eg, producing fifteen thousand units of each commodity, then more of both goods can be produced simultaneously. If the economy is at this point because of heavy unemployment then measures that succeed in reducing unemployment will allow the economy to have more of both goods. If, on the other hand, the economy is inside the boundary because, although existing resources are fully employed, they are being used inefficiently, then measures that increase the efficiency of resource utilisation will allow the economy to produce more of both goods. To produce beyond the production possibilities curve something has to happen to cause economic growth. This may be growth across the economy as a whole or just in one sector of the economy.

**FOR DISCUSSION**

Use a Production Possibilities Frontier to investigate one of the trade-offs you make in your lives. For example, you can discuss the time you spend studying versus the time you spend working at an after school job.

**Activity 1** **(20 minutes)**

A country is capable of producing the following combinations of goods and services per period of time, assuming that it makes full use of its resources of land, labour and capital.

| Goods (units) | 100 | 80 | 60 | 40 | 20 | 0 |
|---|---|---|---|---|---|---|
| Services (units) | 0 | 50 | 90 | 120 | 140 | 150 |

(a) Draw the production possibility curve for this country.

(b) Is it possible for this country to produce the following combinations of goods and services?

(i) 80 units of goods and 50 units of services
(ii) 70 units of goods and 90 units of services
(iii) 40 units of goods and 100 units of services

(c) What is the opportunity cost (in terms of services) of producing twenty extra units of goods when this country is initially producing:

(i) 60 units of goods
(ii) 70 units of goods

**Activity 2** **(10 minutes)**

In the diagram overleaf PQ is the community's production possibility curve. The point R represents:

A An optimum combination of capital and consumer goods
B Less than full employment output
C An output that can only be achieved at the cost of inflation
D A combination of capital and consumer goods that is not attainable

**Activity 2 (cont'd)**

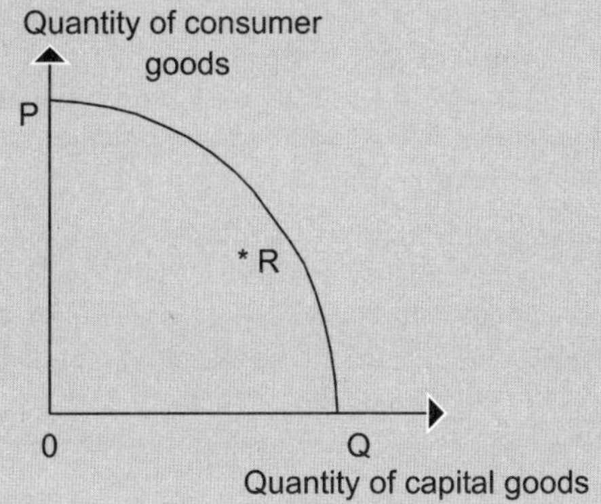


## 2 ECONOMIC SYSTEMS

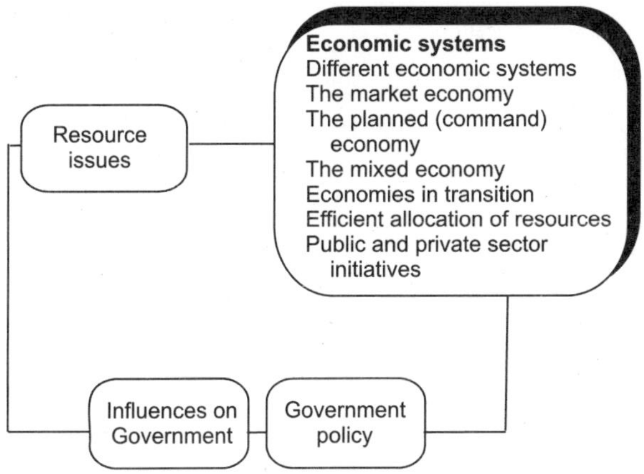


### 2.1 Different economic systems

In advanced economies there are various ways to deal with the question of scarcity. Different countries use different approaches or types of economic system.

**Definitions**

(a) **Free market economy** – sometimes called capitalism. In this type of economy most decisions are taken through the operation of the market mechanism. Supply and demand and the ability to pay influence decision-making. There is very little government intervention in business decision-making.

(b) **Command economy** – sometimes referred to as state controlled. In this type of economy decisions are taken collectively, usually by central planning committees. The government controls what is produced, how much is produced, the price and who the goods are available to. Decisions are intended to benefit all members of society. Citizens all contribute to the common good of the state. There is a lot of state intervention in this type of economic system.

(c) **The mixed economy**. In this type of economy there is a balance between market forces and state intervention. The view is taken that certain activities need to be regulated by the state while others can be left to the influence of the market. A mixed economy usually comprises:

- A free enterprise sector, where economic decisions are based on market forces
- Public ownership and control of key central industries
- Welfare sector to provide a minimum level of medical, social and educational services for all citizens regardless of wealth

Arguments about the merits of markets and planning proceed at different levels. For example, opponents of the market system are often found really to be attacking 'capitalism'. Private ownership of the means of production leads, they claim, to an inequitable distribution of income and wealth and to the exploitation of labour by the capitalist class. That was the basic thinking of Karl Marx in his monumental work. *Capital,* published in 1867.

At the other end of the political spectrum there are those who are fundamentally opposed to socialism and planning on the grounds that it restricts the freedom of individuals to choose where they work and invest, what they produce and what they consume.

No country uses one system to the exclusion of the other; every society has a mixed economy and, particularly since the demise of the socialist regimes of Central and Eastern Europe, the argument focuses much more on the extent of government intervention in the economy.

### 2.2 The market economy

The market economy is based upon an ideology that assumes that consumer choice will influence market forces to ensure an optimum allocation of resources with no need for interference from government. The only role for government is to ensure that the 'invisible hand' of market forces is free to operate via the price mechanism or forces of supply and demand.

The assumptions of a free market system include the following:

(a) Firms seek to maximise profits.

(b) Consumers seek the greatest benefit for least cost.

(c) Workers seek to maximise their wage relative to the cost of working.

(d) Individuals are free to make their own decisions, eg where to work, what to buy. Firms are free to choose what to produce and who to sell to.

(e) The 'Price Mechanism' decides prices in the free market. Prices rise if there are shortages of a good or service (supply) and fall if there is a surplus.

(f) Prices will also rise if consumers suddenly wish to purchase a large quantity of the good (demand) and fall if the good suddenly becomes unpopular.

(g) If there is an excess of supply then the price of the good will fall. As the price falls consumers will get more benefits for less cost and thus demand more. The price will eventually reach a point at which all the excess supply will have been bought up.

(h) Because of the interaction of supply and demand, prices will fluctuate. But they will always tend towards the 'equilibrium price' where the amount consumers wish to buy equals the amount producers wish to supply.

Using markets to allocate resources is diametrically opposed to planning. In a pure market system decisions about what is produced, how and who gets what is produced are decentralised. All these things would be the outcome of millions of separate individual decisions made by consumers, producers and owners of productive services. As such, of course, they reflect private preferences and interests.

Suppose both food and furniture were bought and sold in free and competitive markets. This means that there is no attempt by the government to influence or regulate the decisions of individual buyers and sellers and that there are large numbers of them with no one sufficiently powerful to 'corner' the market. Essentially, the two product markets will be self-regulating through the medium of prices.

---

**EXAMPLE: INDIRECT DISCRIMINATION**

Imagine that we start at point D in Figure 5.2, overleaf, with production of 14 thousand units of food and 13.5 thousand units of furniture. Producers of both goods are making adequate profits at the current prices and buyers too can obtain all they want at those prices. In other words, there is a matching-up of supply and demand.

Then, suppose more people want to buy furniture. At the current price they now want to buy, say, 18 thousand units. We know that, so long as food output stays at 14 thousand units, the economy cannot meet this extra demand for furniture; resources will have to be diverted out of food into furniture production along the production possibilities curve. In a market economy the increased demand for furniture will drive up the price, making furniture production more profitable than food. Firms making furniture will therefore expand their output and will attract factors of production out of the food industry by offering higher wages for labour and bigger rents for land. Equally, some food producers might be induced to move into furniture production instead.

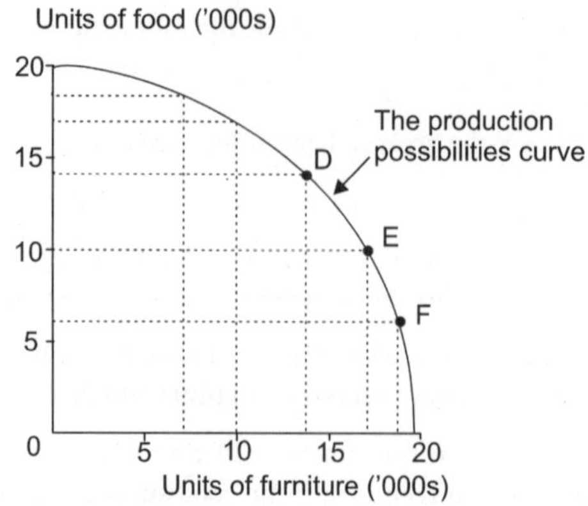


*Figure 5.2: Production possibilities curve*

The outcome is that the rise in furniture prices will divert resources into furniture and out of food. In the graph production will thus move away from D towards F. Also, the rise in furniture prices will choke off some of the demand to, say, 16.5 thousand units. Point E, in fact, could be a new point of 'equilibrium' at which firms in both industries are again satisfied with their profitability and buyers can obtain precisely what they want of both goods at the new prices.

This adjustment of supply to demand takes place purely as a result of the independent decisions of producers, consumers and resource owners in response to an automatic change in the relative price of food and furniture and with no need for intervention by some external planning agency.

---

**Problems with the market economy – reasons for market failure**

According to free market theory, if consumers desire a good they are willing to pay a high price for it, and producers sensing a chance for profit, increase or start production. Thus the allocation of resources and mix of goods available is in accordance with society's wants. But can the invisible hand of supply and demand and producers' desire for profit be relied upon in all instances? Not always.

(a) There is an unwillingness on the part of consumers to pay for 'merit goods' or 'public goods'

(b) Goods and services provided by the government (or public sector) are called public goods and those by the market system (private sector) private goods. Merit goods are goods whose social benefit to the community exceeds their benefit to thc individual. A good example is education. If schools charged the full rate for their services then many families would withhold their children, as they are unable or unwilling to pay. Governments on the whole believe that schooling is beneficial for its people and the economy and therefore steps in.

Public goods and merit goods are mainly provided by the government and are funded through taxation.

In the price system, people demand and purchase goods and services because they personally wish to consume them. This exclusion principle applies to what are termed 'private goods'. There is another category of goods – public goods – like defence, law and order, and street-lighting where if they are provided everyone can consume them, ie, the provider does not have the ability to exclude others from consuming them and hence is not able to charge others for their enjoyment of the goods concerned. As a result, it is unlikely that such goods would be produced in a totally free economy. If the State feels that a more substantial provision is socially desirable then it must intervene to ensure an increased supply.

(c) Willingness on the part of consumers to pay for 'demerit goods'

The opposite of goods that the government thinks are under-consumed are those that are over-consumed (de-merit goods). Governments may wish to intervene to discourage the use of resources in the production of demerit goods such as tobacco because the social costs exceed the private costs. (The private cost means the price at which such goods would be sold in a free market.)

(d) Inequality of power in the market place

Resources gravitate to the production of those goods with the highest profit margins that, by implication, are those in greatest demand. However, if the distribution of income and wealth is uneven, those sections of society blessed with the greatest monetary muscle are in a position to outbid others in the determination of prices and, consequently, the allocation of resources. Hence, the pattern of production may not be a reflection of what society as a whole wants produced, but of what the richest elements are able to ensure is produced.

(e) Barriers restricting entry to the market place and the immobility of factors of production

The working of the free market depends on an increased demand for a good causing an increase in production, with existing producers raising output levels and new producers entering the market. Given that producers aim to maximise profits they may be tempted to combine with each other to restrict the supply of goods and thus drive up prices and profits. This exploitation of the consumer can also arise when producers take over their competitors, resulting in a similar increase in monopolisation.

Also, in practice, resources do not always move quickly between uses. Firstly, there may be insufficient information available about employment and entrepreneurial opportunities in other sectors of the economy. Secondly, resources currently being used in one sector may be unsuited for use elsewhere: accountants cannot become solicitors overnight, it requires years of training to qualify for either occupation. By the same token, if there is a surplus in wheat production one year but a shortage of dairy produce, it takes a full growing season for farmers to adjust their supplies. These problems are referred to as friction, or immobility of factors.

(f) Producers may ignore 'externalities'

When producers determine the amount they wish to supply, they weigh up the expected benefit from selling the good, ie, price, against the expected cost of production. When they consider the cost of production, they will only consider the *private* cost, ie, the money they have to lay out to produce the good, ignoring any external cost or spill over effect on society, such as increased smoke, noise or congestion. If an activity confers substantial social costs of this sort, the good concerned may be over-supplied from society's point of view. Conversely, some activities may provide net social benefits as a result of 'good' externalities and may thus be underprovided by a market economy.

**Activity 3** **(20 minutes)**

Explain the concept of 'opportunity cost' and illustrate its importance in economic theory.

### 2.3 The planned (command) economy

A command economy is one in which the fundamental economic questions; what, how, and for whom to produce, are answered by reference to state determined priorities rather than the interaction of supply and demand in the market place. It is based on an ideology, which assumes that left alone the market will create an unjust and undesirable allocation of resources; consequently the state must take over the running of the economy and dictate the use of the factors of production.

Usually we associate command economies with socialist countries but they could equally well be right wing dictatorships. At the present, the only remaining socialist command economies are North Korea and Cuba.

The state plans at three levels:

(a) At the **macroeconomic** level central authorities decide between allocating resources for (a) current consumption goods that raise living standards in the present, and (b) investment goods that will help build for the future. This answers the 'what to produce' question.

(b) At a **micro** level it plans the output of each industry and firm. Once the level of output is decided calculations can be made to determine the inputs required. For example if 200 bicycles are needed then the inputs will be 400 wheels, 200 handlebars, 200 chains etc. If 400 wheels are needed then 1200 steel spokes are required. If 400 spokes are required then 200 metres of steel wire needs to be made. This means that there are thousands of calculations needed just to produce one bicycle. This answers the 'how to produce' question.

(c) It plans the **distribution of output between consumers**. This will depend on a government's aims. In many socialist countries the basis of this decision is 'for each according to their needs'. This means that the product of the economy is distributed equitably, eg a family of four would receive more than one person living alone. Goods and services may be given out directly eg flats and houses are allocated to citizens, or it may allow some degree of choice by paying workers salaries.

In the latter case the state may influence the distribution of these goods or services by setting prices. Goods the authority wishes to encourage are priced cheaply and goods that are to be discouraged are priced more expensively. This answers the 'for whom to produce' question.

Resource allocation decisions are generally made by a central committee, which determines both the target level and composition of output in accordance with a medium-term plan, usually expressed on a five-year timescale. To meet the requirements of the plan, detailed decisions have to be made concerning the resource requirements of each industrial sector. In assessing these, the planners have to predict the impact on all other sectors , for example, a scaling-up of output in certain sectors, to identify any likely resource bottlenecks. To take a simple example, the steel industry requires input of coal equivalent to 50% of its own output. Therefore to double steel output, the coal industry must double the proportion of coal production which is required for steel making. However, the increased output in the steel industry has resource requirement implications elsewhere and a further set of secondary resource requirements can be determined.

In a complete command economy it is possible to guarantee everyone a job. Ostensibly, the elimination of unemployment is a major advantage of planning. However, the corollary of this is that the government will also have to determine the allocation of labour to different occupations. The planners will therefore need to predict the requirements for the many types of skills to fulfil their overall production targets. People will have to be educated and trained appropriately and directed or induced into particular jobs. Restrictions might have to be imposed on individual freedom of choice of jobs and places of work. Finally, the government will have to decide the distribution of income. This is often claimed as another major advantage of planning since, in principle, the national income can be shared out on an equitable basis of what people need rather than on their luck in inheriting wealth or intelligence. The reality, however, is likely to be different as those in power, including the planners, use their influence to secure privileges for themselves.

The main failings of command economies include:

(a) **Lack of investment** – the main stimulus to investment is competition; the threat that if you do not improve your product or your production process, your rivals will, and they will take your market share. In the East all organisations were state monopolies and the stimulus of competition was absent. While competition led West Germany to develop the Mercedes, the BMW and the Volkswagen, East Germany had a single car maker – Trabant – producing an antiquated and unreliable vehicle which sold for more second hand than it did new because of its enormous waiting list.

(b) **No incentive to productivity** – in the West it is necessary to cut costs and raise output per person in order to compete, and those who can achieve this are rewarded. In the East success meant not the maximisation of production but the achievement of the planned target. There were no rewards for over-filling the plan, only penalties for under-filling it. Accordingly a manager's first task was always to get the target reduced. He then met the target whether it was sensible or not. If the plan said your factory should send ten machines a year to the state repair shop, you sent ten machines, even if only eight were actually broken.

(c) **Wastage of resources** – inevitably a planned economy needs to divert resources into planning, rather than actually producing. In the USSR *Gosplan,* the state planning organisation, needed to calculate 12 million prices a year, and plan the output of 24 million products. Inefficiency was rife, waste and pollution at alarming levels, the lack of high quality information for the planners and the ability to be able to communicate the plans effectively all led to economic decline and, as the eighties drew to an end, the gap between the wealth and economic power of the West and that of the Soviet Union was rapidly widening.

(d) **Black markets** – have a way of coming into existence wherever wants are unsatisfied, and if you are willing to pay, someone will find a way of supplying what you want. In some parts of Eastern Europe the black markets were fairly open affairs.

**Activity 4** **(20 minutes)**

Describe the economic problems of planning that have led to its declining popularity as a means of allocating resources.

### 2.4 The mixed economy

**Definition**

A **mixed economy** is one which combines elements of both private enterprise, where individuals have the freedom to set up in business in their own right and personally reap the rewards of their enterprise (or suffer the penalties of their mistakes) and intervention, in varying guises, by the state.

In reality no such thing as a 100% planned or 100% free market economy exists. The Western industrialised economies are all mixed, with the governments being involved in economic activity to varying degrees. There is probably no optimum degree of mixture of an economy – it rather depends on the political persuasion of the government and how badly it wishes to correct the drawbacks of the market economy.

There are two broad strategies for governments to pursue – replacing the market or augmenting the market. The three main types of intervention are:

(a) **Provision or prohibition** – public goods are provided at zero prices to maximise consumption and increase social benefit. Alternatively the worst demerit goods, such as heroin and paedophile literature, may be judged to be so harmful, both to individuals and society, that it is banned.

(b) **Subsidy or taxation** – merit goods are encouraged by subsidies to increase their consumption. Conversely, some demerit goods are taxed heavily, eg tax on spirits to deter excessive consumption and reduce the social costs. The government also gives public health information at zero prices because there is no incentive for the private sector to do so.

(c) **Regulation** – price and quantity controls can be used to change production and consumption patterns. Externalities that are bad, eg river pollutants, may be taxed, illegalised or limited by quality/quantity. In contrast, good external benefits, eg, home improvements may be subsidised. Regulation has been extensively used in post-war Britain to limit monopolies and cartels. Since 1979 there has been deregulation in many sectors of the British economy.

### 2.5 Economies in transition

The vastly superior performance of market economies explains the drive to introduce market mechanisms in the states of the former Soviet Union and in Eastern Europe following the collapse of their communist governments since 1989. Thus, the majority of these countries are now termed transition economies, that is, they are committed to programmes of transition from central planning to market systems.

However, the path to a market economy is by no means smooth, not least because of the resistance to transition from powerful groups such as former communist party members and bureaucrats with vested interests in the maintenance of the old system. Transition means replacing the old planning system with the key elements of a market economy. This requires fundamental institutional, legal and cultural change together with massive investment in neglected infrastructure, production, distribution and finance. Some of the main elements of reform include:

(a) **Price liberalisation** – with removal of price controls to establish free and competitive markets

(b) Removal of subsidies

(c) **Privatisation** – the transfer of ownership of enterprises from the state to the private sector. This is essential to establish the private profit motive, the driving force of the market economy

(d) **Trade liberalisation** – provides competition for domestic monopolies

(e) **Exchange rate convertibility** – interest rates must be decontrolled and the foreign exchange market liberalised

(f) **Reform of the financial sector** – is essential to mobilise savings for investment and to channel funds into the most productive investment projects

(g) **Institutional reforms** – requires setting up commercial banks and other financial institutions such as stock markets together with heavy investment in training workers in the new institutions

The troubled experience of countries, such as Poland, Hungary and Russia, which have embarked on reform, illustrates the enormous obstacles to successful transition. In the first stages, countries have invariably suffered steep declines in output and soaring unemployment as inefficient enterprises are closed down or workers laid off to improve productivity. In Poland unemployment rose from near zero in 1989 to around 15% of the workforce in 1994.

Price liberalisation has led to surges in inflation, reaching hyperinflation levels in some cases – in Russia inflation rose to 1300% in 1992; in 1994 it was still running at over 200% but by 2008 had fallen to 9%. Increased government spending in establishing welfare benefits for the newly unemployed contributed to inflationary pressures. In all countries the privatisation programme has been less than smooth – in parts of Russia political resistance threatens to halt or even reverse privatisations.

Transition inevitably involves, at least in the short term, enormous costs and hardship for the general population in the shape of sharp cuts in living standards and rising unemployment. Unless governments can convince people that the sacrifices from establishing a market system will eventually be worthwhile, there is the risk of a loss of vital popular support for reform and of a political backlash with a return to power of the old guard.

### 2.6 Efficient allocation of resources

Mixed economies are intended to combine the best of both command and market systems and to avoid the worst. To some extent they succeed. For example, social security is often provided as a command style safety net to avoid the market failure of starvation of the poor, and free education and health care, are provided in the UK because left to itself the market would under produce these goods. At the same time there may be compulsory competitive tendering for public service projects to avoid the command failure of inefficiency, the hiring of private security firms to run prisons, or the private finance initiative applied to infrastructure developments such as the Skye Bridge.

In the last quarter of the 20th century, the failures of the command system led to privatisation and moves towards more market-oriented systems in most parts of the world.

There has, however, been increasing criticism of alleged profiteering or inefficiency amongst privatised firms and utilities, for example the record profits of £18 billion declared by the privatised BP for 2008, or the severe disruption of the privatised railways following the Hatfield crash in 2000. In late 2001 the privatised Railtrack was placed into administration, following the refusal of further state funding to meet safety requirements, and in 2002 the rail infrastructure was transferred to a not-for-profit body, Network Rail. However by 2003 it was clear that the new supplier had an even greater appetite for state subsidy than had the old.

There has been controversy over public private partnerships that have been used to introduce private finance into the provision of merit goods. There were accusations that profits had been placed ahead of the interests of workers and consumers.

### 2.7 Public and private sector initiatives

Development of a strong and dynamic private sector is crucial to long-term economic growth. Experience over the past two decades has shown that when properly regulated and operating under competitive market conditions, the private sector can generally use resources more efficiently than the public sector. Private enterprises can deliver goods and services to meet growing consumer demands, and create new job opportunities at the same time. Public-private partnerships in infrastructure projects can reduce pressure on public budgets and enable governments to redirect more resources to social spending. Private sector participation in infrastructure and utilities can also improve and extend the delivery efficiency of essential services. Private sector involvement in the delivery of education and health services to higher income groups can free-up government resources for the needs of lower income groups.

The challenge to government is to create and maintain the legal and market institutional infrastructure needed to enable private sector activities to act as the engine of economic growth, in other words, to support and strengthen an 'enabling business environment'.

**Definition**

> An **enabling business environment** is one where the set of conditions that affect private sector behaviour encourage the growth of private sector activity and enterprise development.

To create an enabling business environment, public policy should be directed at removing the constraints that impede private sector growth and creating new opportunities for private sector investment and business development.

**Private finance initiatives**

Public Private Partnerships (PPP) is the umbrella name given to a range of initiatives that involve the private sector in the operation of public services. The Private Finance Initiative (PFI) is the most frequently used initiative. It is a mechanism developed by the Government to raise money to pay for new buildings and services.

PFI is only used where it can meet the following requirements.

(a) Commitment to efficiency, equity and accountability

(b) Delivery of clear value for money without sacrificing the terms and conditions of staff.

A typical PFI project will be owned by a company set up specially to run the scheme. These companies are usually a consortium including a building firm, a bank and a facilities management company. While PFI projects can be structured in different ways, there are usually four key elements: Design, Finance, Build and Operate.

The concept of Public Private Partnership is based upon the premise that there are some activities that the public sector does best and other activities where the private sector or the voluntary and community sector may have more to offer. The public sector is looking to the private sector for expertise, innovation and management of appropriate risks. The private sector is looking for business opportunities, a steady funding stream and a good return on its investment. For the partnership to work each party must recognise the objectives of the other and be prepared to build a good, long-term relationship. It is argued that only by allowing each sector to focus upon what it does best can government provide the quality services and outcomes that the public want and expect in an economically efficient manner. Public Private Partnerships aim to create diversity in the way in which public services are delivered and projects procured, thereby promoting choice, innovation, competition and skills transfer.

| Roles might include: | Responsibilities might include: |
|---|---|
| • The delivery of a public service, eg street cleaning or issuing of vehicle licences<br>• The performance of an internal or cross departmental service or function, eg catering or information technology support<br>• The planning and implementation of major projects or infrastructure initiatives, eg the construction of bridges or container terminals | • Resource provision, eg expertise or technology<br>• Costs and budget management<br>• Income generation<br>• Investment and project financing<br>• Asset ownership, eg buildings or equipment; and risk management |

Private sector involvement in the delivery of public services is not new and in areas such as the provision of rural postal services, ophthalmic services and residential care, private sector service providers have been active for many years. The emergence and development of Public Private Partnerships needs to be viewed in this wider context and in many senses these arrangements not only give rise to an increase in the scope and scale of private sector involvement in public service delivery, but they also allow this involvement to become much more focused and structured.

The key differences between Public Private Partnerships and privatisation are as follows.

(a) **Responsibility** – in a privatisation responsibility for the delivery and funding of services passes to the private sector. Consumers generally buy these services using their own resources and the individual service providers are responsible for making resource allocation decisions. Under a Public Private Partnership arrangement, responsibility for services remains with the public sector, which then delegates the delivery of the services to the private sector. The public sector remains in control of the quality and amount of services purchased.

(b) **Ownership** – in a privatisation ownership rights or interests in public sector assets are sold to private sector investors and the benefits and responsibilities associated with asset ownership are vested in private shareholders. In a Public Private Partnership arrangement, legal ownership of any assets can be retained by the public sector.

(c) **Service nature** – in a privatisation the nature and scope of service provided by a privatised enterprise is determined largely by that enterprise itself and the public sector retains a purely regulatory role. In a Public Private Partnership arrangement, the nature and scope of service provided by the private sector is determined by the public sector as client on the basis of contractually specified outputs.

(d) **Service level and quality** – in a privatisation the level and quality of service delivered is shaped by the degree of competition (or lack of it) in the market, with market forces dictating prices, volumes and quality. In a Public Private Partnership arrangement, the level and quality of service delivered is shaped by the contract and output specification. Service pricing, volumes and quality are specified in detail and the public sector client then holds the private sector contractor responsible for the delivery of these specified outputs over the term of the arrangement.

(e) **Risk and reward** – in a privatisation the private sector accepts all of the risks inherent in a business and shareholders are exposed to the profits and losses arising from that business. In a Public Private Partnership arrangement, risks are shared between the public and private sectors, with individual risks being allocated to the party best able to manage them. Rewards and benefits are shared between the public and private sectors.

(f) **Service monitoring** – in a privatisation the ability of the public sector to easily monitor and influence the nature and quality of service delivery over time is limited. In a Public Private Partnership arrangement, the public sector retains the ability through the contract to monitor and influence service delivery over time.

**Types of PFI projects**

There are three types of PFI project:

(a) **Financially free-standing projects,** where the private sector undertakes the project on the basis that costs will be recovered entirely through charges for services to the final (generally private sector) user. Public sector involvement is limited to enabling the project to go ahead, for example by undertaking some of the initial planning, licensing, awarding works concessions, providing ancillary works or assisting with statutory procedures. Examples of such projects include toll bridges and the provision (and operation) of visitor centres at sites of public interest.

(b) **Services sold to the public sector**, where the cost of the project is met wholly or mainly by charges from the private sector service provider to the public sector body that let the contract eg, privately financed prisons.

(c) **Joint ventures**, where the costs of the project are not met entirely through charges on the end users, but are subsidised from public funds. In many cases, the public sector subsidy secures wider social benefits.

## 3 GOVERNMENT POLICY

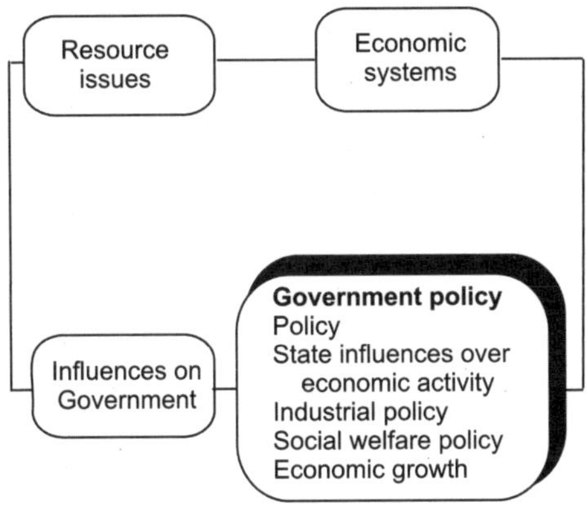


### 3.1 Policy

**Definition**

> **Policy**: a way of expressing the broad purposes of government activity in a particular field, with some desired outcome in mind. The word 'policy' is used in a variety of ways.
>
> (a) A policy may be a *specific* proposal (eg to raise revenue by indirect as opposed to direct taxation).
>
> (b) A policy may *establish procedures* to achieve specific objectives such as parental choice in education (eg enabling schools to opt out of local authority control).
>
> (c) A policy can also be a vague direction for change with no *specific* outcome intended.

In the UK, political parties direct government policy and state activity.

Policies often end up as compromises between different interest groups. Political decision-making on a national scale cannot really be compared to the decision-making framework in a business. This is because governments have to take into account the interests of all citizens. Public sector policies, therefore, always have some element of overt political choice attached to them. Responsibility for the actions taken by the public sector ultimately rests at the highest political level (ie the Cabinet and its committees). Ministerial decisions are made within an agreed policy framework. At this level the Treasury is also involved to assess the financial implications of policy.

The government can solicit advice from a number of sources, or in turn it may be lobbied.

(a) The civil service exists to advise the government.
(b) Academics and 'think tanks', for example, may be asked for their views.
(c) Royal Commissions may be set up.
(d) Special interest groups may also pitch in.

Few policies are 'new'. They may be built upon an existing set of policies that are not working or are no longer relevant. The policy-making process is a pattern of continuous readjustment. Few policies run their course to the full without change.

**Policy formulation** is not always the responsibility of one single ministry. (In launching major initiatives the Prime Minister may be flanked by ministers who are associated with the bundle of policies aimed at dealing with particular problems.)

**Policy implementation** is not always the responsibility of a single organisation either. For example, the release of long-term patients from psychiatric hospitals into the community means the co-ordination of a number of policy areas (the organisations responsible for health, social welfare, housing and employment). The funding for these organisations may not be properly related to or co-ordinated with the policy objectives.

With the intermingling of policies, and of the agents who implement them, it may be difficult to identify clearly the impact of a particular policy or its implementation. Policies that have elements of political and resource choice in them may be strong on rhetoric but weak on funding, as the power system for allocating funds is not the same as that for getting the issues onto the political agenda. The Treasury wishes to control public spending in the interests of managing the economy, whereas other departments of state can think of good reasons for spending more money. For example, the Chancellor of the Exchequer may wish to implement tax cuts in the next Budget in order to enhance the government's image before the next election. However, the Treasury will want to know how the shortfall in 'income' can be made up.

***The election manifesto and the voting process are the links between the parties and the policies underlying them.***

### Political parties

The apparatus of government is headed by ministers who, unlike the civil servants advising them, are elected, and whose jobs as ministers can be terminated periodically by the electorate. Ministers direct the apparatus of government.

**Definition**

> **Party**: 'a body of men and women united for promoting, by their joint endeavours, the national interest according to principles upon which they are all agreed'. (*Adapted from Edmund Burke*)

In the UK a political party is an organisation whose members share:

(a) Values or interests

(b) Views as to how society should be run

(c) A desire to work together to ensure that they achieve control over policy making and the apparatus of government

In the UK, political parties compete for representation in Parliament and local government.

(a) They are normally organised at constituency level – in order to promote their candidate for that particular seat.

(b) However, all parties have a central organisation (eg Conservative Central Office).

A political party:

(a) Aims to take over the whole of government, and be in charge of a variety of public policy areas from crime prevention to arts sponsorship.

(b) Draws its members from any section of society.

The national parties in Britain are governed on different bases.

(a) The **Labour Party** is composed of local parties, which send delegates to the party conference. The party conference also contains representatives from trade unions. The conference elects a **National Executive Committee**, responsible for most policy-making. The leader is elected by MPs, party members and trade unionists.

(b) The **Conservative Party** is in theory a federation of local associations that select candidates, normally from a short list, for the parliamentary seat.

(c) The **Liberal Democratic Party** has no trade union connection. Its formal constitution requires the leader be elected by a national conference. The Liberal Democrats maintain separate organisations for England, Scotland and Wales. They form a federal party.

### 3.2 State influences over economic activity

Government economic policy affects organisations in many ways. The varieties of influences are outlined in the following table.

| Government | Organisations |
|---|---|
| Overall economic policy | Market demand<br>Cost of finance<br>Taxation |
| Industry policy | Protection v free trade<br>Grants, incentives, sponsorship<br>Regulation eg, investor protection, company law<br>Entry barriers, capacity |
| Environment and infrastructure policy | Distribution |

| Government | Organisations |
|---|---|
| Social policy | Workplace regulation, employment law<br>Labour supply, skills, education |
| Foreign policy | Trade promotion, export credits<br>EU and WTO obligations<br>Export promotion to allies, aid recipients |

The state influences economic activity in the UK in three ways, through:

(a) taxation and interest rate policies
(b) public spending on goods and services
(c) regulation

Government economic policy is conducted with at least three aims in mind:

(a) Economic growth is desired in order to provide employment for the national increase in the population and to improved living standards

(b) Full employment (that is, the economy's resources are fully employed, and there are very few people out of work – just those between jobs, for example)

(c) Price stability (ie no inflation)

These aims often conflict with each other, and so it can be very difficult to achieve a balance between these aims. Unemployment and inflation are dealt with below.

**Inflation**

Inflation is the name given to an increase in price levels generally. It is also manifest in the decline in the purchasing power of money.

Why is a *high* rate of price inflation harmful and undesirable?

(a) **Redistribution of income and wealth**

Inflation leads to a redistribution of income and wealth. In general, in times of inflation those with economic power tend to gain at the expense of the weak, particularly those on fixed incomes. Their nominal income will stay the same but the purchasing power of it will fall.

(b) **Balance of payments effects**

If a country has a higher rate of inflation than its major trading partners, its exports will become relatively expensive and imports relatively cheap. Eventually, the exchange rate will be affected.

(c) **Uncertainty of the value of money and prices**

If the rate of inflation is imperfectly anticipated, no one has certain knowledge of the true rate of inflation. As a result, no one has certain knowledge of the value of money or of the real meaning of prices.

(d) **Wage bargaining**

Wage demands will be increased in times of high inflation. If they are successful then a wage/price spiral will take hold, which will reinforce the problem.

(e) **Consumer behaviour**

People may stockpile goods fearing price increases later. This could create shortages for other people who haven't already stockpiled themselves.

### Causes of inflation

There are three main causes of inflation:

- Demand pull factors
- Cost push factors
- Excessive growth in the money supply (quantity theory of money)

**Demand pull inflation** occurs when the economy is buoyant and there is a high aggregate demand, in excess of the economy's ability to supply.

(a) Because aggregate demand exceeds supply, prices rise.

(b) Since supply needs to be raised to meet the higher demand, there will be an increase in demand for factors of production, and so factor rewards (wages, interest rates, and so on) will also rise.

There are two main causes of demand pull inflation.

(a) **Fiscal**. For example, an increase in government spending or a reduction in taxes and interest rates will raise demand in the economy.

(b) **Credit**. If levels of credit extended to customers increase, expenditure is likely to follow suit. In this case, inflation is likely to be accompanied by customers increasing their debt burdens.

**Cost push inflation** occurs where the costs of factors of production rise regardless of whether or not they are in short supply, and where the rise in costs is not matched by an increase in productivity. This appears to be particularly the case with wages. **Import cost push** inflation occurs when the cost of essential imports rise regardless of whether or not they are in short supply.

### Expectations and inflation

A further problem is that once the rate of inflation has begun to increase, a serious danger of **expectational inflation** will occur. This means, regardless of whether the factors that have caused inflation are still persistent or not, there will arise a generally held view of what inflation is likely to be, and so to protect future income, wages and prices will be raised now by the expected amount of future inflation. This can lead to the vicious circle known as the **wage-price spiral**, in which inflation becomes a relatively permanent feature because of people's expectations that it will occur.

### Unemployment

The **rate of unemployment** in an economy can be calculated as:

$$\frac{\text{Number of unemployed}}{\text{Total workforce}} \times 100\%$$

The number of unemployed at any time is measured by government statistics. If the flow of workers through unemployment is constant then the size of the unemployed labour force will also be constant.

Unemployment results in the following problems.

(a) **Loss of output**. If labour is unemployed, the economy is not producing as much output as it could. Thus, total national income is less than it could be, because economic resources are not being fully used.

(b) **Loss of human capital.** If there is unemployment, the unemployed labour will gradually lose its skills, because skills can only be maintained by working.

(c) **Increasing inequalities in the distribution of income.** Unemployed people earn less than employed people, and so when unemployment is increasing, the poor get poorer.

(d) **Social costs.** Unemployment brings social problems of personal suffering and distress, and possibly also increases in crime such as theft and vandalism.

(e) **Increased burden of welfare payments.** This can have a major impact on government fiscal policy, because governments will have to pay out more in state benefits whilst collecting less through tax revenue.

The causes of unemployment can be summarised as follows:

| Category | Comments |
|---|---|
| Demand deficient | A fall in demand for goods and services means that the equilibrium level of output falls to below the full employment position.<br>The fall in aggregate demand could come from a fall in consumer expenditure; business investment; exports or government expenditure. |
| Structural change | The demand for labour falls as a result of a significant change in the structure of an industry.<br>This may result from:<br>• Technological change (with machines and computers replacing people)<br>• Shifts in the industry (for example, the decline in manufacturing industry in developed countries as it was relocated to cheaper, developing countries). |
| Supply side problems | Supply side problems are all effects that prevent the market for labour from working efficiently. They include powerful trade unions and employment protection legislation which can discourage employers from taking on staff; other labour market regulations such as minimum wage rates; social security systems which allow workers to be better off by not working than working and skill shortages caused by poor education and a lack of training. |

**Government employment policies**

Job creation and reducing unemployment should often mean the same thing, but it is possible to create more jobs without reducing unemployment.

(a) This can happen when there is a greater number of people entering the jobs market than there are new jobs being created, as has been the case in the UK in recent years because of high net immigration.

(b) It is also possible to reduce the official unemployment figures without creating jobs. For example, individuals who enrol for a government financed training scheme are taken off the unemployment register, even though they do not have full-time jobs.

A government can try several options to create jobs or reduce unemployment.

(a) **Spending more money directly on jobs** (for example hiring more civil servants)

(b) **Encouraging growth** in the private sector of the economy. When aggregate demand is growing, firms will probably want to increase output to meet demand, and so will hire more labour.

(c) **Encouraging training in job skills**. There might be a high level of unemployment amongst unskilled workers, and at the same time a shortage of skilled workers. A government can help to finance training schemes, in order to provide a 'pool' of workers who have the skills that firms need and will pay for.

(d) **Offering grant assistance to employers** in key regional areas

(e) **Encouraging labour mobility** by offering individuals financial assistance with relocation expenses, and improving the flow of information on vacancies.

The state uses various policy tools to try to achieve its aims, including **fiscal policy** and **monetary policy**.

### Fiscal policy

Fiscal policy involves:

(a) Taxation and other sources of income
(b) Government spending
(c) Borrowing whenever spending exceeds income
(d) Repaying debt when income exceeds expenditure

A feature of fiscal policy is that a government must plan what it wants to spend, and so how much it needs to raise in income or by borrowing. It needs to make a plan in order to establish how much taxation there should be, what form the taxes should take and so which sectors of the economy (firms or households, high income earners or low income earners etc) the money should come from. This formal planning of fiscal policy is usually done once a year. The taxation aspects are set out in the Budget.

This annual review of taxation means that a government's review of its fiscal policy can normally only be done once a year. In between Budgets, a government must resort to other non-fiscal policy instruments to control the economy, such as influencing interest rate levels.

Fiscal policy then covers a government's income and expenditure. In the UK the policies adopted are intended to promote high and stable levels of growth and employment.

### Monetary policy

Monetary policy involves attempts to influence economic activity through:

(a) Interest rates
(b) Exchange rates
(c) Control of the money supply
(d) Controls over bank lending and credit

The main aim of UK monetary policy for many years has been the **control of inflation**.

Monetary policy can be made to act as a subsidiary support to fiscal policy and demand management. Since budgets are usually once-a-year events, a government must use non-fiscal measures in between budgets to make adjustments to its control of the economy.

(a) **A policy of low interest rates** or the absence of any form of credit control might stimulate bank lending, which in turn would increase expenditure (demand) in the economy. This can lead to increased inflation.

(b) **High interest rates** might act as a deterrent to borrowing and so reduce spending in the economy. This can lead to reduced inflation

(c) **Strict credit controls** (for example, restrictions on bank lending) might be introduced to reduce lending and so reduce demand in the economy.

Alternatively, monetary policy might be given prominence over fiscal policy as the most effective approach by a government to achieving its main economic policy objectives. This might not however be possible: from 1990 to 1992, for example, monetary policy in the UK was heavily constrained by the need to set interest rates at levels which maintained sterling's position in the European exchange rate mechanism (ERM). From 1998, the government gave the Bank of England the role of setting interest rates, although it is still the government that sets an inflation target. If the UK joined a single European currency, interest rates would largely be determined at the European level.

*Framework for monetary policy*

In almost his first action as Chancellor of the Exchequer in May 1997, Gordon Brown unveiled 'the most radical reform of the Bank of England since it was established in 1694'. He set up a Monetary Policy Committee (MPC) to **decide the level of interest rates.** This means that the government no longer has any direct say on interest rates but it still sets inflation targets. The Bank of England must then set interest rates at a level consistent with achieving the target.

The Bank's monetary policy objective is to deliver price stability (as defined by the government's inflation target) and, without prejudice to that objective, to support the government's economic policy, including its objectives for growth and employment. The government's inflation target will be confirmed in each Budget statement. The price stability objective is to achieve the inflation target of two per cent, as measured by the twelve-month increase in the Consumer Prices Index (CPI).

The MPC meets on a monthly basis and decisions are made by a vote of the Committee on a one-person one-vote basis, with the Governor having the casting vote if there is no majority. The Treasury has the right to be represented in a non-voting capacity. Decisions on interest rates are announced immediately.

**Quantitative easing**

Economic growth requires expansion of the money supply in order to finance it. A low level of inflation, such as the government's target of two percent, should ensure that there is always money available to finance increased levels of economic activity. In normal times, this target level of inflation is achieved by the MPC's setting of interest rates.

The financial crisis that started in 2007 led to huge losses by banks in the USA, the UK and much of the rest of the western world. This meant that the funds available to finance existing levels of economic activity were insufficient. The response of central banks such as the Bank of England and the US Federal Reserve was to cut interest rates to levels not very much above zero. Generally, this would have stimulated borrowing and demand and thus boosted economic activity. However, the banks' losses were such that they used whatever funds they could obtain to rebuild their balance sheets and lending fell to very low levels. The result was continuing recession.

**Quantitative easing** is the tool that central banks use in an attempt to overcome this problem. Interest rates cannot be cut any further, so cash is injected directly into the economy in the hope that this will allow expansion of business. The method and its effects can be described in simple terms.

(a) The central bank creates new money by making entries in its own books of account. This is an entirely computerised process: no new banknotes are printed or put into circulation.

(b) The new money is used to buy assets. This puts the money into the hands of those who sell the assets.

(c) Generally, the assets are variable rate government debt instruments (gilts) and the sellers are banks. This combination has two desirable effects.

  (i) The banks have increased funds available for lending.

  (ii) The increased demand for gilts forces down their effective interest rate. This leads to a fall in long-term interest rates generally, thus reducing the costs of debt such as mortgages and releasing even more spending power into the economy.

## Impact of fiscal policy

Businesses are affected by a government's fiscal or tax policy. The levels of taxation and the methods through which they are collected – on individual earnings, on savings, through VAT, on business profits or upon inheritance of wealth – illustrate the power of the state to determine the operating environment and thus the strategy of firms at any given time.

**Activity 5** **(2 minutes)**

'Fiscal policy' means

A The control of incomes and prices to restrain inflation

B Government measures to restrict imports and encourage exports

C The adjustment of public expenditure and taxation so as to affect aggregate demand

D The use of the power of the central bank to influence interest rates

*Fiscal policy and macroeconomic objectives*

Fiscal policy is concerned with government spending (an injection into the circular flow of income) and taxation (a withdrawal).

(a) If government spending is increased, there will be an increase in the amount of injections, expenditure in the economy will rise and so national income will rise (either in real terms, or in terms of price levels only ie the increase in national income might be real or inflationary).

(b) If government taxation is increased, there will be an increase in withdrawals from the economy, and expenditure and national income will fall. A government might deliberately raise taxation to take inflationary pressures out of the economy.

Achieving growth in national income without inflation has been a problem bedevilling governments for many years. Certainly, government spending and government taxation policies can affect economic growth (ie the national income level in real terms) but it can also stimulate further inflation.

Fiscal policy can be used to reduce unemployment and provide jobs.

(a) More government spending on capital projects would create jobs in the construction industries.

(b) Government-funded training schemes are a means of spending by government to improve training, so as to make people more qualified for jobs in private industry.

(c) A government might tax companies on the basis of the numbers and pay levels of people they employ (as with employers' national insurance contributions). Lower 'employment taxes' would possibly make employers more willing to take on extra numbers of employees.

Government spending, however, might create inflationary pressures, and inflation tends to create more unemployment. Fiscal policy must therefore be used with care, even to create new jobs.

Since government spending or tax reductions might be inflationary, and higher domestic prices make imports relatively cheaper and exports less competitive in foreign markets, fiscal policy has possible implications for the balance of payments.

If macroeconomic objectives are economic growth, full employment, low or no inflation and equilibrium in the balance of payments, fiscal policy can certainly influence those objectives, and governments use fiscal policy to do so (as well as to help achieve other non-economic objectives). However, the impact of changes in fiscal policy is not always certain, and fiscal policy to pursue one aim (eg lower inflation) might for a while create barriers to the pursuit of other aims (eg employment).

*Taxes on business*

Taxation is effectively a cost. It is resources generated by the business and then appropriated by the state.

Many countries offer low taxation in certain regions as an incentive for businesses to locate their activities there.

*Taxes on people (eg income tax)*

A high proportion of tax reduces the amount people have to spend on certain kinds of goods rather than others. In other words, low tax might mean more spent on consumer goods and less, say, on education provided by the state.

Certain types of tax, such as Employers' National Insurance Contributions, make it more expensive for employers to hire workers.

**Activity 6** **(10 minutes)**

(a) Mrs A earns £30,000 per annum and Mr B earns £10,000 per annum. Calculate the amount of tax each would pay if:

(i) a flat rate of 20% applied

(ii) there were a tax allowance of £5,000 with the remaining earnings taxed at 25%

(b) If the government wanted to increase the spending on luxury goods, which method of taxation ((i) or (ii)) would be most likely to achieve this?

(c) If the government wanted to safeguard the net income of people on low earnings, which method ((i) or (ii)) would be most likely to achieve this?

*Public spending*

The economist *John Maynard Keynes* claimed that if the economy is operating at less than full employment there is scope for increasing national income, preferably through new investment. If the private sector will not invest enough, the government can. According to this view, government policies for boosting extra government spending financed by borrowing need not cause off-setting reductions in total domestic consumption, industrial investment or imports, and so national income will grow.

**What form does government spending take?**

Governments, like other organisations, spend money on the following:

(a) Payments of **wages and salaries** to employees, and pensions to old age pensioners

(b) Payments for materials, supplies and services

(c) Purchases of **capital equipment**

(d) Payments of **interest** on borrowings and repayments of capital

Expenditure has to be allocated between departments and functions – eg health, social services, education, transport, defence, grants to industry, and so on. Expenditure decisions by government are of great significance to companies that are major suppliers to the government – eg producers of defence equipment, medicines and medical equipment, and school textbooks.

More indirectly, government spending decisions affect companies and other organisations. Government spending has a 'knock-on' effect throughout the economy – companies supply companies, which in turn supply the government. A lot of government work is subcontracted to private sector firms. For example, recently the British arms industries have been heavily affected by government cutbacks in arms expenditure and contracts.

**Fiscal policy and the budget**

A feature of fiscal policy is that a government must **plan** what it wants to spend, and so how much it needs to raise in income or by borrowing. It needs to make a plan in order to establish how much taxation there should be, what form the taxes should take and so which sectors of the economy (firms or households, high income earners or low income earners) the money should come from. This formal planning of fiscal policy is usually done once a year and is set out in the **budget**.

The two components of the budget that the government determines and through which it exercises its fiscal policy are:

(a) **Expenditure**. The government, at a national and local level, spends money to provide goods and services, such as a health service, public education, a police force, roads, public buildings and so on, and to pay its administrative work force. It may also, perhaps, provide finance to encourage investment by private industry, for example by means of grants.

(b) **Revenues**. Expenditure must be financed, and the government must have income. Most government income comes from **taxation**, albeit some income is obtained from **direct charges** to users of government services such as National Health Service charges.

A third element of the fiscal policy is:

(c) **Borrowing**. To the extent that a government's expenditure exceeds its income it must borrow to make up the difference. The total amount that public sector bodies, including the government, must borrow each year can be recorded in different ways. The most important difference between these methods is whether they relate to movements of actual cash or to accrued book assets and liabilities. For many years accounting was on the cash basis. The expression **Public Sector Borrowing Requirement (PSBR)** was replaced by the term **Public Sector Net Cash Requirement (PSNCR)** in order to emphasise the strictly cash basis of the measure. The problem with this approach is that the complexity of the government's finances can lead to sudden, large movements of cash that do not reflect any change in the underlying debt. The redemption of an index-linked issue of government debt, for example can produce a sharp increase in interest payments, even though the level of debt and interest rates may not have changed. In 1998 the British government decided to use the accruals basis for its presentation of borrowing, and adopted the term **Public Sector Net Borrowing (PSNB)**, which is used in the EU 1995 European System of Accounts.

**Private sector and public sector investment**

Extra investment means an increase in total expenditure in the economy, which in turn means an increase in national income. There are certain differences between public sector and private sector investment however.

(a) Investment by the public sector will tend to be directed towards industries, in which the public sector is involved, and towards industries supplying public sector industries (eg new roads) or on fulfilling social needs.

(b) Public sector investments might have a longer time scale (eg health) or have fewer quantifiable economic benefits (eg education, basic research) than the private sector is willing or able to accept.

(c) Public sector investment is financed differently from private-sector investment. In the public sector, investment could be financed even if the government did not have sufficient income from taxation. To pay for a budget deficit, the government can borrow large amounts of money.

(d) Increasingly, the UK Government is involving the private sector in the funding of public sector projects. This is the Private Finance Initiative (which we have seen earlier in this chapter). An example of this is the railway link to the Channel Tunnel and the building of the Millennium Dome.

### 3.3 Industrial policy

In the UK the government's industrial policy allows it to take an active role to support investment and encourage a faster rate of economic growth in industry and to halt the decline of the manufacturing sector.

The government can give assistance to those industries with the highest growth potential; this is referred to as picking winners or 'indicative planning'. This also includes identifying bottlenecks – areas in the economy where there are supply side problems.

Government **industrial policy** might either hamper or promote the growth of new industries.

(a) **Restraining growth**: 'green belt' policies prevent the location of industry in certain areas.

(b) **Encouraging an emerging industry**: for example the decision by the UK government some years ago to adopt the BBC microcomputer in state schools.

Government policy might make it difficult for new firms to gain entry into an industry or market. Examples of how this could be done are as follows.

(a) By placing **restrictions** on foreign firms that wish to set up business in the country, or by putting import tariffs on the goods of overseas suppliers

(b) By **subsidising**, directly or indirectly, domestic firms that are already in the industry

(c) By **imposing product standards** requiring a particular level of safety. One of the aims of EU harmonisation is the elimination of national differences, and hence the creation of economies of scale. However, this will also mean that products previously banned as not meeting UK safety requirements will be brought up to the correct standard and so can enter the UK market.

***Government may also seek to encourage or discourage new products.***

### New products

In some industries, governments regulate the adoption of new products.

(a) In the pharmaceuticals industry new drugs or medicines must undergo stringent testing and obtain government approval before they can be marketed. (The stringency of controls varies from country to country, and so drugs companies may sell a product in one country that has been banned in others.)

(b) The food industry is subjected to strict controls on products and also manufacturing processes. Consequently, companies in the food industry have less freedom to move to any new technology, or to change material mixes, than firms that are in other industries. A current issue in this area is the recent debates about the safety of genetically modified food products.

### Competition

***Government can influence the degree and nature of competition within an industry.***

As a buyer, controller and supplier in a mixed economy, the government can bring considerable pressure to bear on competition within an industry. Moreover, changes in policy can result in a change in the industry and competition. As an example, the government in the UK decides what television and radio companies are permitted to broadcast; changes in policy – eg, to permit more local commercial radio stations or to take away the franchises of existing ITV companies – have brought about significant changes in the industry. The government sometimes has the right to determine the structure of an industry, to ensure competition.

**Definition**

> **Substitute product** (or service): a product or service that can stand in for another product or service in satisfying a customer need. For example, should you wish to travel from London to Paris you can go by boat, plane or train (via the Channel Tunnel). These are substitutes.

Government policy can affect the position of products in one industry with respect to the position of substitute products. More stringent safety regulations on one type of product might weaken its competitive position against substitute products. For example, strict controls over products that use asbestos would weaken the position of asbestos producers against producers of substitute materials. On the other hand, subsidies for one industry would put that industry at an advantage against other industries producing substitute products.

**Definitions**

> **Global industry** and **global competition** imply an industry in which producers in different countries compete with each other, with the emergence of multinational or international companies. A government can put restrictions on global competition by favouring its domestic industries.

Just as a government can put restrictions on global competition, it can encourage it too, by removing the restrictions and regulations. For example, it has been the removal of exchange controls by various countries such as the UK that has permitted the international money markets and capital markets to develop rapidly from the 1980s onwards.

### Industrial competitiveness policy

The new approach to industrial policy is to focus on improving the factors that shape the nation's competitiveness. Initiatives may include:

(a) Investment in physical and human capital – a sound skills base is crucial for attracting global business

(b) Reductions in non-wage employment costs – these costs are seen as limiting competitiveness and employment creation

(c) Support for small- and medium-sized enterprises – because they create employment opportunities and contribute to skills development, especially in high-tech areas

(d) Promotion of R&D and innovation

(e) Improvements to infrastructure – physical transport as well as information highways

(f) Reinforcing the laws on copyright and patents to encourage enterprises to develop new products

These initiatives represent a shift in the government's role from direct intervention in the form of subsidies and protecting industry from competition to one of focusing on the external business environment and pinpointing the conditions that influence its competitiveness.

**Regional policy**

Industrial policy is complicated by regional policy. England, for example, is divided into nine regions, each with its own regional development agency (RDA). Each RDA fosters a development strategy for its own region. Matters dealt with by these strategies include, in addition to economic matters, housing, public services and environmental protection. The RDAs for the north-east, north-west and Yorkshire and Humber have combined to devise a long-term strategy for the north of England as a whole.

The election of a new government in 2010 may lead to significant changes in regional policy.

**Training and skills policy**

The Department for Business Innovation and Skills promotes measures to improve skills at all levels.

(a) Skills and training support are available to employers via Train to Gain, Apprenticeships, Business Link and Job Centre Plus.

(b) The Skills Funding Agency is now the single funding provider for adult skills outside of higher education. It is responsible for routing approximately £4 billion to employers and further education colleges.

### 3.4 Social welfare policy

**Definition**

> **Social Welfare Policy** seeks to protect and directly improve people's standard of living.

In the UK the name 'social policy' is used to apply to:

(a) the policies that government uses for welfare and social protection, and
(b) the ways in which welfare is developed in a society

In the first sense, social policy is particularly concerned with social services and the welfare state. In the second, broader sense, it stands for a range of issues extending far beyond the actions of government – the means by which welfare is promoted, and the social and economic conditions which shape the development of welfare.

Welfare is an ambiguous term:

- It commonly refers to 'well-being'. In welfare economics, welfare is understood in terms of 'utility'; people's well-being or interests consist of the things they choose to have.
- It also refers to the range of services which are provided to protect people in a number of conditions, including childhood, sickness and old age. The idea of the 'welfare state' is an example. This is equivalent to the term 'social protection' in the European Union.

Current welfare policy emphasises individual responsibility and biases the role of the state towards promotion of equality of opportunity and the provision of services targeted on specific lower income or disadvantaged groups. However, some policy-makers and professionals in the public services adhere to a different understanding of the operation of state welfare that identifies problems as the outcome of structural inequalities and not as the failure to grasp opportunities. They therefore reject the emphasis on enhancing equality of opportunity promoted by the government.

Social policy expenditure accounts for between 50% and 60% of government spending and includes:

- old age programmes (eg, pensions)
- unemployment
- sickness/disability
- social assistance/ poverty alleviation
- health/medical care
- environmental policy

**Universality and selectivity**

Universal benefits and services are benefits available to everyone as a right, or at least to whole categories of people (like 'old people' or 'children'). Selective benefits and services are reserved for people in need.

Universal services can reach everyone on the same terms. This is the argument for public services, like roads and sewers: it was extended in the 1940s to education and health services. The main objection to universal services is their cost. Selectivity is often presented as being more efficient: less money is spent to better effect. There are problems with selective services, however: because recipients have to be identified, the services can be administratively complex and expensive to run, and there are often boundary problems caused by trying to include some people while excluding others. Selective services sometimes fail to reach people in need.

**Social security**

**Contributory benefits** are benefits that an individual has paid for, rather like an insurance policy. Payment is made by national insurance contributions (NICs), which are compulsory deductions.

(a) **Retirement pension** *is* a taxable benefit. Broadly, the level of pension depends on the number of years for which NICs have been paid (the individual's **contributions record**).

(b) **Incapacity benefit** is paid when an individual cannot work because of incapacity (eg illness, disability etc).

(c) **Maternity allowance** is a tax-free benefit paid to mothers for eighteen weeks. It can start between six and eleven weeks before the expected date of the birth.

(d) **Jobseekers' allowance** is for those who are looking for work.

In addition, there are several *non-contributory benefits,* available regardless of whether or not the claimant has made contributions. These include the following.

(a) The **Child Tax Credit** and **Working Tax Credit** are for working people on low income who have children.

(b) **Housing benefit** is a tax-free contribution to rent paid by local authorities to people on low incomes.

(c) **Council tax benefit** is a tax-free contribution to the council tax liabilities of people on low incomes.

(d) The **Social Fund** is a source of tax-free payments for specific needs, such as things for a new baby. Loans may also be made from the fund.

(e) **Child benefit** is a tax-free weekly payment to people bringing up children. *Guardian's allowance* may be added to child benefit.

(f) **Attendance allowance** is a tax-free benefit for people disabled after age 65 who need a lot of help. **Disability living allowance** is a tax-free benefit for people disabled while under 65 who need a lot of help.

(g) **Invalid care allowance** is a taxable benefit for people aged between 16 and 65 who spend at least 35 hours a week caring for a sick or disabled person, subject to an income test.

(h) **Industrial injuries disablement benefit** is a tax-free benefit paid to people disabled by accidents at work or by industrial diseases.

***The social security system provides a safety net for those on low incomes. It has the effect of redressing some of the inequalities in society as a whole.***

**Health and social protection**

The **welfare state** seeks to provide citizens with benefits they would find it hard to purchase as individuals. The National Health Service was set up to provide health care free at the point of delivery, funded by taxation. People are free to purchase private medical insurance if they so wish.

Life expectancy has increased steadily since 1901, when it was 45.5 years for males and 49 years for females; it now it stands at around 77 year for males and 81 for females. This is likely to add significantly to the cost of the welfare state. This is why the government is seeking to encourage people to make their own pension arrangements rather than relying on the state. The 'ageing' of the population will put significant pressure on the existing health system and other social benefits.

In 2008, just under 11.6 million people were in receipt of a retirement pension, an overall increase of 31% since 1981/2. Furthermore, demands on the health service have increased. For example, total public spending on the NHS in England has increased from £45 billion in 2001 to £90 billion in 2007.

The National Health Service has now been re-organised. At one time, it was managed centrally. Hospitals and doctors did what they were told to do by regional health authorities. Now, many hospitals are managed independently, as NHS Hospital trusts. Area health authorities and some 'fund-holding' general practitioners (GPs) now purchase services from hospitals. The aim is to ensure that 'market' mechanisms ensure an efficient allocation of resources.

A problem is that hospitals are more 'glamorous' than preventative medicine, which might improve people's health more effectively in the long term.

---

**FOR DISCUSSION**

In the UK the state provides welfare services. Some politicians in Asia regard this as decadent, arguing that extended families should do this job.

What do you think? How do the previous Government's views on 'care in the community' fit with this? Does the current Government propose any changes?

---

### 3.5 Economic growth

Economic growth is measured by increases in any of the following:

(a) Total expenditure in the economy – ie 'aggregate demand'
(b) Total income for individuals and companies in the economy
(c) Total output in the economy

There are various measures available:

**Definitions**

(1) **Gross Domestic Product** (GDP) is the result of all economic activity in the economy (even though UK citizens or organisations may receive income from assets abroad, or make payments to foreign individuals or organisations).

(2) **Gross National Product** (GNP) is GDP inclusive of amounts earned by the UK from overseas assets, but exclusive of amounts paid to overseas holders of UK assets.

(3) A formula for measuring total national expenditure is:

$E = C + I + G + (X - M)$ where:

E is the total national expenditure
C is the total domestic consumption
I is the total industrial investment
G is the total government spending
X is total exports
M is total imports

We live in an increasingly global economy, where what happens in the world economy affects our national economy, and so we must be able to maintain price and non-price competitiveness. Economic growth is important because it is closely linked with technical innovation, profitability, investment and a healthy trade balance. Growth will also create more jobs in the economy and so lower unemployment.

If the economy has a high rate of growth then it is more likely to produce new innovative enterprise, and in turn further efficiency gains. A good example of this is the so-called 'tiger economies' of the Far East. If firms are growing rapidly, taking more market share, then their additional profitability can be used to finance further development. This is more relevant today when the life cycle of products is shortening, and companies must be more adaptable.

In the most basic sense when we talk about the growth of the economy we mean by how much national income is increasing usually on annual basis. We can describe this as actual growth.

However, some of the increases in output that we see in the economy are cyclical in nature, which means that they may simply be a 'catching up' in the economy, where following an earlier downturn the economy is in reality recovering. Growth in the stricter sense is concerned with the longer-term changes in the economy to do with the underlying capacity of the economy to produce; this is therefore concerned with the increases in output that can be sustained in the long run; economists sometimes call this the potential or sustainable growth rate.

**Definition**

> **Potential growth** is the speed at which the economy could grow. It is the percentage annual increase in the economy's capacity to produce: the rate of growth in potential output.

The distinction between actual and potential growth can be illustrated using the production possibilities diagram. A production possibility curve shows potential output and potential growth would be shown by a shift outwards of the curve (from A to B in diagram below). Actual growth is represented by a movement outwards of the production point eg, from S to T to U to V in the diagram below:

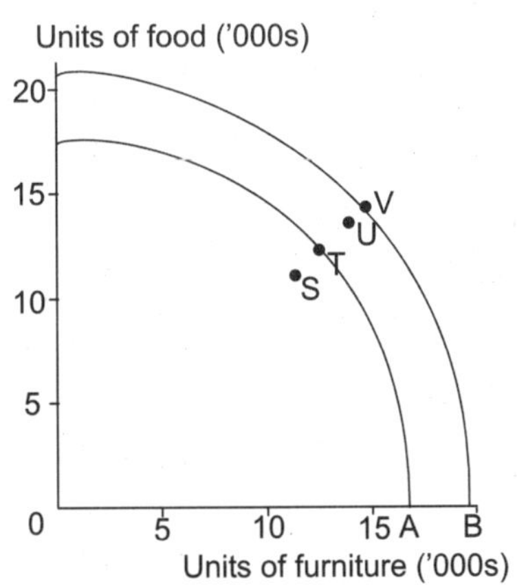


*Figure 5.3: Production possibilities*

Sustainable output is the level of output corresponding to stable inflation. The difference between the actual growth of the Gross Domestic Product (GDP) and its sustainable or trend growth line is called the **output gap** in the economy. For the UK this trend growth rate is about 2.5%. In the short-term the economy can grow faster than this, thus opening up a negative output gap, but this will lead to rising inflation. Policy makers therefore try to raise the trend growth rate, thus increasing the rate at which the economy can grow without raising the inflation rate.

### Measuring trends

The Monetary Policy Committee considers a range of surveys provided by business organisations such as the Confederation of British Industry (CBI) and the British Chambers of Commerce (BCC). These surveys can provide additional indications of business trends and conditions. As a way of measuring the output gap, the **CBI Industrial Trends Survey** asks manufacturing firms how optimistic they are. The balance of responses from firms saying they are 'more' or 'less' optimistic about the future than previously has tended to have a fairly good relationship in the past with the annual growth of GDP.

A typical survey will ask companies or individuals a range of questions relating to current economic and business conditions – for example, questions on a firm's output, orders, employment and prices – or about confidence in the future in a more general sense. Responses are often in the form of whether something like output or prices is higher or lower than at the time of the previous survey. For example, a firm might be asked 'compared with the situation three months ago, are the prices you charge higher, lower or about the same?' We are interested in how these responses alter over time, ie, how the total number of firms responding 'higher', 'lower' or 'same' is changing. For example, if a larger number of firms report that output is now higher than at the time of the previous survey, this might be a sign that the growth in output is increasing.

Survey responses may also provide forward-looking information. For example, answers to questions about order books may tell us something about future output, and responses about investment intentions may tell us about future investment spending. Similarly, firms' expectations of prices, employment and output in the near future can be a useful indication of short-term prospects.

Unfortunately, survey evidence tends to focus on specific sectors that might or might not be indicative of the capacity position of the economy as a whole. It could be that firms in one sector of the economy are working above normal capacity eg, by working overtime, while firms in another sector might have plenty of spare capacity to continue expansion.

### How can governments raise the level of national income?

They can do it by raising the level of aggregate demand.

The most obvious way of doing so using fiscal policy is to increase government expenditure, which has a direct effect.

The other aspect of fiscal policy is taxation, with tax cuts being the appropriate response to deflationary conditions. A cut in income tax, for instance, would leave individuals with more disposable income to spend on consumption goods, tending to cause the demand for goods and services to rise. A cut in corporation tax would give companies higher post-tax profits, which they could either retain for investment or pay out as increased dividends to shareholders (giving them higher disposable incomes and leading, as with income tax, to higher demand for goods).

The government sometimes likes to limit the amount of money that people spend, to ensure economic growth without doing too much too quickly. This is known as demand management. In the formula $E = C + I + G + (X - M)$ described above, this involves the manipulation of E (ie, achieving economic growth) by influencing C, I, G or net imports/exports. People's consumption can be limited by taking more in taxation.

Other measures to encourage investment include:

(a) Lower interest rates

(b) **Tax incentives** such as capital allowances for firms

(c) Improved **access to capital** such as loan guarantees or new forms of raising share capital

(d) Encourage a **higher savings ratio,** and more savings through the stock market. The UK savings ratio since the war has tended to be relatively low by international standards; this puts a limit on the level of investment that can be financed through the capital markets.

(e) Help for small firms

(f) **Improvements to the labour force** – addressing the skills gap. Most educational experts agree that the main gap in the UK is at technician grade – our numeracy and literacy levels at sixteen tend to be below comparable economies. Government can allocate money to education according to normal investment criteria ie where it produces the highest rate of return. This tends to be in part-time (vocational) courses.

Government policy and laws can have a direct influence on the total volume of market demand and hence the total demand for the products of individual firms and industries. For example, the tax differentials on lead-free petrol have increased demand for lead-free petrol as a whole and reduced demand for leaded petrol.

Policies can also encourage firms to increase the amount of goods they are able to produce ie, by increasing their output capacity.

**Definition**

**Capacity**: the maximum amount of goods a firm can make. A bakery whose ovens are big enough to bake 3,000 loaves a day would have a daily output capacity of 3,000 loaves. A firm (or industry) with overcapacity is able to produce more than it actually needs to satisfy customers. A firm that is operating at less than full capacity is producing less than it can. If there is undercapacity in a firm or industry then the firm or industry is unable to produce enough to meet the demand.

The range of policies available include the following.

(a) The government might offer cash grants or tax incentives to firms to invest more money in new plant and equipment ('capital spending'). However:

  (i) Firms might invest too much in order to get the grant or incentives, with the result that over-capacity builds up in the industry

  (ii) Such incentives might discourage employment, by making it cheaper to buy labour-saving equipment than to hire workers

  (iii) If overseas governments offer investment support, foreign firms trading in the UK will have a possible advantage as they will be able to access this source, whereas locally based firms may not

(b) To avoid paying for imports, government might want to build up an industry based in the home country (eg by granting it all the government's purchase contracts). To achieve economies of scale, the home-based industry might require an output capacity that would force it to produce more than the domestic market could take, and to try to sell the excess output on world markets. This might result in a short-term over-capacity in world output. The less efficient or protected firms will eventually fail.

(c) Governments might be prepared to subsidise excess capacity in the interests of keeping people in work.

(d) Inward investment (ie investment in the UK by overseas firms) may be encouraged.

***A number of groups can influence government policy. We shall go on now to look at these***

## 4 INFLUENCES ON GOVERNMENT

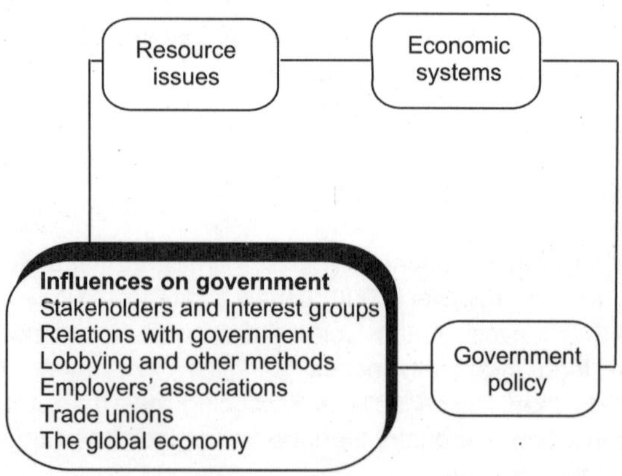


### 4.1 Stakeholder and interest groups

**Stakeholders**

We have already discussed the stakeholders of a firm – they include customers, employees, shareholders, suppliers, lenders and the local and national communities.

The supporters of a stakeholding economy argue that these interest groups ought to have a say in the decisions of the firm. **Trade unions or workers' councils** ought to be included in decisions affecting the workforce, or indeed all company decisions. They could be represented on decision-making bodies and perhaps have seats on the board of directors. Alternatively, the workforce might be given the power to elect managers.

**Banks or other institutions lending to firms** ought to be included in investment decisions. In Germany, where banks finance a large proportion of investment, banks are represented on the boards of most large companies.

**Local communities** ought to have a say in any projects (such as new buildings or the discharge of effluent) that affect the local environment. **Customers** ought to have more say in the quality of products being produced: for example, by being given legal protection against the production of shoddy or unsafe goods. Where interest groups cannot be directly represented in decision-making, companies ought to be regulated by the **government** in order to protect the interests of the various groups. For example, if farmers and other suppliers to supermarkets are paid very low prices, then the purchasing behaviour of the supermarkets could be regulated by some government agency.

But is this vision of a stakeholder economy likely to become reality? Trends in the international economy suggest that the opposite might be occurring. The growth of multinational corporations, with their ability to move finance and production to wherever it is most profitable, has weakened the power of employees, local interest groups and even national governments.

**Employees** in one part of the multinational may have little in the way of common interests with employees in another. In fact, they may vie with each other: for example, over which plant should be expanded or closed down. What is more, many firms are employing a larger and larger proportion of casual, part-time, temporary or agency workers. With these new 'flexible labour markets', such employees have far less say in the company than permanent members of staff: they are 'outsiders' to decision-making within the firm.

Also, the widespread introduction of share incentive schemes for managers (whereby managers are rewarded with shares) has increasingly made profits their driving goal. Finally, the policies of opening up markets and deregulation – policies that have been adopted by many governments round the world in recent years – have again weakened the power of many stakeholders.

### Interest groups

#### Definitions

**Interest group** a group that represents the wider interests of a particular group of people such as a Trade Union.

**Pressure group** a collection of people promoting some particular course or objective. Examples are Greenpeace and Friends of the Earth.

A **pressure group** can be described as an organised group that does not put up candidates for election, but seeks to influence government policy or legislation. They can also be described as 'interest groups', 'lobby groups' or 'protest groups'. Some people avoid using the term 'pressure group' as it can inadvertently be interpreted as meaning the groups use actual pressure to achieve their aims, which does not necessarily happen. In Britain, the number of political parties is very small, whereas the number of pressure groups runs into thousands. As the membership of political parties has fallen, that of pressure groups has increased. The Royal Society of the Protection of Birds (RSPB), for instance, has more members than the Labour, Conservative and Liberal Democratic parties combined.

The term pressure group is a very wide definition that does not clearly distinguish between the groups that fall under the term. For example, a pressure group can be a huge organisation like the CBI (Confederation of British Industry), which represents 150,000 businesses, and it can also be a single-issue locally based organisation. The definition also does not distinguish between the more extreme pressure groups such as the Animal Liberation Front, whose campaigns include illegal activities such as planting bombs, and the pressure groups such as the Institute for Public Policy Research (IPPR), which has links to the Labour Government and regular contact with cabinet ministers.

The aim of all pressure groups is to influence the people who actually have the power to make decisions. Pressure groups do not look for the power of political office for themselves, but do seek to influence the decisions made by those who do hold this political power. Often pressure groups find themselves competing with rival pressure groups with the aim of gaining an advantage over them, but sometimes groups work together to achieve a common aim.

A pressure group can use a variety of different methods to influence law. First, it can merely inform legislators of its members' preferences. Second it may well give money or time to help with an election campaign. Third, its members may threaten, as a group, to vote as a bloc. By doing this they promise to help a co-operative legislator, and threaten to harm a non-co-operative legislator. Fourth, a pressure group may speed up legislation by writing bills and helping legislators make progressive agreements. Finally, a pressure group my attempt to influence members of the executive, who have some law making input and who can partly decide the strength and effectiveness of law enforcement.

The main associations reflecting economic interests are as follows.

(a) **Businesses**: Confederation of British Industry (CBI), Institute of Directors (IOD). There are also smaller more specific trade associations in particular industries, which group together to promote common interests (eg newspapers to oppose VAT on the press). There are many other organisations such as chambers of commerce and specialised areas such as the food and drink industry, chemicals, motor manufacturing and engineering.

**EXAMPLE: CBI**

An example of an interest group representing business is the Confederation of British Industry (CBI).

**Objectives** – to support and represent industrial and commercial organisations in the private sector.

**Activities and concerns**

- Government relations – Draft legislation; economic policy; and training and education
- Commercial opportunities – Exports; inward investment and regional development
- Inter-organisational relations – Professions; trade unions; local governments
- Public relations – Research; publications; and media appearances

(b) **Professional associations** are groups of people who do the same job or have the same skill, for example:

(i) Accountants (with several professional bodies)

(ii) Doctors (British Medical Association)

(iii) Professional associations are generally involved in setting standards of skill and enforcing adherence to good practice (eg through disciplinary schemes).

(c) **Trade unions** are similar to professional associations, in that they represent people who work. Their function is to negotiate terms and conditions of employment for their members. They are described in more detail later.

(d) **Consumers' associations** represent people as consumers, campaigning on issues such as product pricing, safety and quality. Consumers' associations have campaigned for labelling on food, for example.

**Activity 7** **(30 minutes)**

Under the procedures of the European Union, interest groups such as the CBI and the Trade Unions are recognised as 'social partners' in the process of creating economic policy and legislation. Does this idea accord with UK practice? Identify UK practices to support or contradict the assumption that social partnership has an economic function.

### 4.2 Relations with government

We can identify the general factors that determine the success of particular groups as far as the government is concerned:

(a) **The status they enjoy with the government** – this in turn is dependent on the compatibility between the objectives of the group and those of the government, and the dependency of the government on that particular group for such things as expertise and service delivery. Labour Governments have traditionally been sympathetic to the wishes of trades unions, (TUC) while Conservative Governments have been sympathetic to industry, (CBI). A distinction that is sometimes made is that of insider and outsider groups. Insider groups are those that have a privileged position in their dealings with the government and Whitehall departments. This came about usually because those groups were considered vital for the running of a particular service or because they offered specialised advice. The British Medical Association was traditionally regarded as playing this role. However, in the 1980s many of these insider groups lost a lot of their influence as first the Conservative party and later New Labour, gave up the policies of the post-war consensus and adopted a more free market approach to the economy and public services such as health and education. So the older groups such as the TUC, CBI, BMA, and local government associations have lost influence, while at the same time there has been a rise in the importance of local groups, such as educational campaigners.

(b) **The points of contact in the policy-making process** – traditionally this is what gave insider groups their influence, since they were involved at an early stage in policy formulation. These days there are few if any of these older styles of groups and therefore groups must make contact as they can. At one extreme there are those cases of outside interests having access to Cabinet ministers. Bernie Ecclestone had direct access to Tony Blair in 1997 over the ban on advertising in Formula One racing; such direct access is rare, but one link is through so-called 'political advisers', of which there has been an increase in numbers under the Labour Governments since its first election in 1997.

The role of interest and pressure groups is controversial. Some argue that their existence means that power is diffused widely and that they are an informal check on the ever-increasing power of the state. However, some interest groups representing business may be more influential than others and this can be anti-democratic. For example, some supporters of rail transport believe that the 'road lobby' has undue influence on UK transport policy.

### 4.3 Lobbying and other methods

**Definition**

**Lobbying**: a method used to influence political decision-making. It involves maintaining regular contact with ministers or members of parliament, to put forward a case.

The UK government has itself issued details on how to influence government bodies – in this case the EU processes of the European Commission, but it applies at national level too.

It is much better to influence the drafting process of new regulations than to try and get them changed once they have been implemented.

**Step 1** **Get in early**. Make your views known at the drafting stage. Work with officials rather than ministers.

**Step 2** **Work with others**. 'A spread of opinion carries more weight than a lone voice.' UK businesses should thus work with European trade associations.

**Step 3** **Think 'politically'**. A firm's lobbying will be more effective if it can be demonstrated that the issue is relevant to government or EU policy (eg single market program).

**Step 4** **Be prepared**. Monitor what is going on, and the issues that are being dealt with by the Commission and Government.

**Step 5** **Think long-term**. A long-term presence (eg in Brussels) can be of immense benefit, given that the lobbying process can be a long-standing one.

Interest groups can use a number of techniques when dealing with their own national government.

(a) They can employ **lobbyists** to put their case to individual ministers or civil servants.

(b) Businesses can give MPs **non-executive directorships**, in the hope that the MP will take an interest in all legislation that affects them. This is now subject to Parliamentary rules. However, it should be noted that a business is just as entitled to approach its constituency MP as any other constituent is.

(c) They can sit on consultative committees.

(d) They can **donate money** to (or withdraw funds from) the political party they support. Companies spending such funds must report the amounts involved. Rules on donations are now stricter than ever to prevent allegations of bribery.

(e) Some businesses have considerable **influence/contact with government**, as they are involved in contracts directly with them, eg the defence industry.

The Department of Trade and Industry also recommends that having a long-term presence in Brussels to influence the European Commission can be of immense benefit, given that the lobbying process can be a long-standing one. Moreover, a business might be in a position to initiate the legislative process if it has unique information about a particular trading issue.

However, all businesses should be very careful when taking part in such activities – there are now strict boundaries imposed as a result of the various 'sleaze' allegations concerning MPs and others who were felt to be too highly influenced.

Some interest groups can act as both insiders and outsiders. When not walking up and down the corridors of power, members of an interest group can do the following to influence government policy.

(a) They can try to influence public opinion and the legislative agenda by **advertising**. The RSPCA advertised (unsuccessfully) for a dog registration scheme in the UK. This was more than just an appeal for donations. The advertising was specifically designed to change government policy.

(b) Few organisations can afford expensive press advertising. However, there are other ways of getting publicity.

   (i) **Demonstrations** get media publicity, and are a means by which sufficiently committed people can demonstrate support. Involvement by celebrities can also add to media interest.

   (ii) **Petitions** are a way of dramatising a problem.

   (iii) **Direct action,** as practised by Greenpeace against whalers, puts certain issues on the agenda.

   (iv) Effective **public relations** are important. An interest group might try to convince journalists or major newspapers, or indeed television producers, that its story is newsworthy.

These methods may or may not have a direct impact. If the action is public, ministers might not wish to be seen to 'lose face' by giving in. However, they can create a climate of opinion to which politicians can later respond. The adoption of environmental issues by politicians is the result of many years of campaigning by pressure groups.

**Activity 8** **(45 minutes)**

Find a recent press article that concerns pressure-group activity designed to make either the government or a business organisation change its policy. Précis the article, listing the main points made by the pressure group.

***We now discuss interest groups directly related to the business and the workplace.***

### 4.4 Employers' associations

**Definition**

**Employers' associations** have a role similar to that of trade unions, insofar as they protect and promote the interests of their members; however, their membership and aims are very different. They represent the employers (the 'management side' of the industry), they promote the interests of the industry as a whole and they protect their businesses in relation to the workforce.

Eligibility for membership depends on:

(a) Participating in the relevant industry
(b) Acceptance of the policy of the association
(c) The member having a 'reputable business'

Discipline over members is exercised by the threats of: exclusion from membership, loss of the member's share of the association's strike fund, and denial of other services.

Sometimes labour and trade matters are managed by two different associations.

(a) On labour matters, associations are organised by industry. These issues fall into two categories:

   (i) Collective bargaining, in which employers in an industry meet employees' representatives to hammer out pay, productivity and conditions agreements

   (ii) Assistance to individual firms on management/labour issues

(b) Their trade related activities include:

   (i) Representing employers' interests to government and the European Commission

   (ii) Collating and publishing information and statistics

   (iii) Providing joint training arrangements

   (iv) Engaging in joint research and development activities

   (v) Drawing up codes of conduct (eg to avoid regulation being imposed by the state)

As well as associations for particular industries there are wider bodies, such as the Confederation of British Industry, which exist to promote the aims of industry as a whole to government.

***Trade unions represent the other side of industry, although they have diminished in influence in recent years.***

## 4.5 Trade unions

**Definition**

> **Trade unions** are organised associations of working people in a trade, occupation or industry (or several trades or industries) formed for protection and promotion of their common interests, mainly the regulation and negotiation of pay and conditions.

There are four main types of trade union.

(a) **Craft or occupational unions**. Mainly catering for skilled workers, such as printers, engineers, building trade craftsmen, for example the Amalgamated Union of Engineering and Electronic Workers.

(b) **General workers' unions**. Mainly semi-skilled and unskilled workers across the full range of industry, for example the Transport and General Workers Union, which has about one million members.

(c) **Industrial unions**. Covering many of the workers of all grades and occupations within a single industry, for example the Rail and Maritime Transport and the National Union of Mineworkers.

(d) **White collar unions**. A growing sector of trade unionism covering technical, professional, supervisory and managerial staffs. Since 1945 white collar unions have been the main growth area in trade union membership. Trade union membership as a whole has been in severe decline since 1979.

### 4.6 The global economy

The world economy over the last three decades has seen an increasing concentration of economic production resulting from the formation of transnational corporations (TNCs) – multinational corporations (MNCs), which operate trans-nationally. It is now estimated that some 50% of world production (including exports, overseas production, home production and sales) is undertaken by TNCs.

**Definition**

> **Globalisation** is the process by which national economies become increasingly integrated, often as a result of power wielded by TNCs.

According to prophets of globalisation such as Japanese commentator *Kenichi Ohmae* TNCs have reached the status of 'stateless corporations'. They are able to move production round the globe, make mergers and acquisitions and foreign investments where they please and manage to pay few taxes. The combination of changes in communication and the inexorable rise of these corporations means that there are no effective controls on the movement of capital – there is a truly globalised economy.

**Comparison of the World's 25 Largest Corporations with the GDP of Selected Countries (2007)**

| Company/Country | Revenues/GDP ($ billions) |
|---|---|
| **Greece** | **360** |
| Wal-Mart Stores | 351 |
| Exxon Mobil | 347 |
| Royal Dutch Shell | 319 |
| **Denmark** | **308** |
| **South Africa** | **278** |
| BP | 274 |
| **Argentina** | **262** |
| General Motors | 207 |
| **Hong Kong** | **207** |
| Toyota Motor | 205 |
| Chevron | 201 |
| DaimlerChrysler | 190 |
| **Malaysia** | **181** |
| ConocoPhillips | 172 |
| Total | 168 |
| General Electric | 168 |

| **Nigeria** | **166** |
|---|---|
| Ford Motor | 160 |
| ING Group | 158 |
| Citigroup | 147 |
| **Pakistan** | **144** |
| AXA | 140 |
| Volkswagen | 132 |
| Sinopec | 132 |
| Crédit Agricole | 128 |
| **Egypt** | **128** |
| Allianz | 125 |
| Fortis | 121 |
| Bank of America Corp. | 117 |
| HSBC Holdings | 115 |
| American International Group | 113 |
| China National Petroleum | 111 |
| **Peru** | **109** |
| BNP Paribas | 109 |
| *Sources:* Fortune *magazine, July 23, 2007 & World Bank, 2007* | |

A new **international division of labour** has emerged, with workers in Asia producing components for computers assembled in Ireland and call centres in India answering the queries of banking customers in London. The TNCs are seen as an alternative institution to the nation state as organisers of production. The sheer size of their operation is increasing the weight of these corporations in relation to other institutions.

The number of these corporations has increased but so too has the concentration of assets. Seventy per cent of all foreign direct investment is made by the top 300 TNCs and 25% of all capital is held by them. The MNCs and the major financial institutions like pension funds and insurance companies have become more powerful than national governments. Their influence over economic and financial affairs is extremely limited as a result. The power of these corporations means that even rich nation states are unable to withstand the pressure. For instance, Canada's policy of allowing generic copies and encouraging the provision of cheap medical drugs fell victim to pressure from the pharmaceutical industry.

This extended global reach is not confined to trading. Global restructuring has occurred on a huge scale through acquisition and mergers and the increasing use of **joint ventures** (especially in the developing capitalist economies). The injection of capital investment can rejuvenate an area, and often spawns a multitude of connected industries.

**EXAMPLE**

The M4 corridor is one of globalisation's most successful ventures in Britain.

Governments vie with each other to attract foreign investment, in order to boost the economy on a local and national scale. Consequently, there is less unemployment and deprivation, and more TNCs may be encouraged to cluster round the area. This leads to regeneration, as component suppliers are established, and improvements in infrastructure are made. Production does not necessarily move to less developed countries. But increasingly it moves within the developing trade and investment blocs or between them.

---

**EXAMPLE**

Examples abound: Grand Metropolitan moved Green Giant food production from Canada to Mexico; Japanese and South Korean components' manufacture has moved to a low wage, subsidised, South Wales area in the UK.

---

Agencies such as the World Trade Organisation, World Bank, and the International Monetary Fund, bolstered by agreements like NAFTA and GATT are putting more and more power into the hands of TNCs by putting the squeeze on national governments. The primary mechanism of control is debt. For decades, developing countries have depended on foreign loans, resulting in increasing vulnerability to the transnational corporate strategy for the global economy. Access to international credit and aid is given only if governments agree to certain conditions known as 'structural adjustment'.

In a nutshell, structural adjustment requires cuts in social services, privatisation of state-run industry, repeal of agreements with labour about working conditions and minimum wage, conversion of multi-use farm lands in cash crop agriculture for export, and the dismantling of trade laws which protect local economies. Under structural adjustment, police and military expenditures are the only government spending that is encouraged.

Recent protests against the IMF and the World Bank have put the spotlight on the way the institutions put the interests of wealthy corporations in the developed world above the interests of the planet's poor majority.

---

**FOR DISCUSSION**

'A global economy is emerging' claim those who depict a world in which multinational trade, production, investment, and financing moves in and out of countries ever more easily.

---

The 'globalists' tell us that as a result, governments and states are losing their capacity to control economic interactions. This is partly because the quantity and rapidity of flows make it more difficult for governments to regulate trade, investment or capital. Equally important is the fact that firms and investors can more easily take their business elsewhere puts new constraints on governments trying to retain and encourage investment. The argument here is that TNCs will simply exit from a country if a government does not pursue liberalising policies that foster corporate profitability and flexibility. For this reason, governments are under pressure to reduce taxes and to cut back state expenditure on health, education, pensions and so forth.

## Chapter roundup

- In a mixed economy, total economic activity is managed by both the private and public sectors.
- The state has grown in size and function in this century. The state contains a variety of institutions serving a number of purposes. The relationships between the state and other areas of the public sector are characterised by varying degrees of regulation and control.
- Politics influences decision-making processes in the public sector.
- Government influences business indirectly through its general conduct of economic policy affecting investment and demand, and directly through company law, corporation tax and other regulations.
- The government can also be a major buyer from, or supplier to, particular industries.
- Interest and pressure groups use direct and indirect means to influence government.

## Quick quiz

1 List three different types of economy.

2 What are the policy tools used by the state to regulate the economy?

3 What are stakeholders?

4 What is meant by policy?

5 Who directs government policy in the UK?

6 List some sources of advice for government.

7 What do interest groups do to influence legislation?

8 List some ways in which government could promote or hamper the growth of new industries.

9 List the two types of relationship a pressure group can have with government.

10 How can business influence government?

11 Give some examples of bodies that represent employers.

12 Give some examples of bodies that represent employees.

## Answers to quick quiz

1 Free enterprise economy, command economy, mixed economy

2 Fiscal policy and monetary policy.

3 Stakeholders are people whose interests are affected by the activities of a firm.

4 Policy is a way of expressing the broad purposes of government activity.

5 Political parties.

6 The Civil Service, 'Think Tanks', academics, Royal Commissions etc.

7 They can lobby, sit on committees, donate money, influence public opinion, take direct action.

8 Restrain growth, place restrictions on import tariffs, subsidise domestic firms, impose standards.

9 They can be 'insiders' or 'outsiders'.

10 Lobbying, representing members of employers' associations, joining committees, non-executive directorships.

11 CBI, Institute of Personnel Development, industry-wide associations.

12 Trade Unions, Staff Associations, TUC, Professional Bodies.

## Answers to activities

1 (a)

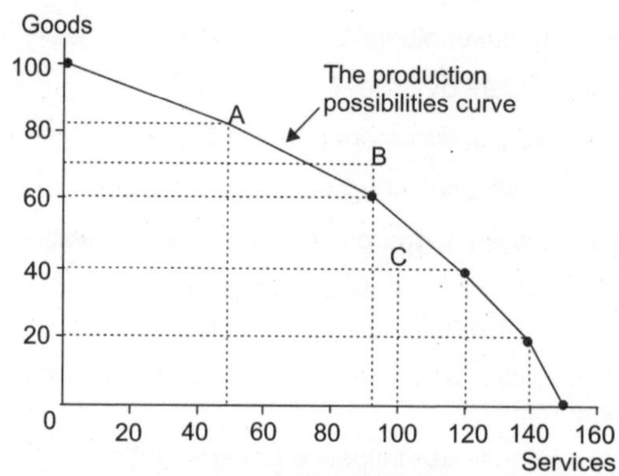


(b) (i) 80 units of goods and 50 units of services – Yes (point A)
(ii) 70 units of goods and 90 units of services – No (point B)
(iii) 40 units of goods and 100 units of services – Yes (point C)

(c) (i) producing 60 units of goods allows 80 units of services

producing 80 units of goods allows 50 units of services

The opportunity cost of producing an extra 20 = 40 units of services

(ii) producing 20 units of goods allows 140 units of services

producing 40 units of goods allows 120 units of services

The opportunity cost of producing an extra 20 = 20 units of services

2 B less than full employment output.

3 Economics as a subject is primarily concerned with choice: choosing how resources are allocated at a personal or corporate level and in relation to society generally. Resources on the whole are scarce, but demand for resources is infinite, thus if individuals and/or governments choose to consume or produce additional units of a good or service, it will probably be necessary to reduce the consumption or production of others. Thus the cost of increasing consumption must be the forgone consumption of other products. At a social level, the cost of enhanced resources devoted to strengthening the army might be a reduction in the school building programme. The economist's term for expressing costs in terms of foregone alternatives is opportunity cost.

The concept of opportunity cost has a widespread application throughout micro and macroeconomic theory. As far as macroeconomic theory is concerned, reference has already been made to the cost of specific aspects of government expenditure but a distinction needs to be made between capital and current opportunity cost. What the cost will be depends very much on what resources the government project uses and from where they are drawn. If they are away from the production of consumer goods and services, the opportunity cost is necessarily borne by the present generation in terms of reduced consumption of goods produced by the private sector. In so far as they are obtained by reducing the production of capital goods the opportunity cost will affect not only present but also future generations.

At a micro level it is usually believed that the current cost of using a factor of production owned by a company is related to the price that was paid when the factor was originally purchased, ie, historical costs are paramount in this calculation. However, this is not the case. A company deciding what course of action to pursue at a moment in time must consider the relevance of costs associated with the alternative courses of action – bygones are bygones and should have no influence on present and future decisions. Thus the cost of using various factors of production should be measured in terms of the value of output they would have produced if such factors had been used in alternative ways. Again the concept of opportunity cost is the most relevant in these circumstances.

It is clear that opportunity cost is of considerable importance throughout the whole of economic theory in relation to the decision-making of consumers, enterprises and government.

4 If markets can 'fail' so can central planning. Major problems with the centrally planned economies of Eastern Europe have recently led to a decisive move away from total state control of the economy. Some of the more obvious problems include:

(a) Shortages – where the price mechanism is not used to allocate goods, supply and demand cannot easily be brought into balance. Deliberate under-pricing of consumer goods (to suppress inflation) leads to shortages and queues and to black markets where goods are (illegally) sold at high but market-clearing prices.

(b) Informational problems – the information necessary for central planners to make optimal decisions is beyond the ability of any organisation to process and understand. In any case, enterprise managers have an incentive to suppress information when it is to their advantage. (For example, under-reporting plant capacity means factories are set easier targets to achieve.)

(c) Lack of appropriate incentives – there is no simple relationship between effort and economic reward in many centrally planned economies, where political status may be a more important influence on the living standards of individuals. Ordinary workers, even those with quite high incomes, have been denied access to many goods reserved for the political elite. Even where there exist economic incentives for effort, they may not be appropriate to the economy's needs. For instance, reliance on physical targets (so many shoes, so many tons of steel) may mean workers and managers are rewarded for quantity irrespective of quality.

(d) Inefficient use of resources – because wages and the cost of capital equipment do not reflect supply and demand considerations, and because prices of output do not reflect costs of production, managers have little incentive to use resources efficiently. This often results in overstaffing of factories, shops and service industries and the under-utilisation of valuable machinery and plant.

(e) Limitations on personal freedom – control over resource allocation implies controls over employment, and free movement between jobs and between areas is often tightly controlled.

5 'Fiscal policy' means:

C the adjustment of public expenditure and taxation so as to affect aggregate demand

6 (a) **Mrs A – £30,000**

Method (i) £30,000 – 20% = £24,000 net
Method (ii) £30,000 – £5,000 allowance = £25,000 taxable.

£25,000 – 25% =£18,750

£18,750 + £5,000 = £23,750 net

**Mr B – £10,000**

Method (i) £10,000 – 20% = £8,000 net
Method (ii) £10,000 – £5,000 allowance = £5,000 taxable.

£5,000 – 25% = £3,750

£3,750 + £5,000 = £8,750 net

(b) Method (i) would be best for ensuring maximum expenditure on luxury items.

(c) Method (ii) would be best for safeguarding the net income of people on low earnings.

7 Many multinational companies have complied with the EU's Works Council Directive to provide for consultation with employees – but the argument and debate continues as to whether there are 'social partners' in the economy. Read the business press to follow the debate between the British Government, industrial organisations such as the CBI, TUC etc and the European Commission's proposal for social and employment legislation about minimum standards and consultative processes in the workplace.

8 You might have found an article on any of the following (or on another issue):

- Animal Aid and the National Anti-Vivisection Society (NAVS) have launched a High Court challenge to the decision by First Secretary of State John Prescott to allow a massive primate research laboratory to be built in the Cambridgeshire green belt. The appeal describes Prescott's decision as perverse, unreasonable and unfair.

- Campaigners who are urging people to put pressure on the government to banish GM crops from the whole of Britain. Friends of the Earth are arguing that genetic engineering is imprecise and unpredictable. But most testing is carried out by the very biotech companies that have the most to gain from results that say GM food is safe.

# Chapter 6:
# MARKET DEMAND

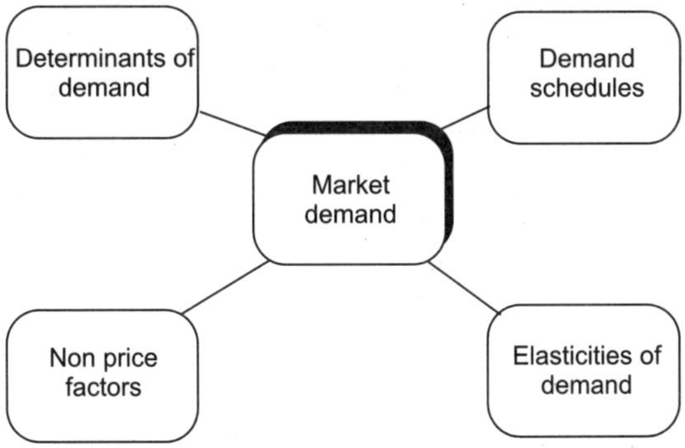


**Introduction**

Businesses cannot sell anything unless there is a demand for it. People must both want a product and have the money to buy it. How much people will buy depends on several things, not just the price. In this chapter we will see what affects the demand for goods and services.

**Your objectives**

In this chapter you will learn about:

(a) What determines demand

(b) Constructing a demand schedule

(c) The concept of price elasticity of demand

(d) Other measures of elasticity

## 1 DETERMINANTS OF DEMAND

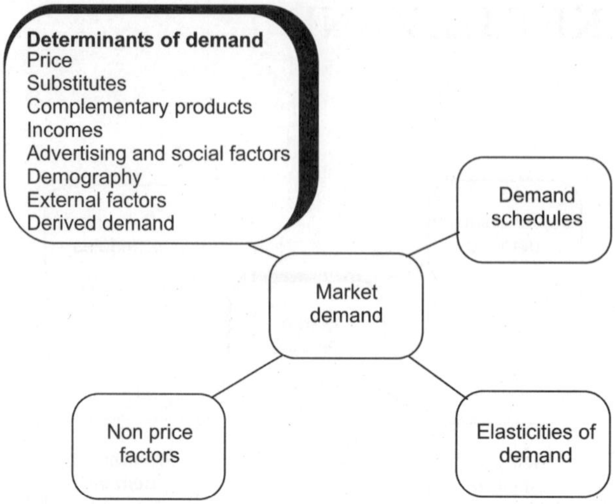


**Activity 1** **(10 minutes)**

What do you think determines the demand for lager?

You should have come up with several factors. All the following are likely to be relevant.

(a) The **price of lager**. The higher the price of lager, the less will be demanded.

(b) The **price of substitutes**. The prices of other beers, spirits and soft drinks will have a bearing on the demand for lager. For example, if the price of substitutes increases while the price of lager remains the same, then people will tend to switch to lager.

(c) The **price of complementary goods**. These are goods which go with lager. Thus a rise in the price of curry should reduce the demand for lager drunk with it.

(d) The **level of incomes**. If people earn more than they used to, then they will tend to buy more of most things, including lager.

(e) **Advertising and social factors**. If lager is heavily advertised, or if it becomes a fashionable drink, demand for it will rise. People who have not drunk lager before may try it and, possibly, like it. People who already drink lager may drink it on more occasions.

(f) **Demography**. If the population consists largely of people who are of the right age and lifestyle to go out to pubs for a drink, demand for lager is likely to be high.

(g) **External factors**. In hot weather, demand for lager is likely to increase.

***The conclusions reached above are a little simplistic. We will now analyse the factors affecting demand more closely.***

### 1.1 Price

It seems likely that as the price of something rises, the quantity demanded will fall. Eventually, it will become so expensive that no-one will buy any of it. However, it does not follow that as the price falls, more and more will be demanded with no upper limit. There are two reasons for this.

(a) People will only want a certain amount of anything. You cannot drink an infinite amount of lager, because you will first become ill and then become unconscious.

(b) Many people assume that price indicates quality. If lager is offered at 20p a pint, people may assume that it is of poor quality, and not buy it.

### 1.2 Substitutes

People may change from one product to another, as the relative prices change, but they may not. Some people simply like lager, and will not change to bitter just because it becomes relatively cheap.

### 1.3 Complementary products

It could be suggested (rather facetiously) that if the price of curries rises, the demand for lager would fall. However, this might not happen. People might choose to eat cheaper bar snacks in pubs instead of curries, and they might then drink as much lager as before. They might even drink more, because they would be spending less on food than before.

### 1.4 Incomes

If someone's income rises, their spending will also rise. Economists identify two important factors in relation to increases in income: the propensity to consume and the propensity to save. These are given numerical values by measuring the percentage of any extra income that is spent and the percentage that is saved. Looked at overall, these propensities differ over time and between nations. Germany and Japan, for example have higher propensities to save than does the USA. In the UK, the propensity to save seems to have fallen in times of economic boom and risen again in times of recession. This is quite reasonable, as booms usually depend on spending and recession causes people to spend less. As a lager drinker's income rises, his or her spending on lager is likely to rise at first. However, beyond a certain point their spending on lager may actually start to fall. This is because there may be enough money to change to more expensive drinks, such as fine wines. Thus we have the paradox of demand for a product going down in spite of increased buying power.

This effect can be seen in reverse, when incomes fall and demand for cheaper products increases. People cease to be able to afford expensive products and switch to cheaper ones.

### 1.5 Advertising and social factors

Advertising and other sales promotional activities can greatly affect the level of demand. However, if a brewer runs a successful advertising campaign for lager, we should not automatically conclude that overall consumption of lager has risen. The campaign may simply have persuaded people to switch from other brands of lager to that brewer's brand.

Fashion can certainly affect the demand for products. It is closely linked with advertising: many advertisements deliberately suggest that in order to be fashionable, you need to buy the advertised product.

### 1.6 Demography

Lager is often seen as a drink for younger people. One might therefore expect that as the population ages, with fewer younger people because people were not having many babies twenty years earlier, demand for lager would fall. However, this might not happen. Current lager drinkers could continue to drink lager as they age, so that demand does not fall.

### 1.7 External factors

Demand for lager is likely to increase during a spell of hot weather. However, alcohol affects people more quickly when they are dehydrated, so if it is very hot demand for lager might fall.

### 1.8 Derived demand

Some items are not demanded for their own sake, but because of a demand for something else. For example, the demand for farming land is derived from the demand for food which will grow on the land.

**Activity 2** **(5 minutes)**

Consider mountain bikes and suggest how demography and social factors may affect demand for them.

***It is very important to be able to map out and understand how demand works, as we will later see how demand interacts with supply to determine whether price information demand is represented in demand schedules.***

## 2 DEMAND SCHEDULES

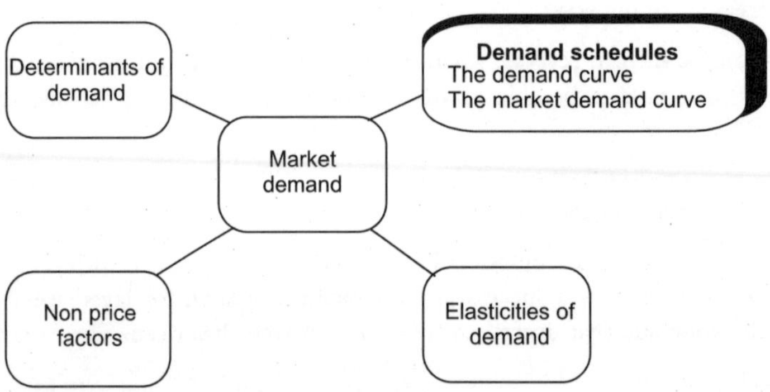

## 2.1 The demand curve

As we have seen, if the price of something goes up the quantity demanded is likely to go down. The relationship between the quantity demanded and the price is known as a demand schedule. It can be shown graphically as a demand 'curve'. The demand schedule for an individual is found by finding out how much of an item he or she would want to buy at various prices. Figure 6.1 is an example of a household's demand schedule for cheese and the corresponding demand curve. The curve has price on the vertical (y) axis and quantity on the horizontal (x) axis.

| *Price per kg* | *Quantity demanded each month* |
|---|---|
| £ | kg |
| 1 | 9.75 |
| 2 | 8 |
| 3 | 6.25 |
| 4 | 4.5 |
| 5 | 2.75 |
| 6 | 1 |

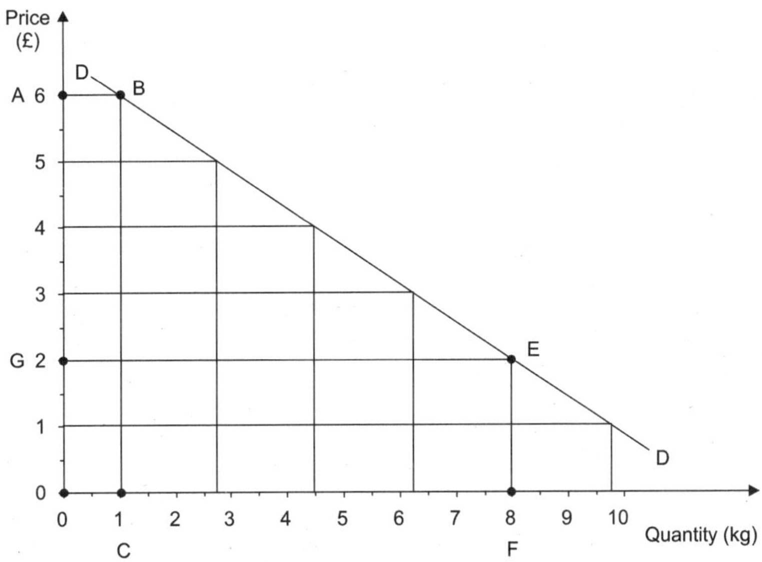


*Figure 6.1: The demand curve*

The extra horizontal and vertical lines are not necessary if we just want the demand curve. We have drawn them so as to see how much money in total would be spent on cheese each month at different price levels. For example, at a price of £6, demand would be 1 kg and total spending would be £6. This is represented by the area of the rectangle ABCO. Similarly, at a price of £2, demand would be 8 kg and the total spending of £16 is represented by the area of GEFO.

**Activity 3** **(10 minutes)**

Choose a product that you buy frequently and estimate how much you would buy at three different price levels.

***Although the demand schedule for one person or household may be interesting, a business needs to know how much will be demanded by the whole population: it needs to see the total market demand curve.***

### 2.2 The market demand curve

The market demand curve shows the total quantities of a product that all consumers would buy together at each price level. A market demand curve is therefore the sum of all individual demand curves.

As with the individual demand curve, the market demand curve generally slopes down from left to right, reflecting the fact that at lower prices more will be sold. This is for the following reasons.

(a) For the individual consumer, a fall in the price of an item makes it cheaper compared to other goods. The individual only has a limited amount of money to spend, so expenditure will be switched to the item whose price has fallen. It is the relative price of the item that is important: a fall in the relative price of an item increases demand for it.

(b) A fall in the item's price means that people with lower incomes will also be able to afford it. The overall size of the market for the item increases. The reverse applies so far as increases in prices are concerned. As the price goes up, consumers on low incomes will no longer be able to afford the item, and the size of the market will shrink.

**Activity 4** **(20 minutes)**

Repeat Activity 3, but compile demand schedules for five of your friends. Add up all their demands for the product at each price level to produce a demand schedule for the group as a whole. Plot your findings on a graph, to give the demand curve.

***A demand curve shows how the quantity demanded will change in response to a change in price provided that all other conditions affecting demand are unchanged. This means that there is no change in the prices of other goods, or consumers' tastes and expectations, or in the distribution of household income. This condition is known as*** **ceteris paribus** ***(Latin for 'all other things being equal'). We now look at what can happen to demand when things other than the price of the item we are interested in change, that is when all other things are not equal.***

# 3 NON-PRICE FACTORS

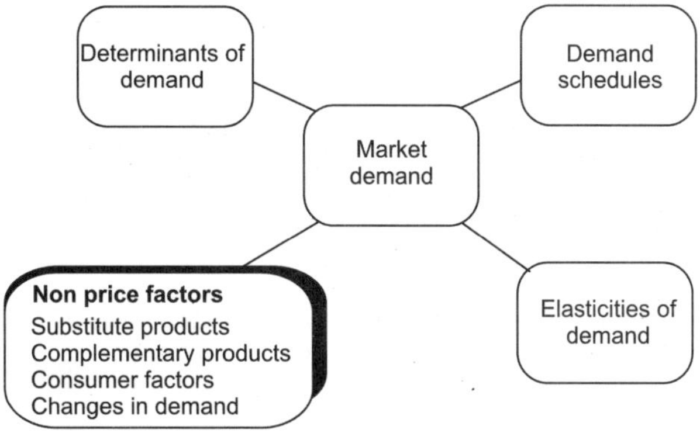


## 3.1 Substitute products

Most products have alternatives. These are known as substitute goods. Some are very close, for example tea and coffee, and some are not so close, such as a new car and a luxury holiday. Goods should be treated as substitutes if an increase in demand for one of them should result in a decrease in demand for the other.

Examples of substitute goods and services, to a greater or lesser extent, are:

(a) Rival brands of the same commodity, for example Coca-Cola and Pepsi-Cola
(b) Lager and bitter
(c) Rail travel and car travel
(d) Films and plays

**Activity 5** **(10 minutes)**

For someone who commutes from a suburban home to a city centre office each day, are rail travel and car travel close substitutes? Give reasons for your view.

***The next category is complementary products. When demand for a product goes up, demand for its substitutes goes down but demand for its complementary products goes up as well.***

## 3.2 Complementary products

These are goods that tend to be bought and used together. Thus a change in demand for one item should lead to a similar change in demand for the other related product.

Examples of complements are:

(a) Cups and saucers
(b) Bread and butter
(c) Motor cars and replacement exhausts

In the case of cups and saucers, the maker tends to supply both goods at the same time. With the other examples the link is less close. A supplier of replacement exhausts will have to monitor the quality of the original exhausts closely so as to forecast demand for replacements.

**Activity 6** **(10 minutes)**

If the ownership of domestic deep freezers increased, would this have any effect on the demand for perishable food products?

***We will now look at the effects on market demand that household income, fashion, consumer expectations and the distribution of incomes will have.***

### 3.3 Consumer factors

#### Household incomes

More income will give people more to spend, and they will want to buy more goods at existing prices. However, a rise in incomes will not increase market demand for all goods and services. The effect of a rise in income on demand for an individual product will depend on its nature.

Demand and the level of income may be related in different ways.

(a) A rise in income may increase demand for a good. This is what we would normally expect, and goods like this are called *normal goods*. For instance, a rise in income may increase demand for moderately priced wine.

(b) Demand may rise with income up to a certain point but then fall as income rises further. Goods whose demand eventually falls as income rises are called *inferior goods*. An example is cheap wine. The reason for falling demand is that as incomes rise, demand switches to superior products, for example better quality wines instead of cheap 'plonk'.

#### Fashion and consumer expectations

As already mentioned, a change in fashion will alter the demand for a product. For example, if it becomes fashionable for middle class households in the UK to drink wine with their meals, expenditure on wine will increase. There may be passing crazes, such as rollerblades or Power Rangers, and long-term trends, such as the move away from red meat for health reasons (even before the BSE scare).

If consumers believe that prices will rise, or that shortages will occur, they may try to stock up on the product, thereby creating excess demand in the short term which will increase prices. This can then lead to panic buying. Some years ago, a rumour was spread that the Siberian salt mines were closed. This caused panic buying of salt in the UK to the extent that most shops ran out of supplies, even though salt for the UK is supplied from enormous deposits in Cheshire and not from Siberia at all!

#### The distribution of incomes

Market demand for products is influenced by the way in which income is shared among households.

In a country with many rich and many poor households and few middle income ones, we might expect relatively high demand for luxury cars and yachts, and also for basic necessities such as bread and potatoes. In a country with many middle-income households, we might expect high demand for TV sets and medium-sized cars.

**Activity 7** **(15 minutes)**

A food supermarket chain known for its service, up-market goods and fairly high prices is looking to build a new store in the North East. They have narrowed down their choice of area to two sites and now have to make a decision. The sites are 75 miles apart and one of their criteria is distribution of income within a five-mile radius of the new store. Site A has many large, new executive housing estates within the area, but also many run down older areas with high unemployment. Site B has many well established private and council housing estates within the area. Unemployment is around average in this area.

(1) Where do you think the supermarket chain might choose to build a new store and why?

(2) Can you name one factor for and against each area?

***Finally in this section we look at how to show the effect of changes in demand, using the demand curve.***

## 3.4 Changes in demand

### Changes in price

If the price of a good goes up or down, given no changes in the other factors that affect demand, then there will be a change in the quantity demanded, shown as a movement along the demand curve (the demand curve itself does not move).

### Shifts of the demand curve

When there is a change in other factors that affect demand, the relationship between quantity demanded and price will also change, and there will be a different demand; schedule and so a different demand curve. For example, suppose that at current levels of income, the total UK demand for cheese at a price of £4 per kg is 150,000 tonnes. This will be a point on the demand curve. If incomes increase by 10%, the total demand at £4 per kg might rise to 160,000 tonnes. This will be a point on the new demand curve, which will be further to the right on a graph than the old curve.

We refer to such a change as change in demand, so as to distinguish it from a change in the quantity demanded. A change in demand involves a new demand curve. A change in quantity demanded, resulting from a price change, simply involves a movement along the old demand curve.

Figure 6.2 depicts a rise in demand at each price level, with the demand curve shifting to the right from $D_0$ to $D_1$. For example, at price $P_1$ , demand for the good would rise from X to Y. This shift could be caused by any of the following.

(a) A rise in household income

(b) A rise in the price of substitutes
(c) A fall in the price of complements
(d) A change in tastes towards this product
(e) An expected rise in the price of the product

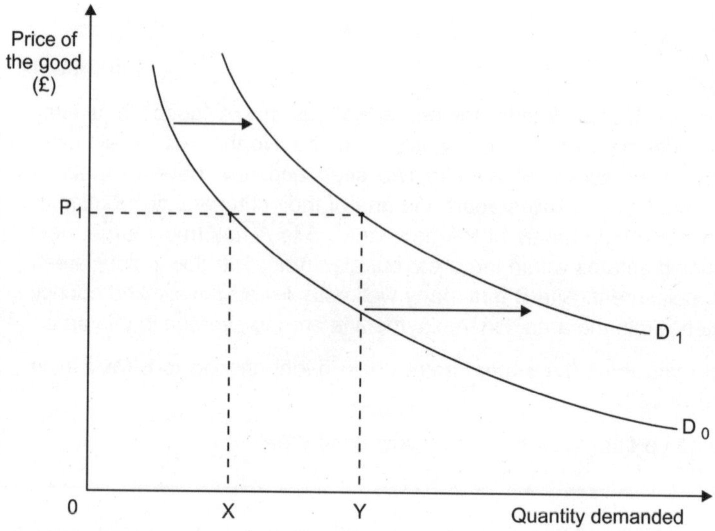


*Figure 6.2: Shift of the demand curve*

A fall in demand at each price level would lead to a shift of the demand curve in the opposite direction: towards the left of the graph. Such a shift could be caused by the reverse of the changes described in the previous paragraph.

**Activity 8** **(5 minutes)**

Can you think of three reasons why it is important for a company to know how demand for their products will be affected by income changes?

***We have looked at the factors affecting demand, but we have so far only discussed their effect in general terms. We will now see how to measure their effect.***

# 4 ELASTICITIES OF DEMAND

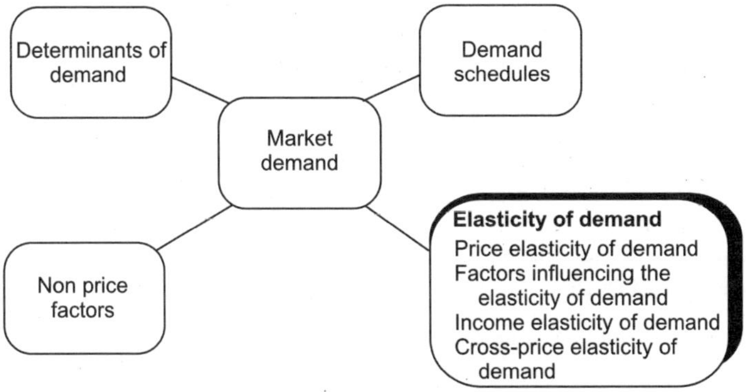


## 4.1 Price elasticity of demand

The price elasticity of demand measures how far the quantity demanded changes as the price changes. As explained later, the price elasticity of demand for a product is likely to be different at different prices.

The formula for the price elasticity of demand is as follows:

$$\frac{\text{Percentage change in the quantity demanded}}{\text{Percentage change in price}}$$

Because demand usually increases when the price falls and decreases when the price rises, price elasticity of demand normally has a negative value. However, it is usual to ignore the minus sign when looking at the price elasticity of demand.

Here are some examples.

(a) Price rises from £10 to £11, a 10% rise, and demand falls from 4,000 units to 3,200 units, a 20% fall: the elasticity is 20/10 = 2.

(b) Price rises from £15 to £18, a 20% rise, and demand falls from 1,000 units to 800 units, a 20% fall: the elasticity is 20/20 = 1.

**Activity 9** **(5 minutes)**

Price rises from £5 to £6.25, a 25% rise, and demand falls from 8,000 units to 7,000 units, a 12.5% fall. What is the price elasticity of demand?

Note the following points.

(a) A product is said to have an elastic demand if the elasticity is greater than 1. A small change in price (up or down) leads to a large change in quantity demanded.

(b) If the elasticity equals 1, then a given percentage change in price leads to an equal percentage change in demand: this is called unit elasticity.

(c) A product is said to have an inelastic demand if the elasticity is less than 1. A large change in price (up or down) leads to only a small change in quantity demanded.

### Why is price elasticity of demand important?

The price elasticity of demand is important when working out how much to charge for a product. If a company has a good idea of the price elasticity of demand for its products, that can help it to make sensible decisions on prices.

If demand is inelastic, then a company should seriously consider increasing the price, because it will not lose many sales: in fact, its total revenue will go up, even though it is selling less than before and therefore incurring lower costs. If you go back to the last example, where a price rise from £5 to £6.25 caused a fall in quantity from 8,000 units to 7,000 units, total revenue was 8,000 × £5 = £40,000 at a price of £5 and 7,000 × £6.25 = £43,750 at a price of £6.25.

Conversely, if demand is elastic, then a price rise may not be a good idea, because sales will fall fast and total revenue will fall. (Total costs will fall as well if less is being made, so a price rise might not be a disaster.) A price cut may be a good idea, because it will lead to a lot of extra sales, but of course costs will rise as well.

To find the elasticity of demand, a company may conduct market research to find out how much of a product people would buy at different prices.

**Activity 10** **(20 minutes)**

The elasticity of demand generally changes as the price changes. Here is the demand schedule from section 2.1 with the elasticity of demand worked out for the first price. Work out the elasticity of demand for the other prices and complete the table.

| *Price per kg* | *Quantity demanded each month* | *Price elasticity of demand* |
|---|---|---|
| £ | kg | |
| 1 | 9.75 | |
| 2 | 8 | 0.158 |
| 3 | 6.25 | |
| 4 | 4.5 | |
| 5 | 2.75 | |
| 6 | 1 | |

***We now need to analyse what factors are at play in determining how elastic demand for a product is.***

### 4.2 Factors influencing the elasticity of demand

The elasticity of demand for any product depends mainly upon the availability of substitutes. If close substitutes are readily available then demand will be elastic: a small increase in price will cause many consumers to switch to the close substitutes, resulting in a fall in demand. If the price of canned spaghetti increases then people may switch to a close substitute – baked beans. If there are no close substitutes demand will be less elastic, because consumers will find it harder to switch to another product. If the price of milk goes up, people are likely to go on buying it in much the same quantities as before, because the closest substitutes (such as orange juice) are not really that similar.

**Activity 11** **(10 minutes)**

Do you think that demand for each of the following products is price elastic or inelastic: tick the appropriate box?

| | *Price elastic* | *Price inelastic* |
|---|---|---|
| Petrol | ☐ | ☐ |
| Commuter rail tickets | ☐ | ☐ |
| Holidays in Spain | ☐ | ☐ |
| Mars bars | ☐ | ☐ |

***We have looked at the price elasticity of demand, making the assumption that other factors remain unchanged. We will now see how to measure the effect on demand of a change in incomes.***

### 4.3 Income elasticity of demand

The responsiveness of demand to changes in household incomes is known as the **income elasticity of demand**. The formula for the income elasticity of demand for any one product is as follows.

$$\frac{\text{Percentage change in the amount demanded}}{\text{Percentage change in income}}$$

The income elasticity of demand may be positive, zero or negative.

(a) Demand for a good is **income elastic** if income elasticity is greater than 1 so that quantity demanded rises by a larger percentage than the rise in income. For example, if the demand for compact discs will rise by 10% if household incomes rises by 7%, we would say that the demand for compact discs is income elastic.

(b) Demand for a good is **income inelastic** if income elasticity is between 0 and 1 and the quantity demanded rises less than the proportionate increases in income. For example, if the demand for books will rise by 6% if household income rises by 10%, we would say that the demand for books is income inelastic.

(c) If the income elasticity is negative, then as people's incomes rise, they buy less of the product. This could happen if people switch to more expensive products. For example, as incomes rise people might switch from lager to wine: the income elasticity of demand for lager would then be negative.

Goods whose demand is positively income elastic or income inelastic are said to be **normal goods**, which means that demand for them will rise when household income rises. If income elasticity is negative, the commodity is said to be an inferior good since demand for it falls as income rises.

**Activity 12** **(20 minutes)**

Complete the table to show the income elasticity for each product.

| | Positive elasticity | Zero elasticity | Negative elasticity |
|---|---|---|---|
| White bread | ☐ | ☐ | ☐ |
| Croissants | ☐ | ☐ | ☐ |
| Salt | ☐ | ☐ | ☐ |
| Bars of chocolate | ☐ | ☐ | ☐ |
| Boxes of Belgian chocolates | ☐ | ☐ | ☐ |

***We have seen that both prices and incomes may cause people to switch from one product to another. We will now look at the relationship between the demand for one product and the price of another.***

## 4.4 Cross-price elasticity of demand

The way in which the price of one product affects demand for another is measured by the *cross-price elasticity of demand*. The formula is as follows.

$$\frac{\text{Percentage change in the demand for product X}}{\text{Percentage change in the price of product Y}}$$

The result may be positive, zero or negative.

(a) If it is positive, then X and Y are substitutes, like butter (X) and margarine (Y). If the price of margarine goes up, the demand for butter will rise because some people will switch from margarine to butter. A margarine maker would have to consider the sales he would lose in consequence before going ahead with a price rise.

(b) If it is zero, then the products are unrelated. For example, a change in the price of newspapers (Y) is unlikely to affect the demand for holidays (X).

(c) If it is negative, then the goods are **complements**, like tyres (X) and petrol (Y). If the price of petrol goes up, then people will drive less. This means that they will not have to replace their tyres so often, so the demand for tyres will fall.

## Chapter roundup

- There are several factors that determine demand. These are price; the price of substitutes and complementary products; the level of household incomes; advertising and social factors; demography; and external factors.
- A demand schedule shows the quantity demanded of a product at each price level. The figures can be plotted on a graph, to give a demand curve.
- The market demand curve is found by adding up the demand curves of individual consumers.
- Shifts in the demand curve can be caused by many non-price factors.
- The responsiveness of the quantity of a product demanded to changes in its price is measured by the price elasticity of demand.
- The effect of changes in consumers' incomes on demand is measured by the income elasticity of demand.
- Demand for a product is affected by changes in the prices of related products. This is measured by the cross-price elasticity of demand.

## Quick quiz

1. Why might the quantity demanded of a good fall as its price falls?
2. What are complementary products?
3. What is a demand schedule?
4. What is shown by a demand curve?
5. Which way does a demand curve normally slope? Why?
6. What does *ceteris paribus* mean?
7. Give some examples of substitute products.
8. How do substitute products differ from complementary products?
9. What are the social factors affecting demand?
10. How will a change in quantity demanded as a result of a price change be shown on the demand curve?
11. How will a change in demand, due to something other than a change in the price of the product concerned, be shown on the demand curve?
12. What is the formula for the price elasticity of demand?
13. Why might a company want to know the price elasticity of demand for one of its products?
14. What is the formula for the income elasticity of demand?
15. If the cross-price elasticity of demand for a product measured against another product were negative, what would that tell you about the two products?

## Answers to quick quiz

1 People only want a certain amount of anything; price indicates quality.

2 Products bought and used together.

3 The relationship between quantity demanded and price.

4 The demand schedule.

5 Downwards from left to right because the lower the price, the more will be demanded.

6 All other things being equal.

7 Lager and bitter; films and plays.

8 Complementary tend to be bought and used together; substitute goods are alternatives.

9 Household incomes; fashion and consumer expectations; distribution of income.

10 Move of quantity demanded along demand curve.

11 New demand curve.

12 $$\frac{\text{Percentage change in quantity demanded}}{\text{Percentage change in price}}$$

13 To know how much to charge for a product.

14 $$\frac{\text{Percentage change in amount demanded}}{\text{Percentage change in income}}$$

15 They are unrelated.

## Answers to activities

1 The answer is given in the text following the activity.

2 As the population ages it is likely that demand will fall, but as the present fashion is for health and fitness, it may be that demand will remain fairly static but with ageing customers.

3 The answer will depend on the product you have chosen and your own tastes and income.

4 Again, the answer will depend on the product and on the individuals' tastes and incomes. Did you find that everyone had a similar demand schedule? Were there any cases of demand going up as the price fell?

5 On the face of it the two products should be closely related. They both satisfy the same need, to get the commuter to and from work. There are, however, some big differences. Driving into a city and finding somewhere to park is difficult and stressful. On the other hand, trains only run at set times, which may not be convenient for the commuter. A commuter may not be able to afford the capital outlay for a car at all.

6 Domestic deep freezers and perishable food are complements, because people buy deep freezers to store perishable food. Perishable food may be supplied fresh or ready frozen. If more people have freezers, the demand for frozen produce will rise. The demand for fresh food may fall, but on the other hand it might keep up because people may buy fresh food and freeze it.

7 You may have chosen site A but B is equally possible. They may choose site B. At site B, people will have been in homes longer and may have more money to spend than those who have just taken out large mortgages. However, Site A has high income families but high unemployment in some parts. Site B may have middle income families but no pockets of high unemployment.

8 The company may wish to make substitutes, they know whether it is possible to put up prices without losing too many sales and they may decide to switch to other products.

9 12.5/25 = 0.5

10

| *Price per kg* | *Quantity demanded each month* | *Price elasticity of demand* |
|---|---|---|
| £ | kg | |
| 1 | 9.75 | 0.179 |
| 2 | 8 | 0.437 |
| 3 | 6.25 | 0.84 |
| 4 | 4.5 | 1.556 |
| 5 | 2.75 | 3.182 |
| 6 | 1 | 10.5 |

11 The demand for petrol is likely to be inelastic within a modest range of prices: people will not cut back on their motoring significantly just because petrol goes up by 5p a litre. However, if the price were to rise a lot, people might cut back significantly, and demand would then be elastic.

The demand for commuter rail tickets is likely to be inelastic in a city with serious traffic congestion: people have to get to work, and they will pay quite a lot more to do so rather than switch to driving to work. Where car journeys take less time, there may be more substitution and demand for rail tickets will be more elastic.

The demand for holidays in Spain is likely to be elastic: many people go there simply for a beach holiday with reliable sunshine, and will happily switch to Greece or some other country if Spain becomes relatively more expensive.

The demand for Mars bars might be elastic, because there are many alternative chocolate bars which people could switch to. On the other hand, they might stick with Mars bars, because they have been made highly aware of the brand by advertising and because the cost of buying them is only a very small part of income.

12 White bread: negative, because as incomes rise people will switch to more expensive alternatives.

Croissants: positive, because people will only switch to them as incomes rise.

Salt: zero, because income levels are not likely to have much effect on consumption.

Bars of chocolate: as incomes rise, positive at first, because people feel able to indulge in chocolate more often; then negative, as people feel able to afford 'luxury' chocolates.

Boxes of Belgian chocolates: positive, because people will only switch to them as their incomes rise.

# Chapter 7:
# MARKET SUPPLY AND PRICE

## Introduction

In the last chapter we looked in detail at demand – what the customer is willing to buy. In this chapter we will look at supply – what businesses are willing to sell. We will go on to see how supply and demand fit together to establish the market price. We will also consider how to decide what price to charge for a product.

## Your objectives

In this chapter you will learn about:

(a) The factors that affect market supply

(b) How to assess the impact of changes in supply

(c) The interaction between supply and demand

(d) Other considerations which affect pricing

# 1 MARKET SUPPLY

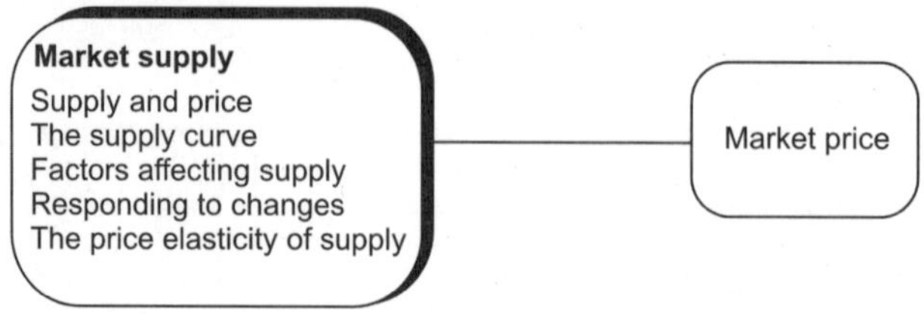


## 1.1 Supply and price

**Definition**

> **Supply** is the quantity of a product that existing or would-be suppliers would want to produce at a given price. As with demand, supply is measured per time period – for example 17,000 kg of cheese a week, or 50,000 tonnes of coal a year.

As you would expect, supply depends largely on price. The higher the price that a product can be sold for, the more of it businesses will be willing to supply. The quantity of the product on offer may change because existing businesses choose to increase production as the selling price rises, or because new businesses are attracted into the market by the prospect of good profits. Conversely, if the price falls, some businesses will reduce their production and others will go out of business altogether (voluntarily or because they have gone bust).

Although a high price will attract producers, it will put consumers off. Thus a high price may result in over-supply, which means that more is being produced than consumers want. One possible result is a price war, with each producer cutting his price in the hope of attracting enough consumers. In the very short term, one producer (probably the first one to reduce the price) may benefit, but other producers will follow suit in order to win back some customers. The result is that all producers will suffer. In the long-term, some producers may choose to withdraw, reducing supply and solving the problem, but before that happens some producers may run out of cash to pay their bills and be forced into liquidation. This is what happened in the package holiday business when Intasun, one of the three largest tour operators, went out of business.

> **Activity 1** **(20 minutes)**
>
> The retail grocery industry suffers from some over-supply. The major supermarkets have specifically avoided using price as a weapon to beat their competitors in the fight for customers. How have they avoided this? What would happen if they decided to compete aggressively on price?

As with demand, we must distinguish between the total market supply and the individual business' supply.

(a) The total market supply is the total quantity that all firms in the market would want to supply at a given price.

(b) An individual business's supply is the quantity which that business would want to supply to the market at a given price.

We will sometimes find a business charging prices which are higher than those charged by other businesses in the same market, that is non-market prices. There may be many reasons why this is so. Here are two.

(a) Individual businesses may be able to use marketing, and particularly brand names, to ensure that even if they charge high prices, they can still get customers. Thus for example, Marks & Spencer can charge more than the major supermarkets for many foods, because people associate the St Michael brand with high quality.

(b) Reciprocal buying may occur, in order to maintain good business links. For example a manufacturer of computer chips may buy computers from important customers even if there are cheaper alternatives available elsewhere. Reciprocal buying may also take place between members of the same group of companies.

### 1.2 The supply curve

We can draw up a supply schedule and supply curve:

(a) For an individual supplier, or
(b) For all suppliers together

A supply curve is constructed in the same way as a demand curve (from a schedule of quantities supplied at different prices), but it shows the quantity suppliers are willing to produce at each price. It slopes upwards from left to right, because greater quantities will be produced at higher prices.

Suppose, for example, that the supply schedule for television sets of a given type is as follows.

| *Price per unit* | *Quantity that suppliers would supply at this price* |
|---|---|
| £ | Units |
| 100 | 10,000 |
| 150 | 20,000 |
| 300 | 30,000 |
| 500 | 40,000 |

The relationship between output and price is shown as a supply curve in Figure 7.1.

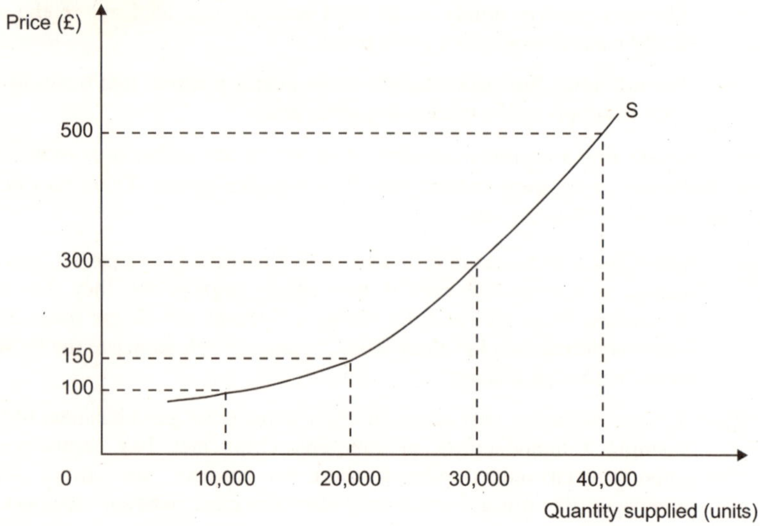


*Figure 7.1: A supply curve*

***In the next section we look at the main factors that affect supply. Some of these are similar to those that affect demand.***

### 1.3 Factors affecting supply

The quantity supplied of a good depends both on the market selling price and on the supplier's costs. There are five main factors as follows.

(a) The **price** obtainable for the product.

(b) The **prices of other products**. Increases in the prices of other products would make the supply of a product whose price does not rise less attractive: if other products become more profitable, suppliers will be tempted to switch to producing them, if they are able to. Of course, some products are produced as by-products of others, and a rise in the price of one will then increase the supply of the other. For example, if the price of beef rises, suppliers will decide it is worthwhile to supply beef and the supply of beef will rise. One effect of this will be an increase in the supply of leather.

(c) The **costs of making thc product**, including wages, raw materials and the cost of money to run the business (the interest rate). If any of these costs rise, some producers will be put off and will go out of business, reducing the total supply. They may not go out of business entirely, of course. They may simply change to products which are not so affected by the increase in production costs. Thus the jeweller, faced with a sharp rise in the cost of gold, might decide to stop making gold jewellery and switch to silver jewellery instead. See below on *productivity,* which affects cost

(d) **Changes in technology**. Technological developments which reduce costs of production will increase the quantity of a product supplied at a given price.

(e) **Other factors**, such as changes in the weather (very important for agriculture), natural disasters and strikes.

> **Activity 2** **(5 minutes)**
>
> Think of specific examples of products whose supply has been affected by the following: the weather, a natural disaster and a strike.

### Productivity

**Definition**

> **Productivity** is a measure of the *efficiency* with which output has been produced.

Suppose that an employee is expected to produce three units in every hour that he works. The standard rate of productivity is three units per hour, and one unit is valued at ${}^{1}/_{3}$ of a standard hour of output. If, during one week, the employee makes 126 units in 40 hours of work the following comments can be made.

(a) **Production** in the week is 126 units.

(b) **Productivity** is a relative measure of the hours actually taken and the hours that should have been taken to make the output.

| | | |
|---|---|---|
| (i) | *Either*, 126 Units should take | 42 hours |
| | But did take | 40 hours |
| | Productivity ratio = 42/40 × 100% = | 105% |
| (ii) | *Or alternatively*, in 40 hours, he should make (× 3) | 120 units |
| | But did make | 126 units |
| | Productivity ratio = 126/120 × 100% = | 105% |

A *productivity ratio* greater than 100% indicates that actual efficiency is better than the expected or 'standard' level of efficiency

Management will wish to **plan** and **control** both production levels and labour productivity.

(a) Production levels can be raised as follows.

- Working overtime
- Hiring extra staff
- Sub-contracting some work to an outside firm
- Managing the work force so as to achieve more output.

(b) Production levels can be reduced as follows.

- Cancelling overtime
- Laying off staff

(c) Productivity, if improved, will enable a company to achieve its production targets in fewer hours of work, and therefore at a lower cost.

**Labour cost control** is largely concerned with **productivity**. Rising wage rates have increased automation, which in turn has improved productivity and reduced costs.

**The supply curve and changing supply conditions**

The supply curve shows how the quantity supplied will change in response to a change in price, provided that all other conditions affecting supply remain unchanged (the *ceteris paribus* assumption which we also made in connection with demand). If supply conditions (such as the prices of other products, costs of production or changes in technology) alter, a different supply curve must be drawn. In other words, a change in price will cause a shift along the supply curve, which we call a change in the quantity supplied. A change in supply conditions will cause a shift in the supply curve itself, which we call a change in supply. We are here making the same distinction that we made in the last chapter between a change in the quantity demanded and a change in demand.

Figure 7.2 shows a shift in the supply curve from $S_0$ to $S_1$

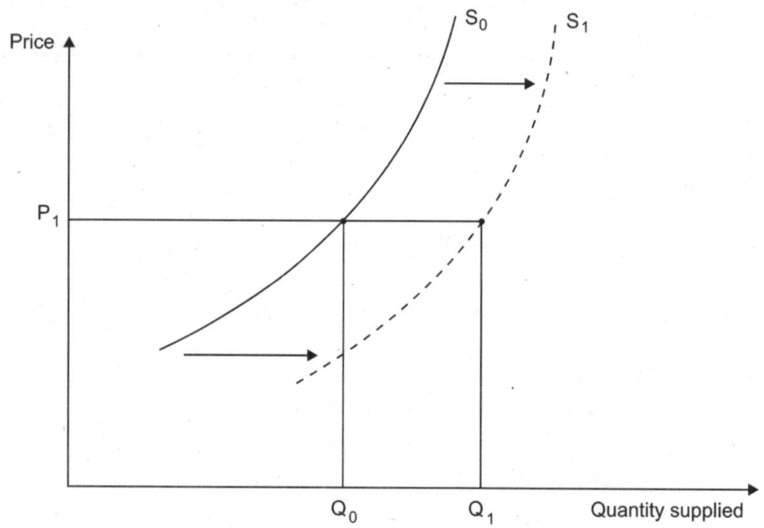


*Figure 7.2: A shift in the supply curve*

This diagram shows a rightward shift of the curve, representing an expansion of supply. If the market price of the product is $P_1$, suppliers would be willing to increase supply from $Q_0$ to $Q_1$ because of the new conditions of supply. The change in conditions might be:

(a) A fall in costs of production
(b) A fall in the prices of other products
(c) Technological progress

Suppliers need to be able react to changed conditions of supply.

### 1.4 Responding to changes

The factors which affect supply can change very quickly. Unfortunately, suppliers may not be able to adapt to changed conditions instantly. For example, a prolonged hot sunny spell may cause a shortage of suntan lotion. The makers may be able to run their machines for longer periods, perhaps working nights and weekends, but they may already be working at full capacity. If the increase in demand were permanent, they would in due course enlarge their factories and install new machines, but that cannot be done in a few days. Even if production can be increased in the short-term, it takes a little while to get the extra output to the shops.

With goods which do not deteriorate rapidly, one solution to this kind of problem is to hold substantial stocks, which can be used in weeks when demand exceeds supply and then be built up again once demand falls. Often these stocks will not be held by the manufacturers, but by wholesalers and distributors who stand between the manufacturers and the shops.

This is not a solution with products which deteriorate rapidly, such as fresh fruit, or with products which for some other reason must be sold straightaway or thrown away, such as newspapers. (How much would you pay for yesterday's newspaper?) In these cases, someone has to take the risk of either oversupplying the market, or leaving some consumers unsatisfied. With newspapers, the publisher normally takes the risk. Newsagents take more than enough copies to satisfy the customers, and then return the unsold copies to the publisher for a full refund. If the publisher refused to take this risk, newsagents would order the lowest number of newspapers they thought they would need, and some customers would not be able to buy their preferred newspapers. The result would be immediate lost sales, and possibly the loss of previously loyal customers as they changed to other newspapers.

***We have seen how to calculate the responsiveness of demand to price changes using elasticity. We will now see how to do the same thing for supply.***

### 1.5 The price elasticity of supply

The price elasticity of supply is calculated as follows:

$$\frac{\text{Percentage change in quantity supplied}}{\text{Percentage change in price}}$$

(a) If this exceeds 1, for example when a 10% price rise leads to a 20% quantity rise (elasticity = 2), supply is **elastic**.

(b) If it equals 1, we have unit **elasticity**.

(c) If it is less than 1, for example when a 10% price rise leads to a 6% quantity rise (elasticity = 0.6), supply is **inelastic**.

**Activity 3** **(5 minutes)**

The makers of a particular type of television set are prepared to supply 15,000 sets a year if the price per set is £200. If the price were to rise to £300, they would be prepared to supply 20,000 sets a year. What is the price elasticity of supply? (Calculate the percentages as percentages of £200 and 15,000, not £300 and 20,000.)

***When we talk about the quantity supplied in the formula for elasticity, we mean the quantity which suppliers would be happy to supply at a given price. This might not be the same as the quantity they will end up supplying, because while a price rise encourages suppliers, it also puts customers off. We will now look at how supply and demand interact to set the market price and the quantity supplied and consumed.***

## 2 THE MARKET PRICE

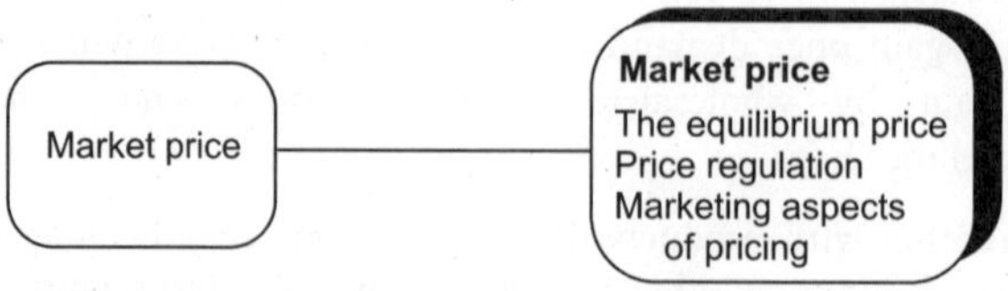


### 2.1 The equilibrium price

We have seen how, as price rises, more of a product is supplied but less is demanded. If supply exceeds demand, then suppliers will cut their prices in an attempt to win customers. This may lead to some suppliers going out of business, reducing the supply. It may also attract some new consumers, increasing demand. Conversely, if demand exceeds supply, some suppliers will raise their prices. This may put some customers off, reducing demand, and may also attract new suppliers into the market, increasing supply.

The end result of these changes will be that both price and quantity will settle down to equilibrium. The equilibrium is the point at which there are no longer any pressures to change the price or the quantity, because at the equilibrium price suppliers want to sell the same quantity as consumers want to buy.

We can find the equilibrium by showing the supply curve and the demand curve on the same graph: the equilibrium is the point where they cross (Figure 7.3).

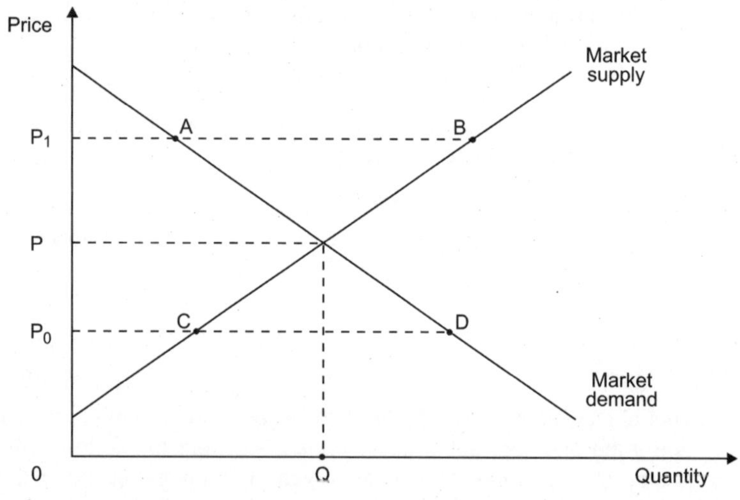


*Figure 7.3: Point of equilibrium*

At price P the amount that sellers are willing to supply is equal to the amount that customers are willing to buy (Q). There will be no unusual variation in stocks and, so long as nothing else changes, there will be no change in price. Customers will be willing to spend a total of £(P × Q) on buying Q units of the product. Suppliers will supply Q units and earn a revenue of £(P × Q). P is the equilibrium price.

At price $P_1$ sellers want to supply more than customers want to buy. The gap between supply and demand is represented by the length AB. At price $P_0$ customers want to buy more than sellers want to supply, and the gap between supply and demand is represented by the length CD. In either case, the market is said to be in disequilibrium. Suppliers and customers will behave as explained above, in order to get to the equilibrium price P and quantity Q.

Supply and demand can be seen working in this simple manner in commodity markets, such as the markets for gold and coffee, where prices move rapidly in response to deals done. In most markets, the mechanism may not be so obvious or efficient. For example, if car manufacturers are selling more cars than they can make, they may not increase prices straightaway because it may take them a while to realise what is happening, and because a sudden price rise may look bad. They may let waiting lists grow for a while instead.

**Activity 4** **(20 minutes)**

Use the following supply and demand schedules to draw supply and demand curves on the same graph, and find the equilibrium price and quantity.

| *Unit price* | *Monthly supply* | *Monthly demand* |
|---|---|---|
| £ | Units | Units |
| 15 | 60,000 | 150,000 |
| 25 | 90,000 | 120,000 |
| 35 | 120,000 | 90,000 |
| 50 | 150,000 | 60,000 |
| 75 | 180,000 | 30,000 |

We have seen how if a market is in disequilibrium, the price will change, leading the quantity supplied and the quantity demanded to change until they are equal. Once the market is in equilibrium, we can expect it to stay there unless either the supply curve or the demand curve shifts: a change in supply or a change in demand. Either of these could happen for any of the reasons we have already covered, for example a change in consumer tastes or a change in the weather.

**Activity 5** **(10 minutes)**

Suggest three conditions which you think determine the supply and demand curves in a retail fruit and vegetable market.

**Activity 6** **(15 minutes)**

Customers may be prepared to wait for some products. A sports car company has chosen to supply only a fixed quantity a month which is below the current demand level. A waiting list build up and people sell their places on the list.

How do you think the price of a place on the list is determined? How do you think that the price of a place is related to the price which the company should charge to make demand equal supply? Why does the company not simply charge that price and make more money?

***Prices are not always left to find their own equilibrium levels. We will now see what can happen when governments interfere.***

## 2.2 Price regulation

A government may wish to regulate prices. This is normally done for one of two reasons.

(a) The government may want to control inflation. It may do this by setting maximum prices for certain goods, or by ruling that prices may only rise by (for example) 4% a year.

(b) The government may want to help suppliers. It may do this by setting minimum prices.

### Maximum prices

If a **maximum price** for a product is set, but this maximum is above the market equilibrium price, there will be no immediate effect. However, people will read the maximum as a warning of future government intervention.

If the maximum price is lower than the equilibrium price, then there will be an excess of demand over supply. This is shown in Figure 7.4.

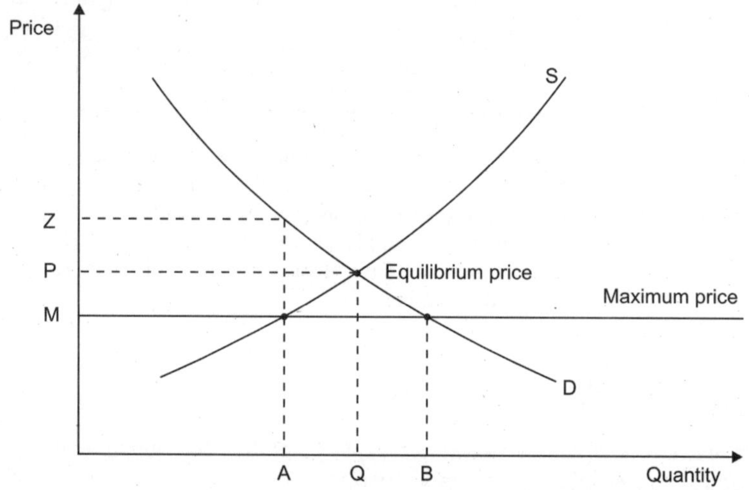


*Figure 7.4: Maximum prices*

The low price will attract buyers, but it will deter suppliers. The amount supplied will fall from Q, the market equilibrium quantity, to A. The quantity demanded will increase from Q to B. Demand will exceed supply by the gap AB.

The result of this gap is that some consumers will have to go without. To prevent an unfair allocation of the available supply the government might introduce rationing (so that each consumer gets something, but less than they want), or alternatively a waiting list. Unfortunately such systems rarely work perfectly. There will always be people who are willing to pay more than the maximum price, and other people (black marketeers) who will find ways to supply what they want. If only quantity A is available in the market, consumers will be prepared to pay price Z, and so black marketeers can supply at this price.

**Minimum prices**

Minimum prices are introduced for the benefit of suppliers. Minimum prices are the basis of the Common Agricultural Policy of the European Union: farmers are guaranteed a minimum price for their output if they cannot get a higher price on the free market. If the minimum price is set below the market price there is no effect. However if it is set higher it will result in excess supply.

The effect of a minimum price which is above the market equilibrium price is shown in Figure 7.5.

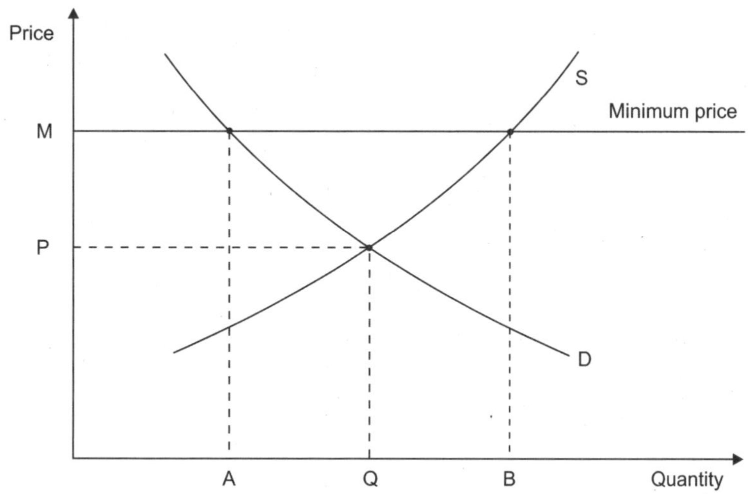


*Figure 7.5: Minimum prices*

The minimum price M is set above the market price P. The quantity demanded falls from Q to A but the quantity supplied increases to B. There is excess supply, represented by AB.

The excess supply caused by the Common Agricultural Policy led to the notorious beef mountains, butter mountains and wine lakes of the 1970s and 1980s. Some of these have had to be sold very cheaply to countries outside Europe. To try to prevent this oversupply, quotas have been set (limiting the amounts farmers are allowed to produce) and set-aside payments have been offered to farmers who take land out of production.

With all these problems, you may wonder why the Common Agricultural Policy exists at all. The historical reasons may be largely political, but we can say that the result has been fairly stable food prices. One of the problems which all farmers face is the danger that the weather will lead to a very good harvest, leading to excessive supply and very low prices, or a very bad harvest, leading to excessive demand and very high prices. The Common Agricultural Policy has helped to control these price fluctuations.

**Activity 7** **(15 minutes)**

If there were no price regulation in agriculture, what would the implications of a very good harvest be for farmers? You should look beyond the obvious fact that prices would fall, and consider the consequences of price falls.

***We have now looked at how prices are set as the result of supply, demand and government intervention. It is now time for us to focus again on marketing and look at how an individual producer should set prices.***

## 2.3 Marketing aspects of pricing

### Brand loyalty

The basic economic theory of supply and demand suggests that prices are fixed in a simple way, and that there is not much an individual supplier can do about them. If, of course, the supplier is a monopolist (sole supplier) he has a freer hand and can set prices without fear that competitors will undercut him and take all his customers away. However, even a monopolist does not have a totally free hand because if prices are too high consumers will use their ingenuity to find acceptable substitute products or will simply do without. A supplier who wants a bit of freedom in setting his prices can do so by creating the impression that he has a unique product, so that he is a bit like a monopolist. For example, Ford do not have a monopoly on cars, but they do have a monopoly on Ford cars. If they can build up brand loyalty, so that some consumers would rather buy a Ford than any other brand of car, then they have a bit of freedom in setting their prices. In practice this is not difficult, because different makes of car are in fact different: they have different engine powers, different size boots, different safety features and so on. A Vauxhall may be a close substitute for a Ford, but it is not an exact substitute.

### Price perceptions

As well as using brand loyalty, a business needs to consider **consumers' perceptions of prices**. Consumers very often feel that a given product ought to cost a certain amount: they would not expect an ordinary family car to cost as little as £5,000 or as much as £20,000. They are likely to go out shopping with the intention of spending a certain amount of money and a company which does not charge a price within the expected range is unlikely to attract many customers.

Consumers also take **price to be an indication of quality**. A very cheap product may fail to sell, not because there is really something wrong with it but because consumers assume that there must be something wrong with it.

### Competitors' prices

Competitors' prices are important factors. If a business charges more than its competitors for a product which consumers see as being the same, then it cannot expect to sell much. Similarly, sales can suffer if a business puts up its prices but its competitors do not do so. Sometimes all businesses within an industry have a reason to raise prices at the same time, as when the cost of a raw material rises such as the price of oil. When this happens all the oil companies put up the price of petrol. However, no one business can rely on its competitors putting up their prices. Some will be tempted to keep their prices the same, in the hope of taking customers from those who put up their prices.

As well as considering what competitors will do before changing its own prices, a business should consider how competitors will react to its actions. In particular, a price cut which is meant to attract customers away from competitors may fail, if the competitors respond by cutting their prices: the result may be a price war, in which all the businesses involved suffer.

**Maximising profit**

Most businesses want to maximise their profits, or at least make reasonably large profits. The choice of prices will certainly have an effect on profits, but the effect can be hard to determine in advance. If prices are raised, revenue per unit sold will rise, but fewer units will be sold. Total revenue may rise or fall, depending on the price elasticity of demand.

Profit is revenue minus costs. If total output falls, then costs will fall, but they may not fall by much. For example, if a business needs expensive machines, the cost of those machines will stay the same even if they are not used much. The raw materials which the same company uses might be quite cheap, so that a fall in their use caused by a fall in output may make little difference to total costs. Another business with cheap machines but expensive raw materials, such as a jeweller, might find that costs change much more quickly as output changes.

The conclusion to be drawn is that before making any decisions about price changes, a business should find out what it can both about price elasticity of demand and about its own costs.

**Chapter roundup**

- Supply is the amount of a product that suppliers would like to produce at a given price.
- As a general rule, if the price rises, suppliers will be happy to produce more. This can be shown by a supply curve, plotting quantity supplied against price, which slopes upwards from left to right.
- Supply does not only depend on price. It is affected by the prices of other products, by the costs of production and by technology.
- The factors which affect supply can change very fast, but it can take some time for suppliers to respond.
- The responsiveness of the quantity of a product supplied to price changes is measured by the price elasticity of supply.
- The equilibrium price is determined by the interaction of demand and supply. It can be found by drawing the supply and demand curves on the same graph, and seeing where they cross.
- Price regulation can lead to excess demand or excess supply.
- When a business is working out what prices to charge, it must consider several factors, including customers' perceptions, competitors' behaviour and its own costs.

## Quick quiz

1. What is a price war, and what are the likely consequences?
2. Why can some businesses get away with charging higher prices than their competitors for the same goods?
3. How can the prices of some products affect the supply of others?
4. Define reciprocal buying.
5. What is the difference between a change in the quantity supplied and a change in supply?
6. Why is holding large stocks not always a sensible response to the problem of fluctuating demand?
7. What is the formula for the price elasticity of supply?
8. Describe how price and quantity settle down to equilibrium.
9. In what types of market can supply and demand best be seen interacting to reach the equilibrium price and quantity?
10. How does a black marketeer exploit maximum prices for products?
11. What sorts of preconception held by consumers are important to producers when setting their prices?
12. If a producer doubles his output, does it follow that his costs will double? If not, why not?

## Answers to quick quiz

1. Price war: each producer cuts prices in hope of attracting enough consumers when there is oversupply. Consequences: other producers follow, some withdraw from the market, some go into liquidation.
2. Brand names and reciprocal buying.
3. When some are by-products of others.
4. Buying in order to maintain good business links, or from other members of your group of companies.
5. Quantity supplied depends on suppliers' costs and selling price. Change in supply is due to other factors such as the weather.
6. Some stocks deteriorate rapidly and some go out of date.
7. $\dfrac{\text{Percentage change in quanitity supplied}}{\text{Percentage change in price}}$
8. As price rises demand falls so supply is reduced. This recurs until equilibrium is reached.
9. Commodity markets.
10. Some consumers are always prepared to pay more for goods in short supply.
11. They feel certain products ought to cost a certain amount and see price as an indication of quality.
12. No. Fixed costs remain the same.

## Answers to activities

1 The major groups such as Sainsbury, Safeway and Tesco have avoided using price as a key marketing device even in the face of competitive pressures because they need high profits in order to fund their superstore programmes. Low price ranges are available, but they are not heavily promoted. Marketing strategies have been based upon quality as indicated by the range of goods and services offered to customers. If you compare the range of goods available as recently as five years ago to that available today you will see a marked change. The quality of service offered has improved to include such things as a range of different styles of shopping trolleys, more efficient checkouts, cafés and mother and baby rooms.

A price war would reduce profits. This would cause shareholders to look to invest in sectors offering a better return. They would sell their shares and the share price would fall as supply exceeded demand. A lower share price would affect the ability of companies to raise more capital to fund expansion plans. A loss of profitability could also lead to store closures, job losses and even company failures. This would lessen consumer choice.

2 The supply of coffee has been affected by frosts in Brazil. Natural disasters such as earthquakes and tornadoes affect the supply of holiday accommodation in the stricken areas. Strikes have practically closed the British Rail network.

3 The price elasticity of supply is 33%/50% = 0.67.

4 Your graph should look like this.

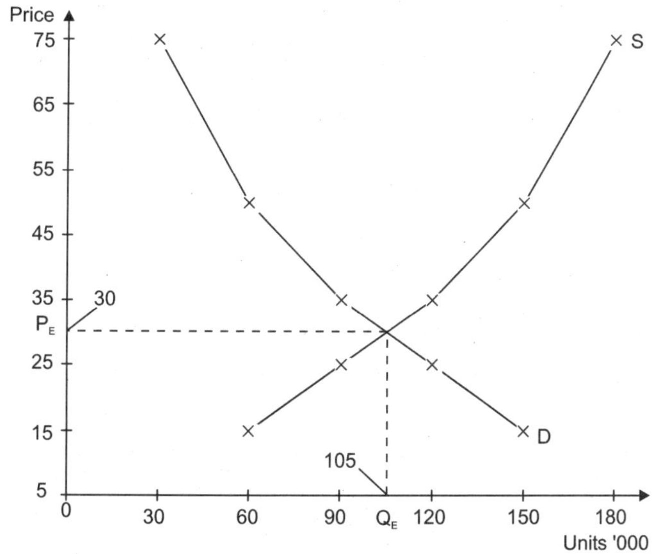


The equilibrium price, $P_E$ is £30 and the market quantity exchanged at this price is $Q_E$ 105,000 units.

5 A retail fruit and vegetable market will probably consist of many small traders, each with their own stall and competing directly with one another.

The conditions determining the supply curve include:

(a) Costs: the main cost to the traders will be the cost of their own wholesale supplies; although there will also be costs of renting a stall and costs of labour

(b) Availability of stalls: the prices that traders can charge will depend to some extent on the number of stalls that there are and the ease with which new traders can acquire stalls and thus enter the market

The conditions determining the demand curve include:

(a) Prices of similar goods in supermarkets

(b) Shopping habits: some people are in the habit of using markets, while others prefer supermarkets

(c) How much money shoppers have to spend

6 The price may be determined by adding a mark-up for profit on to the total costs. If the price was determined by demand it would rise until demand = supply. The company could set prices by demand and make a much higher profit which could be invested in the business. However, it may be that the company feels the cars are good value at the price they are and this is why they are so popular. By making them so desirable they are sure of sales and customers know they can obtain a good second-hand price for them. If the price were to rise, they might not appear such good value.

7 Oversupply is likely to lead to a serious fall in prices. While more may be sold at the reduced prices, it is likely that large quantities of produce will not be sold at all: the fact that food is cheap does not mean that everyone will eat much more, because each person still only has one stomach of a given size! Thus farmers' incomes may fall drastically. This may drive some farmers out of business. The result may be to reduce the supply in the following year, causing an abnormal price rise.

# Chapter 8:

# PRODUCTION AND COSTS

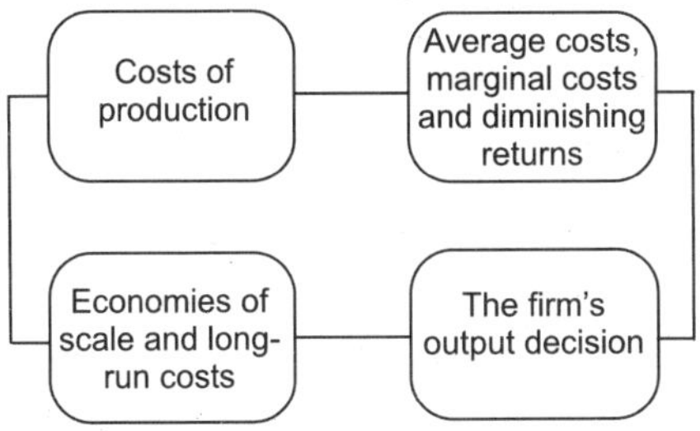


### Introduction

In this chapter we shall be looking at the costs and output decisions of an *individual* firm. In other words, we shall look at what the costs of production are for a single firm, and how these are affected by both short-run and long-run factors.

We contrast the concept of *opportunity cost*, which was introduced in Chapter 5, with financial cost as seen from the accountant's point of view.

We also consider how much output a firm will produce at a given market price.

The aggregate amount of goods supplied by every individual firm adds up to the market supply. By studying an individual firm we are looking at the 'building blocks' of market supply.

### Your objectives

In this chapter you will learn about:

(a) The behaviour of costs in the short-run and the long-run

(b) Concepts of costs

(c) Economic profits and opportunity costs

(d) Profit maximisation

(e) Law of diminishing returns

(f) Economies and diseconomies of scale

## 1 COSTS OF PRODUCTION

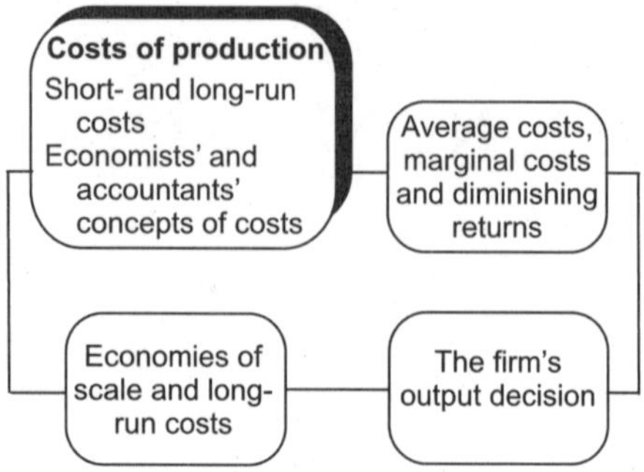


### 1.1 Short- and long-run costs

Production is carried out by firms using the factors of production which must be paid or rewarded for their use. The cost of production is the cost of the factors used.

| Factor of production | Its cost |
|---|---|
| Land | Rent |
| Labour | Wages |
| Capital | Interest |
| Enterprise | Normal profit |

**Notice that normal profit is viewed as a cost.** This may seem odd to an accountant, who thinks of profit as the difference between revenue and cost – a point we shall return to later. Any profit earned in excess of the profit needed to reward the entrepreneur (in other words, the **opportunity cost** of keeping the entrepreneur from **going elsewhere**) is called **supernormal, abnormal or excess profit.**

The behaviour of costs is usually analysed under two sets of conditions: the short-run and the long-run.

**Definitions**

> The **short-run** is a time period in which the amount of at least one input is fixed. The **long-run** is a period sufficiently long to allow full flexibility in all the inputs used.

#### Fixed costs and variable costs

In the short-run, certain costs are fixed because the availability of resources is restricted. Decisions must therefore be taken for the short-run within the restriction of having some resources in fixed supply. In the longer-run, however, most costs are variable, because the supply of skilled labour, machinery, buildings and so on can be increased or decreased. Decisions in the long-run are therefore subject to fewer restrictions about resource availability.

Inputs are variable at the decision of management. For example, management might decide to buy more raw materials, hire more labour, start overtime working and so on.

(a) **Labour is usually considered to be variable** in the short-run. Inputs which are treated as **fixed** in the short-run will include **capital items**, such as buildings and machinery, for which a significant lead time might be needed before their quantities are changed.

(b) All inputs are variable in the long-run. A decision to change the quantity of an input variable which is fixed in the short-run will involve a change in the **scale of production**.

**Short-run costs: total costs, average costs and marginal costs**

Let us now turn our attention to short-run costs: the costs of output during a time period in which only some resources of production are variable in availability and the remaining resources of production are fixed in quantity.

Figure 8.1 shows how the various elements of cost vary as output changes.

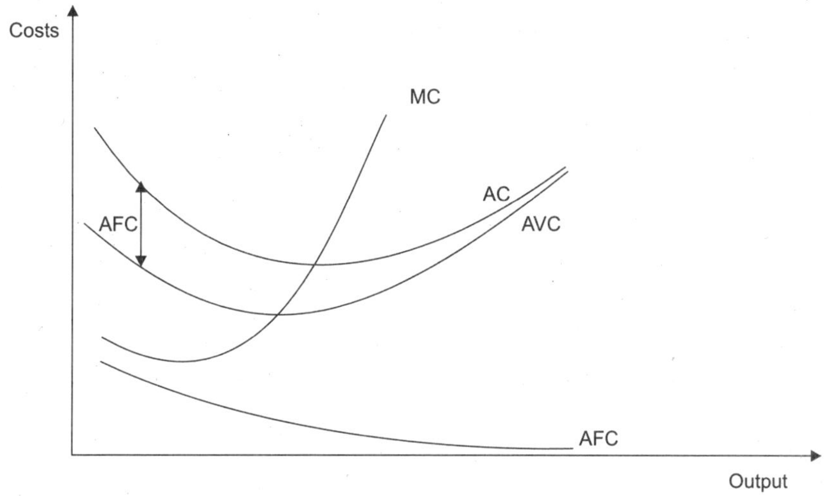


*Figure 8.1: Components of a firm's short-run costs*

**Definition** 

- **Total cost** (TC). Total cost for a given level of output comprises total fixed cost (TFC) and total variable cost (TVC).
- **Average cost** (AC). Average cost for a given level of output is simply the total cost divided by the total quantity produced.

  **Average cost** is made up of an average fixed cost per unit plus an average variable cost per unit.

  $$AC = \frac{TC}{N} = \frac{TFC}{N} + \frac{TVC}{N}$$

  AC = AFC + AVC

**Definition continued**

Average fixed cost per unit (AFC) will get smaller as more units (N) are produced. This is because TFC is the same amount regardless of the volume of output, so as N gets bigger, AFC must get smaller.

Average variable costs per unit (AVC) will change as output volume increases.

- **Marginal cost** (MC). This is the addition to total cost of producing one more unit of output. For example, the marginal cost for a firm of producing the 50th unit of output is the total cost of making the first 50 units minus the total cost of making the first 49 units.

**Activity 1** **(15 minutes)**

To test your understanding of these concepts, look at the three definitions given below. Which one(s) of them, if any, correctly describes the marginal cost of producing one extra unit of output?

(a) MC = increase in total cost of production
(b) MC = increase in variable cost of production
(c) MC = increase in average cost of production

## EXAMPLE: NUMERICAL ILLUSTRATION

Let us suppose that a firm employs a given amount of capital which is a fixed (invariable) input in the short-run: in other words, it is not possible to obtain extra amounts of capital quickly. The firm may combine different amounts of labour with this capital, which we assume to be an input that is variable in the short-term. Thus fixed capital and variable labour can be combined to produce different levels of output.

Here is an illustration of the relationship between the different definitions of the firm's costs. (The figures used are hypothetical.)

| *Units of output* | *Total cost* | *Average cost* | *Marginal cost* | |
|---|---|---|---|---|
| *n* | *TC* | *AC* | *MC* | |
| | £ | £ | £ | |
| 1 | 1.10 | 1.10 | 1.10 | |
| 2 | 1.60 | 0.80 | 0.50 | (1.60 – 1.10) |
| 3 | 1.75 | 0.58 | 0.15 | (1.75 – 1.60) |
| 4 | 2.00 | 0.50 | 0.25 | (2.00 – 1.75) |
| 5 | 2.50 | 0.50 | 0.50 | (2.50 – 2.00) |
| 6 | 3.12 | 0.52 | 0.62 | (3.12 – 2.50) |
| 7 | 3.99 | 0.57 | 0.87 | (3.99 – 3.12) |
| 8 | 5.12 | 0.64 | 1.13 | (5.12 – 3.99) |
| 9 | 6.30 | 0.70 | 1.18 | (6.30 – 5.12) |
| 10 | 8.00 | 0.80 | 1.70 | (8.00 – 6.30) |

(a) *Total cost* is the sum of labour costs plus capital costs, since these are by assumption the only two inputs.

(b) *Average cost* is the cost per unit of output, ie $AC = \frac{TC}{output} = \frac{TC}{n}$

(c) *Marginal cost* is the total cost of producing n units minus the total cost of producing one less unit, ie (n – 1) units.

Note the following points on this set of figures.

(a) *Total cost.* Total costs of production carry on rising as more and more units are produced.

(b) *Average cost.* AC changes as output increases. It starts by falling, reaches a lowest level, and then starts rising again.

(c) *Marginal cost.* The MC of each extra unit of output also changes with each unit produced. It too starts by falling, fairly quickly reaches a lowest level, and then starts rising.

(d) *AC and MC compared.* At lowest levels of output, MC is less than AC. At highest levels of output, though, MC is higher than AC. There is a 'cross-over' point, where MC is exactly equal to AC. In this example, it is at five units of output.

---

### 1.2 Economists' and accountants' concepts of cost

As we have already mentioned, to an economist, cost includes an amount for normal profit which is the reward for entrepreneurship. **Normal profit is the opportunity cost of entrepreneurship,** because it is the amount of profit that an entrepreneur could earn elsewhere, and so it is the profit that he must earn to persuade him to keep on with his investment in his current enterprise.

A further feature of **cost accounting** is that costs can be divided into fixed costs and variable costs. Total fixed costs per period are a given amount, regardless of the volume of production and sales. Cost accountants usually assume that the variable cost per unit is a **constant amount,** so that the total **variable cost** of sales is directly proportional to the **volume** of sales.

Economists do not take this approach. In the short-run, there are fixed costs and variable costs, but the variable cost of making an extra unit of output need not be the same for each extra unit that is made. As a result, the marginal cost of each extra unit is not constant, either.

**Accounting profits** consist of sales revenue minus the **explicit costs** of the business. Explicit costs are those which are clearly stated and recorded, for example:

- Materials costs – prices paid to suppliers
- Labour costs – wages paid
- Depreciation costs on fixed assets
- Other expenses, such as rates and building rental

**Economic profit** consists of sales revenue minus both the explicit costs and the **implicit costs** of the business. Implicit costs are benefits forgone by not using the factors of production in their next most profitable way.

It is a well-established principle in accounting and economics that relevant costs for decision-making purposes are **future costs incurred as a consequence of the decision.** Past or 'sunk' costs are not relevant to our decisions now, because we cannot change them: they have already been incurred. Relevant future costs are the **opportunity costs** of the input resources to be used.

---

## EXAMPLE: ECONOMIC PROFITS AND OPPORTUNITY COSTS

Suppose that a sole trader in 20X7 sells goods worth £200,000. He incurs materials costs of £70,000, hired labour costs of £85,000, and other expenses of £20,000. He has no fixed assets other than the building, on which depreciation is not charged. In accounting terms, his profit would be as follows.

| | £ | £ |
|---|---|---|
| Sales | | 200,000 |
| Materials | 70,000 | |
| Labour | 85,000 | |
| Other expenses | 20,000 | |
| | | (175,000) |
| Profit | | 25,000 |

But suppose the buildings he uses in his business could have been put to another use to earn £15,000, and his own labour as business manager could get him a job with a salary of £20,000. The position of the business in economic terms would be as follows.

| | £ |
|---|---|
| Sales less explicit costs | 25,000 |
| Implicit costs | (35,000) |
| Loss | (10,000) |

In economic terms, the business has made a loss. It would pay the trader to put his buildings and capital to their alternative uses, and employ his own labour another way, working for someone else at a salary of £20,000.

---

**Activity 2** **(20 minutes)**

Wilbur Proffit set up his business one year ago. In that time, his firm has earned total revenue of £160,000, and incurred costs of £125,000, including his own salary of £12,000. Before, he had been a salaried employee of Dead End Ventures Ltd, earning an annual salary of £20,000.

To finance the business, Wilbur had to sell his investment of £200,000 in government securities which earned interest of 10% pa. He used £80,000 of this to buy a warehouse, whose annual commercial rental value would be £11,000 pa. The remaining £120,000 has been used to finance business operations.

*Required*
Calculate

(a) The accounting profit earned by Wilbur in the last year
(b) The economic profit or loss earned

## 2 AVERAGE COSTS, MARGINAL COSTS AND DIMINISHING RETURNS

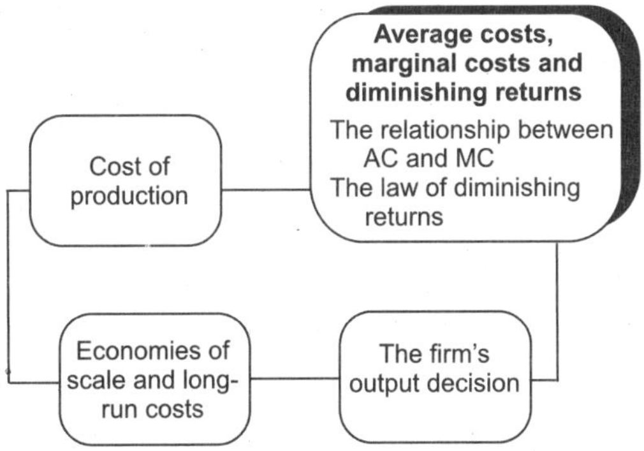


### 2.1 The relationship between AC and MC

The relationships between average and marginal costs are important.

(a) **When the average cost schedule is rising, the marginal cost will always be higher than the average cost**. If the cost of making one extra unit of output exceeds the average cost of making all the previous units, then making the extra unit will clearly cause an increase in the average unit cost.

(b) In our example in section 1.1, the average cost schedule rises from six units of output onwards and MC is bigger than AC at all these levels of output (six to ten units).

(c) **When the average cost curve is falling, marginal cost lies below it**. This follows similar logic. If the cost of making an extra unit is less than the average cost of making all the previous units, the effect of making the extra unit must be a reduction in average unit cost. In our example, this happens between production of one and four units.

(d) **When the average cost curve is horizontal, marginal cost is equal to it.** In our example, when there are five units of output, the average cost stays at £0.50 and the marginal cost of the fifth unit is also £0.50.

**Activity 3** **(10 minutes)**

(a) It is possible for the average total cost curve to be falling while the average variable cost curve is rising. True or false?

(b) Marginal fixed costs per unit will fall as output increases. True or false?

The marginal cost curve always cuts through the average cost curve at the lowest point of the average cost curve (see Figure 8.1 earlier).

The short-run average cost curve (AC in Figure 8.1) is U-shaped. We now consider why.

Fixed costs per unit of output, ie average fixed costs, will fall as the level of output rises. Thus if fixed costs are £10,000 and we make 10,000 units, the average fixed cost (AFC) will be £1 per unit. If output increases to 12,500 units the AFC will fall to 80p (10,000 ÷ 12,500) and if output increases to 15,000 units, the AFC will fall again to 67p (10,000 ÷ 15,000), and so on. Spreading fixed costs over a larger amount of output is a major reason why (short-run) average costs per unit fall as output increases.

Variable costs are made up from the cost of the factors of production whose use can be varied in the short-run – for example wages, fuel bills and raw material purchases. **Total variable costs therefore vary with output in the short-run as well as in the long-run.**

(a) The accountant's assumption about short-run variable costs is that **up to a certain level of output, the variable cost per unit is more or less constant** (eg wages costs and materials costs per unit of output are unchanged). If the average fixed cost per unit is falling as output rises and the average variable cost per unit is constant, it follows that the average total cost per unit will be falling too as output increases.

(b) However, there are other reasons for the initial fall in average total cost. The first are the effects of the **division of labour** and **specialisation**. Imagine a small but fully equipped factory, with a variety of machinery and equipment and a workforce of, say, ten. If each person attempts to perform all the operations on a single item, production is likely to be low.

   (i) They will be unable to develop a high level of skill at every one of the jobs

   (ii) Time will be lost as they move from machine to machine

   (iii) Individual variability will produce a high rate of defects, perhaps with each person tending to produce different faults

   (iv) Individuals will work at different rates on different operations; as a result, queues will form at some machines and others will be under-utilised

   If there is a degree of specialisation, expertise and speed will rise, machines will be run at optimum rates and output will rise. Average costs will therefore fall.

(c) **The second reason is the utilisation of indivisibilities.** If a machine has an output capacity of 100 units per day but is only used to produce 50 units per day, the machinery cost of each of those 50 units will be twice the level it would be if the machine was used to capacity. Operation of a plant below normal output is uneconomical, so there are cost savings as production is increased up to capacity level.

### 2.2 The law of diminishing returns

**Definition**

Eventually, as output increases, average costs will tend to rise. **The law of diminishing returns** says that if one or more factors of production are fixed, but the input of another is increased, **the extra output generated by each extra unit of input will eventually begin to fall**. In our factory, as we add staff, we start to see queues forming at machines; it becomes more difficult to co-ordinate work; machinery starts to break down through over-use and there simply is not enough space to work efficiently.

The law of diminishing returns states that, given the present state of technology, as more units of a variable input factor are added to input factors that are fixed in supply in the short-run, the resulting increments to total production will eventually and progressively decline. In other words, as more units of a variable factor (eg labour) are added to a quantity of a fixed factor (eg a hectare of land), there may be some **increasing returns** or **constant returns** as more units of the variable factor (eg labour) are added, but eventually, **diminishing returns** will set in. Putting more people to work on a hectare of land will increase the yield up to a point, but eventually it will be costing more to employ additional labour than is being earned in additional yield. Observation of agriculture is the origin of the law of diminishing returns.

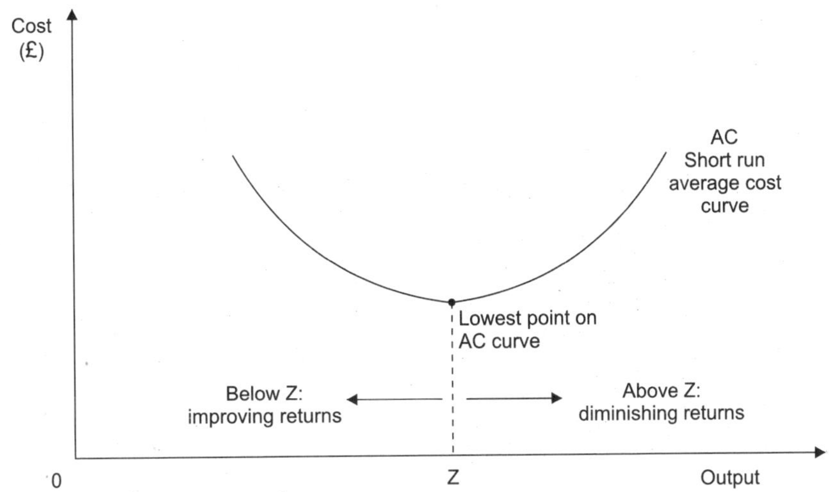


*Figure 8.2: U-shaped short-run cost curve and diminishing returns*

***Remember that this is a short-run phenomenon; at least one factor of production is fixed.***

The law of diminishing returns is expressed in production quantities, but it obviously has direct implications for short-run average and marginal **costs**. Resources cost money, and the average and marginal costs of output will depend on the quantities of resources needed to produce the given output.

**Activity 4** **(10 minutes)**

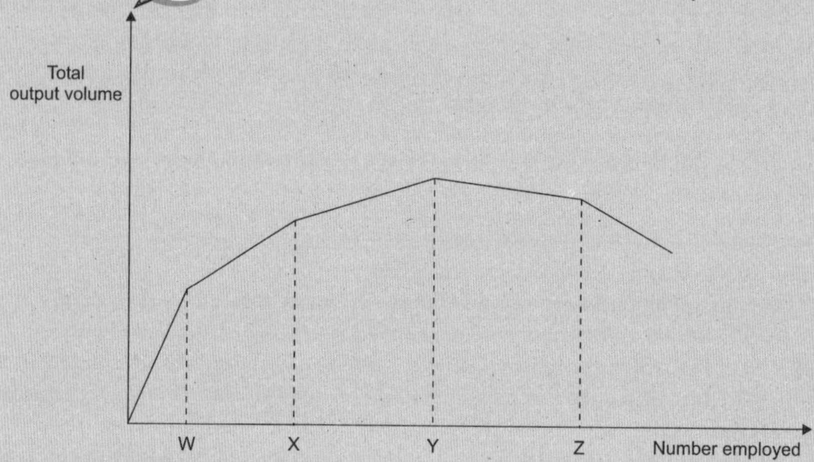


In the diagram above, from what level of employment do diminishing returns start to occur?

## 3 THE FIRM'S OUTPUT DECISION

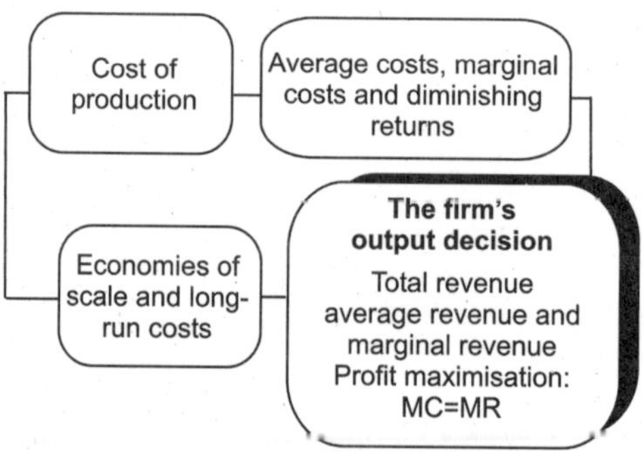


### 3.1 Total revenue, average revenue and marginal revenue

The assumption of **profit maximisation** provides a basis for beginning to look at the output decisions of individual firms.

**Definition**

> **Profit** is equal to total revenue minus total cost of any level of output.

There are three aspects of revenue to consider.

(a) **Total revenue** (TR) is the total income obtained from selling a given quantity of output. We can think of this as quantity sold multiplied by the price per unit.

(b) **Average revenue** (AR) we can think of as the price per unit sold.

(c) **Marginal revenue** (MR) is the addition to total revenue earned from the sale of one extra unit of output.

When a firm can sell all its extra output at the same price, the AR 'curve' will be a straight horizontal line on a graph. The **marginal revenue** per unit from selling extra units at a fixed price must be the same as the **average revenue** (see Figure 8.3).

If the price per unit must be cut in order to sell more units, then the marginal revenue per unit obtained from selling extra units will be less than the previous price per unit (see Figure 8.4). In other words, when the AR is falling as more units are sold, the MR must be less than the AR.

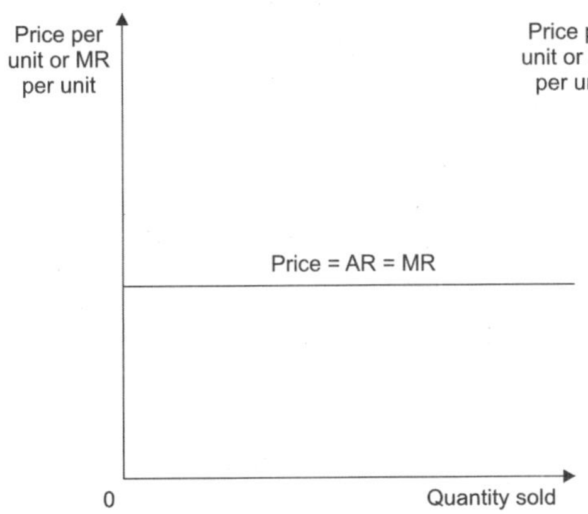


*Figure 8.3*

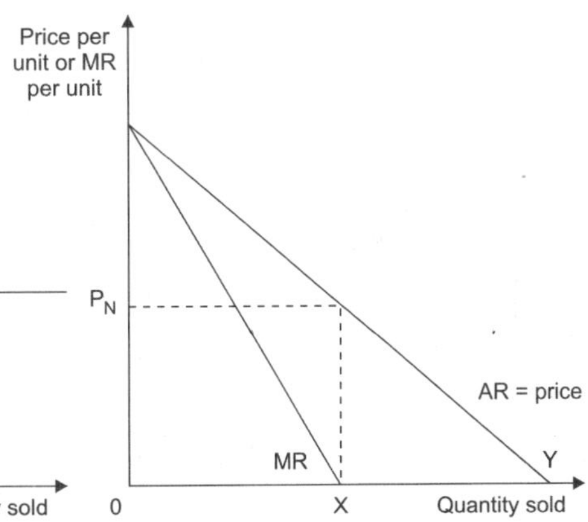


*Figure 8.4*

In Figure 8.4, with straight line MR and AR curves, the length OX is exactly half of the length OY.

***Figure 8.4 is another important diagram and forms the basis of other more detailed illustrations.***

Note that in Figure 8.4, at any given level of sales, **all units are sold at the same price**. The firm has to reduce its price to sell more, but the price must be reduced for *all* units sold, not just for the extra units. This is because we are assuming that all output is produced for a single market, where a single price will prevail.

When the price per unit has to be reduced in order to increase the firm's sales the marginal revenue can become negative. This happens in Figure 8.4 at price $P_N$ when a reduction in price does not increase output sufficiently to earn the same total revenue as before. In this situation, demand would be price inelastic.

We have defined profit as TR minus TC.

(a) Figure 8.5 shows, in simplified form, how TR and TC vary with output. As you might expect, TC increases as output rises. The effect of increasing marginal cost (caused by diminishing returns) is that the rise in TC accelerates as output increases and so the TC curve becomes steeper.

(b) Conversely, the gradient of the TR curve reduces as output and sales increase. This is because most firms operate under the conditions illustrated in Figure 8.5. That is to say, they must reduce their prices in order to sell more. The rate of growth of TR therefore declines.

(c) Notice carefully that the vertical axis of Figure 8.6 shows total values whereas in Figures 8.4 and 8.5, it shows value per unit.

(d) Profits are at a maximum where the vertical distance AB between the TC and TR curves is greatest.

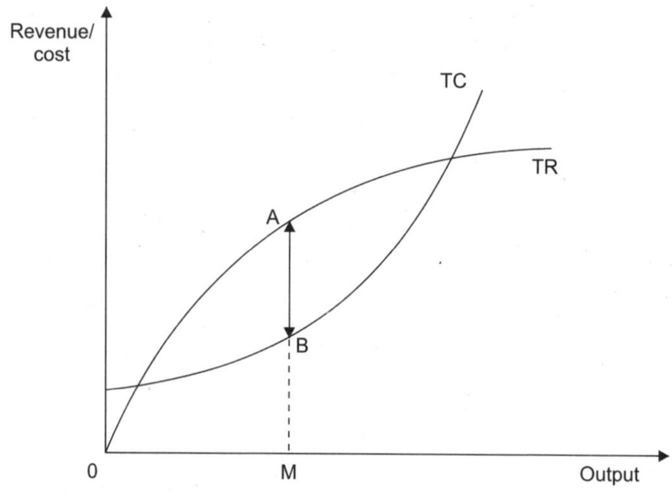


*Figure 8.5: Profit maximisation*

### 3.2 Profit maximisation: MC = MR

As a firm produces and sells more units, its total costs will increase and its total revenues will also increase (unless demand is price inelastic and MR has become negative).

(a) Provided that the extra cost of making an extra unit is **less than** the extra revenue obtained from selling it, the firm will increase its profits by making and selling the extra unit.

(b) If the extra cost of making an extra unit of output **exceeds** the extra revenue obtainable from selling it, the firm's profits would be reduced by making and selling the extra unit.

(c) If the extra cost of making an extra unit of output is **exactly equal** to the extra revenue obtainable from selling it, bearing in mind that economic cost includes an amount for normal profit, it will be worth the firm's while to make and sell the extra unit. And since the extra cost of yet another unit would be higher (the law of diminishing returns applies) whereas extra revenue per unit from selling extra units is never higher, the profit-maximising output is reached at this point where MC = MR.

(d)

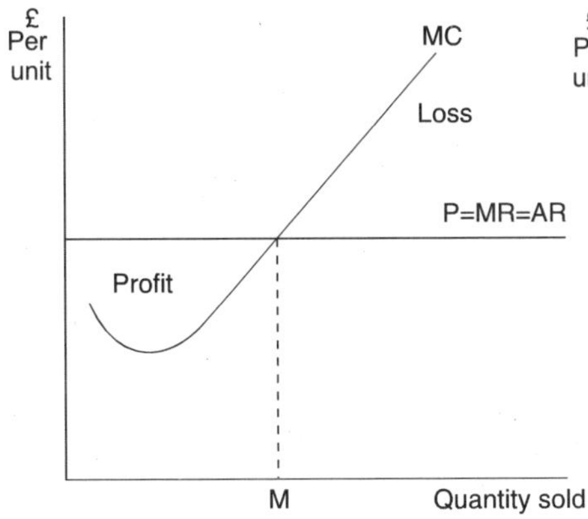


*Figure 8.6*

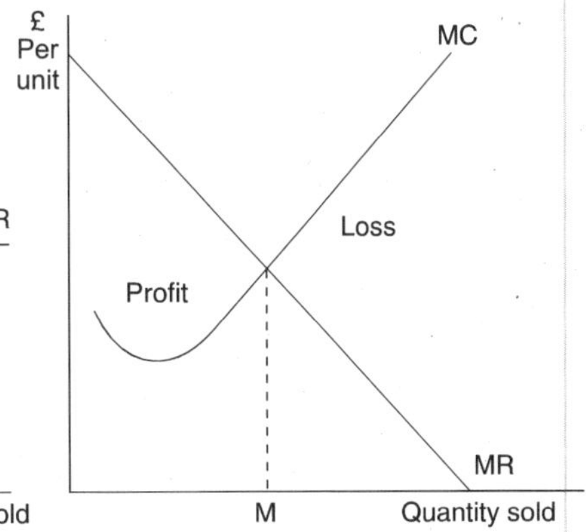


*Figure 8.7*

(d) Figures 8.6 and 8.7 show the profit maximising output quantity M for the two types of firm shown in Figures 8.3 and 8.4. In both cases, the marginal cost function is as discussed earlier in this chapter. The firm makes a profit on each extra item it produces, albeit a smaller one, until output M is reached. At this level of output the MC and MR curves cross. The addition to total revenue from the next unit is less than the increase in total cost which it causes. This level of output corresponds to the level M shown in Figure 8.5.

In other words, given the objective of profit maximisation there are **three possibilities**.

(a) If MC is less than MR, profits will be increased by making and selling more.

(b) If MC is greater than MR, profits will fall if more units are made and sold, and a profit-maximising firm would not make the extra output.

(c) If MC = MR, the profit-maximising output has been reached, and so this is the output quantity that a profit-maximising firm will decide to supply.

**Activity 5** **(20 minutes)**

The following data refer to the revenue and costs of a firm.

| Output | Total revenue | Total costs |
|---|---|---|
| | £ | £ |
| 0 | – | 110 |
| 1 | 50 | 140 |
| 2 | 100 | 162 |
| 3 | 150 | 175 |
| 4 | 200 | 180 |
| 5 | 250 | 185 |
| 6 | 300 | 194 |
| 7 | 350 | 229 |
| 8 | 400 | 269 |
| 9 | 450 | 325 |
| 10 | 500 | 425 |

*Required*

(a) Calculate the marginal revenue for the firm and state which sort of market it is operating in.

(b) What level of output will the firm aim to produce and what amount of profit will it make at this level?

# 4 ECONOMIES OF SCALE AND LONG-RUN COSTS

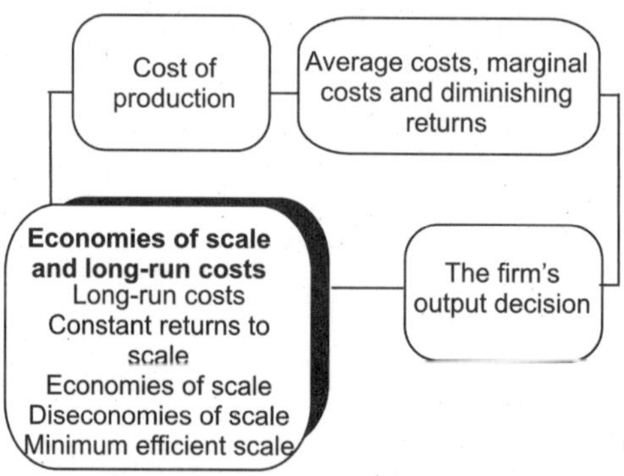


## 4.1 Long-run costs

We have not yet considered a firm's long-run costs of output. In the long-run, all inputs are variable, so the problems associated with the diminishing returns to variable factors do not arise; in other words, the law of diminishing returns applies only to short-run costs and not to long-run costs. Whereas short-run output decisions are concerned with diminishing returns given fixed factors of production, **long-run output decisions** are concerned with **economies of scale** when all factor inputs are variable.

Output will vary with variations in inputs, such as labour and capital.

(a) If output increases in the **same proportion** as inputs (for example, doubling all inputs doubles output) there are **constant returns to scale.**

(b) If output increases **more than in proportion** to inputs (for example, doubling all inputs trebles output) there are **economies of scale** and in the long-run average costs of production will continue to fall as output volume rises.

(c) If output increases **less than in proportion** to inputs (for example, trebling all inputs only doubles output) there are **diseconomies of scale** and in the long-run average costs of production will rise as output volume rises.

Returns to scale are, for example, concerned with improvements or declines in productivity **by increasing the scale of production**, for example by mass-producing instead of producing in small batch quantities.

### 4.2 Constant returns to scale

A feature of constant returns to scale is that **long-run** average costs and marginal costs per unit remain constant. For example:

| *Output* | *Total cost (with constant returns)* | *Average cost per unit* | *Marginal cost per unit* |
|---|---|---|---|
| | £ | £ | £ |
| 1 | 6 | 6 | 6 |
| 2 | 12 (2 × 6) | 6 | 6 |
| 3 | 18 (3 × 6) | 6 | 6 |
| 4 | 24 (4 × 6) | 6 | 6 |

In the real world, the duplication of all inputs might be impossible if one incorporates qualitative as well as quantitative characteristics in inputs. One such input is entrepreneurship. Doubling the size of the firm does not necessarily double the inputs of organisational and managerial skills, even if the firm does hire extra managers and directors. The input of entrepreneurship might be intangible and indivisible.

### 4.3 Economies of scale

**Definition**

> **Economies of scale**: factors which cause average cost to decline in the long-run as output increases.

The effect of economies of scale is to shift the whole cost structure downwards and to the right on the graph. A long-run average cost curve (LRAC) can be drawn as the 'envelope' of all the short-run average cost curves (SRAC) of firms producing on different scales of output. The LRAC is tangential to each of the SRAC curves. Figure 8.8 shows the shape of such a long-run average cost curve if there are increasing returns to scale – economies of scale – up to a certain output volume and then constant returns to scale thereafter.

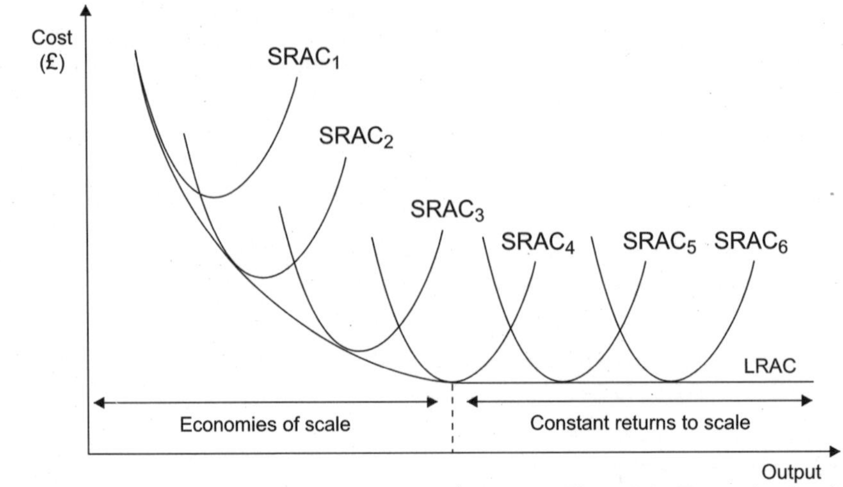


*Figure 8.8: Economies of scale*

### 4.4 Diseconomies of scale

It may be that the flat part of the LRAC curve is never reached, or it may be that diseconomies of scale are encountered. Diseconomies of scale might arise when a firm gets so large that it cannot operate efficiently or it is too large to manage efficiently, so that average costs begin to rise.

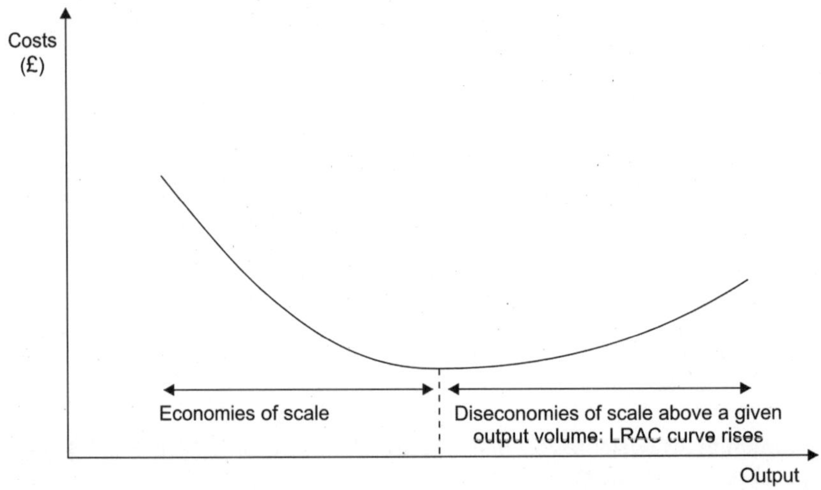


*Figure 8.9: Diseconomies of scale*

A firm should try to minimise its average costs in the long-run, and to do this it ought to try to produce output on a scale where the LRAC curve is at its lowest point. While there are economies of scale, a firm should always be trying to grow.

**Reasons for economies of scale**

The economies of scale attainable from large scale production fall into two categories.

(a) **Internal economies**: economies **arising within** the firm from the organisation of production

(b) **External economies**: economies attainable by the firm because of the growth of the industry as a whole

**Internal economies of scale**

*Technical economies*

Technical economies arise in the production process. They are also called **plant economies of scale** because they depend on the size of the factory or piece of equipment.

Large undertakings can make use of **larger and more specialised machinery**. If smaller undertakings tried to use similar machinery, the costs would be excessive because the machines would become obsolete before their physical life ends (ie their economic life would be shorter than their physical life). Obsolescence is caused by falling demand for the product made on the machine, or by the development of newer and better machines.

**Indivisibility of operations**

(a) There are operations which must be carried out at the same cost, regardless of whether the business is small or large; these are fixed costs and **average fixed costs always decline as production increases.**

(b) Similarly, other operations' costs vary a little, but not proportionately, with size (ie having 'semi-fixed' costs).

(c) Some operations are not worth considering below a certain level of output (eg advertising campaigns).

**Dimensional economies of scale** arise from the relationship between the volume of output and the size of equipment (eg storage tanks) needed to hold or process the output. The cost of a container for 10,000 gallons of product will be much less than ten times the cost of a container for just 1,000 gallons.

*Commercial or marketing economies*

**Buying economies** may be available, reducing the cost of material purchases through bulk purchase discounts. Similarly, **stockholding** becomes more efficient. The most economic quantities of inventory to hold increases with the scale of operations, but at a lower proportionate rate of increase.

*Organisational economies*

When the firm is large, centralisation of functions such as administration, R&D and marketing may reduce the burden of overheads on individual operating locations.

*Financial economies*

Large firms may find it easier to obtain loan finance at attractive rates of interest. It is also feasible for them to sell shares to the public via a stock exchange.

**Activity 6** **(15 minutes)**

The above list is not exhaustive. Can you add to it?

**External economies of scale**

External economies of scale occur as an **industry** grows in size. Here are two examples.

(a) **A large skilled labour force is created** and educational services can be geared towards training new entrants.

(b) **Specialised ancillary industries will develop** to provide components, transport finished goods, trade in by-products, provide special services and so on. For instance, law firms may be set up to specialise in the affairs of the industry.

**The effect of size**

The extent to which both internal and external economies of scale can be achieved will vary from industry to industry, depending on the conditions in that industry. In other words, big-sized firms are better suited to some industries than others.

(a) **Internal economies of scale** are potentially more significant than external economies to a supplier of a product or service for which there is a large consumer market. It may be necessary for a firm in such an industry to grow to a certain size in order to benefit fully from potential economies of scale, and thereby be cost-competitive and capable of making profits and surviving.

(b) **External economies of scale** are potentially significant to smaller firms who specialise in the ancillary services to a larger industry. For example, the development of a large world-wide industry in drilling for oil and natural gas off-shore has led to the creation of many new specialist supplier firms, making drilling rigs, and various types of equipment. Thus, a specialist firm may benefit more from the market demand created by a large customer industry than from its own internal economies of scale.

**Diseconomies of scale**

Economic theory predicts that there will be **diseconomies of scale** in the long-run costs of a firm, once the firm gets beyond an ideal size. The main reasons for possible diseconomies of scale are human and behavioural problems of managing a large firm. In a large firm employing many people, with many levels in the hierarchy of management, there may be a number of undesirable effects.

(a) Communicating information and instructions may become difficult.

(b) Chains of command may become excessively long.

(c) Morale and motivation amongst staff may deteriorate.

(d) Senior management may have difficulty in assimilating all the information they need in sufficient detail to make good quality decisions.

There will not usually be **technical** factors producing diseconomies of scale. The technology of higher volume equipment, on the contrary, is more likely to create further economies of scale.

The implication of diseconomies of scale is that companies should achieve a certain size to benefit fully from scale economies, but should not become too big, when cost controls might slacken and organisational inefficiency is likely to develop.

### 4.5 Minimum efficient scale

Given the idea of economies of scale, it is generally accepted that in any industry, there is a **minimum efficient scale** of production which is necessary for a firm to achieve the full potential economies of scale.

Just what this **minimum efficient scale** (MES) is will vary from industry to industry. In the paint manufacturing industry, for example, it might be necessary to have a 15% share of the market in order to achieve maximum scale economies, whereas in frozen food production, a 25% share of the market might be necessary, and so on. If a firm has a production capacity below the minimum economic scale, its unit costs of production will be higher than the unit costs of its bigger competitors, and so it will not compete successfully and it will make lower profits, or even losses. A profit maximising firm should be attempting to minimise its unit costs, and this means striving to achieve maximum scale economies, which in turn may mean having to grow bigger.

**Activity 7** **(15 minutes)**

Explain in detail the difference between economies of scale and diminishing returns to a factor.

## Chapter roundup

- It has been emphasised that economic costs are different from accounting costs, and represent the opportunity costs of the factors of production that are used.
- A firm's output decisions should be seen in both the short-run, when some factors of production are fixed and the long-run, when all factors of production can be varied.
- In the short-run, a firm's average cost (SRAC) curve is U-shaped, due to diminishing returns beyond a certain output level. In the short-run, a firm will maximise its profits where MR = MC.
- In the long-run, a firm's SRAC curve can be shifted, and a firm's minimum achievable average costs at any level of output can be depicted by a long-run average cost (LRAC) curve.
- The shape of the LRAC depends on whether there are increasing, constant or decreasing returns to scale. There are some economies of scale, and even if increasing returns to scale are not achievable indefinitely as output rises, up to a certain minimum efficient scale of production (MES) there will be increasing returns to scale. Firms will reduce their average costs by producing on a larger scale up to the MES.
- Whether there are constant or decreasing returns to scale beyond the MES will vary between industries and firms. Similarly, whether economies of scale are significant will vary between industries.
- Technological progress results in shifts in the LRAC, and since technology changes are continual, a firm's LRAC can probably never be 'stabilised' and unchanging for long.
- If economies of scale are significant, there is a strong argument in favour of growth by firms, which might occur either through organic growth (building up the firm's own resources) or through mergers and takeovers.
- Before going on, make sure that you understand two things.

  The concepts of fixed and variable costs and their relationship to average and marginal costs.

  The relationships between price, average revenue and marginal revenue
- Questions in the examination may require you to make calculations from limited cost and revenue data.

## Quick quiz

1 Explain the distinction between long-run and short-run costs.

2 What is the law of diminishing returns?

3 How can the prices of some products affect the supply of others?

4 Why might there be diseconomies of scale?

5 Which of the following is an example of an external economy of scale?

A Increased wage costs due to falling unemployment in the region.

B The employment of specialist managers by a firm to cope with higher output levels.

C The extension of low-cost telecommunication links to an area of the country not previously served by such links.

D Cheaper finance in recognition of the firm's increased share of the market and therefore its stability.

6 Which of the following cannot be true? In the short-run as output falls:

A Average variable costs falls

B Average total cost falls

C Average fixed cost falls

D Marginal costs falls

7 The tendency for unit costs to fall as output increases in the short-run is due to the operation of:

A Economies of scale

B The experience of diminishing marginal returns

C Falling marginal revenue

D Increasing marginal returns

8 Which of the following cannot be true in the short-run as output rises?

A Average variable cost rises

B Average total cost rises

C Average fixed cost rises

D Marginal cost rises

9 Harold Ippoli employs 30 people in his factory which manufactures sweets and puddings. He pays them £10 per hour and they all work maximum hours. To employ one more person he would have to raise the wage rate to £11 per hour. If all other costs remain constant, the marginal cost of labour is:

A £41.00

B £30.00

C £11.00

D £1.00

10 Which of the statements below best defines the difference between the short-run and the long-run?

A Labour costs are fixed in the short-run and variable in the long-run.

B Economies of scale are present in the long-run but not in the short-run.

C At least one factor of production is fixed in the short-run but in the long-run it is possible to vary them all.

D None of the factors of production is fixed in the short-run.

## Answers to quick quiz

1 The distinction between the short-run and the long-run is that in the long-run, all resource inputs are variable. In the short-run, probably only the amount of labour input is variable.

2 If one or more factors of production are fixed, but the input of another is increased, the extra output generated by each extra unit of input will eventually begin to fall.

3 At the level of output at which marginal cost equals marginal revenue

4 Diseconomies of scale are problems of size and tend to arise when the firm grows so large that it cannot be managed efficiently. Communications may become difficult, motivation may deteriorate because of alienation and senior management may find it difficult to identify the information they need in the vast volumes available.

5 C This is an external economy of scale.

A is a diseconomy of scale.

B is an internal economy of scale.

D is an internal economy of scale.

6 C Factual knowledge. The key to this question is to draw a diagram of the cost curves.

7 D The benefits of specialisation and the division of labour.

Economies of scale only operate in the long-run.

B results in rising unit costs in the short-run.

C is nothing to do with costs.

8 C Average fixed cost must continue to fall as output rises in the short term. This is a mathematical fact.

9 A

| | £ |
|---|---|
| Cost of 31 people (at £11 per hour) | 341.00 |
| Cost of 30 people (at £10 per hour) | 300.00 |
| Marginal cost | 41.00 |

10 C

## Answers to activities

1 (a) and (b) are correct; (c) is incorrect. An example might help. Suppose a firm has made 100 units of output, and now goes on to produce one more. The costs might be as follows.

| | *Cost of 100 units* | *Cost of 101 units* |
|---|---|---|
| | £ | £ |
| Total variable cost | 200 | 202 |
| Total fixed cost | 100 | 100 |
| Total cost | 300 | 302 |
| Average cost | £3.00 | £2.99 |

Marginal cost = 302p – 300p = 2p.

2 (a) Accounting profit

| | £ |
|---|---|
| Revenue | 160,000 |
| Costs | 125,000 |
| Profit | 35,000 |

(b) Economic profit

| | £ | £ |
|---|---|---|
| Revenue | | 160,000 |
| Accounting costs | 125,000 | |
| Opportunity cost of owner's time – extra salary forgone from alternative employment (20,000 – 12,000) | 8,000 | |
| Rental of factory (opportunity cost of £80,000) | 11,000 | |
| Opportunity cost of other capital tied up in the business (10% of £120,000) | 12,000 | |
| | | 156,000 |
| Economic profit | | 4,000 |

3 (a) True. Average total cost (AC) comprises average fixed cost (AFC) and average variable cost (AVC). AFC falls as output rises, and the fall may be sufficient to outweigh a possible increase in AVC. In such a case, AC will fall while AVC rises.

(b) False. It is *average* fixed costs per unit that fall as output increases. *Marginal* fixed costs = 0.

4 Diminishing returns occur when the marginal physical product of extra units of labour starts to decline. This begins to happen at output W, when the rate of increase in total output starts to decline as the number employed continues to increase.

5

| *Output* | *Total revenue (TR)* | *(a) Marginal revenue* $TR_n - TR_{(n-1)}$ | *Total costs (TC)* | *(b) Marginal costs* $TC_n - TC_{(n-1)}$ | *Total profit TR - TC* |
|---|---|---|---|---|---|
| | £ | £ | £ | £ | £ |
| 0 | – | – | 110 | – | (110) |
| 1 | 50 | 50 | 140 | 30 | (90) |
| 2 | 100 | 50 | 162 | 22 | (62) |
| 3 | 150 | 50 | 175 | 13 | (25) |
| 4 | 200 | 50 | 180 | 5 | 20 |
| 5 | 250 | 50 | 185 | 5 | 65 |
| 6 | 300 | 50 | 194 | 9 | 106 |
| 7 | 350 | 50 | 229 | 35 | 122(max) |
| 8 | 400 | 50 | 269 | 50 | 131(max) |
| 9 | 450 | 50 | 325 | 56 | 125 |
| 10 | 500 | 50 | 425 | 100 | 75 |

(a) Marginal revenue is the additional revenue which results from the sale of the last unit of output.

The figures in the table above show that marginal revenue is a constant £50 at all levels of output given. This means that average revenue (price) must also be a constant £50. The firm's demand curve is perfectly elastic, indicating that the firm is operating in a perfectly competitive market.

(b) The fixed costs of the firm are those costs which do not vary with output. The level of fixed costs are therefore the total costs of £110 at the output level of zero.

Marginal cost is the change in total cost arising from the production of the last unit of output. The marginal cost for each level of output is shown in the table.

(c) As stated in (a) above, the firm is operating in a perfectly competitive market. The firm will seek to maximise profits by producing at a level of output at which marginal cost equals marginal revenue. It can be seen from the table that this occurs at output level 8. Total profit (total revenues minus total costs) at this levels of output is £131.

6 (a) Large firms attract *better quality employees* if the employees see better career prospects than in a small firm.

(b) Specialisation of labour applies to management, and there are thus *managerial economies*; the cost per unit of management will fall as output rises.

(c) *Marketing economies* are available, because a firm can make more effective use of advertising, specialist salesmen, and specialised channels of distribution.

(d) Large companies are able to devote more resources to *research and development* (R & D). In an industry where R & D is essential for survival, large companies are more likely to prosper.

Large companies find raising finance easier and can often do so more cheaply. Quoted public limited companies have access to the Stock Exchange for new share issues. They are also able to borrow money more readily.

7 *Diminishing returns*. In the short-run, some factors of production are fixed, and some are variable. This means that a firm can increase the volume of its output in the short-run, but only within the constraint of having some fixed factors. As a result, the short-run average cost curve is U-shaped, because of increasing and then diminishing marginal returns. Diminishing marginal returns occur within a given production capacity limit.

*Economies of scale*. In the long-run, all factors of production are variable and so a firm can increase the scale of its output in the long-run without any constraints of fixed factors. By increasing output capacity in this way, a firm might be able to reduce its unit costs, for example by mass-producing with bigger and more efficient machines or more specialised machines. These cost reductions are economies of scale.

If economies of scale are sufficiently great, average costs and more particularly marginal unit costs will fall to the point where suppliers are able to reduce their selling prices and still maximise profits at the lower selling price. MC has fallen, and so MR will fall too, at the profit-maximising output level.

Economies of scale explain the L shape of a firm's long-run average cost curve.

# Chapter 9:

# MARKET TYPES AND MARKET FORCES

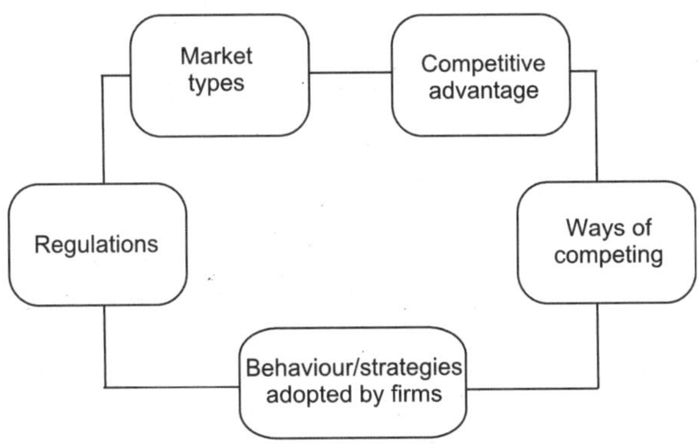


## Introduction

The degree and nature of competition faced by firms varies enormously. Firms which dominate the market for their goods enjoy substantial freedom in setting prices and other marketing variables such as advertising. By contrast, a high level of competition tends to curb prices and profits and the firm's long-run survival may depend on such factors as successful product development and innovation. So in this chapter we look at the implications for the firm of different market structures.

We go on to describe aspects of the competitive environment and the forces that make it hard or easy for businesses to compete before looking at the behaviour adopted by firms in imperfect market situations.

The last part of the chapter concentrates on the various methods of regulating the market.

## Your objectives

In this chapter you will learn about:

(a) Different market types
(b) The five competitive forces
(c) The marketing mix
(d) Competition and collusion
(e) Cartels
(f) Self-regulation
(g) Government regulation

## 1 MARKET TYPES

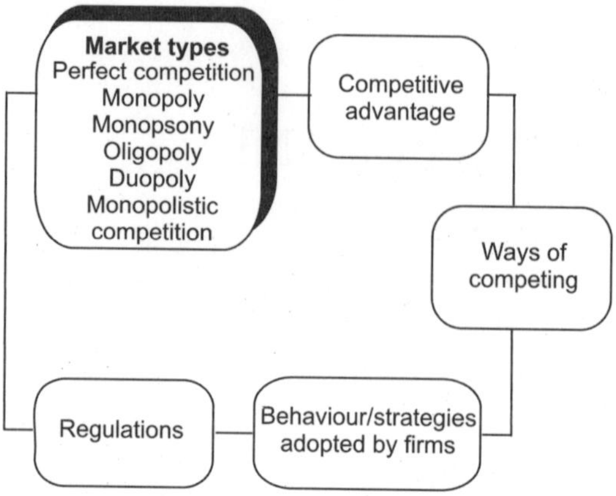


Economics is concerned with where money comes from and where it goes to: with buying and selling, with wages and profits and with wealth. Economists try to work out general laws which can be applied in a wide variety of businesses. The area of economics which is most relevant to us looks at how businesses and consumers behave in markets. The most important thing for an individual business or consumer is the number of rivals there are in the market. If you run the only supermarket in a town, you have a lot of power: people will come to you even if your prices are a bit high. If, however, another supermarket is opened next door to yours, you may have to cut your prices to keep your customers.

***We will now look at the types of market which economists identify. We will start with one which has lots of businesses and lots of consumers, so that no-one has much power, and go on to consider markets with a few big players.***

### 1.1 Perfect competition

**Definition**

> **Perfect competition** exists when there are so many people in the market, and other conditions are such, that no-one can influence the price, all other things being equal.

Perfect competition exists when all the following conditions are fulfilled.

(a) There are lots of buyers and lots of sellers. None of them can have any significant effect on the total quantity for sale (the *quantity supplied*) or the total amount which buyers want (the *quantity demanded*).

(b) The market price is fixed by the total quantity supplied and the total quantity demanded. If buyers want more, the price goes up. If businesses offer more for sale, the price goes down. This happens pretty well automatically. Suppose, for example, that you run a cake shop. You can only make 200 cakes a day, and you normally sell just that number at £1 each. Cakes then become more popular, and you find that 300 people come into your shop each day, each wanting a cake. You have to send the last 100 customers away empty-handed. The obvious thing to do is to increase the price, perhaps to £1.40. This will put off some of your customers (ideally 100 of them), so that you are back to 200 customers a day, but you get £280 a day instead of £200.

(c) There are no barriers to entry or exit. This means that if someone wants to come into the market, or leave it, they can without incurring high costs. Thus the market for legal advice is not perfect, because it takes a long time to qualify as a solicitor and start offering your services to the public. Ease of entry and exit helps to keep prices under control: if the quantity demanded goes up, prices will go up and businesses will start to make good profits. This will attract new businesses into the market, increasing the quantity supplied and bringing prices back down again.

(d) The product is standardised, so that customers do not care who they buy from. For example, if you are buying ingots of pure gold, you can buy them from anyone: one ingot is the same as another. This means that there is no point in promoting a brand: customers will only look at the price. Petrol companies have this problem – a litre of four star petrol is much the same thing, no matter who you buy it from. They therefore try to create artificial differences, using the image of the company, shops at filling stations, free gifts and so on.

(e) There is good exchange of information: everyone knows what everyone's prices are. Real life is not like this: when you look at a bag of sugar in Sainsbury's, you cannot find out straightaway how much Tesco's would charge you for the same product.

The consequence of all the above is that there is a single market price, and there is nothing anyone can do on their own to change it. Any business charging more than the market price will lose all its customers to its rivals, and any business charging less than the market price will be swamped with customers whom it cannot satisfy.

**Activity 1** **(10 minutes)**

Think about the market for new motor cars. In what respects is it like a perfect market, and in what respects is it unlike a perfect market?

***It probably strikes you that the conditions required for perfect competition to exist are pretty unrealistic and in fact it would be difficult to point to a truly perfect market. In the past in the UK it has certainly been a lot easier to point to the other extreme of market structure, monopoly.***

### 1.2 Monopoly

**Definition**

A **monopoly** exists when there is only one supplier of a product or service.

There are now few true monopolists. Most of those that existed were state-owned: for example, British Rail once had a monopoly on the provision of rail travel in most parts of Britain, but the government has sold rail travel operations to private operators. Even where we do find monopolies, they may not be as complete as they seem – it depends on how you define the market. British Rail certainly never had a monopoly on long-distance public transport, because people could choose to use coaches or air travel instead of trains. However, some companies control large shares of their markets, and they may then be almost as powerful as genuine monopolies. The water industry is close to being a monopoly. While there are many water companies, they hold a monopoly position in the area they serve. Consumers are only able to purchase from their local water provider. They cannot choose one of the other water companies no matter how better their service or cheaper their product. However, the government has recently stated that it intends to introduce competition to the water industry.

A business which has a monopoly on something which people really need could in theory charge what it liked, and still make sales, without any marketing effort. In practice, businesses cannot behave quite as badly as that. If something is really expensive, people will find substitutes. If, for example, electricity became too expensive, people would go back to gas for lighting although substitution is more difficult with water. In addition, marketing efforts are still needed to make sure that the product is what customers need, and to persuade customers to buy a bit more than they need.

Because monopolies could charge high prices, there are laws which try to control them, such as the Fair Trading Act of 1973 and the Enterprise Act 2002. **A company controlling 25% of the UK market is considered to be a monopoly**. The Director General of Fair Trading who can investigate unfair trade practices and monopolies and mergers which may put a company in a monopolistic position. Most service monopolies, such as water and gas, have regulators to look after the consumer's interest.

If a monopoly abuses its power and makes big profits, other businesses will want to move into the market and make big profits themselves. Thus for monopoly power to exist in the long run, **the monopoly must be able to set up barriers to entry**, to keep other businesses out. The most common types of barriers to entry are as follows.

(a) The business owns a **key resource** without a close substitute. For example, De Beers controls most of the world's supply of diamonds.

(b) There are **government restrictions**. For example, the Post Office had a legal monopoly on the delivery of letters for less than £1. In March 2001 the Post Office lost its monopoly after more than 150 years.

(c) Patents can give **exclusive rights** to exploit an invention for twenty years. For example, Black & Decker has enjoyed a monopoly on the WorkMate, and has been able to take legal action to stop the sale of similar, competing products. The patent for the WorkMate has now expired, but the trademark, WorkMate, first registered in 1969 is still in existence – which means that although other manufacturers can produce similar workbenches, none of them can be called the WorkMate.

(d) The huge amount of **capital** required to enter some markets can be a severe limitation. For many years the high cost of specialist cheese slicing equipment deterred competitors from entering the cheese slice market and gave Kraft a monopoly. This monopoly was lost when the cost of machinery fell dramatically.

**Activity 2** **(10 minutes)**

Can you think of three ways a monopoly may abuse its power to the detriment of the customer?

Sometimes a company's monopoly power is weak, because the barriers to entry are not really effective. For example, if the monopoly is based upon product differentiation which is primarily cosmetic, for example a brand name or fancy packaging, competitors could probably enter the market quite easily even though they could not legally copy the brand name or packaging. Only Heinz can sell baked beans under that name, but other companies can sell them under other names: if the customers do not see any significant difference between the contents of the tins, then there is no monopoly. This sort of threat may lead to the monopolist not charging too high a price, so as not to tempt competitors into the market. If a competitor does enter, a likely response is increased promotional activity. This is often in the forms of new advertising and price cuts.

### 1.3 Monopsony

**Definition**

**Monopsony** arises when there is only one buyer for a product.

The buyer may then be able to dictate terms to suppliers. For example the manufacturers of hydraulic mining equipment at one time only had British Coal as a customer in the UK. For some manufacturers, Marks and Spencer is the sole buyer of their products. Monopsonists must remember that they need a good quality supply: if they force prices down, they may end up getting shoddy goods.

### 1.4 Oligopoly

**Definition**

There is an **oligopoly** when there are a few large suppliers, whose business decisions affect each other.

We can distinguish oligopoly from monopoly by asking **whether the businesses in the market can set their own prices** (monopoly) or must take account of the prices set by other businesses (oligopoly). If an oligopolist sets a price higher than that charged by others, the company can expect to lose a lot of sales (but not necessarily all sales, unlike perfect competition).

The UK soaps and detergents market is an oligopoly, with Procter & Gamble and Unilever dominating the market. However, this does not mean that they set out to exploit customers, nor that they could do so if they wanted to. They are both acutely conscious of the German company Henkel and have not so far set prices for their products at the level where Henkel would consider it worthwhile to compete.

Like monopolies, oligopolies can only last for a long time if they are protected by barriers to entry.

**Activity 3** **(30 minutes)**

Is the United Kingdom grocery market an oligopoly? With the big four supermarket chains – Tesco, Wal-mart (Asda), Sainsbury and Morrisons – holding a combined market share of over 50%, how easy would it be for another retail grocery chain to enter the market? What specific obstacles are there?

An **oligopsony** is the buyers' equivalent of an oligopoly, when there are very few customers in the market.

### 1.5 Duopoly

Oligopoly, as we have just noted, is a market in which a small number of large firms make up the industry; in the case of there being just two firms this is called a duopoly.

Duopoly is a market with two sellers competing with each other with a homogenous good. The output of the other firm is assumed to be fixed. It is a case between competition and monopoly.

In the former the firms take the price as given; in the latter the monopolist can set the price. In duopoly each firm has an influence on the price but must take into account that the other firm also has an influence on the price. The profits of each firm depend on the decisions of both firms – and they must both take that into account when taking their decisions. Picture a beach with just two ice cream stands. While the vendors may start out anywhere, eventually they will locate in the middle of the beach where they will each be closest to half the bathers. In addition, as long as they can keep out any other competition, they can jointly act to raise their prices, lower the quality of their ice cream, and even take a holiday at the same time. An investor can come along and give both vendors a lot of money to sell only one kind of ice cream, or to keep another brand from being sold. As long as this is the only beach to swim at, the bathers will be the losers.

Between the two firms there will be strategic interaction as opposed to collusion. Each business must ask how its rival will react to changes in key business decisions. For example, if British Airways (BA) lowers its transatlantic fares, how will Virgin react? Suppose BA has determined that if it cuts its fares by 10% its profits will rise as long as Virgin does not match the price cuts but will fall if they do. BA must make an educated guess as to how Virgin will respond to its price move. Its best approach is to estimate how Virgin would react to each of its actions and then to maximise profits with strategic interaction recognised. Game Theory is used to do this – it can analyse situations involving two or more interacting decision-makers who have conflicting objectives.

## 1.6 Monopolistic competition

**Definition**

**Monopolistic competition** occurs when a large number of firms sell closely related, but not homogenous products. Instead, the products are said to be 'differentiated' and not seen as perfect substitutes by consumers. There is a heavy reliance on non-price actions eg, advertising, to differentiate the product.

The market has some features of competition and some of monopoly. Monopolistic competition resembles perfect competition in three ways:

(a) There are many buyers and sellers
(b) Entry and exit are easy
(c) Firms take other firm's prices as given

The distinction is that products or services are identical under perfect competition while under monopolistic competition they are differentiated. As a result the firm can raise its price without losing all of its customers.

To say that products are differentiated is to say that the products may be (more or less) good substitutes, but they are not perfect substitutes. The differentiated product sold by a firm in monopolistic competition has some features that make a customer prefer it to the available similar products of other firms. The power of any firm over price stems from this very fact that products are not perfect substitutes. Non-price actions are necessary to make the products differentiated. This action is either product development or advertising. Product development is sometimes only cosmetic to give the illusion of novelty. There are some arguments in favour of advertising:

- advertising is informative,
- advertising increases sales and permits economies of scale,
- advertising increases sales and contributes to economic growth,
- advertising supports the media,
- advertising increases competition and lowers prices.

Some of the arguments against advertising are:

- advertising is not informative but competitive,
- the economies of scale are illusory,
- advertising raises the cost curve,
- advertisers may use their influence to bias the media,
- advertising is used as an entry barrier, and
- advertising is not a productive activity.

Petrol stations, builders, restaurants, books, breakfast cereals, shampoos, frozen foods, piano lessons and hairdressers are all examples of monopolistic competition. The monopolistic competition form of market is extremely common. Almost all retail operations are in this form of market. Small businesses in all sectors fall in this category. Starting a business is relatively easily, but staying in business is not: that requires an ability to convince customers that the product is different and better than that of competitors.

**EXAMPLE**

Hairdressing illustrates the point – there are many of them in the country, and most of them are quite small. There is free entry to the market and it is at least possible that people know enough about their hairdressing options so that the 'sufficient information' condition is fulfilled. But the products of different hairdressers are not perfect substitutes. At the very least, their services are differentiated by location. A hairdresser in the city centre is not a perfect substitute for a hairdresser in the suburbs – although it may be a good substitute from the point of view of a customer who lives in the suburbs but works in the city centre. Hairdressers' services may be differentiated in other ways as well. Their styles may be different; the decor of the salon may be different, and that may make a difference for some customers; and even the quality of the conversation may make a difference.

The large number of firms in monopolistic competition implies that the firms are small in comparison to the entire market. Although they have some power over price (to the extent that their products are differentiated), they do not have sufficient power to retaliate if another firm changes its price. This is the major distinction between this market form and oligopoly.

***The context within which a business and its market operates is known as the environment. The business environment can be analysed to reveal a wide range of factors that influence success or failure in addition in addition to the theory of markets described above.***

## 2 COMPETITIVE ADVANTAGE

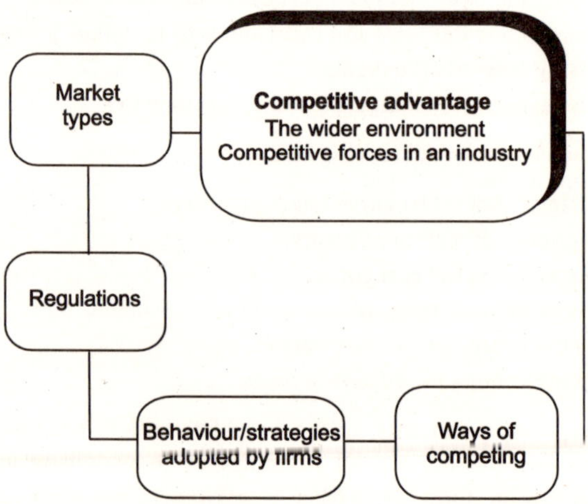

### 2.1 The wider environment

The wider business environment may be analysed into six segments using the PESTEL framework.

- political
- economic
- socio-cultural
- technological
- environmental protection
- legal

**Note**. The acronym **PESTEL** is sometimes replaced by **SLEPT**, in which the environmental protection aspect is folded into the other five, or even by **STEEPLE**, where the extra E stands for **ethics**.

**The political environment**

*Government policy*

Government is responsible for providing a stable framework for economic activity and, in particular, for maintaining and improving the physical, social and market infrastructure. Public policy on **competition** and **consumer protection** is particularly relevant to business strategy.

However, it is **political change** which complicates the planning activities of many firms.

(a) The governing party's election **manifesto** should be a guide to its political priorities, even if these are not implemented immediately.

(b) The government often publishes advance information about its plans for consultation purposes.

*Political risk*

The political risk in a decision is the risk that political factors will invalidate the strategy and perhaps severely damage the firm. Examples are wars, political chaos, corruption and nationalisation.

**The economic environment**

The **economic** environment affects firms at national and international level, both in the general level of economic activity and in particular variables, such as exchange rates, interest rates and inflation.

| **Factor** | **Impact** |
|---|---|
| Overall growth or fall in gross domestic product | Increased/decreased demand for goods (eg dishwashers) and services (holidays). |
| Local economic trends | Type of industry in the area. Office/factory rents. Labour rates. House prices. |
| Inflation | Low in most countries; distorts business decisions; wage inflation compensates for price inflation. |
| Interest rates | How much it costs to borrow money affects cash flow. Some businesses carry a high level of debt. How much customers can afford to spend is also affected as rises in interest rates affect people's mortgage payments. |

| Factor | Impact |
|---|---|
| Tax levels | Corporation tax affects how much firms can invest or return to shareholders. Income tax and VAT affect how much consumers have to spend, hence demand. |
| Government spending | Suppliers to the government (eg construction firms) are affected by spending. |
| The business cycle | Economic activity is always punctuated by periods of growth followed by decline, simply because of the nature of trade. The UK economy has been characterised by periods of boom and bust. Government policy can cause, exacerbate or mitigate such trends, but cannot abolish the business cycle. (Industries which prosper when others are declining are called counter-cyclical industries.) |

The **forecast state of the economy** will influence the planning process for organisations which operate within it. In times of boom and increased demand and consumption, the overall planning problem will be to **identify** the demand. Conversely, in times of recession, the emphasis will be on cost-effectiveness, continuing profitability, survival and competition.

Fairly obviously, there is constant and large scale interaction between government and economy through the various aspects of **government economic policy**.

**The sociocultural environment**

The social and cultural environment features long-term social trends and people's beliefs and attitudes.

**Factors of importance to organisational planners**

| Factor | Comment |
|---|---|
| **Growth** | The rate of growth or decline in a national population and in regional populations. |
| **Age** | Changes in the age distribution of the population. In the UK, there will be an increasing proportion of the national population over retirement age. In developing countries there are very large numbers of young people. |
| **Geography** | The concentration of population into certain geographical areas. |
| **Ethnicity** | A population might contain groups with different ethnic origins from the majority. In the UK, about 5% come from ethnic minorities, although most of these live in London and the south east. |
| **Household and family structure** | A household is the basic social unit and its size might be determined by the number of children, whether elderly parents live at home and so on. In the UK, there has been an increase in single-person households and lone parent families. |
| **Social structure** | The population of a society can be broken down into a number of subgroups, with different attitudes and access to economic resources. Social class, however, is hard to measure (as people's subjective perceptions vary). |

**Implications of demographic change**

(a) **Changes in patterns of demand**: an ageing population suggests increased demand for health care services: a young growing population has a growing demand for schools, housing and work.

(b) **Location of demand**: people are moving to the suburbs and small towns.

(c) **Recruitment policies**: there are relatively fewer young people so firms will have to recruit from less familiar sources of labour.

(d) **Wealth and tax**. Patterns of poverty and hence need for welfare provisions may change. The tax base may alter.

**Culture**

Through contact with a particular culture, individuals learn a language, acquire values and learn habits of behaviour and thought.

Knowledge of the culture of a society is clearly of value to businesses in a number of ways.

(a) **Marketers** can adapt their products accordingly, and be fairly sure of a sizeable market. This is particularly important in export markets.

(b) **Human resource managers** may need to tackle cultural differences in recruitment. For example, some ethnic minorities have a different body language from the majority, which may be hard for some interviewers to interpret.

Culture in a society can be divided into **subcultures** reflecting social differences. Most people participate in several of them.

Cultural change might have to be planned for. There has been a revolution in attitudes to female employment, despite the well-publicised problems of discrimination that still remain.

**The technological environment**

**Technology contributes to overall economic growth**. The **production possibility curve** describes the total production in an economy. There are three ways in which technology can increase total output.

(a) Gains in **productivity** (more output per units of input)
(b) Reduced **costs** (eg transportation technology, preservatives)
(c) New types of **product**

**Effects of technological change on organisations**

(a) **The type of products or services that are made and sold.**

(b) **The way in which products are made** (eg robots, new raw materials).

(c) **The way in which services are provided**. For example, companies selling easily transportable goods, such as books and CDs can offer much greater consumer choice and are enjoying considerable success over the Internet.

(d) **The way in which markets are identified**. Database systems make it much easier to analyse the market place.

(e) **The way in which firms are managed**. IT encourages delayering of organisational hierarchies, homeworking, and better communication.

(f) **The means and extent of communications with external clients**. The financial sector is rapidly going electronic – call centres are now essential to stay in business, PC banking is on the way, and the Internet and interactive TV are starting to feature in business plans.

---

**EXAMPLE:** *ETHANOL IN BRAZIL*

The need to consider the general environment as an integrated whole and not as a group of separate influences is illustrated by the history of the ethanol fuel industry in Brazil.

Ethanol as an alternative or supplement to petroleum products for motor vehicle fuel came back into prominence in 2005 because of major demand-driven rises in the global price of oil. In January 2006, *The Financial Times* reported that the Brazilian ethanol industry had been established in response to the oil crises of the 1970s. Subsidies for cane mills and price controls had helped to create a major industry. Here we see a problem that combines politics and economics being solved with a combination of politics, economics and technology.

During the 1980s, nearly all cars in Brazil were running on ethanol, so there was clearly a significant social effect in terms of acceptance. Unfortunately, in 1989, world sugar prices spiked and ethanol producers shifted their raw material (sugar cane) to the production of sugar. The price of ethanol was still controlled, so the inevitable result was a major shortage of fuels, which prejudiced consumers against it for a decade. Once again, politics, economics and social factors interact. A further prejudice was created against ethanol-fuelled cars, focusing on their inferior performance. This has only recently been overcome by the introduction of higher technology 'flex fuel' cars that utilise a mix of ethanol and petrol to boost performance.

---

**Environmental protection**

The **physical** environment is important for logistical reasons, as a source of resources, and because of increasing regulation.

The impact of business activity on the physical environment is now a major concern. Companies are under pressure to incorporate measures to protect the environment into their plans. This presents both challenges and opportunities, since some measures will impose costs, but others will allow significant savings. There is also a new range of markets for goods and services designed to protect or have minimum impact on the environment.

**The legal environment**

Laws come from common law, parliamentary legislation and government regulations derived from it, and obligations under EU membership and other treaties.

**Legal factors affecting all companies**

| Factor | Example |
|---|---|
| General legal framework: contract, tort, agency | Basic ways of doing business; negligence proceedings; ownership; rights and responsibilities, property |
| Criminal law | Theft; insider dealing; bribery; deception; industrial espionage |
| Company law | Directors and their duties; reporting requirements; takeover proceedings; shareholders' rights; insolvency |
| Employment law | Trade Union recognition; Social Chapter provisions; possible minimum wage; unfair dismissal; redundancy; maternity; Equal Opportunities |
| Health and Safety | Fire precautions; safety procedures |
| Data protection | Use of information about employees and customers |
| Marketing and sales | Laws to protect consumers (eg refunds and replacement, 'cooling off' period after credit agreements); what is or isn't allowed in advertising |
| Environment | Pollution control; waste disposal |
| Tax law | Corporation tax payment; Collection of income tax (PAYE) and National Insurance contributions; VAT |
| Competition law | General illegality of cartels |

### 2.2 Competitive forces in an industry

We make a distinction between two groups of factors.

(a) Environmental factors that characterise the nature of competition in one industry compared with another (eg in the chemicals industry compared with the clothing retail industry) and make one industry as a whole potentially more profitable than another (ie yielding a bigger return on investment).

(b) Factors that characterise the nature of competition within a particular industry.

**Activity 4** **(15 minutes)**

Jaspal is considering opening a new balti restaurant in Birmingham. He has seen the growth in the number of restaurants of this type over the past two years and has noticed that they all seem to be very popular. He wants to get in on the act. He realises that it is a competitive market, but is keen to join. What could influence the success of his venture?

*Michael Porter (Competitive Strategy)* suggests there are five basic competitive forces that influence the state of competition in an industry. Some industries have a bigger profit potential than others, since keener competition leads to lower profits. The five competitive forces are as follows.

(a) The **threat of new entrants** to the industry
(b) The **threat of substitute products** or services
(c) The **bargaining power of customers**
(d) The **bargaining power of suppliers**
(e) The **rivalry** amongst current competitors in the industry

We now describe each of them in turn.

**Definition**

1 **Capacity**: how much a firm (or industry) is capable of producing.

2 **Market share**: the sales of a good or service by one firm in the industry as a percentage of the sales of the good or service by all companies in the industry. For example, if VW had a 9% share of the European car market in 2008, this means that 9% of all cars sold in Europe in 2008 were VWs.

3 **Economy of scale**: the more of an item you make the cheaper it becomes to produce each item. For example, if you produce enough, you might save money on raw materials by buying in bulk.

***A new entrant into an industry will bring extra capacity. The new entrant will have to make an investment to break into the market, and will want to obtain a certain market share.***

### The threat of new entrants

The strength of the threat from new entrants is likely to vary from industry to industry, depending on two factors:

(a) The strength of the barriers to entry
(b) The likely response of existing competitors to the new entrant

**Definition**

**Barriers to entry**: a term used in economics to describe the factors that make it difficult for a new entrant to gain a foothold in an industry.

Barriers to entry can be categorised as shown in Figure 9.1.

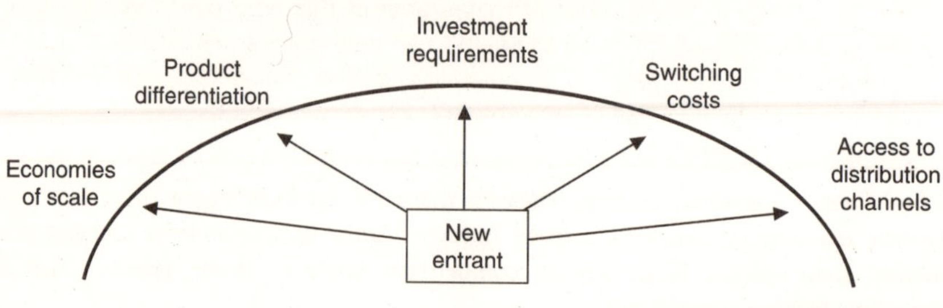


*Figure 9.1: Barriers to entry*

(a) **Economies of scale**. If the industry is one in which significant economies of scale can be obtained by producing more than certain volumes of output, existing firms in the industry should have a big advantage over any new entrant.

(b) **Product differentiation**. Existing firms in an industry may have built up a good image for their products through advertising, product quality etc. Customers may see no reason to change product. New entrants would have to spend heavily to overcome existing brand loyalties and to build up a brand image of their own.

(c) **Investment requirements**. The amount of capital for investment that is needed by a new entrant varies from one industry to another. When capital requirements are high, the barrier against new entrants is strong, particularly when the investment might be high-risk.

(d) **Switching costs**. A customer may have to incur costs when they switch from one supplier's products to another's. These costs are not just financial – time and inconvenience are costs in this context. The consequences of a switch might include the following.

  (i) Having to buy new ancillary equipment that is compatible with the equipment of the new supplier

  (ii) The loss of the existing supplier's after-sales service, which might include the provision of technical support

  (iii) The risk that the new supplier will be less reliable than the existing supplier.

  When customers think that switching costs will be high, there is a strong barrier to entry against new competitors in the industry.

(e) **Access to distribution channels**. Distribution channels are the means by which a manufacturer's products reach the end buyer. In some industries new distribution channels are difficult to establish, and existing ones hard to gain access to. For example, food products in the UK are largely sold through supermarket chains; it can be difficult for a new producer to get supermarket organisations to agree to stock his or her product. As the supermarkets become more powerful they are placing greater demands on food producers: failure to comply can mean exclusion from the channel of distribution.

(f) **Other cost advantages of existing producers**. These include the following.

  (i) *Patent rights*. A patent is a type of intellectual property. If you invent something new you can take out a patent to prohibit other people from copying your invention without your permission. Patents expire after a certain time, but they do give an innovating firm a breathing space in which to establish their product.

  (ii) *Experience and know-how.*

  (iii) *Government subsidies.*

  (iv) *Access to sources of raw materials on favourable terms.*

Entry barriers are not permanent. Firms in an industry try to strengthen them; potential new entrants may seek to lower them (eg through the use of new technology or by bypassing them).

---

**EXAMPLE: CLASSIFICATION AND EXAMPLES**

*Michael Porter* classifies the markets into four general cases:

- High barrier to entry and high exit barrier – eg telecommunications, energy
- High barrier to entry and low exit barrier – eg consulting, education
- Low barrier to entry and high exit barrier – eg hotels, siderurgy
- Low barrier to entry and low exit barrier – eg retail, e-commerce

Those markets with high entry barriers have few players and thus high profit margins. Those markets with low entry barriers have lots of players and thus low profit margins. Those markets with high exit barriers are unstable and not self-regulated, so the profit margins fluctuate very much along time. Those markets with a low exit barrier are stable and self-regulated, so the profit margins do not fluctuate along time.

The higher the barriers to entry and exit the more prone a market tend to be a natural monopoly. The reverse is also true. The lower the barriers the more likely to become a perfect competition.

---

***Competition can come not just from other firms but from other industries.***

### The threat from substitute products

The products or services that are produced in one industry may have substitutes that are produced by another industry.

---

**EXAMPLE: CROSS-CHANNEL TRANSPORT**

If you want to go from London to Paris there are a number of options open to you:

(a) Planes (London to Paris flight)
(b) Trains (Channel Tunnel) from London Waterloo to Paris (Gare du Nord)
(c) Automobiles (via car ferry or tunnel)

---

***Customers can set the pace by refusing to pay above a certain amount.***

### The bargaining power of customers

The profitability of an industry also depends on the strength of the bargaining power of its customers. Are the customers in a position to drive a hard bargain? At the moment, supermarkets find it hard to increase prices as customers are unable – or unwilling – to pay more. At the same time, the supermarkets themselves are in a very powerful position with respect to their own suppliers.

The following factors can influence the relative strength and weakness of customers and sellers.

(a) Customers are in a strong position relative to the seller when the seller makes a high proportion of their sales to that one customer.

(b) If most of a customer's supplies come from a single industry, the customer is in a weaker bargaining position than if only a small proportion do so.

(c) Customers who find it hard to switch products are in a weaker position.

(d) Suppliers may try to increase their bargaining power over customers by creating a strong brand image, making customers reluctant to move.

(e) A customer who makes low profits will be forced to insist on low prices from suppliers.

(f) Customers may take over sources of supply if suppliers charge too much.

(g) The skills of the customers' purchasing staff, or the price-awareness of consumers, can be a strength.

(h) When product quality is important to the customer the customer is less likely to be worried about price.

***Just as customers can influence the profitability of an industry by exerting pressure for higher quality products or lower prices, suppliers can also influence profitability by exerting pressure for higher prices.***

**The bargaining power of suppliers**

The ability of suppliers to get higher prices is influenced by the following factors:

(a) There being just one or two dominant suppliers to the industry, able to charge monopoly or oligopoly prices

(b) Suppliers being threatened by new entrants to the market, or by substitute products

(c) Whether or not the suppliers have other customers outside the industry and do not rely on the industry for the majority of their sales

(d) The importance of the suppliers' products to the customers' business

(e) The supplier having a unique product that buyers need to obtain but that cannot be found elsewhere

(f) The existence of high switching costs for buyers

**EXAMPLE**

Until the advent of personal computers (PCs), the computer industry was dominated by a small number of suppliers, led by IBM and followed by companies like Burroughs, Sperry and Data General. The equipment supplied by a manufacturer was generally incompatible with that made by a competitor, nor were software applications easily transportable across ranges and makes of machines. The computer firms were able to 'lock in' their customers, as switching costs were so high, and could charge high prices for upgrades. Customers could not mix and match, and so competition as to price was largely irrelevant when it came to system upgrades.

Recently, however, user organisations, supported sometimes by government agencies (The Department for Business, Enterprise and Regulatory Reform in the UK, and also the EU), have banded together in support of open systems so that machines can be connected, through the use of a common set of standards. This process has been aided by other changes in competitive conditions (eg the reduction in the cost of microchip technology). Customers now have more bargaining power. Furthermore, the adoption of MS-DOS, Windows and so on as de facto operating systems for PCs has meant a great deal more competition in that market.

---

**Activity 5** **(15 minutes)**

Assess the relative bargaining power of customers and suppliers in the following industries:

(a) The manufacture of fighter aircraft
(b) The production of computer hardware to business users
(c) Fresh fruit and vegetables

***The intensity of competitive rivalry within an industry affects the profitability of the industry as a whole.***

**Intensity of competition**

Competition can do one of two things.

(a) It can help the industry as a whole to expand, stimulating demand with new products and advertising.

(b) It can leave demand unchanged, in which case individual competitors simply spend more money, charge lower prices and so make lower profits, without getting any benefits except maintaining or increasing market share.

The intensity of competition depends on the following factors, some of which may be more important than others.

(a) Industries with **a large number of firms** are likely to be very competitive; but when the industry is dominated by a small number of large firms, competition is likely to be less intense, or is restricted.

(b) When firms are all benefiting from **growth in total demand**, their rivalry is less intense.

(c) In the short-run, **any revenue from sales is better than none at all**, if the firm incurs costs it cannot avoid. This encourages competition just to bring in cash.

(d) **Ease of switching** will encourage suppliers to compete (eg between Coke and Pepsi).

(e) When an industry is characterised by economies of scale from **substantial increases in capacity**, the industry may face recurring periods of over-capacity and price cutting. People invest too much, produce too much, flood the market, and prices fall.

(f) When one firm is not sure what another is up to, there is a tendency to respond to the **uncertainty** by formulating a more competitive strategy that assumes the worst.

(g) If a firm in the industry has put a lot of capital and effort into achieving certain **targets**, it will be likely to act very competitively in order to ensure that its targets are achieved.

(h) **Exit barriers** make it difficult for an existing supplier to leave the industry.

**Activity 6**  **(10 minutes)**

What types of barrier exist to prevent a car manufacturer from closing down a plant producing small family cars?

## 3 WAYS OF COMPETING

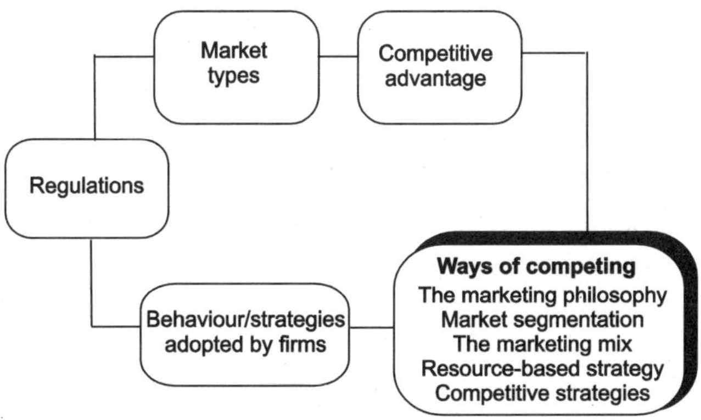


### 3.1 The marketing philosophy

*Marketing* has been defined by the Chartered Institute of Marketing as follows.

**Definition**

> **'Marketing** is the management process which identifies, anticipates and supplies customer requirements efficiently and profitably.'

Marketing is thus more than selling. It starts with the customer: what does the customer want? Once this has been discerned, then a product or service can be designed to satisfy these wants. It can then be promoted to those customers.

***Earlier sections have suggested that firms compete in a single market, mainly on price. This model helps us to understand how prices are set, but the real world is more complex. A market is not a single entity, but is composed of many individuals with different needs and aspirations. The segmentation approach, described below, recognises this fact.***

### 3.2 Market segmentation

**Definition**

> **Market segment**: a group of customers with certain things in common whose needs can be met with a distinct marketing mix.

A market is not a mass homogeneous group of customers, each wanting an identical product. Instead it can be analysed into segments.

(a) Although the total market consists of widely different groups of consumers, each group consists of people (or organisations) with common needs and preferences, who perhaps react to 'market stimuli' in much the same way.

(b) Recognition of segmentation enables a company to adopt the proper approach to selling to a given group of potential customers. This is more successful than an undifferentiated market approach to all customers.

An important initial marketing task is the identification of segments within the market. Typical market segments relate to the following.

(a) **Geographical area.** The needs and behaviour of potential customers in South East England may differ from those in Scotland or Italy.

(b) **End use**. Use in the consumer market might refer to leisure or work use. For example, the men's shirts market can be divided into leisure wear, formal wear and shirts to wear at work.

(c) **Age**. A useful age division might be 0 to 3 years, 4 to 6, 7 to 11, 12 to 19, 20 to 34, 35 to 49, 50 to 64 and over 64.

(d) **Sex**. For example, cosmetics.

(e) **Family size or family life cycle**. For example, young and single, young and married with no children, with one, two or more children, older and single, older and married with one, two or more children.

(f) **Income**. For example, the market for luxury goods.

(g) **Occupation**. For example, the market for men's suits might be segmented according to occupation.

(h) **Education**. For example, segment by education may be relevant to the marketing of newspapers.

(i) **Religion or religious sect**. For example, this form of segmentation may be important for marketing by charities.

(j) **Ethnic background**. For example, the market for music, records and tapes.

(k) **Nationality**. For example, the market for food.

(l) **Social class**. Socio-economic groupings appear to provide reliable indicators of different consumer attitudes and needs for a wide range of products.

(m) **Life style**. Differences in personality, activities, interests and opinions etc may be condensed into a few categories of life style.

(n) **Buyer behaviour**. For example, the usage rate of the product by the buyer, whether purchase will be on impulse, customer loyalty, the sensitivity of the consumer to marketing mix factors (described later in this chapter).

---

**FOR DISCUSSION**

Consider your own college. How might the market for its services be segmented? Suggest some segments that would be worth considering when deciding which types of course are to be offered.

---

**Marketing research**

While segmentation can give a basis for marketing, any marketing decision is inevitably made under conditions of uncertainty and risk. The information system for marketing is referred to as marketing research.

**Definition**

1 **Marketing research**: the objective gathering, recording and analysing of all facts about problems relating to the transfer and sales of goods and services from producer to consumer or user.

2 **Market research**: finding out information about a particular product or service.

You may have been stopped in the street by a market researcher with a clipboard and a number of questions. Many organisations use market-research techniques. For example, London Underground employ researchers to assess customer satisfaction with train cleanliness.

***Having established what customers want we can now decide on how they can be satisfied. The marketing mix does this job.***

### 3.3 The marketing mix

The last word of the Chartered Institute of Marketing's definition of marketing is *profitably*. After all, many customers would be absolutely delighted if you were to satisfy all their needs for exotic holidays, caviar, champagne, private jets and so forth, for nothing. The marketing orientation is a business orientation that seeks to provide satisfaction of customer wants at a profit.

There is thus a balance to be struck between organisational capacity and customer requirements. This balance is expressed in the *marketing mix*, which is the framework in which the customer and the business deal with each other.

| | |
|---|---|
| Product | Promotion |
| Place | Price |

*Figure 9.2: The marketing mix*

These are known as the 4 'P's: product, place, promotion, price.

**Product**

The product element of the marketing mix is what is being sold, whether it be 'widgets', power stations, haircuts, holidays or financial services. Product issues in the marketing mix include such factors as:

(a) Design (size, shape)
(b) Features
(c) Quality and reliability
(d) After-sales service (if necessary)
(e) Packaging

Some issues related to products are as follows.

(a) *Core and augmented products*. The core product is a product's essential features. As a simple example, the core product of a credit card is the ability to borrow up to a certain limit and pay off in varied instalments. Augmentations are extra features. A common augmentation to credit cards is free travel insurance.

(b) Marketing managers make the following distinctions.

(i) **Product class**: a broad category of product, such as 'cars'. This corresponds to the core product identified above.

(ii) **Product form**: the different types of product within a product class. The product form 'cars' may have several classes, including five-door hatchbacks, four-wheel drive vehicles, hearses and so forth.

(iii) **Brand or make**: refers to the particular brand or make of the product form. For example, the Nissan Micra, Vauxhall Corsa and VW Polo are, broadly speaking, examples of the same product form.

### Place

The place element of the marketing mix deals with how the product is distributed – how it reaches its customers. Examples of issues relating to place are as follows.

(a) Where are products sold? In supermarkets or corner shops? Which sales outlets will be chosen?

(b) Will products be sold by mail order? (This might generate cost savings.)

(c) The location of warehouses and efficiency of the distribution system. (A customer might have to wait a long time if the warehouse is far away.) Arguably the **speed of delivery** is an important issue in place.

### Promotion

Promotion in the marketing mix includes all marketing communications that let the public know of the product or service. Promotion includes the following.

(a) Advertising (newspapers, billboards, TV, radio)

(b) Direct mail (or 'junk mail')

(c) Sales promotion (eg special displays in stores, coupons, special offers)

(d) Direct selling by sales personnel (a more common feature of industrial markets than consumer markets, with the exception of certain products such as financial services)

### Price

The price element of the marketing mix is the only one that deals with revenue. Factors affecting price include the following.

(a) Competitors' prices. High price is often taken as being synonymous with quality, so pricing will reflect part of a product's image. (Stella Artois has been marketed as 'reassuringly expensive'.)

(b) Discounts.

(c) Payment terms (eg offering a period of interest-free credit).

(d) Trade-in allowances.

(e) The need to make a profit.

**Activity 7** **(20 minutes)**

Identify the marketing mix for the following two products and say why you think that the manufacturer of each product chose the mix you have identified:

(a) Teletubby figures

(b) A Ferrari car

***There is little point in simply copying competitors, and many firms develop a distinct marketing mix of their own. Now we can integrate what we have discussed in the earlier sections of this chapter and identify ways in which businesses compete with each other.***

### 3.4 Competitive strategies

Competitive advantage is anything that gives one organisation an edge over its rivals in the products it sells or the services it offers. Much of the competitive advantage that an organisation might hope to achieve is provided by the nature/quality/price of its products.

(a) One company's product may have a definite edge over its rivals because it is better in quality, or cheaper in price.

(b) Where rival products are much alike (eg petrol, many processed foods etc), competitive advantage may be sought by making the product seem different and more desirable than a rival producer's similar product, or by augmenting it in particular ways. For example, in 2001 Shell developed Optimax, a high performance unleaded fuel, that sells for a few pence more than standard unleaded petrol.

The type of competitive strategy that a firm adopts depends on the competitive strategies adopted by rivals and has implications for product design and quality, pricing and advertising.

(a) A **cost leadership strategy** seeks to achieve the position of lowest-cost producer in the industry as a whole. By producing at the lowest cost, the manufacturer can compete on price with every other producer in the industry, and earn the highest unit profits.

(b) A **differentiation strategy** is based on the assumption that competitive advantage can be gained through particular characteristics of a firm's products or brands. These differences might be real (for example, design differences) or largely imaginary, created mainly by advertising and brand image (for example, 'designer label' clothing and washing powders). The customer is prepared to pay more for this distinguishing characteristic. Types of characteristic that may be relevant include:

    (i) Colour differences

    (ii) Size differences

    (iii) Different wrappings or containers

    (iv) Variants of the product for different market segments (eg children, adults etc)

    (v) Small changes in the products' formulations to maintain their novelty value

    (vi) Different technical specifications

(c) A **focus strategy** is a strategy based on **segmenting** the market and focusing on particular market segments. The firm will not sell its products industry-wide (in contrast to a differentiation strategy), but will focus on a particular type of buyer or geographical area.

(i) A **cost-focus strategy** involves selecting a segment of the market and specialising in a product (or products) for that segment. The firm, by specialising in a limited number of products, or by concentrating on a small geographical area, can keep costs to a minimum. This type of strategy is often found in the printing, clothes manufacture and car repairs industries, for example.

(ii) A **differentiation-focus strategy** involves selecting a segment of the market and competing on the basis of product differentiation for that segment. Luxury goods are the prime example of such a strategy.

**Activity 8** **(10 minutes)**

What strategy is being used by the holiday firm described below?

*Club 18–30:* Targeted at a specific age group, this company promises 'fun' or 'activity' holidays in or around beach resorts. A poster advertising campaign in 1994/5 had to be suspended as a result of complaints that it was too 'raunchy'. Holidays are fairly cheap.

### 3.5 Resource-based strategy

The resource-based approach to strategy starts from a consideration of capabilities and, in particular, of distinctive **competences** and **resources**.

**Position-based strategy** seeks to develop competitive advantage in a way that responds to the **nature of the competitive environment**: the firm **positions** its offering in response to the opportunities or threats it discerns.

A fundamentally different approach is **resource-based strategy**. This was developed in response to two problems with the positioning method.

(a) Many environments are too complex and dynamic to permit continuing effective analysis and response.

(b) Once an opportunity is discerned and an offering made, it is very easy for competitors to make similar offerings, thus rapidly eroding competitive advantage.

The resource-based view is that sustainable competitive advantage is only attained as a result of the **possession of distinctive resources**. These may be **physical resources**, such as the effective monopolisation of diamonds by *De Beers*, or, more typically in today's service economies, they may be **competences**.

### Terminology

As is so often the case, the terminology used in the literature of resource-based strategy is not yet formalised. Johnson, Scholes and Whittington use their own very clear and specific set of terms when discussing resources and competences.

a) **Strategic capability** is the adequacy and suitability of the resources and competences of an organisation for it to survive and prosper.

b) **Tangible resources** are the physical assets of an organisation, such as plant, labour and finance.

c) **Intangible resources** are non-physical assets such as information, reputation and knowledge.

d) **Competences** are the activities and processes through which an organisation deploys its resources effectively.

e) **Threshold capabilities** are essential for the organisation to be able to compete in a given market.

f) **Threshold resources** and **threshold competences** are needed to meet customers' minimum requirements and therefore for the organisation to continue to exist.

g) **Unique resources** and **core competences** underpin competitive advantage and are difficult for competitors to imitate or obtain.

To some extent, the resource-based approach is diametrically opposed to the marketing concept since, instead of approaching strategy on the basis of giving customers what they want, it concentrates on exploiting what the business already has to offer.

In fact, this distinction is largely theoretical, but it leads to some important ideas.

(a) Where the marketing concept is adopted, it will still be necessary to deploy threshold capabilities in all critical areas and the possession of unique resources and core competences will enhance the market offering.

(b) Conversely, where strategy is built on unique resources and core competences, marketing activities must be carried out with at least threshold competence if the customer is to be satisfied.

(c) As a result, when a company clearly adheres to one approach or the other, the reasons for this may be more cultural than reasoned.

**Innovation and competitive advantage**

For many organisations, product innovation and being the **first mover** may be a major source of competitive advantage. However, the first mover also has particular problems.

- Gaining regulatory approval where required
- Uncertain demand
- High levels of R&D costs
- Lower cost imitators
- Costs of introduction such as training sales staff and educating customers

Research data indicate that there is a **negative correlation** between **profitability** and a high level of expenditure on **R&D**, perhaps because of the costs associated with these problems.

**New product development**

The development of new products might be considered an important aspect of a firm's competitive and marketing strategies.

(a) New and innovative products can lower **entry barriers** to existing industries and markets, if new technology is involved.

(b) The interests of the company are best met with a balanced product portfolio. Managers therefore must plan when to introduce new products, how best to extend the life of mature ones and when to abandon those in decline.

A strategic issue managers must consider is their approach to new product development.

(a) **Leader strategy**. Do they intend to gain competitive advantage by operating at the leading edge of new developments? There are significant implications for the R&D activity and the likely length of product life cycles within the portfolio if this strategy is adopted. Also, **R&D costs** are likely to be heavy, with a significant reduction in potential profitability as a result.

(b) **Follower strategy**. Alternatively they can be more pro-active, adopt a follower strategy, which involves lower costs and less emphasis on the R & D activity. It sacrifices early rewards of innovation, but avoids its risks. A follower might have to license certain technologies from a leader (as is the case with many consumer electronics companies). However, research indicates that this can be a **more profitable strategy** than being an innovator, especially when the follower is able to learn from the leader's mistakes.

**Research and development**

Here are some definitions culled from Statement of Standard Accounting Practice 13.

a) **Pure research** is original research to obtain new scientific or technical knowledge or understanding. There is no obvious commercial or practical end in view.

b) **Applied research** is also original research work like (a) above, but it has a specific practical aim or application (eg research on improvements in the effectiveness of medicines etc).

c) **Development** is the use of existing scientific and technical knowledge to produce new (or substantially improved) products or systems, prior to starting commercial production operations.

**Product and process research**

There are two categories of R&D.

a) **Product research** is based on creating new products and developing existing ones, in other words the organisation's 'offer' to the market.

b) **Process research** is based on improving the way in which those products or services are made or delivered, or the efficiency with which they are made or delivered.

**Product research – new product development**

The new product development process must be carefully controlled; new products are a major source of competitive advantage but can cost a great deal of money to bring to market. A screening process is necessary to ensure that resources are concentrated on projects with a high probability of success and not wasted on those that have poor prospects.

**Process research**

Process research involves attention to how the goods/services are produced. Process research has these aspects.

(a) **Processes** are crucial in service industries (eg fast food), where processes are part of the services sold.

(b) **Productivity**. Efficient processes save money and time.

(c) **Planning**. If you know how long certain stages in a project are likely to take, you can plan the most efficient sequence.

(d) **Quality management** for enhanced quality.

An important aspect of process research is that advances are much more difficult to imitate then are product developments. Competitors can purchase and **reverse engineer** new products. With good physical security in place, they will find it much more difficult to imitate new processes.

**The strategic role of R&D**. R&D should support the organisation's chosen strategy. To take a simple example, if a strategy based on high quality and luxury has been adopted, it would be inappropriate to expend much effort on researching ways of minimising costs. If the company has a competence in R&D, this may form the basis for a strategy of product innovation. Conversely, where product lifecycles are short, as in consumer electronics, product development is fundamental to strategy.

***Economists identify a number of industry structures that act as models to explain the characteristics of markets and the behaviour of firms within these markets.***

## 4 BEHAVIOUR/STRATEGIES ADOPTED BY FIRMS

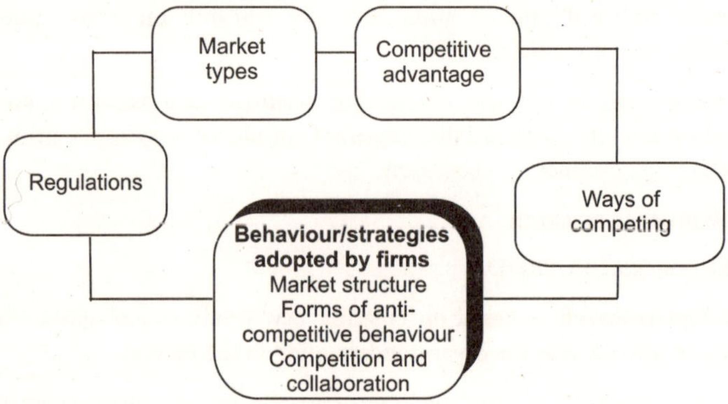


### 4.1 Market structure

The term market structure is used to describe:

(a) The number of buyers and sellers operating in a market

(b) The extent to which the market is concentrated in the hands of a small number of buyers and/or sellers

(c) The degree of collusion or competition between buyers and/or sellers

Market structures range from the theoretical extremes of perfect competition and pure monopoly. In practice, examples of the extremes are rare.

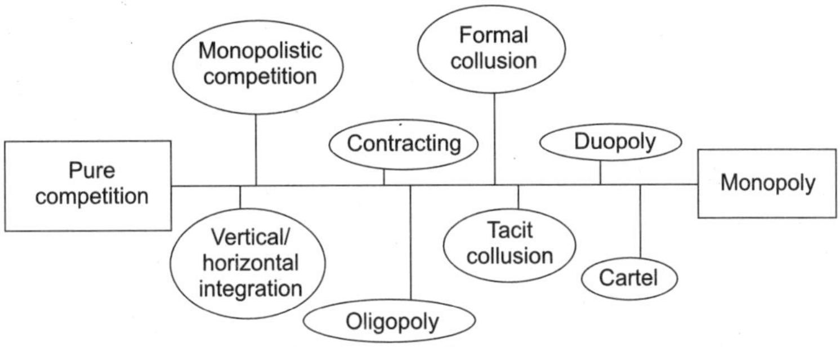


*Figure 9.3: Perfect competition to perfect monopoly spectrum*

Very few markets can be classified as perfectly competitive or as pure monopoly. Most markets lie between the two extremes – in the realm of 'imperfect competition'.

Most firms would like to be in the position of a monopolist and able to control the price level and output of their market. This is an unrealistic aim, but, in practice, firms can create imperfections in markets that give them limited monopoly power over their customers.

In its purest extreme, monopoly in a market occurs where there is only one supplier to the market, perhaps because of regulatory, technical or economic barriers to entry. However, this rarely occurs in practice. Sometimes, monopoly control over supply comes about through a group of suppliers acting in collusion together in a 'cartel'.

Many real world markets have a relatively small number of competing firms. Where there are large numbers of competing firms an individual firm's output and pricing decisions are unlikely to have a major effect on its rivals. By cutting price slightly it may significantly increase its market share, while only taking a negligible share from each of its rivals, thus reducing the likelihood of retaliatory behaviour. However, where there are relatively few firms, then an increase in output/reduction in price by one will firm will have a marked impact on the sales of its rivals and they are likely to react. The essential feature of oligopolistic markets is that firms recognise that their actions will influence the behaviour of their rivals, ie they recognise that they are interdependent.

### 4.2 Forms of anti-competitive behaviour

The main types of anti-competitive behaviour include:

(a) Collusion
(b) Cartels
(c) Price fixing
(d) Predatory or destroyer pricing
(e) Vertical restraints
(f) Insider dealing/trading

### Collusion

The uncertainty that exists in oligopolistic markets and the high costs of non-price competition can lead to collusive behaviour by firms. Collusion may be explicit in the form of formal agreements or understandings (cartel) or it may be tacit. Although the consequences of both formal and tacit collusion are the same, they are treated differently under competition law.

**Tacit collusion** is difficult with more than a very small number of firms, particularly if they sell a variety of different products. Establishing mutually beneficial prices on a wide range of products given likely differences in cost structures can be difficult without some form of explicit understanding. Even under formal collusive arrangements, firms face incentives to cheat. In the absence of complete communications firms are imperfectly informed about market conditions and rivals' intentions. In such circumstances actions by rivals may be misunderstood as 'cheating' provoking a response and making tacit collusion difficult to maintain. In order to overcome such problems firms may engage in 'facilitating practices'. However, such practices may themselves fall foul of competition law.

### Cartels

A cartel is a formal agreement among firms in an oligopolistic industry. Cartel members may agree on such matters as prices, total industry output, market shares, allocation of customers, allocation of territories, establishment of common sales agencies, and the division of profits or combination of these. Cartel in this broad sense is synonymous with 'explicit' forms of collusion. Cartels are formed for the mutual benefit of member organisations.

The theory of 'co-operative' oligopoly provides the basis for analysing the formation and the economic effects of cartels. Generally speaking, cartels attempt to emulate that of a monopoly by restricting industry output, raising or fixing prices in order to earn higher profits.

For the cartel to work effectively the producers must control supply to maintain an artificially high price. Collusion is easier to achieve when there is a relatively small number of firms in the market and a large number of customers, market demand is not too variable and the individual firm's output can be easily monitored by the cartel organisation.

There are two common forms of cartel:

(a) The price fixing cartel;
(b) The market sharing cartel.

### Price fixing cartel

The aim of price fixing is to **maximise joint profits** and act as if the market was a pure monopoly. It is the practice by the government, or a private business, of setting the price for a particular commodity. The government may set prices to eliminate price fluctuations for commodities for which demand is relatively stable, but if private businesses engage in the practice to obtain artificially high prices for commodities, it is illegal.

Price-fixing agreements can take many forms. In addition to the obvious case of agreements to charge the same price, they can also include agreements on discounts, margins, price differentials, price increases or minimum prices.

Why do price fixing arrangements generally collapse? Some economists believe that price-fixing cartels are inherently unstable and that at some point they inevitably come under pressure and finally break down. There are a number of sources of potential instability for price fixing cartel arrangements.

- **Falling demand** creates tension between firms eg during an economic downturn
- The **entry of non-cartel firms** into the industry increases market supply and puts downward pressure on the cartel price
- **Exposure of illegal price fixing** by the government or other regulatory agencies causes an arrangement to end
- **Over-production and excess supply** by cartel members breaks the price fixing

The Prisoners' Dilemma game suggests that all collusive agreements tend to fall eventually because although price fixing is in the joint interests of all members of a cartel, it is not a profit maximising equilibrium for each individual firm.

**Market sharing cartel**

Market sharing agreements are an alternative to a price-fixing cartel. They involve firms **dividing up the market between them and agreeing not to sell in each other's designated area**. This enables each firm to set prices knowing that its 'rivals' will not undercut them. A market-sharing cartel may be no more than an agreement among firms not to approach each other's customers or not to sell to those in a particular area. It may involve secretly allocating specific territories to one another or agreeing lists of which customers are to be allocated to which firm.

Firms participating in a cartel have a strong incentive to cheat by offering secret discounts to customers to increase sales. Where there are only a small number of firms it may be easier to detect cheating and ensure that the participants adhere to any cartel arrangement. International experience indicates that cartels involving large numbers of firms are often organised by trade associations who 'police' the agreements to prevent cheating.

A distinction needs to be drawn between public and private cartels. In the case of **public cartels**, the government may establish and enforce the rules relating to prices, output and other such matters. Export cartels and shipping conferences are examples of public cartels. In many countries depression cartels have been permitted in industries deemed to be requiring price and production stability and/or to permit rationalisation of industry structure and excess capacity. In Japan for example, such arrangements have been permitted in the steel, aluminum smelting, shipbuilding and various chemical industries. Public cartels were also permitted in the United States during the depression in the 1930s and continued to exist for some time after World War II in industries such as coal mining and oil production. Cartels have also played an extensive role in the German economy during the inter-war period. International commodity agreements covering products such as coffee, sugar, tin and more recently oil (OPEC: Organisation of Petroleum Exporting Countries) are examples of international cartels, which have publicly entailed agreements between different national governments.

Crisis cartels have also been organised by governments for various industries or products in different countries in order to fix prices and ration production and distribution in periods of acute shortages. In contrast, **private cartels** entail an agreement on terms and conditions from which the members derive mutual advantage but which are not known or likely to be detected by outside parties. Successful cartels, be they public or private, require 'concurrence', 'coordination' and 'compliance' among members. This means that cartel members need to be able to detect when violations of an agreement take place and be able to enforce the agreement with sanctions against the violators. These conditions are not easily met and this often explains why cartels tend to break down over time.

**Activity 9** **(20 minutes)**

What do you know about OPEC?

### Predatory pricing

The predatory pricing argument is very simple. The predatory firm first lowers its price until it is below the average cost of its competitors. The competitors must then lower their prices below average cost, thereby losing money on each unit sold. If they fail to cut their prices, they will lose virtually their entire market share; if they do cut their prices, they will eventually go bankrupt. After the competition has been forced out of the market, the predatory firm raises its price, compensating itself for the money it lost while it was engaged in predatory pricing, and earns monopoly profits for a time.

Predatory pricing is used by large businesses that give massive discounts. This practice helps to destroy independent small businesses, which cannot compete by selling for low prices. When the small businesses are forced to leave, the large ones often increase prices to higher than they were previously set by the small businesses.

Another example of predatory pricing occurs when firms who have market power in more than one market set prices below cost in one period in order to drive out rivals and restrict entry. Having done so, it once again raises price.

### Vertical restraint in the market

Generally, vertical restraints are limitations placed on retailer activities by the manufacturer or distributor. First are agreements in which a seller attempts to control a factor relating to the eventual resale of the product. The second broad category includes efforts by a seller to limit a buyer's purchases from sellers of competing products. The impact of these restraints is on competition between brands.

(a) *Exclusive dealing*

This occurs where a retailer undertakes to sell only one manufacturer's product and not the output of a rival firm. These may be supported with long-term contracts, which bind a retailer to a supplier and can only be terminated by the retailer at great cost.

Vertical restraints on distribution can be of the price or non-price variety. Those in the first category include minimum and maximum resale prices. Non-price restraints appear in a number of forms, but typically involve the allocation of particular geographic areas or classes of customers to specified resellers. Distribution agreements may seek to prevent parallel trade between EU countries (eg from lower-priced to higher priced countries) – this lay at the heart of the decision by the EU to fine Nintendo in October 2002.

(b) *Territorial exclusivity*

Territorial exclusivity happens when a particular retailer is given sole rights to sell the products of a manufacturer in a specified area.

(c) *Quantity discounts*

Where retailers receive progressively larger discounts the more of a given manufacturer's product they sell – this gives them an incentive to push one manufacturer's products at the expense of another's.

(d) *A refusal to supply*

Where a retailer is forced to stock the complete range of a manufacturer's products or else he receives none at all.

**Insider dealing**

Insider dealing is a criminal offence and happens when individuals use, or encourage others to use, information about a company which is not generally available (that they have got through inside knowledge or contacts), to deal for their own profit. The law applies to transactions on the Stock Exchange and to off-market trading. The Stock Exchange has its own rules reinforcing the law on insider dealing.

The Companies Act prohibits individuals and companies who are connected with the company from using non-public price-sensitive ('inside') information to deal in securities of that company. Examples of the type of information that may be considered to be 'inside information' include details of interim and final results, mergers, acquisitions and takeovers.

**Horizontal and vertical integration**

*Horizontal integration*

When two firms in the same business merge, there is horizontal integration. Horizontal integration tends to create monopolies, or at least firms with a disproportionate share of the market. If, for example, All-England Chocolate plc with a 15% share of the UK chocolate market were to merge with British Choc plc which has a 20% share of the UK market, the enlarged company might expect to hold a 35% market share. A recent example is the merger between the Nationwide and Portman building societies in August 2007.

*Vertical integration*

Two firms operating at different stages in the production and selling process might merge. When they do, vertical integration occurs. For example, the stages in the production of petrol for cars are as follows.

- Oil extraction
- Shipping (in tanker fleets, or by pipeline)
- Refining
- Distribution (to petrol stations)
- Retail sales (at petrol stations)

A company that operates exclusively in oil refining might take over an oil shipping company, and perhaps an oil extraction company too. This would be backwards vertical integration, ie back through stages in production towards the raw material growing/ extraction stage.

The same company might take over a company with a distribution fleet of petrol tanker lorries, and perhaps a chain of petrol stations too. This would be forwards vertical integration, ie forward through stages in production and selling towards the end consumer sales stage.

### 4.3 Competition and collaboration

Economists argue that strong competition between many firms usually creates the best outcomes for consumers. From the seller's point of view, competition may be viewed as a destructive force that reduces profits in both the long and the short run. It is not surprising therefore, that organisations frequently collaborate with each other, rather than try to put their competitors out of business.

The nature of the collaboration can be wide ranging, and new variations are continually being devised by more adventurous businesses. Some examples of collaboration are given below:

(a) *Collaborations of buyers* – smaller firms are often able to improve the power of buyers by joining consortia that buy in bulk thereby negotiating lower prices. Sometimes, these consortia become so successful that they are able to trade effectively on the open market.

(b) *Collaborations of suppliers* – organisations are able to reduce competitive rivalry and limit new entrants by agreements concerning safety, standards, service etc. Industries as diverse as furniture removal and accountancy protect themselves from outbreaks of low price and quality-based competition that damage profits, and may be against the buyer's best interests.

(c) *Collaborations to reduce competitive pressure* – in industries where there is over-supply, such as the car industry, there are a large number of collaborative arrangements that prevent prices falling as far as they might otherwise do. Weaker players are often kept in business by ensuring that ownership and risks are dispersed throughout the industry.

(d) *Collaborations to reduce risk* – organisations in particularly risky environments frequently collaborate to prevent over exposure to a particular project. The European Aircraft industries have collaborated in the development of large airliners, and pharmaceutical companies frequently create joint ventures to collaborate with their rivals in the development of new drugs. This reduces the financial risk if the drug does not work, and the marketing risks associated with having two similar drugs produced by competing companies at the same time.

(e) *Collaboration to enter new markets* – organisations may enter a new market with some, but not all of the skills and competencies necessary to compete effectively. Often, existing competitors with excess capacity are willing to provide such services as distribution, maintenance and retailing. When establishing a presence overseas, it is often necessary to collaborate with a domestic firm; in fact it is a legal requirement in some countries.

### 4.4 Business behaviour

#### Objectives

Business is primarily an economic activity and our discussions of theoretical economic analysis have been based on this assumption. Nevertheless, we should be aware that the things businesses do cannot always be explained in strictly rational terms. This is because business is a human activity and it is deeply influenced by non-rational aspects of individual and social motivation and behaviour. This is particularly true of business objectives.

We discussed business objectives in some detail earlier in the context of the general nature of organisations. Also, when we have explained the basic theory of market structures, we have assumed that firms set out to maximise profit. However, many businesses seem to pursue other objectives. A very important aspect of this is the way firms seem to pursue growth at all costs.

A possible explanation for this and other aspects of business behaviour lies in the fact that most businesses are not managed by their owners, who depend on profits, but by salaried managers, who have interests of their own.

Managers will not necessarily make decisions that will maximise profits.

(a) They may have no **personal interests** at stake in the size of profits earned, except in so far as they are accountable to shareholders for the profits they make.

(b) There may be a **lack of competitive pressure** in the market to be efficient, minimise costs and maximise profits, for example where there are few firms in the market.

It has been suggested that price and output decisions will be taken by managers with **managerial objectives** in mind. Rather than seeking to **maximise** profits, managers may choose to achieve a **satisfactory** profit for a firm: this is called **satisficing**. Satisficing is also a common managerial response when there are multiple objectives, such as boosting share price, and achieving revenue growth. Similarly, if directors' remuneration schemes are based on criteria such as growth or corporate social responsibility, then they are unlikely to make the maximisation of profit their sole objective.

#### Baumol's sales maximisation model

One managerial model of the firm – *Baumol's* **sales maximisation model** – assumes that the firm acts to **maximise sales revenue** rather than profits. The management of a firm might opt for sales revenue maximisation in order to maintain or increase its market share, ensure survival, and discourage competition. Managers benefit personally because of the prestige of running a large and successful company, and also because salaries and other perks are likely to be higher in bigger companies than in smaller ones.

**Investment**

We have pointed out that capital is one of the basic economic resources. Business makes use of capital by investing it in the anticipation of a satisfactory rate of return: this is profit. Generally, however, businesses do not have enough of their own capital to finance all of the investments they wish to make. Even when the limited liability corporation model is used, shareholders may be unable or unwilling to provide all of the capital that is needed. It is therefore usual for businesses to borrow money.

Banks provide a great deal of capital in the form of overdrafts and various kinds of loan. Capital markets are also capable of bringing together private and corporate investors to lend money. Such debt capital takes various forms and may be known as stock, bonds or debentures. It is important to remember that the providers of such loan capital are not involved in the ownership of the company: they are creditors rather than shareholders and both their capital and the interest it earns are generally much more secure that the capital and dividends of shareholders.

**Risk**

Business is inherently risky, since no-one can guarantee a satisfactory return on the capital it invests – or, indeed, any return at all. The capital provided by owners, including shareholders, is therefore sometimes known as risk capital. Owners invest because they hope to make much greater returns than they can obtain by simply lending at fixed rates of interest. They must accept that they might lose everything.

Business managers must also consider risk in depth and take steps to manage it. Risk management is easy to understand in contexts such as fire precautions, but it is also necessary in more complex business contexts such as banking, insurance and international trade.

We may distinguish between risk and uncertainty.

(a) Risk is the potential variability in a value based on past data (eg how many life assurance policy holders will live beyond the age of 65).

(b) Uncertainty on the other hand, is non-quantifiable (whether a key customer will be retained for the next two years).

In practice, the distinction between risk and uncertainty is blurred. Huge losses by insurance underwriting syndicates show that assessments of risk used in insurance have been compromised by unanticipated events such as flooding and hurricanes from climate change and claims for industrial injury resulting from asbestos and stress.

Despite using terms like risk, many business strategies are actually taking place in situations of uncertainty. A management team that only undertakes strategies in which the likelihood of success or failure can be precisely quantified would launch no new products, enter no new markets, and research no new technologies.

For the purposes of risk management, risk can be defined as the combination of the likelihood of an event and its consequences.

That is:

**Risk = Likelihood × Impact**

**Risk management** has three stages:

(a) **Evaluate the risks** to which its business is subject
(b) **Treat risks** by taking steps to reduce the most serious risks
(c) Ensure that any residual risk falls within the business's **risk appetite**

Risks change and compliance must be continuous. The management of risk is an ongoing business process involving continuous identification, assessment, treatment, monitoring and review of risk. A risk management strategy involves the selection, implementation, monitoring and review of suitable risk treatments for each risk identified.

Risk management strategies include:

(a) Risk avoidance – not undertaking the relevant activity

(b) Risk reduction – taking steps to reduce the severity of the impact

(c) Risk transfer – passing the risk to a third party through hedging or insurance

(d) Risk retention – accepting the loss, if and when it occurs

**Cost of capital**

Commercially-provided capital will not be forthcoming unless there are sound prospects of a return, either as dividends or interest. A basic principle here is that **risk and return should be commensurate**. That is to say, an investment that is regarded as very safe will generally pay the investor a lower return than one that is considered to be riskier. Thus, to give a very simple example, if you make a deposit at a building society, you are likely to earn a lower rate of interest than if you buy a one year bond from the same building society. This is because your can reclaim your deposit on the next working day and put the cash under the bed if you want to, but your money and your return are committed for 12 months with the bond. Thus, your money is 'safer' on deposit.

A similar principle applies when companies borrow from banks or the capital market: large, well-known companies with sound trading histories can borrow more cheaply than smaller, less well-known ones. However, credit-worthiness is a constantly shifting quality: the long-term prospects for BP, for example, must be regarded as much less impressive than they were before the Gulf oil spill hit the headlines; Enron was a very large successful business for several years before its collapse; and Icelandic banks were very popular with investors until the 2007 financial crisis.

Business managers must be constantly aware of the return they are expected to pay to their providers of capital: this is known as the company's **cost of capital**. They should only invest in projects that are likely to produce returns that are at least equal to their cost of capital. In other words, if, after they have paid all the relevant expenses, they cannot consistently pay for their capital, they will go out of business. Clearly, the lower your cost of capital, the easier business life is.

## 5 REGULATIONS

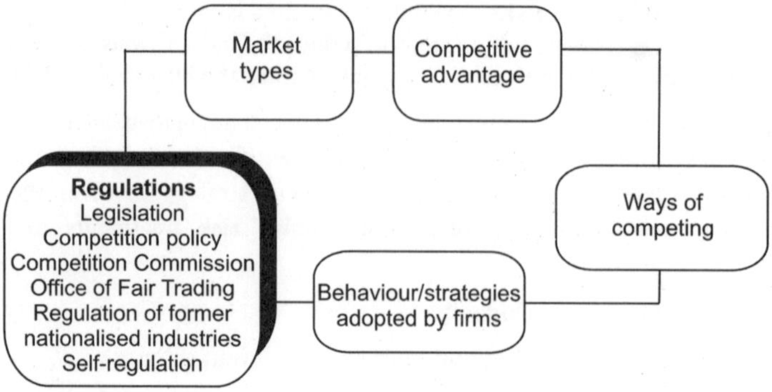


### 5.1 Legislation

Although the examples of collaboration outlined above do not appear to make consumers worse off, most countries nevertheless have a variety of laws and statutory instruments in place to prevent misuse of such agreements to the detriment of buyers. The details of such regulation will vary from country to country, but in the UK collaborative agreements between organisations are regulated by five pieces of legislation:

1. The Fair Trading Act (1973): dealing with monopolies and mergers
2. Restrictive Practices Act (1976): dealing with agreements between individuals that limit freedom to trade
3. The Competition Act (1998) dealing with anti competitive practices
4. The Resale Price Act (1976) dealing with attempts to impose minimum prices
5. Articles 85 and 86 of the Treaty of Rome, where restrictive practices and mergers have an effect on interstate trade

The administration of the UK legislation and the bodies concerned are described below. Competition policy and regulation are dealt with at EU level by a Commissioner with responsibility for competition policy, supported by a Director General and staff. The budget for the Director General for Competition in 2008 was €78.2 million and there were 738 permanent members of staff of whom 179 worked on matters of state aid.

### 5.2 Competition policy

The weaknesses that are the focus of competition authorities include:

(a) Resale price maintenance permitting retail price or a maximum or minimum price to be fixed by the producer

(b) Exclusive distribution agreements demarcating for particular distributors exclusive geographic areas or over a particular type of customer or product

(c) Exclusive dealing arrangements prohibiting dealing with competing producers or distributors

(d) Tie-in sale agreements which require purchase of a certain range of products before the purchase of a particular product

(e) Quantity forcing downstream firms to purchase a minimum quantity of the product.

The Competition Act 1998 came into force on the 1 March 2000. It introduces two main prohibitions.

**Chapter I:** a prohibition of anti-competitive agreements, based closely on Article 81 of the EC treaty; and

**Chapter II:** a prohibition of abuse of a dominant position in a market, based closely on Article 82 of the EC Treaty.

Key aspects of the new legislation are:

(a) Anti-competitive agreements, cartels and abuses of a dominant position are now unlawful from the outset

(b) Businesses which infringe the prohibitions are liable to financial penalties of up to 10% of UK turnover for up to three years

(c) Competitors and customers are entitled to seek damages

(d) The Director General of Fair Trading has new powers to step in at the outset to stop anti-competitive behaviour

(e) Investigators are able to launch 'dawn raids', and to enter premises with reasonable force and

(f) The new leniency policy will make it easier for cartels to be exposed

The intention is to create a regulatory framework that is tough on those who seek to impair competition but allows those who do compete fairly the opportunity to thrive.

### 5.3 Competition Commission

The Competition Commission is an independent public body established by the Competition Act 1998. It replaced the Monopolies and Mergers Commission on 1 April 1999.

The Commission conducts in-depth inquiries into mergers, markets and the regulation of the major regulated industries. Every inquiry is undertaken in response to a reference made to it by another authority: usually by the Office of Fair Trading (OFT) but in certain circumstances the Secretary of State, or by the regulators under sector-specific legislative provisions relating to regulated industries. The Commission has no power to conduct inquiries on its own initiative.

The Enterprise Act 2002 introduced a new regime for the assessment of mergers and markets in the UK. In most merger and market references the Commission is responsible for making decisions on the competition questions and for making and implementing decisions on appropriate remedies. Under the legislation that the Act replaces, the Commission had to determine whether matters were against the public interest. The public interest test is replaced by tests focused specifically on competition issues. The new regime also differs from the previous regime where the Commission's power in relation to remedies was only to make recommendations to the Secretary of State.

### 5.4 Office of Fair Trading (OFT)

The Enterprise Act 2002 established the Office of Fair Trading (OFT) as an independent statutory body with a Board, giving them a greater role in ensuring that markets work well to the benefit of all. The OFT board consists of a Chairman and six other members, appointed by the Secretary of State. The tenure of OFT members (including the Chairman) is determined by the Secretary of State although terms of office may not exceed five years.

The OFT's job is to make markets work well for consumers. Markets work well when businesses are in open, fair and vigorous competition with each other for the consumer's custom. They ensure that consumers have as much choice as possible across all the different sectors of the marketplace.

As an independent professional organisation, the OFT plays a leading role in promoting and protecting consumer interests throughout the UK, while ensuring that businesses are fair and competitive. To carry out this work they are granted powers under consumer and competition legislation.

They have three main operational areas.

(1) Competition Enforcement (CE) – The CE division plays a key role:

- enforcing current legislation including The Competition Act 1998
- stopping cartels and other damaging anti-competitive agreements
- stopping any abuse of a dominant market position
- promoting a strong competitive culture across a wide range of markets
- informing business, through a widespread education programme, about changes in legislation
- working with the European Commission on EC cases

(2) Consumer Regulation Enforcement (CRE) – The CRE team:

- ensures that consumer legislation and regulations are properly enforced
- takes action against unfair traders
- encourages codes of practice and standards
- offers a range of information to help consumers understand their rights and make good choices
- liaises closely with other regulatory bodies that also have enforcement powers.

(3) Markets and Policies Initiatives (MPI) – there are three main areas of activity within MPI.

- economic and statistical advice and financial analysis
- market investigations and competition
- relations with stakeholders, including government departments and public enquiries.

Each branch works closely with the other two, and often in project teams involving colleagues across the OFT.

### 5.5 Regulation of former nationalised industries

Privatisation has had conflicting results. It has allowed the privatised utilities to expand their services into overseas markets. However, there is an argument that it is not so much privatisation as the injection of competition and private sector management techniques that have generated what performance improvement there has been. Where there is no competition, the public is represented by a regulator.

(a) Some economic decisions have been deregulated. The UK government, for example, abolished exchange controls.

(b) In other areas there has been an increase in regulation, supposedly in the public interest.

    (i) Regulatory bodies oversee the activities of privatised utilities such as in telecommunications (for which the watchdog OFTEL, was merged into the new OFCOM at the end of 2003). The Office of Gas Supply (OFGAS) was set up in 1986 to monitor and regulate the newly privatised gas monopoly, British Gas. The Office of Gas and Electricity Markets (Ofgem), working for the Gas and Electricity Markets Authority (GEMA), is the government regulator for the electricity and downstream natural gas markets in Great Britain. It was formed by the merger of the Office of Electricity Regulation (OFFER) and Office of Gas Supply (Ofgas). Its primary duty is to "promote choice and value for all gas and electricity customers".

    (ii) The financial services industry in the City is more heavily regulated than hitherto, even though much of this regulation is carried out by the industry itself.

    (iii) There are far tighter controls on the activities of local authorities and their financial arrangements.

(c) Some of the UK Government's regulating activities have been pooled with the European Union. Aspects of competition policy are managed by the European Union.

**Activity 10** **(1 hour)**

Find out about the most recent activities/reports of OFWAT and OFGEM. What issues have they scrutinised in relation to these two industries?

**Activity 11** **(10 minutes)**

Think about the problems that can arise from privatising industries and services. Is the management accountable to shareholders or to customers?

### 5.6 Self-regulation

**Definition**

**Self-regulation**: where business /industry monitors its own behaviour – often through an agreed code of practice.

Examples include:

(a) **PCC** – Press Complaints Commission

(b) **Portman group** – It was set up in 1989 as part of a campaign to raise awareness of alcohol-related issues, and its members account for the majority of alcohol products sold in the UK. It takes its name from the Portman Square, London, head office of Guinness, one of its co-founders.

There are four main aims of group:

- Promote responsible drinking (and thus lessen binge drinking)
- Help prevent misuse of alcohol
- Encourage responsible alcohol marketing and advertising
- Balance the understanding of alcohol-related issues.

(c) **FSA** – Financial Services Authority – is the independent watchdog set up by Government under the Financial Services and Markets Act 2000 to regulate financial services in the UK, and protect the rights of retail customers. The FSA's aims are to maintain efficient, orderly and clean financial markets and help people get a fair deal. Their funding comes from levies on the firms they regulate.

(d) **BMA** – British Medical Association – is involved with the protection of doctors' professional interests. It represents doctors from all branches of medicine all over the UK. It is a voluntary association with about 80 per cent of practising doctors in membership. The 127,000 memberships include 13,000 medical students and nearly 4,000 members overseas.

The BMA is a democratic organisation and members are encouraged to become actively involved. The extent of their involvement can be completing a BMA survey, attending a mess visit or division meeting, or becoming a local or national representative.

### 5.7 The Civil Aviation Authority

The Civil Aviation Authority is an example of a government sponsored industry regulator that is not primarily concerned with competition; it is concerned, rather, with the safety of flight, though it has other responsibilities. Its website (http://www.caa.co.uk/default.aspx?catid=286) provides the following summary of its role.

The CAA is the UK's specialist aviation regulator. Its specific responsibilities include:

- Air Safety
- Economic Regulation
- Airspace Regulation

- Consumer Protection
- Environmental Research & Consultancy

The CAA:

- Ensures that UK civil aviation standards are set and achieved
- Regulates airlines, airports and National Air Traffic Services economic activities and encourages a diverse and competitive industry
- Manages the UK's principal travel protection scheme, the Air Travel Organisers' Licensing (ATOL) scheme, licenses UK airlines and manages consumer issues
- Brings civil and military interests together to ensure that the airspace needs of all users are met as equitably as possible.

In addition, the CAA advises the Government on aviation issues, represents consumer interests, conducts economic and scientific research, produces statistical data and provides specialist services. The UK Government requires that the CAA's costs are met entirely from its charges on those whom it regulates.

**Chapter roundup**

- The main market structures are perfect competition, monopoly and oligopoly.
- Under perfect competition, no one buyer or seller can influence the price.
- The competitive environment consists of five forces: the threat of new entrants, the threat of substitute products, the bargaining power of customers, the bargaining power of suppliers and the competitive rivalry within the industry.
- A key to success in an industry is to adopt strategies that are superior to, or different from, those of competitors. Generic strategies include cost leadership, differentiation and focus. The marketing mix is a key element in all these strategies.

## Quick quiz

1. What are the main ways of classifying factors in the environment?
2. What are the conditions for perfect competition?
3. Describe barriers to entry.
4. List the components of the marketing mix.
5. What is a segment?
6. List three competitive strategies.
7. What is the relationship between a focus strategy and market segmentation?

## Answers to quick quiz

1. Political, economic, social and technological.
2. There are so many people in the market and conditions are such that no-one can influence the price, other things being equal.
3. Barriers to entry are the factors that make it difficult for a new entrant to gain a foothold in an industry.
4. Product, place, promotion, price.
5. A market segment is a group of customers with certain things in **common** whose needs can be met with a distinct marketing mix.
6. A cost leadership strategy, a differentiation strategy, a focus strategy.
7. A focus strategy is a strategy based on segmenting the market and focusing on particular market segments.

## Answers to activities

1. The market for new cars is like a perfect market in that there are many manufacturers, dealers and customers, and information on products and prices is widely available.

   The market is unlike a perfect market in that the product is not standardised: a Ford and a Honda are not the same. There are also significant barriers to entry: to start making cars, you must make a big investment in machinery.
2. Monopolies may keep prices high in order to make large profits, may limit the distribution system to keep sales costs low and may not update products and services as often as they if there were competitors.
3. Yes, the UK grocery market is an oligopoly. It is hard to enter the market, except perhaps by opening a local store, which is open for very long hours, because the big chains charge very competitive prices. Specific obstacles to overcome include the difficulty of finding suitable sites for stores, the costs of building, stocking and training staff for new stores, and the large amounts of advertising required.
4. Jaspal needs to consider the following issues:
   (a) How many other new entrants are trying to join the industry?
   (b) What substitute products may compete (for example traditional Indian restaurants)?
   (c) Will customers expect low prices/high quality?
   (d) Will suppliers be keen to supply him or will he find it difficult to obtain his raw materials?
   (e) Who are the main competitors? How many of them are there? Where are they situated?
5. *Fighter aircraft:* the customer will be quite influential. They are most likely to be contracts from state governments who wield considerable power in terms of the amount of money they can spend. Manufacturers will rely on orders from them – there are no other customers. In addition, the national government where the factory is situated will have considerable influence over which customers the factory is allowed to sell to – there may be sanctions or trade embargoes against certain countries. A

declaration of war would affect sales, as would disarmament or scaling down of military operations in any of the states that are customers.

*Computer hardware* for business users: here the customer is fairly powerful in terms of the likely sales – there will probably be big orders worth a lot of money. Business customers will have high expectations and will expect good service and reliability. Failure to provide this will lead to custom being taken elsewhere. However, the producer has some influence in the transaction too – they will engage in after-sales services, the supply of components or up-dating items and will be heavily involved in developing new and improved machinery. The majority of business customers will rely heavily on their advice as to the best systems to purchase.

*Fresh fruit and vegetables:* the customer has relatively little bargaining power here. Prices tend to be determined according to demand and supply. The growers decide how much to plant and harvest of each item. They will not know the price until the crop is ready, as it may be affected by factors such as the weather, distribution problems or Delia Smith's latest recommendation for a recipe! Excess demand will push the price up. Excess supply will push the price down.

6 (a) Equipment, factory etc that are hard to sell (eg there may be no other use for them, or they may be old)

(b) The cost of redundancy payments to employees, or the cost of relocating and retraining them

(c) If the business is part of a larger enterprise, its withdrawal from the industry may affect other parts of the group

(d) The reluctance of managers to admit defeat, their loyalty to employees and their fear for their own jobs

(e) Government pressures on major employers not to shut down operations.

7 Teletubbies

*Product*: merchandise linked to a TV series. Product class is toy. Form is various.

*Place*: variety of outlets including multiple toy shops, newsagents, catalogues, discount stores. All places that children and parents frequent.

*Promotion*: linked to a TV series. Almost promotes itself. Promoted via TV adverts, children's comics, catalogues.

*Price*: product is likely to have a limited lifespan so the producer needs to recoup costs quickly. Premium price likely to be charged with considerable reductions at the end of the product's 'saleable' life.

*Ferrari*

*Product:* top of the range car. *Place:* limited number of outlets. Specialist retail garages.

*Promotion:* none. Not really necessary. Cars sell on their reputation/ image. Promoted generally via car programmes and car racing; also product placement in films and television.

*Price:* very expensive. Price reflects image and perceived quality.

8 Club 18 to 30 is using a differentiation focus.

9 The Organization of the Petroleum Exporting Countries (OPEC) is a cartel of twelve countries made up of Algeria, Angola, Ecuador, Iran, Iraq, Kuwait, Libya, Nigeria, Qatar, Saudi Arabia, the United Arab Emirates, and Venezuela. OPEC has maintained its headquarters in Vienna since 1965, and hosts regular meetings among the oil ministers of its Member Countries. Indonesia withdrew its membership in OPEC in 2008 after it became a net importer of oil, but stated it would likely return if it became a net exporter in the world again.

According to its statutes, one of the principal goals is the determination of the best means for safeguarding the cartel's interests, individually and collectively. It also pursues ways and means of ensuring the stabilisation of prices in international oil markets with a view to eliminating harmful and unnecessary fluctuations; giving due regard at all times to the interests of the producing nations and to the necessity of securing a steady income to the producing countries; an efficient and regular supply of petroleum to consuming nations, and a fair return on their capital to those investing in the petroleum industry.

OPEC's influence on the market has been widely criticised, since it became effective in determining production and prices. Arab members of OPEC alarmed the developed world and when they used the "oil weapon" during the Yom Kippur War by implementing oil embargoes and initiating the 1973 oil crisis. Although largely political explanations for the timing and extent of the OPEC price increases are also valid, from OPEC's point of view, these changes were triggered largely by previous unilateral changes in the world financial system and the ensuing period of high inflation in both the developed and developing world.

OPEC's ability to control the price of oil has diminished somewhat since then, due to the subsequent discovery and development of large oil reserves in Alaska, the North Sea, Canada, the Gulf of Mexico, the opening up of Russia, and market modernisation. OPEC nations still account for two-thirds of the world's oil reserves, and, as of April 2009, 33.3% of the world's oil production, affording them considerable control over the global market. The next largest group of producers, members of the OECD and the Post-Soviet states produced only 23.8% and 14.8%, respectively, of the world's total oil production.

10 OFGEM is the regulatory body for gas and electricity suppliers. It has investigated pricing issues, anti-competitive practices and has commented on the pay awards given to top executives of British Gas.

OFWAT is the regulatory body for the water authorities. It has investigated pricing, water metering, problems with cutting off customers' water supplies and problems with supply.

11 Management is accountable to shareholders but must keep in mind the quality of service and value for money offered to customers. This remains a highly political issue. For example, if the water industry is 'private' why do ministers get involved in customer complaints about such matters as the use of garden hoses during summer droughts? One problem is that customers have until recently had little real choice in supplier. Furthermore, the utilities used to be owned by the public, whereas they are now accountable to shareholders. The tension can be managed by increased competition – customers will go to where they get the best service.

Part C

# International Trade and the European Dimension

# Chapter 10:
# INTERNATIONAL TRADE

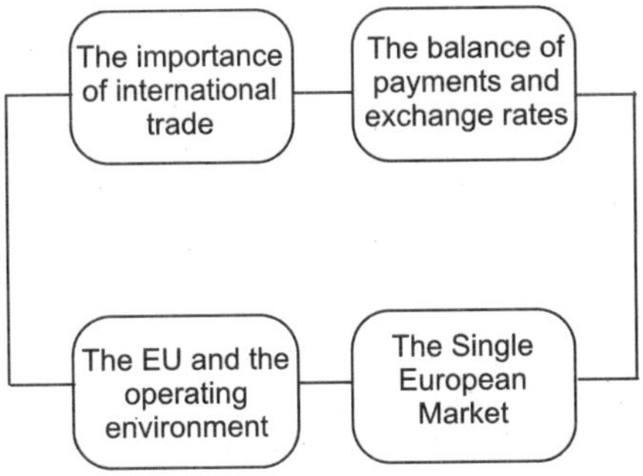


**Introduction**

This chapter begins with an introduction to the international economic environment. We focus first on foreign trade and see how countries can mutually benefit from trade based on differences in their comparative or opportunity costs of producing goods and services. We then look at the balance of payments and exchange rates and examine the UK's trade with the EU and other countries.

Raising finance to fund growth can be a critical issue and rapid growth, which is over-reliant on loan capital, can prove very risky. The merits of organic growth and growth by acquisition are discussed in this chapter.

The second part of the chapter concentrates on the EU and the UK's membership and the economies of Europe.

**Your objectives**

In this chapter you will learn about:

(a) The importance of international trade

(b) Trading blocs throughout the world

(c) The Balance of Payments and the Exchange Rate

(d) The UK membership of the EU

(e) The importance of the EU in world trade

(f) How the single market works for business

# 1 THE IMPORTANCE OF INTERNATIONAL TRADE

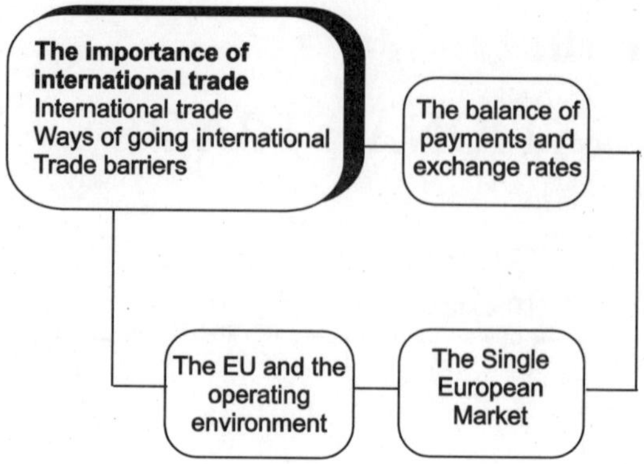


## 1.1 International trade

**International trade** is the exchange of goods and services between countries. An **import** is the UK purchase of a good or service made overseas. An **export** is the sale of a UK-made good or service overseas.

Without international trade we would all be much poorer. There would be some items like tea, coffee, cotton clothes, avocados, foreign holidays and uranium that we would have to do without. There would be other items like spacecraft and wine that we could produce but very inefficiently.

The reasons for international trade are really only an extension of the reason for trade within a nation. Rather than people trying to be self-sufficient and do everything themselves, it makes sense to specialise.

For an individual company, exporting to overseas markets can be attractive for a number of reasons.

(a) Overseas markets represent new market segments.

(b) Saturation of its domestic market can force an organisation to seek overseas markets.

(c) As part of its portfolio management, an organisation may wish to reduce its dependence upon one geographical market.

(d) The nature of a firm's product may require an organisation to become active in an overseas market.

(e) Commercial buyers of products operating in a number of overseas countries may require their suppliers to be able to cater for their needs across national boundaries.

(f) Some goods and services are highly specialised and the domestic market is too small to allow economies of scale to be exploited.

(g) Economies of scale also result from extending the use of brands in overseas markets.

From the perspective of national economies, a number of reasons can be identified for the increasing importance of international trade:

(a) Goods and services are traded to exploit the concept of comparative cost advantage.

(b) The removal of many restrictions on international trade.

(c) Increasing household disposable incomes results in greater consumption of many categories of luxuries, such as overseas travel, which can only be provided by overseas suppliers.

(d) Cultural convergence that has resulted from improved communications.

The benefits of international trade are often quite clear. When a country, perhaps because of its climate, is unable to produce certain goods at home (or can do so only at a very high cost) it will have to import them from abroad and offer other goods which it produces cheaply in exchange. Britain, for instance, could produce bananas and pineapples, but only at a prohibitively high opportunity cost by growing them in hot houses. Similarly, countries like Japan with little or no natural endowment of resources such as oil, coal and other mineral deposits must buy their requirements from overseas. Nevertheless, the basis for trade is less obvious when, say, the USA, which can produce most goods more efficiently than the rest of the world, imports vast amounts of goods like cars, cameras, TVs and other electronic products from countries such as Japan, Taiwan and South Korea.

**Labour costs and international competitiveness**

Globalisation is often perceived as a process of exploiting cheap labour in less developed and developing countries. However, studies indicate that while labour costs per hour in these countries may be lower than in developed countries, when productivity is taken into account, much of the difference disappears. Important differences in labour cost per unit of output still exist, but they appear to be caused by exchange rate movements and differences of industrial structure.

Nevertheless, there is some truth in the concept that low or unskilled workers in developed countries are in competition with equivalent workers in less developed and developing countries. This means that developed countries must promote both productivity improvements in industry and worker training and education in order to provide the skilled workforces required by such improvements.

International competitiveness has other determinants than labour costs and productivity, of course and these have been the subject of much study. Their relative importance is disputed but we might consider the following items to be significant: the list is far from exhaustive.

- Rule of law rather than arbitrary power
- Physical infrastructure especially transport links
- Availability of capital for investment
- Scientific and technological infrastructure
- Vigorous domestic competition
- Innovation
- Minimum of government control over enterprise

**Definitions**

**Absolute advantage** – a country has an absolute advantage in the production of a good if it can produce more of the good with a fixed amount of resources than can any other country (ie when the country uses fewer resources to produce a product than the other country).

**Comparative advantage** is the advantage in the production of a product enjoyed by one country over another when that product can be produced at a lower opportunity cost.

The **opportunity cost** of a product is the alternative products that must be sacrificed to facilitate its production.

The theory of comparative cost advantage states that the world economy will benefit if all countries:

(a) Concentrate on producing what they are good at and export the surplus

(b) Import from other countries those goods that other countries are better able to produce than themselves.

This may best be explained and illustrated with a simple numerical example. This example assumes for simplicity only two nations, each of which can only produce two goods, no transportation costs and no economies/diseconomies of scale. Each nation has the same endowment of resources but their aptitude in producing the two goods (which we will call cars and wheat) differs. If at present, each applies half of its resources to each good, let us suppose that the following pattern of production results:

| | Cars (number) | Wheat (units) |
|---|---|---|
| Nation A | 100 | 50 |
| Nation B | 20 | 80 |
| Total | 120 | 130 |

If we examine the relative or comparative cost of each good in each nation we find in:

A each car produced involves an opportunity cost of ½ a unit of wheat; each unit of wheat involves foregoing two cars

B each car involves foregoing four units of wheat; each unit of wheat involves foregoing ¼ of a car

Clearly, the opportunity cost of car manufacture is least in Nation A, while Nation B enjoys a comparative advantage in wheat growing. If we now persuade the governments of each nation to switch their production capacity to specialising in the good where their advantage is greatest (and remembering the assumption of no scale economies) we find:

| | Cars (number) | Wheat (units) |
|---|---|---|
| Nation A | 200 | 0 |
| Nation B | 0 | 160 |
| Total | 200 | 160 |

Clearly, total world production has increased by 80 cars and 30 units of wheat, and trade is possible within the exchange limits of one car for four units of wheat (B's opportunity cost) and one unit of wheat for two cars (A's opportunity cost). For example, B could offer 60 units of surplus wheat for 20 cars (an exchange rate of 3:1) and still be better off by 20 units of wheat, while A would then have 180 cars and 60 units of wheat, resulting in both nations being better off than without specialisation. However, transport costs in practice will eat into these gains, while diminishing returns may prevent the production gains from being so significant.

This neat theorem may also apply (with modification) even where one nation is more efficient in producing all goods. If the production arrangement prior to specialisation is:

| | Cars (number) | Wheat (units) |
|---|---|---|
| Nation A | 100 (200) | 50 (0) |
| Nation B | 20 (0) | 40 (80) |
| Total | 120 (200) | 90 (80) |

specialisation will result in A producing 200 cars as before and B producing 80 units of wheat so that while the output of cars has risen by 80 the joint output of wheat has fallen by ten units. If we have further information about how the two nations value these goods, eg, if we know that they attach a greater value to 80 more cars than to ten more units of wheat, then this reallocation of resources and output may be deemed acceptable. However, if our aim is to increase the output of some goods without reducing any others, then a more limited specialisation may generate the desired effect.

Overall, we may state that any rearrangement of the pattern of world production that increases the output of all goods or of one good with other outputs unchanged must have a beneficial impact on total welfare.

**Activity 1** **(5 minutes)**

Suppose Germany can produce one ton of sausage with 100 units of resources and a case of wine with 50 units of resources, while France can produce one ton of sausage with 600 units of resources and a case of wine with 100 units of resources.

Therefore:

(a) France has a comparative advantage in exporting wine
(b) France has a comparative advantage in exporting sausage
(c) Germany has a comparative advantage in exporting wine
(d) None of the above

### 1.2 Ways of going international

A new foreign market represents both a potential opportunity and a risk to an organisation. A company's market entry strategy should aim to balance these two elements.

An assessment of risk is required in deciding whether an organisation should enter a foreign market on its own or in association with another organisation. The former maximises the strategic and operational control that the organisation has over its overseas operations, but it exposes it to the greatest risk where the overseas market is relatively poorly understood.

There are a number of entry strategies that a firm can adopt in order to develop international markets and these include:

(a) **Exporting** – it is often possible for a company to gain a feel for a foreign market by exporting to it from its home base. Exporting is likely to be the less satisfactory option for manufacturers who produce high-volume, low-value products for which transport costs could put them at a competitive disadvantage in overseas markets.

Negotiations for the sale of goods can be conducted through local agencies working on a commission basis or through local distributors who purchase the goods from the exporter and then sell them on to the local users. In both cases some degree of exclusivity is normally given in exchange for the local organisations agreeing to certain conditions such as not representing competitors, carrying out a certain amount of local marketing or undertaking the local servicing of products. Alternatively the company may set up a local sales office or form a foreign sales subsidiary to sell, or sell and service, its goods.

(b) **Global e-commerce** – the development of the Internet has offered new opportunities for organisations to enter foreign markets. The service sector has been at the leading edge of developments in electronic commerce, helped by the absence of a tangible content that must be physically delivered.

(c) **Licensing/franchising** – rather than setting up its own operations in an overseas market, a company can license a local company to manufacture and sell a product in the local market. The resources provided include technical know-how, managerial skills and/or patent and trade mark rights and in exchange the licensor receives from the licensee a percentage of the licensed goods sold and/or a lump sum down payment.

A particularly contained form of licensing is **franchising** where the franchiser provides foreign franchisees with a complete package of materials and services, including equipment, products, product ingredients, trademark and trade name rights, managerial advice and a standardised operating system.

Fast food chains such as Kentucky Fried Chicken and McDonald's are good examples of franchising operations. As with licensing, the franchising route offers easy access to international markets.

(e) **Management contracting** – rather than setting up its own operations overseas, a company with a proven track record in a product area may pursue the option of running other companies' businesses for them.

(f) **Overseas production** – which can be achieved by **direct investment** in manufacturing facilities in a foreign country, either totally or partially through a **joint venture** when two or more firms come together to operate in a way that is of value to all concerned. Strategic alliances are agreements between two or more organisations where each partner seeks to add to its competencies by combining its resources with those of a partner. Such activities are becoming more attractive as the rate of environmental change accelerates. Alternatively, the company may set up an overseas **manufacturing subsidiary**, which may be wholly owned or may have some form of local equity participation. In some countries local participation is mandatory – Zambia insists that its state holding companies own at least 51% of any foreign company's subsidiaries.

Direct investment in a foreign subsidiary gives an organisation maximum control over its foreign operations, but can expose it to a high level of risk on account of the poor understanding that it may have of the overseas market. Companies can either set up the overseas subsidiary from scratch or merge with or acquire an existing operation. **Greenfield** development ie, setting up from scratch, is often employed by companies handling products which are highly technical in design or method of manufacture as well as by those desiring direct involvement in the development of new markets and wishing to dispense with intermediate agents. It is also the only method available when breaking into new ground or when there are no suitable companies willing to be acquired or involved in other ways.

Although the final cost may be greater its spread over time is more favourable and realistic. Moreover, it minimises disruption and avoids the behavioural problems associated with acquisitions and mergers.

(g) **Acquisitions and mergers** are preferred to 'Greenfield development' when:

(i) Time is of the essence

(ii) The cost of upgrading internal competencies is greater than acquisition costs

(iii) There is no knowledge/resources on which internal development could be based

(iv) An additional firm operating in the market may create a situation of over supply

Problems associated with acquisitions and mergers involve finding the right firm which is agreeable to a deal, negotiating a fair price and integrating activities in the post acquisition phase.

Having analysed an overseas market and decided to enter it, an organisation must make decisions that will allow it to successfully enter and develop that market. Decisions focus on the extent to which the organisation should adapt its products to the needs of the local market, as opposed to the development of a uniform product that is globally applicable in all of its markets.

Sometimes, products can be exported to a foreign market with little need for adaptation to local needs. Improved communications and greater opportunities for travel have helped create much more uniform worldwide demand for products.

A promotional programme that has worked at home may fail miserably in a foreign market. Usually, this is a result of the target country's differing cultural values, although legislation can additionally call for a reformulation of promotion.

There is usually no reason to assume that the pricing policies adopted in the domestic market will prove to be equally effective in an overseas market. Furthermore, it may be of no great importance to customers that comparability between different markets is maintained.

It is also crucial to consider more operational issues of how a company is going to get its products through to the final consumer.

(a) Consumers' attitudes towards intermediaries may differ significantly in overseas markets.

(b) Differences in the social, economic and technological environments of a market can be manifested in the existence of different patterns of intermediaries.

(c) What is a legal method of distributing goods and services in the domestic market may be against the law of an overseas country.

Adaptation to local regulations governing employment is particularly important for labour intensive service industries.

For relatively straightforward goods and services, a large proportion of staff would be recruited locally, leaving just senior management posts filled by expatriates.

**Activity 2** **(10 minutes)**

A large UK manufacturer of confectionery wishes to expand into European markets. However, the UK style of chocolate is not widely appreciated in Europe. What mode of entry would you suggest for the manufacturer?

### 1.3 Trade barriers

Unfortunately, the principles of comparative cost advantage may sound fine in theory, but it can be difficult to achieve the benefits in practice. In reality, the global ideals described above can become obscured by narrower national interests.

Despite a plethora of international agreements to facilitate trade between nations, minor, and sometimes major, trade disputes occur between nations.

Why do countries impose restrictions on trade? The answer is very simple; the primary reason is to protect domestic workers from competition from abroad. The basis for the decision is mainly political although there is some economic basis for protectionism.

#### Protection

**Definition**

**Protection** is the practice of shielding a sector of the economy from foreign competition.

Protection of domestic industries against foreign competition is often explained by increasing imports displacing domestic production and creating structural unemployment in import-competing industries.

At times of recession and heavy general unemployment, governments may try to stimulate demand for domestic output by import controls to divert spending away from foreign output.

*The case for protection*

(a) Protection saves jobs.

(b) Some countries engage in unfair trade practices. Foreign firms may receive subsidies or other government benefits. They may be **dumping** (selling goods abroad at below cost price to capture a market).

(c) Cheap foreign labour makes competition unfair.

(d) Protection safeguards national security and strategic industries. To protect the manufacture of essential goods.

(e) Protection discourages dependency.

(f) Protection safeguards infant industries. If **sunrise firms** producing new-technology goods (eg computers) are to survive against established foreign producers then temporary tariffs or quotas may be needed.

(g) Reducing imports improves the balance of trade.

(h) Protection safeguards declining industries from creating further structural unemployment.

*Disadvantages of protectionism*

(a) Prevents countries enjoying the full benefits of international specialisation and trade.

(b) Invites retaliation from foreign governments.

(c) Protects inefficient home industries from foreign competition. Consumers pay more for inferior produce.

*Protection methods*

Protection methods include tariffs, quotas, exchange controls, export subsidies and administrative practices that discriminate against imports through customs delays or setting specifications met by domestic, but not foreign, producers.

**Tariffs** (import duties) are surcharges on the price of imports. The effect of the tariff is to:

(a) raise the price of the import;
(b) reduce the demand for imports;
(c) encourage demand for home-produced substitutes;
(d) raise revenue for the government.

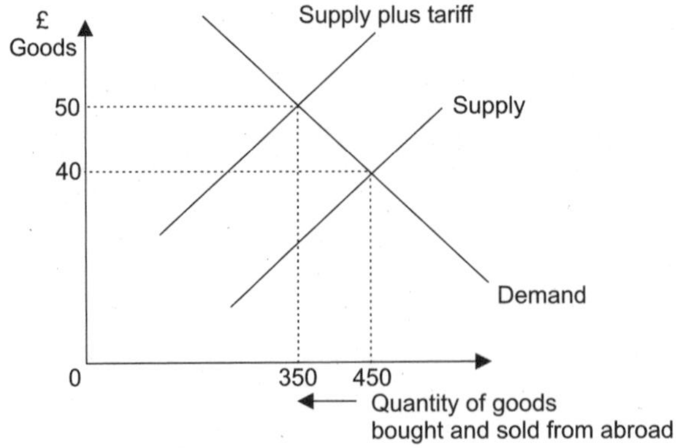


*Figure 10.1: Impact of a tariff*

**Quotas** restrict the actual quantity of an import allowed into a country. Note that a quota:

(a) raises the price of imports
(b) reduces the volume of imports
(c) encourages demand for domestically made substitutes.

**Exchange controls** (currency restrictions) prevent domestic residents from acquiring sufficient foreign currency to pay for imports.

**Export subsidies** are government payments made to domestic firms to encourage exports. Closely related to subsidies is dumping. A firm or industry sells products on the world market at prices below the cost of production.

**Activity 3** **(20 minutes)**

In the USA the steel industry was complaining that foreign steel producers were 'dumping' cheap steel onto the US market rendering US steel producers uncompetitive. President George W. Bush took the decision to impose a tariff on steel imports into the US amounting to 30%; his decision pleased the steel producers but angered the steel users, who therefore faced a choice; continue buying from foreign suppliers and pay a higher price or buy from the US producers. On the face of it the second option looked to be the best but US steel producers took advantage of the protection they had been afforded to raise their prices.

(a) How do you think the steel users reacted to this?
(b) Explain how the tariff works

**The international trading environment**

The environment of international trade may be analysed in the same way as the domestic environment, though it has its own special features, including international political relationships, supranational institutions, a variety of currencies and a wider range of social and economic influences.

Business organisations are subject to a range of international influences.

(a) In times of increasing free trade, firms can expect **incoming competition**. That said, the possibility of competing abroad is also available.
(b) A firm can **attract investment** from overseas institutions. Competing firms from overseas can receive investments from domestic institutions. For example, non-UK banks paid large sums to acquire UK stock brokers and investment firms.
(c) The **barrier** between the domestic and international environment is relatively **permeable**.

Much of the environment of international trade may be analysed using the PESTEL approach.

**Political factors**

*Government attitudes*

The development of plans will depend on the following factors.

(a) **The stability of the government**. Rapid changes or political unrest make it difficult to estimate reactions to an importer or a foreign business.
(b) **International relations**. The government's attitude to the firm's home government or country may affect trading relations.
(c) The **ideology** of the government and its **role in the economy** will affect the way in which the company may be allowed to trade, and this might be embodied in legislation.
(d) **Informal relations** between government officials and businesses are important in some countries. Cultivation of the right political contacts may be essential.

**Political risk** is the possibility of turbulence (eg civil war, revolution, changes in government policy) in the political environment.

*Expropriation and other dangers*

History contains dismal tales of investment projects that went wrong, and were **expropriated** (nationalised) by the local government.

In addition to expropriation, there are other dangers.

- Restrictions on **profit repatriation** (eg for currency reasons)
- **Cronyism** and **corruption** leading to unfair treatment
- Arbitrary changes in **taxation**
- **Pressure group** activity

*Measures to reduce political risk*

- Use **local partners** with good contacts
- **Vertical integration** of activities over a number of different countries
- **Local borrowing** (although not a good idea in high inflation countries)
- **Leasing** rather than outright purchase of facilities in overseas markets
- Take out **insurance**

**Economic factors**

Economic factors affect the demand for, and the ability to acquire, goods and services. Countries generally have larger agricultural sectors in the early stages of economic development (for example India and Africa). As the economy develops, the manufacturing sector increases. Some important economic factors are given below.

- The overall level of **economic activity**
- The relative levels of **inflation** in the domestic and overseas market
- The **exchange rate**
- The **relative prosperity** of individual overseas markets
- **Economic growth** in newly industrialised countries

**Social issues**

- The **culture and social practices** in individual markets
- The **media and distribution** systems in overseas markets
- The differences of **ways of doing business**
- The degree to which **national** cultural differences matter
- The degree to which a firm can use its own **national culture as a selling point**

The higher rate of population growth in **less-developed countries** compared with developed countries has arisen due to a continuing high birth rate and a declining death rate although some populations are being threatened by the HIV virus (for example in South Africa). Social changes (eg attitudes to large families) have not accompanied medical advances imported from developed societies. People are living longer.

**Technological factors**

- The degree to which a firm can **imitate** the technology of its competitors
- A firm's access to domestic and overseas **patents**
- **Intellectual property** protection
- **Technology transfer** requirements
- The relative **cost** of technology compared to labour
- The **competence of potential service contractors** in the target country

Technology, or investment in it, in the narrow sense, cannot on its own promote economic growth. Modern apparatus and techniques have had very uneven success in 'modernising' underdeveloped countries.

(a) The **environmental consequences** of introducing western technology to underdeveloped countries have been ill thought out.

(b) The **economic consequences** have not been as beneficial as might at first be supposed. 'The prestigious new production technologies have not worked optimally or even satisfactorily.' The problems are two-fold.

   (i) **Technological dependency** leading to a heavy foreign currency payments burdens. The country has to import **spare parts**, and even raw materials, to run machinery. It might have to pay for **expatriate technicians**.

   (ii) The inappropriateness of western technology. **Climatic** conditions can affect performance. **Infrastructural** deficiencies such as naturally poor roads affect, for example, the design of a car. The **labour/capital** mix means that in poor countries, with surplus labour, labour intensive industries rather than labour saving capital equipment might be a better use of resources.

### Environmental protection

The environmental and sustainability aspects of the home environment are equally applicable in the international trade environment. The legislative impact may be lower in some foreign countries, but the western media are likely to give enormous publicity to any perceived failings, whether justified or not.

### Legal factors

Legislation is likely to be an important influence on a firm's trade with a particular country. Important elements are listed below.

(a) The nature and principles of the local **legal system**
(b) **Law of ownership**. Especially in developing countries, there may be legislation enquiring local majority ownership of a firm or its subsidiary in that country, for example.
(c) **Acceptance of international trademark, copyright and patent conventions.** Not all countries recognise such international conventions.
(d) The structure of **company law**
(e) **Contract law**

### International agreements

There have been many attempts to develop international agreements for the free movement of trade. At their simplest, international trade agreements comprise bilateral agreements between two countries to open up trade between the two.

The **Organisation for Economic Co-operation and Development (OECD)** works by trying to co-ordinate the economic policies of members, to co-ordinate programmes of economic aid and by providing specialised services, especially information.

The World Bank acts as an adviser to governments in the provision of international finance.

The **International Monetary Fund (IMF)** is essentially a world forum for international negotiations on governments' fiscal policies. Established in 1944 at Bretton Woods, the main aim of the IMF is to stabilise exchange rates and to lend money to countries needing foreign currency. Over 140 member countries pay a sum of their own currency into a pool. The amount paid in depends on the size of their economy. Each country can then borrow foreign currency from the pool according to their contribution to settle temporary balance-of-payments problems. Countries can draw up to 25 per cent of their quota before the IMF begins to set conditions on the loan. In 1967 the IMF created a new international currency called **special drawing rights** (SDRs) that governments use to settle debts with other countries.

**The World Trade Organisation (WTO)** was set up in 1995 and succeeded the General Agreement on Tariffs and Trade (GATT). The aim of the WTO is to help trade flow smoothly, freely, fairly and predictably. It:

(a) Administrates trade agreements
(b) Acts as a forum for trade negotiations
(c) Settles trade disputes
(d) Reviews national trade policies
(e) Assists developing countries in trade policy issues

It has proceeded to reduce tariffs and quotas through several negotiating 'rounds' and has also tried to redress the distortion to world trade and the unfair competitive advantage given to subsidised exporters of agricultural products.

A wide range of other agreements and institutions affect international trading companies. An example in this category is the agreement to set up a European Bank for Reconstruction and Development. On a regional scale groups of countries or trade blocs have also been trying to lower trade barriers between them and stimulate regional trade.

The world's two most powerful economies, the United States, and the European Union, have each wanted to forge links to neighbouring countries and deny access to rivals. Other major trading countries, like the fast growing exporters on the Pacific Rim and the big agricultural exporting nations, have also sought to create looser trade groupings to foster their interests.

The formation of free trade zones and trade blocs is one of the major issues facing the world trading system – whether it will lead to increased protectionism, or whether the trade blocs will promote trade liberalisation. There are a number of types of trade blocs.

(a) **Free Trade Areas** Sovereign countries belonging to the free trade area trade freely amongst them but have individual trade barriers with countries outside the free trade area. All members have most favoured nation status, which means that they are all treated equally. Examples include North American Free Trade Area (NAFTA) between the USA, Canada and Mexico; Asia Pacific Economic Cooperation (APEC) and the Common Market for Eastern and Southern Africa (COMESA)

(b) **Customs Unions** The countries are no longer fully sovereign over trade policy. There will be some degree of unification of custom or trade policies. They will have a common external tariff (CET), which is applied to all countries outside the customs union. The countries will be represented at trade negotiations with organisations such as the World Trade Organisation by supra-national organisations eg the European Union.

(c) **Common Market** This trading bloc is a customs union, which has in addition the free movement of factors of production such as labour and capital between the member countries without restriction. Mercosur is an example of a common market comprising of a number of South American nations.

(d) **Economic Union** This is a common market where the level of integration is more developed. The member states may adopt common economic policies eg the Common Agricultural Policy (CAP) of the European Union. They may have a fixed exchange rate regime such as the ERM of the EMU. Indeed, they may have integrated further and have a single common currency. This will involve common monetary policy. The ultimate act of integration is likely to be some form of political integration where the national sovereignty is replaced by some form of over-arching political authority.

The **European Union (EU)** is the European trading bloc which until May 2004 was composed of Austria, Belgium, Denmark, Finland, France, Germany, Greece, Ireland, Italy, Luxembourg, the Netherlands, Portugal, Spain, Sweden and the UK. On 1 May 2004 a further ten nations joined: Poland, Hungary, Czech Republic, Cyprus, Estonia, Latvia, Lithuania, Malta, Slovakia and Slovenia. Bulgaria and Romania joined the EU on 1 January 2007. Turkey, Croatia, Macedonia and Iceland have applied to join the EU. It has become the most powerful trading bloc in the world with a GDP now exceeding that of the United States. In 2008, its GDP accounted for 22% of the world's total economic output. It is also the largest exporter of goods and the second largest importer. The creation of the euro as a single currency for twelve EU members has led to ever-closer economic links. Slovenia adopted the Euro on 1 January 2007 making Slovenia the first of the trade bloc's new members to take up the currency. The EU has found it difficult to shed its protectionist past based on the idea of self-sufficiency in agriculture, which limits agricultural exports from the other countries.

The United States has linked with Canada and Mexico to form a free trade zone, the **North American Free Trade Agreement (NAFTA)**. The NAFTA agreement covers environmental and labour issues as well as trade and investment, but US unions and environmental groups argue that the safeguards are too weak.

The **Cairns group** of agricultural exporting nations was formed in 1986 to lobby at the last round of world trade talks in order to free up trade in agricultural products. It is named after the town in Australia where the first meeting took place. Highly efficient agricultural producers, including those in both developed and developing countries, want to ensure that their products are not excluded from markets in Europe and Asia. Canada, Brazil and Argentina are other leading members.

The **Asia-Pacific Economic Cooperation forum** is a loose grouping of the countries bordering the Pacific Ocean who have pledged to facilitate free trade. Its 21 members range from China and Russia to the United States, Japan and Australia, and account for 45% of world trade. Progress on free trade initiatives was seriously dented by the Asian crisis, which hurt the economies of the fast-growing newly industrialised countries like South Korea and Indonesia.

The **European Economic Area (EEA)** was created by the signing of a treaty in Oporto in May 1992. It is a free trade area now comprising 30 nations, over 450 million people and is responsible for well over 40% of world trade. The member states are those of the EU plus Iceland, Liechtenstein and Norway.

The purpose of the treaty is to allow the free movement of goods, persons, services and capital throughout the EEA. If a country wishes to join the EU, it must first become a member of the EEA. Areas of EU policy that lie outside of the EEA are relations with other countries (trading and development), fiscal policy, economic and monetary union (EMU) and the common agricultural policy (CAP).

## 2 THE BALANCE OF PAYMENTS AND EXCHANGE RATES

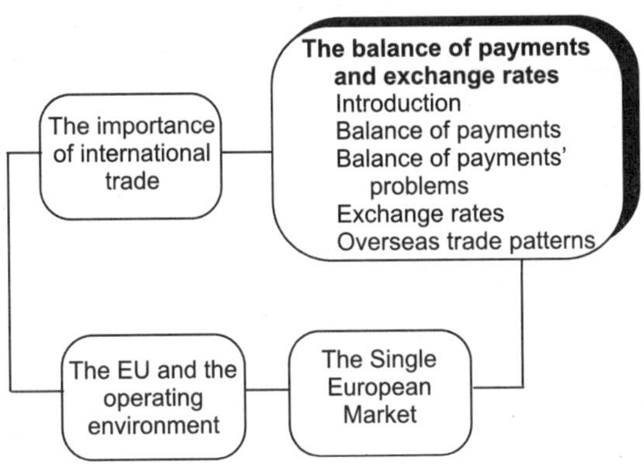

### 2.1 Introduction

We have so far ignored the fact that foreign trade, like domestic trade, is carried out through the intermediary of money. Unfortunately, money denominated in the currency of one country cannot normally be used directly to settle the debts in another country. If I want to buy goods in India I have to exchange my pounds for rupees. International trade means buying and selling foreign currency against the domestic currency and gives rise to international payments problems not encountered in domestic economies. In the long run, if a country wants to import goods or services or wants to invest overseas it must receive enough foreign exchange from exports or from inflows of investment to cover its payments abroad. In the short-run it may have reserves of foreign exchange or it may borrow to finance its payments deficit – an excess of payments over receipts. But when the reserve and credit facilities run out the country must take steps to remove the deficit.

### 2.2 The balance of payments

**Definition**

> The **balance of payments** account is a summary of one country's trade dealings with the rest of the world.

**The nature of the balance of payments**

Confusion of the balance of payments with the government budget is common. Make sure that the distinction is clear in *your* mind. A government cannot correct a balance of payments current account deficit through its own budget. The two are quite separate.

**The balance of payments account**

**Receipts** in the balance of payments come from exports of goods and services and inflows of capital.

**Payments** come from imports of goods and services and outflows of capital.

The balance of payments accounts have three parts:

(a) Current account
(b) Capital account
(c) Financial account

Under the current method of presentation of the UK balance of payments statistics, **current account** transactions are sub-divided into four parts.

- Trade in goods
- Trade in services
- Income (interest, profit, dividends)
- Transfers

Before 1996, the term **visibles** was used in official statistics for trade in goods and the term **invisibles** was used for the rest: services, transfers and repatriated interest, profits and dividends. These terms have now been dropped in order to give more emphasis to the balances for trade in goods and services, although you may still find them mentioned.

Income is divided into two parts.

(a) Income from employment of UK residents by overseas firms
(b) Income from capital investment overseas

Transfers are also divided into two parts:

(a) Public sector payments to and receipts from overseas bodies such as the EU. Typically these are interest payments
(b) Non-government sector payments to and receipts from bodies such as the EU

The **capital account** balance is made up of public sector flows of **capital** into and out of the country, such as government loans to other countries.

The balance on the **financial account** is made up of flows of capital to and from the non-government sector, such as direct investment in overseas facilities; portfolio investment (in shares, bonds and so on); and speculative flows of currency ('hot money'). Movements on government foreign currency reserves are also included under this heading.

If a multinational company invests in Britain this would be shown as an inflow under the investment section of the financial account.

Similarly, if speculators buy up £ sterling in response to interest rate or exchange rate movements, these 'hot money' movements will still be shown as inflows in the financial account even though they are short-term capital movements.

**Net errors and omissions**

A balancing item appears in the balance of payments accounts because of errors and omissions in collecting statistics for the accounts (for example, sampling errors for items such as foreign investment and tourist expenditure and omissions from the data gathered about exports or imports). A positive balancing item indicates unrecorded net exports; a negative one, net imports.

**The sum of the balance of payments accounts must always be zero** (ignoring statistical errors in collecting the figures). This is for the same reason that a balance sheet must always balance: for every debit there must be a credit.

So if the current account is in **deficit** it must be matched by a **surplus** on the capital or financial accounts.

If a country is suffering a current account deficit, it will need to attract additional capital and financial inflows into it. It can do this either by attracting **foreign direct investment** from multinational companies, or attracting foreign funds. It will achieve the latter through having a more attractive level of interest rates than other countries. This could lead to conflict between a domestic need for low interest rates and the need for higher interest rates to attract foreign funds.

**The UK balance of payments accounts**

A recent UK balance of payments account is summarised below, showing how the deficit on the current account is matched by the surplus on capital and financial acocunts.

*UK balance of payments accounts*

| | £ billions |
|---|---|
| **Current account** | |
| Trade in goods | –26,767 |
| Trade in services | 11,538 |
| Income | 8,332 |
| Transfers | –4,084 |
| Current balance | –10,981 |
| **Capital account** | 776 |
| **Financial account** | 5,853 |
| **Net errors and omissions** | 4,352 |
| | 0 |

Given that the balance of payments in principle sums to zero, you may wonder what is meant by a surplus or deficit on the balance of payments. When journalists or economists speak of the balance of payments they are usually referring to the deficit or surplus on the **current account**, or possibly to the surplus or deficit on trade in goods only (this is also known as the **balance of trade**).

Do not, as some students do, equate a trade surplus or deficit with a 'profit' or 'loss' for the country. 'A country is not like a company and the trade balance has nothing to do with profits and losses', commented the Examiner for the old syllabus.

**Equilibrium in the balance of payments**

A balance of payments is in equilibrium if, over a period of years, the exchange rate remains stable and autonomous credits and debits are equal in value (the annual trade in goods and services is in overall balance). However, equilibrium will not exist if these things require the government to introduce measures which create unemployment or higher prices, sacrifice economic growth or impose trade barriers (eg import tariffs and import quotas).

**Surplus or deficit in the current account**

A surplus or deficit on the balance of payments usually means a **surplus or deficit on the current account.**

A problem arises for a country's balance of payments when the country has a deficit on current account year after year, although there can be problems too for a country which enjoys a continual current account **surplus.**

The problems of a **deficit** on the current account are probably the more obvious. When a country is continually in deficit, it is importing more goods and services that it is exporting.

The table below summarises the main reasons why a country might be suffering a current account deficit.

| Increased import penetration | Poor export performance |
|---|---|
| Lower production costs mean overseas competitors can produce goods more cheaply than domestic producers. | Exports are not competitively priced and so overseas demand will fall. |
| Over-valuation of domestic currency makes imports relatively cheaper than domestic products. | Over-valuation of domestic currency makes exports relatively more expensive. |
| High income elasticity of demand for imports increases demand for imports as national income grows. | Low income elasticity of demand in foreign markets, so demand for exports only grows slowly despite foreign national incomes growing.<br><br>Equally it may be true that a country has low exports because its own domestic market is growing, hence its producers will concentrate on domestic sales rather than looking to export. |
| Non-price features of imported goods (eg performance, service care) better than domestic goods. | Non-price features of exported goods (eg performance, service care) worse than those of home-produced goods in target markets. |

Many of these situations explain why Britain has a structural deficit in its balance of payments current account, with a high demand for imports alongside a weak performance in manufacturing exports.

A current account deficit leads to three possible consequences.

(a) A country may borrow more and more from abroad, to build up external **liabilities** which match the deficit on current account, for example encouraging foreign investors to lend more by purchasing the government's gilt-edged securities.

(b) A country may sell more and more of its **assets**. This has been happening recently in the USA, for example, where a large deficit on the US current account has resulted in large purchases of shares in US companies by foreign firms.

(c) **Reserves** of foreign currency held by the central bank may be run down.

Note, however, that none of these three can continue indefinitely, for example because reserves and assets will eventually run out and if liabilities increase too far foreigners will become unwilling to lend fearing their loans will be irrecoverable.

A current account deficit will also mean the demand to buy the country's currency in the foreign exchange markets will be weaker than the supply of the country's currency for sale. As a consequence, there will be pressure on the exchange rate to depreciate in value.

If a country has a **surplus** on current account year after year, it might invest the surplus abroad or add it to official reserves. The balance of payments position would be strong. There is the problem, however, that if one country which is a major trading nation (such as Japan) has a continuous surplus on its balance of payments current account, other countries must be in continual deficit. These other countries can run down their official reserves, perhaps to nothing, and borrow as much as they can to meet the payments overseas, but eventually, they will run out of money entirely and be unable even to pay their debts. Political pressure might therefore build up within the importing countries to impose tariffs or import quotas.

**How can a government rectify a current account deficit?**

The government of a country with a balance of payments deficit will usually be expected to take measures to reduce or eliminate the deficit. A deficit on current account may be rectified by one or more of the following measures.

(a) A depreciation of the currency to make exports more attractive and imports less attractive. This is called a **devaluation** when deliberately instigated by the government, for example by changing the value of the currency within a controlled exchange rate system.

(b) Direct measures to **restrict imports**, such as tariffs or import quotas or exchange control regulations.

(c) Domestic **deflation** to reduce aggregate demand in the domestic economy, and hence reduce the level of imports.

The first two are **expenditure switching** policies, which transfer resources and expenditure away from imports and towards domestic products while the last is an **expenditure reducing** policy.

## 2.3 Exchange rates

**Definition**

> An **exchange rate** is the ratio at which two currencies are traded. The price of one currency in terms of another.

For any pair of countries there is a range of exchange rates that can lead automatically to both countries realising the gains from specialisation and comparative advantage.

Exchange rates determine the terms of trade.

**Foreign currency and international trade**

With international trade, there is often a need for foreign currency for at least one of the parties to the transaction.

(a) If a UK exporter sells goods to a US buyer, and charges the buyer £20,000, the US buyer must somehow obtain the sterling in order to pay the UK supplier. The US buyer will do this by using some of his US dollars to buy the £20,000 sterling, probably from a bank in the USA.

(b) If a UK importer buys goods from Germany, he might be invoiced in euros, say €100,000. He must obtain this foreign currency to pay his debt, and he will do so by purchasing the euros from a UK bank in exchange for sterling.

(c) If a UK investor wishes to invest in US capital bonds, he would have to pay for them in US dollars, and so he would have to sell sterling to obtain the dollars.

Thus **capital outflows**, such as investing overseas, not just payments for imports, cause a demand to sell the domestic currency and buy foreign currencies. On the other hand, exports and capital inflows to a country cause a demand to buy the domestic currency in exchange for foreign currencies.

Exporters might want to sell foreign currency earnings to a bank in exchange for domestic currency, and importers may want to buy foreign currency from a bank in order to pay a foreign supplier.

**Exchange rates and the UK balance of payments**

As in any other market, the market for foreign exchange is a market in which buyers and suppliers come into contact, and 'prices' (exchange rates) are set by supply and demand. Exchange rates change continually. Significant movements in the exchange rate for a country's currency can have important implications for the country's balance of payments.

Changes in the supply of, or demand for, a currency can come about for a number of reasons:

(a) Changes in demand for a nation's currency can result from a significant change in exports from that country.

(b) An increase in imports by UK firms from Japan would have an opposite effect.

(c) Demand for foreign currencies can arise from transactions involving the purchase of assets overseas.

(d) Demand for a currency at any given time is influenced by individuals' confidence about future price levels for a currency.

Fluctuations in exchange rates can cause considerable uncertainty.

A fall in the value of sterling (**depreciation**) means one pound now buys fewer dollars. Sterling depreciates if Americans demand fewer pounds (shown in Figure 10.2 below) or if UK citizens offer more pounds. UK exports become cheaper and UK imports become dearer. Hence, a sterling depreciation improves the balance of payments.

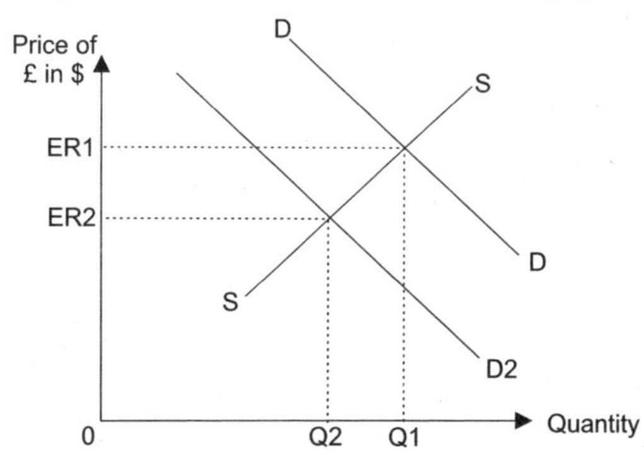


*Figure 10.2: Effect on sterling if Americans demand fewer pounds*

A rise in the value of sterling (**appreciation**) means one pound now buys more dollars. UK exports become dearer and UK imports become cheaper. Hence a sterling appreciation worsens the balance of payments.

The launch of the Euro in 1999 as a common currency for EU member states overcomes problems of fluctuating exchange rates between traders in countries that have adopted the Euro.

Opinion has been divided about the effects of the Euro on UK business organisations. Advocates of the Euro point to the greatly reduced transaction costs involved in trading with other EU countries and the greatly reduced risk of adverse currency movements.

**Activity 4** **(5 minutes)**

Suppose the exchange rate for Yen in terms, of dollars, were to decrease, because Japanese investors no longer want to invest in American securities. Would this?

(a) Make it harder for America to export?
(b) Make it easier for America to import?
(c) Make it easier for America to export?
(d) Reduce the Japanese standard of living?

**Fixed exchange rates**

An alternative to market-based fluctuating exchange rates is a fixed exchange rate system. Here, countries agree to maintain the value of each other's currency, or at least to keep fluctuations within a very narrow range. Where necessary, governments take action to maintain the agreed rates of exchange.

### 2.4 Overseas trade patterns

Trade patterns throughout the world change in response to changes in the economic, political, technological and social environments.

The overseas trade balance of a nation is very much influenced by the structure of its domestic economy. For the UK economy, the deterioration of the visible balance is symptomatic of the declining competitiveness of its manufacturing industries.

An indication of the changing relative competitiveness of UK business sectors can be found by examining ratios of:

(a) Imports as a proportion of home demand and
(b) Exports as a proportion of manufacturers' sales

Trade patterns can also be analysed in terms of the origin and destination of a country's transactions. Our trading performance with other countries has a big effect on prospects for the British economy. Over recent years we have tended to import more goods and services than we have exported.

The economy has run a **trade deficit** since 1983 with the gap widening considerably because of the excessive economic growth in the mid-late 1980s. The deficit shrunk in the early 1990s recession and during three to four years of exchange rate weakness between 1993 and 1996. However the trade gap has widened again.

The long-term growth and development of service sector industries is reflected in an improving trade balance for Britain with the rest of the world. The UK has now overtaken France and Germany to become the second biggest service exporter in the global economy.

Not every service industry makes a net surplus in trade. The UK's main money earner is in business and financial services. Travel and tourism has been in deficit in recent years.

## 3 THE SINGLE EUROPEAN MARKET

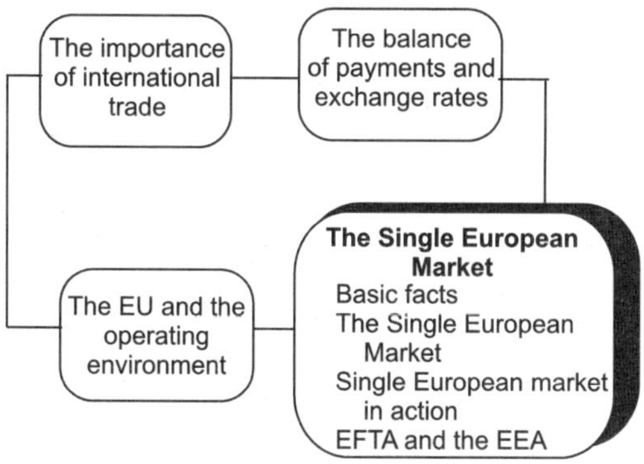


### 3.1 Basic facts

**History**

The idea of creating a single 'common market' goes back to the time when the European Economic Community (EEC) was set up in 1957. This is now referred to as the European Union. Before the EEC was set up, co-operation had commenced with the European Coal and Steel Community in 1955.

The original six member countries of the EEC (Belgium, France, Italy, Luxembourg, Netherlands and West Germany) had removed all restrictions on trade in coal, steel and iron ore between the six countries. The aim had been to gain economies of scale and allow more effective competition with the USA and other foreign producers.

The EEC extended this principle and aimed eventually to be a full common market with completely free trade between members in all products, and with completely free movement of labour, enterprise and capital. By uniting many of the countries of Western Europe, it was hoped too that the EEC could be an effective political and economic force in a world dominated by political giants such as the USA and the USSR, and by economic giants such as the USA (and later Japan).

All internal tariffs between the six members had been abolished and common external tariffs established by 1968. But this still only made the EEC a *customs union,* since a number of restrictions on internal trade remained (legal, administrative, fiscal, etc.). Nevertheless the aim was eventually to create a full common market.

In 1973 the UK, Denmark and Ireland joined; Greece joined in 1981, Spain and Portugal in 1986, and Sweden, Austria and Finland in 1995.

After successfully growing from six to fifteen members, the European Union has now undergone its biggest enlargement ever in terms of scope and diversity. Ten countries – Cyprus, the Czech Republic, Estonia, Hungary, Latvia, Lithuania, Malta, Poland, the Slovak Republic and Slovenia joined on 1 May 2004. They are currently known by the term 'accession countries'. Bulgaria and Romania joined on 1 January 2007. Turkey, Croatia, Macedonia and Iceland have applied to join.

In order to join the Union, they need to fulfill the economic and political conditions known as the 'Copenhagen criteria', according to which a prospective member must:

(a) Be a stable democracy, respecting human rights, the rule of law, and the protection of minorities.

(b) Have a functioning market economy

(c) Adopt the common rules, standards and policies that make up the body of EU law.

The EU assists these countries in taking on EU laws, and provides a range of financial assistance to improve their infrastructure and economy.

### European Council of Ministers

This consists of 27 foreign ministers, one from each country. It receives proposals from the Commission, and has the power to decide on all EU issues. Which ministers are represented on the Council depends on the purpose of the meeting. Thus finance ministers represent their country on economic issues, agricultural ministers on farm policy, etc.

***The main source of power is still the member states (despite 'Brussels-bashing'), which participate in the Council of Ministers. However, government ministers can conveniently blame the EU when things go wrong***

### European Parliament

Constituencies in the member countries elect MEPs to serve in the European Parliament in Strasbourg. Its powers are rather limited in practice, but in theory both the Commission and the Council are answerable to it.

### The European Court of Justice

This meets in Luxembourg and decides on areas of legal dispute arising from the Rome Treaty, whether between governments, institutions or individuals.

### The European Commission

The European Commission is the executive of the EU. The main tasks of the Commission are to:

(a) Ensure that Community rules and the principles of the 'common market' are observed

(b) Make policy proposals to the Council of Ministers

(c) Enforce the implementation of legislation

(d) Administer Community expenditure

The president of the European Commission is the head of the executive body of the European Union. The president leads a college of 27 commissioners, one from each Union member state, who hold specific portfolios. The Commission's term of office is five years, like that of the European Parliament. What is more, the European Parliament is consulted before the member states appoint the President of the commission and the full Commission has to be approved by Parliament before being appointed by mutual agreement by the governments of the member states.

The Amsterdam summit addressed the issue of reviewing the future number of Commissioners but no definitive agreement was reached. A Protocol was produced which leaves the matter open for future resolution.

The general proposal is that the number of Commissioners be reduced to one per state with a weighted voting system. No decisions have been made yet but it is likely that changes will be made when the next enlargement of the Union takes place.

In carrying out their duties, members of the Commission are obliged to be completely independent of their national governments and act only in the interests of the European Union. Only the European Parliament has the right to pass a motion of censure. Each member of the Commission has special responsibility for one or more policy areas, but decisions are taken on the basis of collective responsibility.

The Commission is first and foremost the guardian of the Treaties. It is an impartial body which sees to it that the Treaties, and decisions based on them, are correctly applied. It can initiate infringement proceedings against any member state and may, if necessary, refer matters to the European Court of Justice. It can also impose fines on individuals or companies, notably when they act in breach of the Commission's competition rules.

The Commission is also the catalyst of the European Union. It has the sole right of initiative in the legislative field, and it can exert its influence at every stage of the process preceding the adoption of a new 'European law'. In the area of intergovernmental co-operation, the Commission has the same rights as the individual member states with regard to the submission of proposals.

Finally, the Commission is the executive body of the European Union. This involves issuing rules for the implementation of certain Treaty Articles and administering budget appropriations earmarked for Union operation. The bulk of these fall within one or other of the major funds: the European Regional Development Fund and the Cohesion Fund. In carrying out its executive duties, the commission is often required to seek the opinion of committees of officials from the member states.

The Commission sends proposals, communications, memoranda and reports to the Council. These documents are the product of intensive consultation with political, administrative, economic and social circles. The Commission has an administrative staff based mainly in Brussels (where it has its headquarters) and, to a lesser extent, Luxembourg. It comprises approximately 25,000 officials divided between some 30 *Directorates-General* and other departments. The operating expenditure of the Commission and the other institutions accounts for only 5% of the total community budget, so accusations of waste are not entirely fair.

## EXAMPLE: EUROMYTHS. THE CASE OF THE CURVED BANANA AND OTHER EUROCRAT MADNESS!

The popular press often runs scare stories about plans by 'mad eurocrats' – for example to standardise the sizes of condoms or women's clothes, or ban bendy bananas.

Remember this from the Daily Express? 'The latest EU ruling will see British women expand beyond recognition.' And the story behind it? A mooted standardisation of clothes sizes, based on centimetres not inches. However, there is no such EU ruling – European standards are developed by voluntary agreement between national bodies, with no input from Brussels.

This is just one example of a so-called Euromyth – untrue or distorted information on the EU spread by the media. While some stories are based on facts which are misinterpreted or exaggerated, others are simply made up – like the story published in 'The Sun' on alleged EU plans to change the name of the Indian snack 'Bombay mix' to 'Mumbai mix', for the sake of political correctness. It was dreamt up by the editor of a news agency who said it was 'meant to be funny for the tabloids'.

Euromyths originate most frequently in the British tabloid press. Other tall tales include the harmonisation of condom sizes – as with clothes sizes, the EU has nothing to do with setting these standards – and a ban on 'excessively curved' bananas. This story at least contains a grain of truth: bananas must be 'free from malformation or abnormal curvature' if they are to be sold under the 'extra class' category – but the EU has never attempted to ban them. And it is important to remember that it is industry and consumers who want standards for goods, not a bunch of 'mad Eurocrats' sitting in Brussels!

British journalists are not the only ones with a fertile imagination. When the Danish weekly Søndagsavisen reported on subsidised Viagra pills for eurocrats, another Euromyth was born. What the paper forgot to mention: expenses for Viagra are only covered by EU staff's health insurance for impotence caused by serious illnesses such as cancer. And of the EU's thousands of staff members, medical reimbursements for the drug are currently granted to around ten.

### 3.2 The Single European Market

The EU consists of:

(a) The European Economic Community or EEC (the 'common' market or customs union)

(b) The European Coal and Steel Community (to control iron, steel and coal resources)

(c) The Atomic Energy Community or Euratom (to control the peaceful use of atomic energy)

In addition, there are two more recent areas of intergovernmental cooperation in the fields of Common Foreign and Security Policy (CFSP) and Justice and Home Affairs (JHA).

The European Union has a common market, including a free trade area and a customs union.

(a) A **free trade** area exists when there is no restriction on the movement of goods and services between countries. Such freedom exists on trade within the EU, but there are restrictions on trade between the EU countries and other countries.

(b) The **customs union** of the EU:

   (i) Establishes a free trade area between member states

   (ii) Erects common external tariffs to charge on imports from non-member countries.

The EU thus promotes free trade among member states while acting as a protectionist bloc against the rest of the world.

---

**FOR DISCUSSION**

What does the internal market mean for the EU citizen? Prioritise the following according to your own values:

- Better value for money
- Greater choice of goods and services
- Improved job opportunities
- Trouble-free travel within the EU
- Unlimited cross-border shopping
- Right to work and live in another EU country

---

### Import duties and levies in the EU

No customs duties are levied within the Union. All states levy VAT. All EU countries charge the same duty (which is a tax people have to pay to bring their goods into your country) on imports from elsewhere in the world. This has been very important in opening up national markets to firms in other EU countries. Governments in the past often protected their own industries by charging high duties, which had the effect of making, say, a foreign car too expensive to buy. Such protection led to customers paying higher prices than they needed to. Free competition is basic to good quality, wide variety of choice and value for money. When they face competition, firms have to make sure that they are efficient and are producing what customers want at a price they are prepared to pay.

This has been an issue for the car industry because differential pricing in member states has led to customers buying where it is cheapest and driving the car to their home state in order to save money.

---

**FOR DISCUSSION**

The single European market only benefits firms from the member states of the EU. Do you agree?

---

**How the single market works for business**

A **common market** encompasses the idea of a customs union but has a number of additional features. In addition to free trade among member countries there is also complete mobility of funds and labour. A British citizen has the freedom to work in any other country of the European Union, for example. A common market will also aim to achieve stronger links between member countries, for example by harmonising government economic policies and by establishing a closer political confederation.

The reduction of **frontier controls** on goods and people will affect businesses in a number of ways.

On goods:

(a) An end to customs documentation
(b) No need for traders to submit tax declarations

For people:

(a) Few limits on the amount of purchases that people can carry across borders, for private consumption.

(b) The Schengen agreement abolishes border controls between eight member states, although France is delaying implementation,

(c) No passport checks on EU citizens travelling between member states,

(d) Co-operation between police and immigration authorities.

The internal market might have the following general effects.

(a) Firms learn to compete more effectively, and can benefit from economies of scale.

(b) Open trade policy makes EU firms match the world best.

(c) Stable exchange rates cement the internal market.

(d) Supporters hold that the Social Chapter, which enshrines basic workplace rights, will bring economic prosperity accompanied by better living and working conditions. Others consider it bad for business.

(e) Internal market rules embody a high level of environmental protection.

Elimination of trade restrictions covers the following areas.

(a) European regulations and standards mean that products approved in any one EU country can be freely marketed throughout the Union.

(b) There is a progressive opening up of government and other public body contracts to all EU contractors on an equal basis.

(c) There is more competition and efficiency in Europe-wide services in telecommunications and information technology by developing common standards for equipment.

(d) The road haulage market is being liberalised by eliminating bureaucratic 'red tape'. Shipping services between member countries are to be provided on equal terms. Competition on air routes should increase, resulting in lower fares.

(e) Banks and securities houses authorised in their home country should be free to provide banking and investment services anywhere in the EU. Insurers will have greater freedom to cover risks in other member countries. All restrictions on the movement of capital are being removed.

(f) Protection of ideas will become easier through harmonisation of national laws on patents, trade marks and copyright.

(g) Professional qualifications obtained in one country are generally acceptable in all other countries.

**Activity 5** **(15 minutes)**

Citizens of the European Union are entitled to work in any of the EU countries. In the past, individual countries made rules about residence or qualifications which, in effect, prevented people from other countries getting jobs. What opportunities exist for UK residents to find jobs in other EU countries? List some of the difficulties involved in going to work and live in another country.

***Nearly 300 new laws had to pass through Parliament to complete the single European market. These cover standards for goods (for example food additives and hygiene) and measures to enable EU citizens to carry out their trade or profession anywhere in the EU by ensuring that their qualifications are recognised.***

### 3.3 The Single European Market in action

Elimination of trade restrictions covers the following areas.

(a) Physical barriers (eg customs inspection) on good and services have been removed for most products. Companies have had to adjust to a new VAT regime as a consequence.

(b) Technical standards (eg for quality and safety) should be harmonised.

(c) Governments should not discriminate between EU companies in awarding public works contracts.

(d) Telecommunications should be subject to greater competition.

(e) It should be possible to provide financial services in any country.

(f) There should be free movement of capital and labour within the community.

(g) Professional qualifications awarded in one member state should be recognised in the others.

(h) The EU is taking a co-ordinated stand on matters related to consumer protection.

At the same time, you should not assume that there will be a completely 'level playing field'. There are many areas where harmonisation is a long way from being achieved. Here are some examples.

(a) **Company taxation**. Tax rates, which can affect the viability of investment plans, vary from country to country within the EU. A number of directives on *tax harmonisation* had to be dropped because it was not possible to reach agreement between all member states.

(b) **Indirect taxation (eg VAT)**. While there have been moves to harmonisation, there are still differences between rates imposed by member states.

(c) **Differences in prosperity**. There are considerable differences in prosperity between the wealthiest EU economy (Luxembourg on a per capita basis), and the poorest.

   (i) Grants are sometimes available to depressed regions, which might affect investment decisions.

   (ii) Different marketing strategies are appropriate for different markets.

(d) **Differences in workforce skills**. Again, this can have a significant effect on investment decisions. The workforce in Germany is perhaps the most highly trained, but also the most highly paid, and so might be suitable for products of a high added value.

(e) **Infrastructure**. Some countries are better provided with road and rail than others. Where accessibility to a market is an important issue, infrastructure can mean significant variations in distribution costs.

Below are some examples of issues that affect our everyday lives.

### Trading standards

Many goods within the EU should nowadays have the letter CE (which stands for '*Communauté Européenne*') on them to show that they meet the safety standards recognised by the EU.

### The Food Law programme

The composition of certain food products, such as fruit juice, jam and coffee, has to be shown clearly on the packaging. All ingredients should be listed. Weights and measures are now harmonised across Europe. Goods have to be labelled and sold packaged in metric measures.

### Transport

Laws have been introduced to make aviation, shipping and road transport more competitive. This should lead, among other things, to cheaper air fares.

However, the single market is not just about 'harmonisation' or making everything the same. Above all, it is about maximum choice, achieved by the greatest possible acceptance of each others' products and standards.

### Agriculture

The **Common Agricultural Policy (CAP)** was designed to ensure a stable supply of food at reasonable prices while, at the same time, providing farmers with an adequate income. This was a major priority for the Community in the early post-war years when food shortages were a recent memory. However, the high price paid for food products under the CAP encouraged farmers to expand their production. By the 1970s this had led to large food surpluses – the 'wine lakes' and 'butter mountains'. The high prices paid to farmers for food have placed a considerable burden on the community budget which also has to subsidise sales of surplus food to countries outside the European Union. This has led to complaints from other agricultural trading nations such as Australia and New Zealand, which do not subsidise their agriculture and are suffering as a result.

To tackle this range of problems, the EU has begun to reform the CAP. The prices paid to farmers are being cut, for example by nearly 30% for wheat. This should bring food prices within the EU closer to the levels in the rest of the world, reduce costs to the EU budget and reduce prices in the shops. At the same time, farmers are being compensated for the loss of income (but this is less expensive in the long run than subsidising excess food production).

Further reforms are required, but an important step in the right direction has now been made. This is especially important as cutting agricultural subsidies is a key ingredient of the GATT agreement.

### European Monetary System

The **European Monetary System (EMS)** was set up in 1979. Its purpose is to establish greater monetary stability in the European Union. The exchange rates between currencies can fluctuate considerably. For instance, the number of pounds needed to buy a hundred Deutschmarks changed a lot in the past. This resulted in extra costs for businesses which sold goods or services in more than one country. Exchange rate changes could turn a profit into a loss, or vice versa. Businesses either had to accept this risk or take special measures to reduce it.

At the heart of the EMS was the Exchange Rate Mechanism (ERM). Members of the ERM agreed to make sure that the value of their currencies did not change much in relation to each other. Within the system, a form of money called the European Currency Unit (ECU) was used as a measure of value and a means of making loans between member states. But the ERM did not work for the UK, which withdrew from it in 1992. The UK had pegged its exchange rate too high and the UK entered at the wrong time (just after German re-unification).

### Consequences of membership of an exchange rate system

Exchange rate stability within an exchange rate regime may help dampen inflation by preventing a government from allowing the currency to drift downwards in value to compensate for price inflation. At the same time, it means that interest rate policy must be consistent with keeping the currency stable. If interest rates are too high, foreign investors will buy sterling, leading to capital inflows, much of which may be of short-term 'hot money', and there will be upward pressure on the currency. If interest rates are too low, there will conversely be downward pressure on the currency.

Other possible consequences of stabilisation within an exchange rate system are that there may be effects on people's expectations and on the perceived risk of exchange rate movements between member currencies. As well as allowing firms to plan and forecast with greater certainty, exchange rate stability ought to make a currency less risky to hold.

An important development is the Single European currency. This has been a controversial issue. We discuss this in more detail later.

**The environment and global development**

Pollution respects no frontier, as Chernobyl, acid rain and damage to the ozone layer have all shown. It is crucial that international agreements are reached and acted on.

There is a long way to go on the whole question of protection of our natural environment and the Union has decided to establish the European Environment Agency to help it to develop policies in this area.

The detail below is based on material available from EUROPA, the portal site of the European Union (http://ec.europa.eu)

The EU has participated in the series of UN-sponsored 'Earth Summits' which are conferences intended to promote solutions to perceived global environmental and development problems.

**Climate change**

The EU is promoting a global climate change control agreement and has been taking steps to limit its greenhouse gas emissions since the early 1990s, including the **EU Emissions Trading System**. It is also developing a European strategy for **adapting to climate change**.

The EU was instrumental in the development of the two United Nations climate treaties, the 1992 **UN Framework Convention on Climate Change** (UNFCCC) and the 1997 **Kyoto Protocol**.

'In 2007 EU leaders endorsed an integrated approach to climate and energy policy and committed to transforming Europe into a highly energy-efficient, low carbon economy. They made a unilateral commitment that Europe would cut its emissions by at least 20% of 1990 levels by 2020. This commitment is being implemented through a package of binding legislation.

**Development**

The EU and its member states constitute the world's largest aid donor providing more than half of the global total. This amounted to more than €49 billion in 2008.

'This was the equivalent of 0.40% of EU GNP, and was higher than the per capita aid levels of the United States or Japan. The target for 2010 is 0.56% of GNP, rising to 0.7% in 2015.'

'Since 2001, the EU's Everything But Arms initiative has eliminated all duties and quotas for all products (except arms) originating from the world's least developed countries.'

Most of the EU's aid is in the form of non-repayable grants.

**G20**

The European Union is a full member of both the G8 and the G20.

'The G20 leaders' process was designated the premier forum for international economic cooperation at the Pittsburgh summit in 2009. The June 2010 summit of the G20 focused on the fiscal exit from the crisis and on laying the foundations for sustainable and balanced growth. It will also serve to keep the pressure on leaders to implement previous commitments, notably on financial market reform and the reform of international financial institutions.'

**Employment issues**

The EU's programme for employment and social solidarity is called PROGRESS. Its role is to provide financial support for the implementation of the employment, social affairs and equal opportunities objectives set out in **the Social Agenda**. It also contributes to the Lisbon Growth and Jobs Strategy.

'Working alongside the **European Social Fund** (ESF), *PROGRESS* started in 2007 and will run until 2013. This programme replaces the four previous ones that ended in 2006 covering actions against discrimination, equality between men and women, employment measures and the fight against social exclusion.'

'PROGRESS has a global budget of € 743,25 million for seven years (2007-2013). The EU will use this budget to act as a catalyst for change and modernisation in five areas:

- **Employment**
- Social **inclusion** and **protection**
- **Working conditions**
- **Non-discrimination**
- **Gender equality'**

**Science and technology**

The European Institute of Innovation and Technology (EIT) is intended to be a key driver of sustainable European growth and competitiveness. Its mission is to expand and exploit EU innovation capacity and entrepreneurship through the creation of highly integrated Knowledge and Innovation Communities (KICs), which are highly integrated public-private partnerships of universities, research organisations and businesses.

**Workforce skills**

'Research shows that new and higher levels of skills will be needed for the jobs of tomorrow. The economic crisis and structural factors like globalisation, technological changes, ageing populations and the shift to a low-carbon economy are all contributing to rapid change in European labour markets. As a result of this fast moving evolution, shortages of adequate skills in some sectors or occupations already co-exist with unemployment across the EU.

To provide job opportunities for all and create a more competitive and sustainable economy, Europe needs a highly skilled workforce able to meet current and future challenges. To ensure this, it is urgent to invest in the right skills and improve matching of jobs with these skills in the EU, by effectively anticipating future trends.

A joint policy initiative carried out in cooperation between the European Commission and the EU Member States, New Skills for New Jobs aims to address some of these issues by supporting EU countries and regions in developing more effective ways to analyse and predict which skills will be required in tomorrow's labour markets and, with this knowledge, developing and adapting education and training so that the workers gain the skills required.'

**Education and training**

Each EU member state is responsible for its own education and training systems; however, the EU itself has policies that it believes will support member states. These policies deal with EU wide areas of concern such as ageing societies, workforce skills deficits, and global competition. The strategic framework for co-operation in education and training is known as **ET 2020** since it sets benchmark targets for the year 2020.

The benchmarks for 2020 are:

(a) At least 95% of children between the age of four and the age for starting compulsory primary education should participate in early childhood education.

(b) The proportion of 15-year-olds with insufficient abilities in reading, mathematics and science should be below 15%.

(c) The proportion of early leavers from education and training should be below 10%.

(d) The proportion of 30–34 year olds with tertiary educational attainment should be at least 40%.

(e) On average, at least 15 % of adults (age group 25–64) should participate in lifelong learning.

EU level activities in support of progress towards attaining these benchmarks are being developed for each level of education and training: early childhood, school, higher, vocational and adult education. There are also activities that are relevant to all levels, such as the promotion of multilingualism, innovation and creativity.

**Activity 6** **(30 minutes)**

Find out what objectives were laid down for environment protection within Europe by the Maastricht Summit.

***There are other international trade groups for comparison with the EU. One, EFTA, has become part of the EU. Others are developing for other parts of the world.***

### 3.4 European Free Trade Area (EFTA) and the European Economic Area (EEA)

The **European Free Trade Area (EFTA)** was established in 1960, originally with seven member countries, including the UK. The UK, Denmark, Portugal, Austria, Finland and Sweden have since transferred to the EU. Iceland, Norway, Lichtenstein and Switzerland now constitute EFTA.

EFTA countries account for less than 6% of world export trade. There is free trade between EFTA member countries but there is no harmonisation of tariffs with non-EFTA countries.

**Definition**

The **European Economic Area (EEA)** was established on 1 January 1994 following an agreement between member states of the European Free Trade Association (EFTA), the European Community (EC), and all member states of the European Union (EU). It allows these EFTA countries to participate in the European single market without joining the EU.

The EEA has 10.4 million non-EEA citizens, but nearly 96% of all people in EEA live 'at home'.

Latest estimates by EUROSTAT (the EU statistical office in Luxembourg) indicate that 2.8% of the EEA are non-EEA citizens. They also show that most EEA citizens prefer 'home'. 95.7% of the EEA population are people living in their own country. The remainder, 1.5%, are EEA citizens residing in another EEA country.

The percentages are similar within the EU. Non-nationals form over 4% of total population of the European Union.

You can compare the EEA with the North American Free Trade Association (NAFTA) formed by Canada, the USA and Mexico in 1994. This free trade area covering a population of 360 million is similar in size to the EU. Some countries in Latin America are interested in joining.

Other trading blocs are developing in the Americas, and include Mercosur (Brazil, Argentina, Uruguay and Paraguay), the Andean Community and Caricom.

# 4 THE EUROPEAN UNION AND THE OPERATING ENVIRONMENT

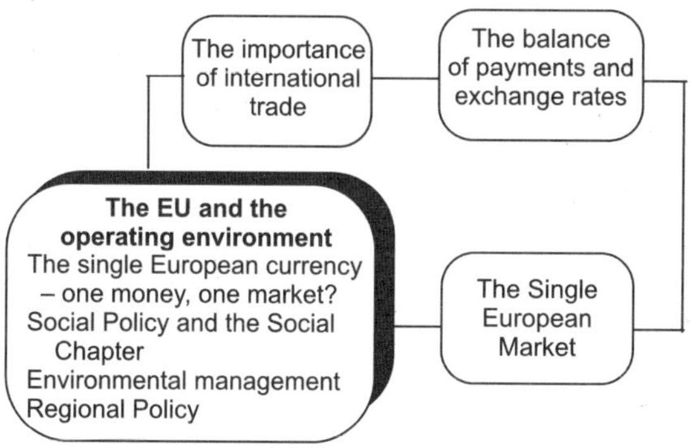


## 4.1 The Single European Currency – one money, one market?

### European economic and monetary union

One of the aims behind the European monetary system has been European economic and monetary union (EMU). This is a long-standing objective of the EU, reaffirmed in the Single European Act of 1985 and in the Maastricht agreement of 1991.

(a) **Monetary union** can be defined as a single currency area, which would require a monetary policy for the area as a whole.

(b) **Economic union** can be described as an unrestricted common market for trade, with some economic policy co-ordination between different regions in the union.

Although the whole package of measures included in European EMU is not paralleled anywhere else in the world, there have been many international monetary unions. For example, the UK and the Republic of Ireland were in currency union up to the 1970s. There are three main aspects to the European monetary union.

(a) A **common currency**. By this, we mean that instead of using the old deutschmarks in Germany and francs in France, a common currency (the 'euro') is used for normal everyday money transactions by everyone in the monetary union.

(b) A **European central bank**. The European Central Bank has the role of:

(i) Issuing the common currency

(ii) Conducting monetary policy on behalf of the central government authorities

(iii) Acting as lender of last resort to all European banks

(iv) Managing the exchange rate for the common currency

(c) A **centralised monetary policy** applies across all the countries within the union. This involves the surrender of control over aspects of economic policy and therefore surrender of some political sovereignty by the government of each member state to the central government body of the union.

The conditions set out at Maastricht were that no EU country could participate in EMU unless the following economic 'convergence criteria' were met.

(a) Consumer price inflation must, over the previous year, have been no more than 1.5 per cent higher than the average of the three best performing EU countries.

(b) Long-term interest rates must, over the previous year, have averaged no more than 2 per cent more than the average of three countries with the best consumer price inflation performance.

(c) A government's deficit should not exceed 5 per cent of GDP (gross domestic product) unless it has declined substantially or continuously or unless it is only temporarily above 3 per cent; additionally, the ratio of government debt to GDP should be no more than 60 per cent (unless it is approaching 60% at a satisfactory rate).

(d) The currency of the country should have remained within the normal bands of the ERM for a minimum of two years, without any devaluation.

**The EMU timetable**

1 May 1998 saw the meeting of those European Union countries wishing to join the monetary union at the outset. Italy, France, Ireland, Germany, Belgium, Luxembourg, the Netherlands, Finland, Spain, Portugal and Austria all signed up for the first phase of EMU starting on 1 January 1999. The UK decided to opt out but retains the right to join at a later stage. The continuing timetable for EMU was as follows.

*1998*. Creation of a European Central Bank (ECB) running a single monetary policy. Fixing of irrevocably locked exchange rates between old currencies of participating countries.

*1 January 1999*. Launch of the single European currency (the 'euro') and the fixing of exchange rates between the old currencies and the euro.

*2002*. Introduction of 'euro' notes and coins.

Under the Copenhagen criteria, it is a condition of entry for states acceding to the EU that they be able to fulfil the requirements for monetary union within a given period of time. The ten new countries that acceded to the European Union in 2004 all intend to join third stage of the EMU in the next ten years, though the precise timing depends on various economic factors. Similarly, those countries who are currently negotiating for entry will also take the euro as their currency in the years following their accession. The euro is thus now an established currency which has entirely replaced the old currencies of the euro zone such as French francs and German marks.

Gordon Brown, when Chancellor of the Exchequer, explained in the House of Commons that in reaching the UK's decision on EMU, the Government Treasury department 'made a detailed assessment of five economic tests' believed to define whether a clear and unambiguous case could be made to support Britain joining a single currency. These are:

(a) Whether there can be sustainable convergence between Britain and the economies of a single currency

(b) Whether there is sufficient flexibility to cope with economic change

(c) The effect on investment

(d) The impact on the financial services industry

(e) Whether it is good for employment

He concluded that applying these economic tests revealed that:

*'It is not in the interest of the UK to join in the first wave of EMU starting on 1 January 1999 and – barring some fundamental and unforeseen change in economic circumstances – making a decision to join, this parliament, is not realistic'.*

The government states that, in principle, it is in favour of UK membership of EMU. In practice it takes the view that the economic conditions must be right. The determining factor stated to underpin any Government decision on membership of the single currency is the national economic interest and whether the economic case for joining is clear and unambiguous. If it is, there is no constitutional bar to joining.

**For and against EMU**

The arguments for and against EMU can be summarised as follows, with particular reference to the UK's position.

| For | Against |
|---|---|
| *Economic policy stability* | *Loss of national control over economic policy* |
| EMU members are required to keep to strict economic criteria. | Under EMU, monetary policy is largely in the hands of the new European central bank. |
| Politicians in member countries are less able to pursue short-term economic policies, for example just before an election, to gain political advantage. | Individual countries' fiscal policies also need to stay in line with European policy criteria.<br>The European economic policy framework puts great emphasis on price stability.<br>Restrictive monetary policies can result in disproportionate unemployment and output effects. |

| For | Against |
|---|---|
| *Facilitation of trade* | *The need to compensate for weaker economies* |
| Eliminates risk of currency fluctuations affecting trade and investment between EMU member countries. | For the UK, the possible benefits of being economically linked to stronger European economies are reduced and possibly even outweighed by the need to compensate for weaker economies. |
| Eliminates need to 'hedge' against such risks. | Stronger economies may be under pressure to 'bail out' member countries which borrow too much in order to hold the system together. |
| *Lower interest rates* | *Confusion in the transition to EMU* |
| Savings in foreign exchange transaction costs for companies, as well as tourists. | |
| Enhances ease of trade with non- EU countries. | |
| Removes risk of inflation and depreciating currencies, reducing interest rates | Introduction of a new currency and coinage can cause confusion to businesses and consumers. |
| Stabilises interest rates at a level closer to that of Germany, reducing interest costs for businesses and government. | Firms have used it as an opportunity to push through price rises. |
| *Preservation of the City's position* | *Lower confidence arising from loss of national pride* |
| If the UK opts out of EMU, the City's position as one of the major European financial capitals will be threatened. | Sterling is a symbol of national cohesion. |
| In turn, the City's role as a leading global financial market would also be jeopardised<br><br>Inward investment from the rest of the EU would also be likely to adversely affect economic performance | EMU puts its members on the road to a federal Europe, it is suggested, making the UK parliament into little more than a regional town hall within Europe, with no more power than local government. Such a move might dent national pride and diminish confidence. |
| | The proposal to have national variants of euro coins and notes is merely a cosmetic attempt to preserve national identities. |

**FOR DISCUSSION**

Do you think a single currency benefits business?

What are the advantages and disadvantages for the UK, as a country, in accepting a single currency?

***The extent of the EU's involvement in social issues is also a matter of dispute, as it is a source of regulation for business.***

### 4.2 Social policy and the Social Chapter

Articles 117 to 128 of the Treaty of Rome, which dealt with social policy, promoted close co-operation between member states, particularly in matters relating to training, employment, working conditions, social security and collective bargaining. They also stated the need to observe the equal pay principle and make provision for the harmonisation of social security measures to accommodate migrant workers. In practice, during the 1980s there was little harmonisation of Community social policy. But in 1989 the European Commission presented a *Social Charter to* the EC heads of state. This spelt out a series of worker and social rights that should apply across the whole Community. These rights were grouped under twelve headings covering the following areas:

1. The right to freedom of movement, eg recognition of qualifications.
2. Employment and remuneration, eg fair remuneration, possible minimum wage.
3. Improvement of living and working conditions.
4. Right to social protection – social security.
5. Right to freedom of association and collective bargaining.
6. Right to vocational training.
7. Right of men and women to equal treatment.
8. Right of workers to information, consultation and participation.
9. Right to health protection and safety in the workplace.
10. Protection of children and adolescents.
11. Protection of elderly – pensions.
12. Protection of disabled people.

However, the Charter was only a recommendation and each element had to be approved separately by the Council.

Then in December 1991 the Maastricht Treaty was signed. This set out a timetable for economic and monetary union for the EC, but also included a 'Social Chapter', which attempted to move the Community forward in implementing the details of the social charter in areas such as maximum hours, minimum working conditions, health and safety protection, information and consultation of workers, and equal opportunities.

The UK Conservative Government refused to sign this part of the Maastricht Treaty. It maintained that such measures would increase costs of production and make EU goods less competitive in world trade. Critics of the UK position argued that the refusal to adopt minimum working conditions (and also a minimum wage) would make the UK the 'sweatshop' of Europe. One of the first acts of the incoming Labour Government in 1997 was to sign up to the Social Chapter.

### 4.3 Environmental management

The EU has been active in raising environmental standards among its member states for many years, for example on lead in petrol and on water pollution levels. The Union wishes to encourage the manufacture of products that are less damaging to the environment.

A product may be awarded an eco-label if its manufacture does not use too much energy and raw materials, or result in harmful emissions into the air, water and soil, or generate too much waste and noise. Clean, lowest-risk, sustainable technologies are to be used.

Waste is one of the main drawbacks for our environment. EU initiatives in this field are as follows.

(a) **List of hazardous waste**. The council has defined a list of different types of hazardous waste.

(b) **Waste packaging**. A new directive covers both new and used packaging. In five years the member states will have to recover between 50% and 65% of waste packaging and between 25% and 45% of it will have to be recycled, with a minimum of 15% for each type of packing material. In order to achieve this target they must set up a collection and recovery system. Each member state can manage its waste according to its own needs as long as it respects European requirements. At the end of ten years the directive will be reviewed and the targets altered.

(c) **Incineration of hazardous waste**. The EU established measurements and methods on how to avoid or reduce as much as possible the harmful effects of the burning of hazardous waste, such as the pollution of the air, the soil, the ground and surface water. Operating conditions and emission limit values were set for factories etc, as were strict conditions on waste water resulting from the purification of flue gases. For plants not specifically designed for that purpose, restrictive conditions under which the incineration of hazardous waste could take place were also set.

**Activity 7** **(5 minutes)**

List three possible advantages to a firm of having an EU eco-label on its product.

**Making EU industry fit for sustainable development**

The Commission has decided to introduce a strategy to implement a system of monitoring and protecting the environment based on two closely related objectives.

(a) To support **sustainable development** in agriculture, energy and transport which will create jobs and improve competition in business while, at the same time, safeguard natural resources.

(b) Second, to establish a 'satellite' national accounting framework to track the development of valuable natural resources and the corresponding environmental statistics as accurately as possible, since Europe-wide statistics are needed.

To achieve these objectives, the Commission intends:

(a) To establish a joint European approach to reporting on the state of the physical environment

(b) To create a European system of environmental pressure indices

(c) To design a report combining economic performance with environmental degradation for each country

The aim is to come up with an idea of the cost of damage caused to the environment and the cost of the restoration work.

In order to provide accurate statistics, EUROSTAT will work with the assistance of the European Environment Agency and various other Commission services and other competent authorities. This new model will make it possible to identify the level of performance in each member state, both in economic terms and in terms of its impact on the environment. The results of this 'green' book-keeping will be available in two years and these statistics will then be used to redefine guidelines for policies such as those for transport, energy and agriculture.

**Air-combating atmospheric pollution – CO2 emissions**

In the context of world-wide efforts to combat climate change, the EU committed itself to stabilising CO2 emissions by the year 2000 at 1990 levels. But the Council failed – due to the opposition of the UK – to reach agreement on a European-wide 'carbon' tax on the use of fossil fuels, such as oil or coal, as proposed by the European Commission.

In March 2007, EU leaders announced a number of initiatives:

(a) A cut to carbon dioxide emissions by 20% from 1990 levels by 2020.

(b) A 20% boost overall in renewable fuel use by 2020.

(c) A possible ban on filament light bulbs by 2010, forcing people to switch to fluorescent bulbs.

(d) A 10% minimum target on the use of bio-fuels in transport by 2020

(e) A commitment to increase use of solar, wind and hydroelectric power

### 4.4 Regional policy

**Definition**

> **Regional policy**: Set of measures aimed at influencing the geographic distribution of economic activity.

The reasons for the geographical disparities in incomes, living standards, (un)employment, etc include:

(a) **Depopulation of rural areas** due to increasing mechanisation of agriculture and the creation of surplus labour

(b) **Decline of traditional manufacturing sectors** (coal, mining, shipbuilding, steel, textiles) and of the regions that concentrated activity in them

(c) **Increasing reliance on services**, that must be located close to markets, so that there develops a vicious circle of small markets – less services – even smaller markets, etc.

A common thread in all the above is the decline in transportation costs and emergence of increasing returns to scale; the former means that proximity to markets is important, and the latter that bigger firms (serving bigger markets) become more productive/ efficient and therefore grow bigger.

Regional policy is an example of small-scale economic planning, with government as an enabler rather than a director. Regional policy can include:

(a) Providing tax incentives for investing in certain areas

(b) Relaxing town planning restrictions to make it easier for businesses to develop

(c) Awarding contracts to companies in one region rather than another (eg dividing operations between shipyards in different parts of the country)

(d) Developing new towns (eg Milton Keynes) to reduce population pressure in major conurbations. The UK Government has examined the issue of whether to encourage inner city developments in order to re-generate rundown areas. They have also considered whether to develop new 'rural towns' to encourage country dwellers to stay in their local area rather than migrate to existing towns and cities.

(e) Making infrastructural developments (eg roads, rail, airports)

The nature of the task facing EU authorities:

(a) How to identify the 'problem areas' – there seems to be a consensus

(b) How to allocate responsibility for regional policies between EU level and national levels/governments

(c) How to engage in regional policy that would be compatible with the goal of completion of the internal market

(d) Where should the support be focused – attracting foreign investment, generating indigenous investment, or R&D, or augmenting the infrastructure?

(e) How to co-ordinate the regional effects of other policies (industrial, CAP, etc).

Regional aid often takes the form of financial subsidy of some kind. This may be provided by the member state under EU rules or by the EU itself. Subsidies are, of course, barriers to free trade and the World Trade Organisation interests itself in such matters to ensure that treaty obligations are complied with. Nevertheless, subsidies of this kind are often available and make a significant contribution to economic development. Effectively, they reduce the organisation's cost of capital (even, often, when in the form of loans, since such loans are often at cheap rates) and thus subsidise activities that might be marginal or impossible under normal commercial conditions.

**Chapter roundup**

- The reasons for international trade are really only an extension of the reason for trade within a nation. Rather than people trying to be self-sufficient and do everything themselves, it makes sense to specialise.
- A new foreign market represents both a potential opportunity and a risk to an organisation. A company's market entry strategy should aim to balance these two elements.
- A country's balance of trade is the difference between the value of its exports and the value of its imports.
- The European Union comprises fifteen member states, with a further enlargement planned. It is a free trade area, and a customs union with a common external tariff.
- The most powerful body is the Council of Ministers representing member states. The Commission does most of the work, in drafting legislation. Parliament has the power to amend legislation and approve the budget; it is also a forum for debate.
- The single market involves a certain amount of standardisation to ensure that consumers benefit from free trade. There is free movement of goods, services, people and capital.
- There are still significant differences between the member states, in terms of GDP per head and hours worked, to mention two examples.

## Quick quiz

1. What is the difference between an absolute and a comparative advantage?
2. Give an example of an international franchising operation.
3. What is a Greenfield development?
4. What does a tariff do to the price of an import?
5. What effect does a quota have on the volume of imports?
6. What is an exchange rate?
7. Distinguish between a free trade area and a customs union.
8. List the members of the EU.
9. What does the European Commission do?
10. List four examples of the single European market in action.
11. List as many as you can of the twelve sets of principles laid down in the Social Charter.

## Answers to quick quiz

1 A country has an absolute advantage when it uses fewer resources to produce a product than the other country. A comparative advantage of a product enjoyed by one country over another is when that product can be produced at a lower opportunity cost.

2 McDonald's

3 Greenfield developments are organisations set up from scratch – when breaking into new ground or when there are no suitable companies willing to be acquired.

4 It raises the price.

5 It reduces the volume.

6 It is the price of one currency in terms of another.

7 Free trade area: restrictions on the movement of goods and services between countries. Customs union: establishes a free trade area between member states only.

8 Austria, Belgium, Bulgaria, Cyprus, Czech Republic, Denmark, Estonia, Finland, France, Germany, Greece, Hungary, Ireland, Italy, Latvia, Lithuania, Luxembourg, Malta, Netherlands, Poland, Portugal, Romania, Slovakia, Slovenia, Spain, Sweden, United Kingdom. (27 in all).

9 It performs the 'executive' function of the government of the EU.

10 Examples include: trading standards, food law, transport, and agriculture.

11 As many as you can from the following.

- The right to freedom of movement, eg recognition of qualifications.
- Employment and remuneration, eg fair remuneration, possible minimum wage.
- Improvement of living and working conditions.
- Right to social protection – social security.
- Right to freedom of association and collective bargaining.
- Right to vocational training.
- Right of men and women to equal treatment.
- Right of workers to information, consultation and participation.
- Right to health protection and safety in the workplace.
- Protection of children and adolescents.
- Protection of elderly – pensions.
- Protection of disabled people.

## Answers to activities

1 (a) France has a comparative advantage in exporting wine

2 The company would probably manufacture overseas, maybe buying an overseas company with existing expertise and available brands.

3 (a) In the USA, steel is a product that is used in a wide variety of different industries for many different purposes. The businesses

react by trying to find a way round the problem. Some steel using businesses are rearranging their supply chain and rather than manufacturing component parts in the US they are transferring the work to Canada. The tariff does not affect steel imports landing in Canada and so getting a Canadian company to manufacture the component and then ship it to the US helps to keep costs low and avoids having to pay the tariff. The impact in manufacturing jobs in steel using businesses in the US though is evident; if the work is transferred to Canada there is no-longer a need for the workers in the US. An attempt to solve a problem in one sector by interfering in the market creates problems elsewhere. The question has to be what is the balance of the costs and benefits, not just in the short term but also in the long-term, for all interested parties?

(b) Tariffs operate as a tax. The exporter pays the tax as the goods enter a country. In the example, steel exporters from, say the UK, would have to pay 30p in tax to the US government for every extra £1 of steel entering the US; this effectively raises the cost of production and so it raises its price to the buyer in the US to cover the cost of the tax. The supply curve shifts to the left by the amount of the tax leading to a rise in the price of steel in the US and a reduction in the amount bought and sold.

4 The answer is (c): it would make it easier for America to export – a dollar price would correspond to fewer Yen. That WOULD make it easier to export!

5 In theory you have the right to work in any EU country, so opportunities ought to be unlimited, but each country has its own rules and procedures (eg for tax and social security). Potential difficulties include unemployment problems across Europe – there may not be a job available, language issues – UK citizens are notorious for being the worst at learning languages, and lifestyle/cultural differences.

6 The Maastricht Summit laid down the following objectives for a EU environment policy:

(i) To preserve, protect and improve the quality of the environment

(ii) To protect human health

(iii) To make prudent and rational use of natural resources

7 Possible advantages could include enhanced reputation for environmental responsibility, ability to charge a premium (higher) price, opportunities for marketing, ability to supply goods to environmentally ethical companies.

# Glossary

**Absolute advantage:** a country has an absolute advantage in the production of a good if it can produce more of the good with a fixed amount of resources than can any other country (ie when the country uses fewer resources to produce a product than the other country).

**Affirmative action:** an approach with a goal to gain representation and upward mobility for ethnic minorities and women. It is focused on special efforts for targeted groups who are under-utilised. It opens up the doors of the organisation to establish the base for diversity.

**Anti-competitive practice (ACP):** a course of conduct that restricts, distorts or prevents competition in the production or acquisition of goods or in the supply of goods and services in the UK.

**Average cost (AC):** Average cost for a given level of output is simply the total cost divided by the total quantity produced.

**Balance of payments:** a record of one country's trade dealings with the rest of the world.

**Balanced scorecard:** 'a set of measures that gives top managers a fast but comprehensive view of the business. The balanced scorecard includes financial measures that tell the results of actions already taken. And it complements the financial measures with **operational** measures on customer satisfaction, internal processes, and the organisation's innovation and improvement activities.' (*Robert Kaplan*, January – February 1992, *Harvard Business Review.)*

**Barriers to entry:** a term used in economics to describe the factors that make it difficult for a new entrant to gain a foothold in an industry.

**Capacity:** the maximum amount of goods a firm can make. A firm (or industry) with overcapacity is able to produce more than it actually needs to satisfy customers. A firm that is operating at less than full capacity is producing less than it can.

**Capital:** money used for investing rather than consumption, although in practice the distinction is not hard and fast.

***Caveat emptor*:** let the buyer beware. There is a duty on customers to be careful in their purchases.

**Central bank:** a bank that acts as banker to the government and other banking institutions; it also acts as the national representative in the international banking community.

**Code of practice:** lays out a set of procedures and policies that a firm will follow. Adherence to the code is sometimes necessary for membership of certain trade associations.

**Collective bargaining:** the terms and conditions under which employees work may be the result of agreements reached between employers and trade unions through the process of collective bargaining between employees, represented by a union, and management.

**Command economy:** sometimes referred to as *state controlled*. In this type of economy, decisions are taken collectively, usually by central planning committees. The government controls what is produced, how much is produced, the price and who the goods are available to.

**Commercial rent:** rent paid to a landlord who owns capital (for example when renting a house, a car or a television). Commercial rent is not the same as the more specific *economic rent.*

**Comparative advantage:** the advantage in the production of a product enjoyed by one country over another when that product can be produced at a lower opportunity cost.

**Constitution:** the fundamental principles by which a state is governed. This includes the organisation and structure of government.

**Consumer credit:** borrowing by individuals for domestic consumption (eg food, cars, hi-fi equipment, holidays, cosmetics).

**Culture:** the sum total of the inherited ideas, belief, values and knowledge that make up the basis of social action.

**De-industrialisation:** often used to describe the long-term decline in the importance of manufacturing industry and the secondary sector in general.

**Demand:** the quantity that potential purchasers could buy if the price was set at a certain level; the number of products that people are willing and able to buy at a certain price.

**Demography:** concerned with the study of population. Demographic information is collected through the national census and is used by many market research organisations to provide a framework for studying how and why consumers buy.

**Dependency ratio:** the number of children and pensioners for every 100 people of working age.

**Diminishing returns:** if one or more factors of production are fixed, but the input of another is increased, the extra output generated by each extra unit of input will eventually begin to fall.

**Disposable income:** the amount of money people have to spend. It includes income from all sources, such as salaries and benefits, after tax and rent or mortgage interest are taken into account.

**Diversity:** 'all the ways in which we are different and similar along an infinite number of lines.' It refers to a broad range of characteristics including: gender, age, race, disability, cultural background, sexual orientation, education, religious belief, class and family responsibilities.

**Divestment:** a firm gets rid of one of its businesses by closing it down or by selling it to another company. This is often the opposite process to diversification.

**Economic rent:** a payment made in excess of the payment needed to keep a factor of production, such as land, labour or capital, in current use.

**Economies of scale:** the reductions in the average cost of producing a commodity in the long run, as the amount of output of the commodity increases. The larger a business is, the more efficiently it can produce.

**Embargo on imports:** an embargo from one particular country is a total ban, ie effectively a zero quota.

**Employers' association:** an interest group that is 'an organisation of employers that seeks to assist, influence or control the industrial relations decisions of member firms and/or engage in trade activities on behalf of members'.

**Empowerment:** a term developed in the US covering the practice of delegating responsibility. Workers are given more control over their own work, with less interference from their supervisors. They also take decisions. In many circumstances it is not so much individuals who are empowered, but teams, which decide collectively how to parcel out the work.

**Enabling business environment:** where the set of conditions that affect private sector behaviour encourage the growth of private sector activity and enterprise development.

**Enforceable code of practice:** a code of practice that is enforceable by means of sanctions falling short of legal proceedings. It will set down codes of conduct that can be enforced against people engaged in a certain trade or business, even though they are not members of the relevant trade body.

**Entrepreneurship:** the organising factor in production. An entrepreneur is someone who undertakes the task of organising the other three factors of production in a business enterprise, and who, in doing so, bears the risk of the venture. He or she creates new business ventures. The reward for the entrepreneurship is profit.

**Equal opportunities:** a generic term describing the belief that there should be an equal chance for all workers to apply and be selected for jobs, to be trained and promoted in employment and to have that employment terminated fairly.

**Equilibrium price:** the price for a good at which the volume demanded by consumers and the volume that firms would be willing to supply are the same.

**European Economic Area (EEA):** EFTA's link with the EU created a European Economic Area (EEA) with a population of 380 million, so extending the benefits of the EU single market to the EFTA member countries (excluding Switzerland, which stayed out of the EEA).

**Exchange rate:** the price of one currency in terms of another. If £1 could buy you 8 French francs, that would be the exchange rate.

**Executive:** implements laws, and perhaps proposes laws to the legislature.

**Firm:** a wide term for any organisation that carries on a business. In spite of their many differences, we treat firms as single, consistent decision-taking units and, for the purposes of economic analysis, we ignore any differences in decision-making procedures and economic structures between them.

**Free market economy:** sometimes called capitalism. In this type of economy most decisions are taken through the operation of the *market mechanism*. Supply and demand and the ability to pay influence decision-making. There is very little government intervention in business decision-making.

**Free trade agreements:** aim to reduce existing barriers to free trade; to eliminate discrimination in international trade; to prevent the growth of protection by getting member countries to consult with others before taking any protectionist measures.

**GDP (gross domestic product):** is the result of all economic activity in the economy (even though UK citizens or organisations may receive income from assets abroad, or make payments to foreign individuals or organisations).

**Global industry and global competition:** imply an industry in which producers in different countries compete with each other, with the emergence of multinational or international companies. A government can put restrictions on global competition by favouring its domestic industries.

**GNP (gross national product):** is *GDP* inclusive of amounts earned by the UK from overseas assets, but exclusive of amounts paid to overseas holders of UK assets.

**Green agenda:** within the *natural environment*, this might involve issues such as: destruction of ecosystems, deforestation, ozone depletion, desertification, global warming, threats to water supplies, energy sources, chemical pollution, air pollution, waste management, animal protection and welfare.

Within the *human environment* concerns would relate to: population growth, displacement of indigenous populations, poverty, appropriate development strategies, health, self determination, education, disastrous impacts of human activities, employment, the arms trade, the global division of wealth between 'North and South', cities, working environments, international debt, health problems and food quality.

**Green consumption:** the decisions directly or indirectly related to consumer choice and usage that involve environmentally related beliefs, values, attitudes, behaviour or choice criteria.

**Green economics:** a form of economics based on alternative ideas, which include: monetary valuation of environmental resources; promoting the quality of life; self reliance; mutual aid; personal growth and human rights.

**High technology:** usually used to refer to very complex equipment, for example an airliner.

**Household:** a person living alone, or a group of people, who have an address as their only or main residence and who either share one meal a day or share the living accommodation. Household size refers to the number of people who normally live there.

**Implied terms:** terms that are automatically part of a contract whether the parties mention them or not. The implied terms of the SGA cannot be removed from a consumer contract.

**Information technology:** the result of the combination of computer technology and communications technology.

**Insolvency:** when a business runs out of cash and cannot pay its debts. The courts may order the business to be closed down and sold off, so that its creditors – people to whom it owes – can be satisfied. Alternatively, the business itself could make the decision to declare itself insolvent before it is forced to do so.

**Interest group:** a group that represents the wider interests of a particular group of people, such as trades unions. Some groups may be both pressure groups and interest groups, and the terms are often used interchangeably.

**Judiciary:** arbitrates between citizens, between the state and citizens, and between the legislature and executive branches of the state.

**Kyoto Treaty of 1997:** assigns 'carbon credits' to countries based on existing economic and environmental factors, which countries can then exchange with other countries. Some countries might end up increasing overall emissions, and the system is open to abuse.

**Labour:** both the mental and the physical resources of human beings. Labour is rewarded with wages (including 'salaries').

**Land:** property (the land element only, buildings are capital) and the natural resources that grow on the land or that are extracted from it. Land is rewarded with rent.

**Legislation:** the act of legislating or the end product of it.

**Legislature:** the body empowered to make or amend legislation.

**Lobbying:** a method used to influence political decision making. It involves maintaining regular contact with ministers or members of parliament, to put forward a case.

**Long run:** a period sufficiently long to allow full flexibility in all the inputs used.

**Managing diversity:** an approach with a goal to improve the full use of all human resources in the organisation. The process is focused on creating a diversity friendly management system. It opens up the whole system to change and questions the policies and practices of the organisation in light of the current diverse environment.

**Marginal cost (MC):** This is the addition to total cost of producing one more unit of output. For example, the marginal cost for a firm of producing the 50th unit of output is the total cost of making the first 50 units minus the total cost of making the first 49 units.

**Market research:** finding out information about a particular product or service.

**Market segment:** a group of customers with certain things in common whose needs can be met with a distinct marketing mix.

**Market share:** the sales of a good or service by one firm in the industry as a percentage of the sales of the good or service by all companies in the industry.

**Marketing:** the management process which identifies, anticipates and supplies customer requirements efficiently and profitably.

**Marketing research:** the objective gathering, recording and analysing of all facts about problems relating to the transfer and sales of goods and services from producer to consumer or user.

**Metatechnology:** technology that can be used in many different ways.

**Mixed economy:** in this type of economy there is a balance between market forces and state intervention. The view is taken that certain activities need to be regulated by the state whilst others can be left to the influence of the market. A mixed economy usually comprises a free enterprise sector, public ownership and control of key central industries and a welfare sector to provide a minimum level of medical, social and educational services for all citizens regardless of wealth.

**Monopolies:** where 25% or more of the goods or services of a particular kind supplied in the UK are supplied either by a single person or to a single person.

**Monopolistic competition:** occurs when a large number of firms sell closely related, but not homogenous products. Instead, the products are said to be 'differentiated' and not seen as perfect substitutes by consumers. There is a heavy reliance on non-price actions eg, advertising, to differentiate the product.

**Monopsony:** a single buyer for a good or service.

**Multinational enterprise** or **company:** one that owns or controls production facilities or service facilities outside the country in which it is based.

**Negligence:** to succeed in an action for negligence, the plaintiff (the person taking the matter to court) must show three things: the existence of a duty of care by the defendant; a breach of that duty by the defendant; which results in injury or damage (or in some cases financial loss) suffered by the plaintiff as a foreseeable consequence of the breach of the duty of care.

**Office of Fair Trading:** a government department which acts on information from the following sources: its own investigations; information provided by local authority trading standards departments; the courts (who inform the DGFT of material convictions); and news media.

**Oligopoly:** oligopoly may result in a market where there are just a very few large competitors. Competition may be restricted because of this, especially if this is supported by informal agreements between the competitors.

**Ombudsman:** used to describe the provision of a final independent appeal that a dissatisfied customer may make against what he or she believes to be unfair or incompetent treatment.

**Opportunity cost** of a product is the alternative products that must be sacrificed to facilitate its production.

**Organisation:** an arrangement of people, pursuing common goals, achieving results and standards of performance.

**Organisation structure:** the way in which work is allocated to individuals; how the work is controlled (eg supervisors); the chain of command from the most senior to the most junior person in the organisation; how people and activities are grouped together.

**Party:** 'a body of men and women united for promoting, by their joint endeavours, the national interest according to principles upon which they are all agreed'. (Adapted from Edmund Burke)

**Perfect competition:** a state in which there are so many people in the market, and other conditions are such that no-one can influence the price, all other things being equal.

**Policy:** a way of expressing the broad purposes of government activity in a particular field, with some desired outcome in mind.

**Polluter pays principle:** aims to relate the damage done by pollution involved in the production of goods and services to the prices of those goods. The intention is to deter potential polluters by making it uneconomic to produce goods and services that also create pollution.

**Potential growth:** the speed at which the economy could grow. It is the percentage annual increase in the economy's capacity to produce: the rate of growth in potential output.

**Pressure group:** a collection of people promoting some particular course or objective.

**Primary objective:** is financial or economic, aimed at optimising the efficiency and effectiveness of the firm's 'total resource conversion process'

**Price cartel:** also known as a price ring, this is created when a group of oligopoly firms combine to agree on a price at which they will sell their product to the market.

**Primary sector:** this sector of industry consists of industries that produce raw materials such as crops and minerals.

**Privatisation:** the transfer of enterprises owned by the state into private hands.

**Productivity:** a measure of the efficiency with which output has been produced.

**Profit:** equal to total revenue minus total cost of any level of output.

**Protectionism:** occurs where governments try to restrict imports, to protect inefficient domestic producers or to enable domestic firms to grow.

**Rationalisation:** the reorganisation of a business's operations, often to cut costs and improve efficiency, or to reduce the number of businesses in which the firm operates.

**Regional policy:** set of measures aimed at influencing the geographic distribution of economic activity.

**Scarcity:** the excess of human wants over what can actually be produced to fulfil these wants .

**Scenario:** an internally consistent view of what the future might turn out to be.

**Secondary sector:** this sector of industry consists of industries that use the raw material produced by the primary sector.

**Self-regulation:** where business/industry monitors its own behaviour – often through an agreed code of practice.

**Shareholder:** a person who owns a share of a company. A share entitles the owner to a share in the company's profits. The management of a company is appointed, indirectly, by shareholders and runs the company on the shareholders' behalf.

**Short run:** a time period in which the amount of at least one input is fixed.

**Social Welfare Policy:** seeks to protect and directly improve people's standard of living

**Society:** the collection of all the institutions that make it possible for individuals to share things in common such as work, leisure and family life. It provides protection, security, continuity and an identity for its members.

**Stakeholders:** the many different groups and individuals whose interests are affected by the activities of a firm.

**Subsidiarity:** the principle that sets the limits of EU action. Decisions should be taken at the lowest possible level.

**Substitute product (or service):** a product or service that can stand in for another product or service in satisfying a customer need.

**Sunrise industries:** rising new industries, such as information technology and genetics. Their importance is increasing worldwide.

**Sunset industries:** gradually dying industries. In the western economies, they include heavy industries such as steel and shipbuilding, whose prices have been undercut for many years by more efficient producers in Korea and other countries in the Pacific.

**Supply:** the quantity of a product or service that existing or potential suppliers would want to produce for a given price.

**Technical complexity:** the extent to which the production process is controllable and its results are predictable.

**Technology:** equipment, the techniques whereby equipment is used, and the organisation of people, techniques and equipment in work processes.

**Tertiary sector:** distribution and service industries. Services include activities as diverse as banking, tourism, hairdressing, teaching, office cleaning, tax advice and the media.

**Total cost (TC):** total cost for a given level of output comprises total fixed cost (TFC) and total variable cost (TVC).

**Trade deficit:** the deficit that occurs when imports are greater than exports.

**Trade description:** any indication, direct or indirect, of any of the following: quantity, size or gauge of goods; method of manufacture, production, processing or reconditioning; composition of goods fitness for purpose, strength, performance, behaviour or accuracy; any physical characteristics not included in the preceding paragraphs; testing by any person and the results of testing; approval by any person or conformity with a type approved by any person; place or date of manufacture, production, processing or reconditioning; person by whom manufactured, produced, processed or reconditioned; other history, including previous ownership or use.

**Trade surplus:** an excess of exports over imports.

**Trade unions:** organised associations of working people in a trade, occupation or industry (or several trades or industries) formed for protection and promotion of their common interests, mainly the regulation and negotiation of pay and conditions.

**Unfair dismissal:** a concept that was created by industrial relations legislation about twenty years ago. It is now an extremely important element of employment protection legislation.

**Valuing diversity:** an approach with a goal to improve the quality of relationships between people. It is focused on understanding the cultural similarities and differences within an organisation. There is strong research evidence (*Meredith Belbin's* 1981 studies on team effectiveness) to support the view that groups that have a diverse mix of experiences, skills, knowledge and working approaches are generally more creative and productive than groups with a more uniform profile. Diversity is therefore a valuable organisational asset, and needs to be perceived as such.

**Voluntary organisations:** can be described as non-profit driven, non-statutory, autonomous and run by individuals who do not get paid for running the organisation.

**Wrongful dismissal:** where the employer has summarily dismissed an employee without notice, or with less notice than the period outlined in the contract (as where the employer becomes insolvent), there may be a claim for damages for wrongful dismissal. However, a claim will not succeed where the employer can show justification (eg breach of contract).

# Bibliography

Ansoff, H. I. (1987) *Corporate Strategy* (2nd edition). London: Penguin.

Johnson, G., Scholes, K., and Whittington, R. (2008) *Exploring corporate strategy* (8th edition). Harlow: Pearson Education Limited.

Kaplan, R. (1992) *Harvard Business Review*. Jan–Feb.

Keynes, J.M. (1997) *The General Theory of Employment, Interest and Money*. London: Prometheus Books

Marx, K. (1867) *Capital*. London: Penguin Classics

Mintzberg, H. (1994) *The Rise and Fall of Strategic Planning*. Harlow: Financial Times/Prentice Hall

Ohmae, K. (1983) *The Mind of the Strategist: The Art of Japanese Business.* New York: McGraw-Hill

Porter, M. (1980) *Competitive Strategy*. New York: Free Press

Sarewitz, D. and Pielke, R. (2000) Breaking the Global Warming Gridlock. *The Atlantic Monthly*. July.

For additional texts and resources, see guidance on pages 334 and 335.

# Index